Lecture Notes in Computer Science   10880

Commenced Publication in 1973
Founding and Former Series Editors:
Gerhard Goos, Juris Hartmanis, and Jan van Leeuwen

Editorial Board

David Hutchison
Lancaster University, Lancaster, UK
Takeo Kanade
Carnegie Mellon University, Pittsburgh, PA, USA
Josef Kittler
University of Surrey, Guildford, UK
Jon M. Kleinberg
Cornell University, Ithaca, NY, USA
Friedemann Mattern
ETH Zurich, Zurich, Switzerland
John C. Mitchell
Stanford University, Stanford, CA, USA
Moni Naor
Weizmann Institute of Science, Rehovot, Israel
C. Pandu Rangan
Indian Institute of Technology Madras, Chennai, India
Bernhard Steffen
TU Dortmund University, Dortmund, Germany
Demetri Terzopoulos
University of California, Los Angeles, CA, USA
Doug Tygar
University of California, Berkeley, CA, USA
Gerhard Weikum
Max Planck Institute for Informatics, Saarbrücken, Germany

More information about this series at http://www.springer.com/series/7412

José Francisco Martínez-Trinidad
Jesús Ariel Carrasco-Ochoa
José Arturo Olvera-López
Sudeep Sarkar (Eds.)

Pattern Recognition

10th Mexican Conference, MCPR 2018
Puebla, Mexico, June 27–30, 2018
Proceedings

 Springer

Editors
José Francisco Martínez-Trinidad
National Institute of Astrophysics,
  Optics and Electronics
Sta. Maria Tonantzintla, Puebla
Mexico

Jesús Ariel Carrasco-Ochoa
National Institute of Astrophysics,
  Optics and Electronics
Sta. Maria Tonantzintla, Puebla
Mexico

José Arturo Olvera-López
Autonomous University of Puebla
Puebla, Puebla
Mexico

Sudeep Sarkar
University of South Florida
Tampa, Florida
USA

ISSN 0302-9743   ISSN 1611-3349   (electronic)
Lecture Notes in Computer Science
ISBN 978-3-319-92197-6   ISBN 978-3-319-92198-3   (eBook)
https://doi.org/10.1007/978-3-319-92198-3

Library of Congress Control Number: 2018944384

LNCS Sublibrary: SL6 – Image Processing, Computer Vision, Pattern Recognition, and Graphics

Printed on acid-free paper

This Springer imprint is published by the registered company Springer International Publishing AG
part of Springer Nature
The registered company address is: Gewerbestrasse 11, 6330 Cham, Switzerland

Preface

The 2018 Mexican Conference on Pattern Recognition (MCPR 2018) was the tenth event in the series organized by the Computer Science Department of the National Institute for Astrophysics Optics and Electronics (INAOE) of Mexico. This year the conference was jointly organized with the University of Puebla, under the auspices of the Mexican Association for Computer Vision, Neurocomputing and Robotics (MACVNR), which is a member society of the International Association for Pattern Recognition (IAPR). MCPR 2018 was held in Puebla, Mexico, during June 27–30, 2018.

This conference aims to provide a forum for the exchange of scientific results, practice, and new knowledge, as well as promoting collaboration among research groups in pattern recognition and related areas in Mexico and around the world.

In this special anniversary edition, as in previous years, MCPR 2018 attracted not only Mexican researchers but it also included worldwide participation. We received contributions from nine countries. In total, 44 manuscripts were submitted, out of which 29 were accepted for publication in these proceedings and for presentation at the conference. Each of these submissions was strictly peer-reviewed by at least two members of the Program Committee, all of them experts in their respective fields of pattern recognition, which resulted in these excellent conference proceedings.

Beside the presentation of the selected contributions, we were very honored to have three outstanding invited speakers:

- Prof. Hamido Fujita, Faculty of Software and Information Science, Iwate Prefectural University, Japan
- Prof. Ventzeslav Valev (IAPR invited speaker), Institute of Mathematics and Informatics of the Bulgarian Academy of Sciences, Sofia, Bulgaria
- Prof. Julian Fierrez, School of Engineering, Universidad Autónoma de Madrid, Spain

These distinguished researchers gave keynote addresses on various pattern recognition topics and also presented enlightening tutorials during the conference. To all of them, we express our appreciation for these presentations.

We would like to thank all the people who devoted so much time and effort to the successful running of the conference. In particular, we extend our gratitude to all the authors who contributed to the conference. We are also very grateful for the efforts and the quality of the reviews of all Program Committee members and additional reviewers. Their work allowed us to maintain the high-quality standard of the conference and provided a conference program of high standard.

Finally, our thanks go to IAPR (International Association for Pattern Recognition) for sponsoring one IAPR Invited Speaker at MCPR2018, and also to the National Council of Science and Technology of Mexico (CONACYT) for providing key support to this event through sponsorship 292930.

We are sure that MCPR 2018 provided a fruitful forum for the Mexican pattern recognition researchers and the broader international pattern recognition community.

June 2018

José Francisco Martínez-Trinidad
Jesús Ariel Carrasco-Ochoa
José Arturo Olvera-López
Sudeep Sarkar

Organization

MCPR 2018 was sponsored by the Computer Science Department of the National Institute of Astrophysics, Optics and Electronics (INAOE).

General Conference Co-chairs

Sudeep Sarkar	University of South Florida, USA
José Francisco Martínez-Trinidad	National Institute of Astrophysics, Optics and Electronics (INAOE), Mexico
Jesús Ariel Carrasco-Ochoa	National Institute of Astrophysics, Optics and Electronics (INAOE), Mexico
José Arturo Olvera-López	Autonomous University of Puebla (BUAP), Mexico

Local Arrangements Committee

Cervantes-Cuahucy Brenda Alicia	National Institute of Astrophysics, Optics and Electronics (INAOE), Mexico
Lopez-Lucio Gabriela	National Institute of Astrophysics, Optics and Electronics (INAOE), Mexico
Palacios-Coatl Edith	National Institute of Astrophysics, Optics and Electronics (INAOE), Mexico

Scientific Committee

E. Alba-Cabrera	Universidad de San Francisco de Quito, Ecuador
M. Alvarado	CINVESTAV, Mexico
A. Asano	Kansai University, Japan
J. M. Benedi	Universidad Politécnica de Valencia, Spain
D. L. Borges	Universidade de Brasília, Brazil
M. Castelan	CINVESTAV, Mexico
H. J. Escalante-Balderas	INAOE, Mexico
J. Facon	Pontifícia Universidade Católica do Paraná, Brazil
M. García-Borroto	CUJAE, Cuba
D. Gatica	Idiap Research Institute, Switzerland
L. Goldfarb	University of New Brunswick, Canada
H. Gomes	Universidade Federal de Campina Grande, Brazil
L. Heutte	Université de Rouen, France
X. Jiang	University of Münster, Germany
M. Kampel	Vienna Univerity of Technology, Austria
R. Klette	University of Auckland, New Zealand
V. Kober	CICESE, Mexico

M. S. Lazo-Cortés	INAOE, Mexico
J. V. Lorenzo-Ginori	Universidad Central de Las Villas, Cuba
J. Martínez-Carranza	INAOE, Mexico
P. Menezes	University of Coimbra-Polo II, Brazil
M. Montes-Y-Gomez	INAOE, Mexico
E. Morales	INAOE, Mexico
A. Morales-Reyes	INAOE, Mexico
P. Pina	Instituto Superior Técnico, Portugal
A. Pinho	University of Aveiro, Portugal
J. Pinto	Instituto Superior Técnico, Portugal
B. Raducanu	Universitat Autònoma de Barcelona, Spain
P. Real	University of Seville, Spain
E. F. Roman-Rangel	University of Geneva, Switzerland
J. Ruiz-Shulcloper	UCI, Cuba
V. Riazanov	Russian Academy of Science, Russia
D. Sanchez	University of Granada, Spain
D. Sanchez-Cortes	HES-SO Valais-Wallis, Switzerland
K. Sang-Woon	Myongji University, South Korea
G. Sanniti di Baja	ICARCNR, Italy
A. Sappa	Universitat Autònoma de Barcelona, Spain
J. H. Sossa-Azuela	CIC-IPN, Mexico
L. E. Sucar	INAOE, Mexico
T. Turki	New Jersey Institute of Technology, USA
V. Valev	University of North Florida, USA
J. Vitria	University of Barcelona, Spain

Additional Reviewers

J. J. Carbajal-Hernández	R. M. Ortega-Mendoza
Fors-Isalguez	G. Sánchez-Díaz
García-Hernández	E. Villatoro-Tello
A. P. López-Monroy	

Sponsoring Institutions

National Institute of Astrophysics, Optics and Electronics (INAOE)
Mexican Association for Computer Vision, Neurocomputing and Robotics (MACVNR)
National Council of Science and Technology of Mexico (CONACYT)

Contents

Computer Vision

Pattern Recognition Principles

Patterns of Go Gaming by Ising Model

Arturo Yee[1](✉) and Matías Alvarado[2](✉)

[1] Facultad de Informática Culiacán, Universidad Autónoma de Sinaloa,
Culiacán, Mexico
arturo.yee@uas.edu.mx
[2] Departamento de Computación, CINVESTAV – IPN, Mexico City, Mexico
matias@cs.cinvestav.mx

Abstract. Go game gaming patterns are very hard to identify. The stochastic interaction during a Go game makes highly difficult the pattern recognition in Go gaming. We use the Ising model, a classic method in statistics physics, for modeling the stochastic interaction among spins that result in well identified patterns of phenomena in this discipline. An Ising energy function is defined; this function allows the formal translation of Go game dynamics: the use of rules and tactics to elaborate the complex Go strategies. The result of Go game simulations shows a close fit with real game scores during the evolution of all the game.

Keywords: Patterns of Go gaming · Ising model · Pattern stochastic formation

1 Introduction

Go is a two players, zero-sum and complete information game [1], that official board is a 19 × 19 grid [2]. Each player places one black/white stone on an empty board cross-point position, black plays first then white and so on. In Go gaming white stones player receives a compensation *komi* by playing the second turn [3]. Same color stones joined in horizontal or vertical line form up one indivisible compound stone. *Connection* of ally stones is by placing one same color stone between them. Stone's *liberty* is a contiguous empty board cross-point in the vertical or horizontal direction. Any stone on board is removed if is adversaries rounded losing all its liberties. For board territory control the way is by means of tactics of *invasion, reduction, nets, ladders* and connections. Stone allocation within an empty board neighborhood is an invasion, and if the adversary places a stone close to invasion it is making a reduction. Same color stones make a net over adversarial stones by surrounding them, and make a ladder by surrounding them and leaving a sole liberty, called Atari condition. A stone is Go *alive* if cannot be captured and is Go dead if cannot avoid be captured. Placement of stone being directly captured is *suicide* that is not allowed. Go strategies are compositions of tactics. The game ends when both players pass turn. The score is computed based on both board territory occupied and the number of adversarial simple stones captured. The usual criteria are that the winner has the largest territorial and number of captures.

A summary of computer Go concepts and definitions follow. A Go gaming state is a configuration that combines black-white-empty board positions. The set of states is

© Springer International Publishing AG, part of Springer Nature 2018
J. F. Martínez-Trinidad et al. (Eds.): MCPR 2018, LNCS 10880, pp. 3–11, 2018.
https://doi.org/10.1007/978-3-319-92198-3_1

the Go state space with cardinality $3^{19 \times 19} \sim 10^{172}$. The game tree records the different paths between the successive states that correspond to the players' decisions from the start to the end so the sequence of moves in the game. Go game tree cardinality is by 10^a, $a = 10^{172}$, that quantifies the huge diversity of paths for Go gaming. As a result, the automation of Go tactics and strategies to efficiently win a match is vastly complex. In average, the branching factor for Go ranges from 200 to 300 possible moves at each player's turn, while 35–40 moves for Chess, which cardinality of state space and game tree is 10^{50} and by 10^{123} [4].

The very difficult task for Go automation is the evaluation of positions for estimating the potential of occupied territory [3, 5, 6]. The challenge is to deal with the huge number of Go gaming patterns in the board, which must be classified prior to deciding on the next advantageous Go move. Advances on computer Go gaming for pattern recognition of Go tactics (eye, ladder, nets) have used Neural Networks, and the Monte Carlo tree search algorithms (MCTS) [7]. The MCTS algorithms ponder an eventual next Go move on the base of the average values from thousands of possibilities since the current state to the game end. Main weakness of the MCTS methods is its extremely high computational cost [8]. AlphaGo is the current top Go player [9]. It uses machine learning and MCTS combined with extensive training, from both human and computer play records. Actually, AlphaGo uses deep neural network (DNN) methodology as a milestone for its meaningful power in complex Go gaming patterns recognition. DNN is a bio-inspired formal abstraction from visual cortex of felines and eagles characterized by an acute vision system [9]; DNN embraces dozens of layers each with a long (deep) number of neurons. The intense correlation and composition, like in visual cortex process, makes DNN a powerful tool for recognition in complex scenarios. DNN uses convolution integral functions for neurons activation.

MCTS lacks an adequate model to represent Go gaming patterns which can be easy used in game heuristic function. Deep neural networks in AlphaGo is truly efficient for pattern recognition but not for a comprehension of the Go game phenomenology.

In this work, for modeling Go gaming, we propose an analytical method based on the Ising model and Hamiltonian, the classics for modeling complex interaction in electromagnetism and thermodynamic phenomena [10]. In the struggling for board area control in Go, the Ising model is relevant for modeling the dynamics of complex interaction, henceforth for designing algorithms to quantify the synergy among allied stones as well as the tension against the adversary ones. Definition of energy function stands back algorithms to compute the power of stones patterns during the successive Go states, so account the each state dominance. Sometimes a phase-transition-like process happens in Go gaming: when after a movement the black - white force equilibrium is broken and emerges pre-eminence of blacks over white or conversely. This Go-game-phase-transition is fine described by the adapted Go Ising energy function.

The rest of this paper is organized as follows: In Sect. 2 the Ising-model-based method to estimate the energy value of Go stones configurations during a match is introduced. Section 3 presents experiments and the analytical description of results. Section 4 is the Discussion, followed by the conclusions.

2 Ising Model for Go Stochastic Interaction

In the 2D Ising model, the energy spin interactions are described by the Hamiltonian in Eq. (1):

$$H = -\sum_{ij} w_{ij} x_i x_j - \mu \sum_i h_i x_i \tag{1}$$

w_{ij} sets for interaction between spin i and j, μ the magnitude of an external magnetic field, and h_i the magnetic field contribution at site i; for a homogeneous external field, $h_i = 1$.

2.1 The Go Energy Function

We use 2-dimensional Ising model for displaying the black – white stones interactions in Go gaming. Our definition of energy function stands back the algorithms to compute the power of the adversary groups of stones in a Go state, so account board dominance. The energy function lets quantify the strength of interaction among allied stone, versus adversaries, and the impact of the involved liberties. Associated to Ising Hamiltonian in Eq. (1), the Go energy function – via the CFG representation of states [17] – embraces the mentioned parameters in the next (1) and (2) that result in tactics (3)–(5):

(1) The numbers of single (atomic) stones in a compound (molecular) stone.
(2) The number of eyes a compound stone has.
(3) The tactic pattern the stone is involved and making.
(4) The synergy strength the ally stones are making among.
(5) The strength of adversary stones that fight against.

The quantitative description of stone i is by means of the elements involved in Eq. (2):

$$x_i = c_i \left(n_i + r_{eye}^{k_i} \right). \tag{2}$$

n_i sets the number of single stones, r_{eye} is the constant to represent the occurrence of an eye, $r_{eye} > 1$, or $r_{eye} = 0$ if no eye; k_i is the number of eyes in stone i, and c_i is the stone color, 1 for white, and -1 for black. Hence, $r_{eye}^{k_i}$ quantifies the eyes' power inside i. If no eye x_i just indicates the i size and color. Observe that $k_i \geq 2$ guaranties these liberties to i, so it cannot be captured.

In Hamiltonian of Eq. (1) for Go, w_{ij} should quantify the ratio of synergy or tension between single or compound stones i, j. So, w_{ij} should encompass the $i - j$ synergy regarding the presence and strength of adversary stones that try to inhibit this synergy. As well, w_{ij} should encompass the presence of allied stones enforcing the mutual strengthen. Hence, up to tactics in Go gaming the interaction among stones is weighed by the next Eq. (3):

$$w_{ij} = \sum_s r_t x_s^{(ij)} \tag{3}$$

$x_s^{(ij)}$ formula describes each stone s lying between i and j, that in turns, is making a Go tactic with allies and against adversaries.

Parameter r_t quantifies the a-priori known power of tactic t: eye (r_{eye}), net (r_{net}), ladder (r_{lad}), invasion (r_{inv}), reduction (r_{red}). Tactic parameters fit a total order > induced by the *a-priori* knowledge of Go tactics power learned from high ranked Go players, and, the proposed definition of the energy function as follows: $r_{eye} > r_{net} > r_{lad} > r_{inv} > r_{red} > r_{sl}$. The single liberty parameter value is $r_{sl} = 1$. We remark that $r_{eye} > r_{net}$, because, given the energy function parameterization, the quantity of stones and the each stone' size seize the influence of each stone in a net. As the usual occurrence, three or more stones are making a net and at least one of large size. So, net power is well pondered. In addition, one compound stone has one or two internal eyes and rarely more. Regarding these facts the influence of net with respect to eyes in the Go Hamiltonian is well tuned. The whole field impact value is $\mu = 1$ in this proposal for simplicity; and, the specific impact h_i from field to stone i is the number of liberties i has.

In the Go game Hamiltonian in Eq. (1) the first term accounts the interaction of collaboration among same color stones, and, the fight against adversaries. In the second term the stone's force from its liberties. Henceforth, given any Go state, by definitions in Eqs. (2) and (3) used in Eq. (1) the Go Hamiltonian quantify the interaction strength among ally and/or against adversarial stones on the base of the each stone's power, that in turns depends on the each other relative position: that's the contribution of each eye, ladder or net pattern; or from invasion, reduction or connection tactics.

Like with changes of matter by heat or pressure transmission in nature phenomena, the evolution leading to territory control it can result a phase transition in Go gaming. The sequentially heated stones placed as a Go move it eventually change the board state abruptly in the evolution of games, similar to matter changes. This sequence of moves yields to a Go phase-transition process that brings sudden board area dominance. In Fig. 3, the sequential placement of red-black-flag stones makes the override over white in this board area, alike local phase transition. Because Go is a zero-sum game where victory for one means defeat for the other, the Go game thermodynamics may be seen as out of the equilibrium.

3   Experiments and Results

AlphaGo machine [9] is the current top Go player and one of the biggest triumphs of Artificial Intelligence. For testing the proposed model both Go games comparisons are made: human *vs* human players, and AlphaGo *vs* humans. Scores from the simulations using as input the logged games files, they close fit with the real games' scores.

3.1 Human Go Games

As a first tough test we simulate classic Go games that have been broadly analyzed. The strength of stones in the successive states and the final result are shown in Figs. 1 and 2. The board in the figure is the game final state. In the following figures blue line is for blacks and red line is for whites.

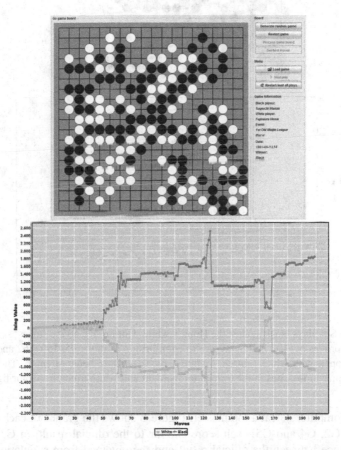

Fig. 1. The winner S. Masao played black versus Fujisawa playing white. From moves 50 to 160 the strength of the groups is quite separated, in move 166–170 the separation is reduced but, from then until game end black is ever strengthen. No phase transition happens. (Color figure online)

3.2 AlphaGo Versus Lee Sedol Games

Lee Sedol is one top Go player since he was 12 years old. AlphaGo – Lee Sedol encounter was a five-game match gamed by March 2016 in Seoul, Korea. Lee Sedol played blacks the odd games and whites the pair games. AlphaGo won the first, second, third and fifth game and Lee Sedol the fourth, so 4/5 games won AlphaGo, being the

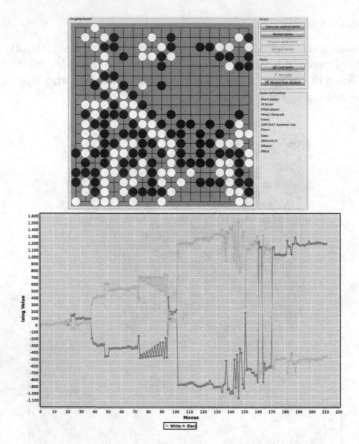

Fig. 2. Yi Se Sol plays black against the Hong's white. Until move 40 the stones' strength is tie; then white improves but late both converge to equilibrium. In move 95, 150, 162 and 171 phase transitions happen with white – black - white – black – white better strength. The successive scores are similar to the ones in the official tournament and white triumph. (Color figure online)

first time a computer defeat a top master. Figure 3 shows the graphs of each of the five games: G1, G2, G4 and G5, each score similar to the official result. In G3 there is a small difference between the official result and the obtained from simulation.

Results shows how the measure of the potential of a stone or army of stones for controlling territory on the board is up to the own stones board position and the made synergy from interaction. Go gaming fix on *long-term influence moves* that strong affect the outcome of later moves, so the relevance on the early correct decision making for playing Go. We showed that Go (stochastic-like) gaming is straightforward treated by Ising model and Hamiltonian, so fair to estimate the each player's board area control and the dominion status at any stage of game evolution. The Ising model for launching interaction of spins in a two-state space is relevant used to define an energy function for accurate Go gaming model.

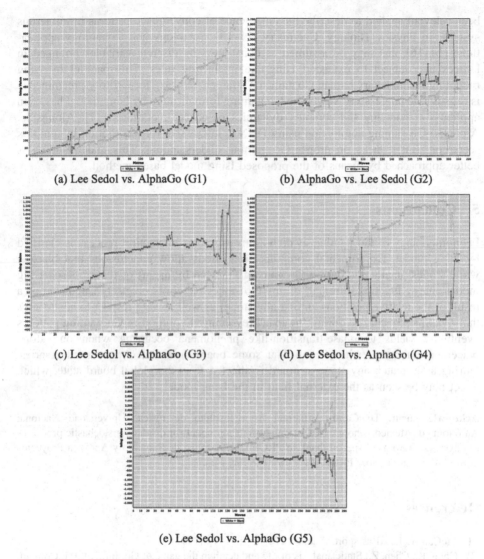

(a) Lee Sedol vs. AlphaGo (G1)   (b) AlphaGo vs. Lee Sedol (G2)

(c) Lee Sedol vs. AlphaGo (G3)   (d) Lee Sedol vs. AlphaGo (G4)

(e) Lee Sedol vs. AlphaGo (G5)

Fig. 3. Lee Sedol vs AlphaGo https://deepmind.com/research/alphago/match-archive/alphago-games-english/. (Color figure online)

4 Discussion

The stones in a Go board are organized into distinct groups or clusters, usually sparsely scattered about or somewhat intermingled. Grouping is regularly the result of proximity of stones of the same color or the predominance of stones of one color in an area making synergy throughout the whole board regarding Go rules. The area subtended by the board is divided into black and white territories, "spheres of influence". Since the interaction rules in the Ising model are very general and simple [10], the model has been relevant applied to describe the emergence of convergence patterns in numerous systems in Physics, Biology, Chemistry [11–13], Sociology and technology applications [14–16], that may be assumed as constituted by discrete variables arranged in lattices and subject to extended Ising-like interacting rules. This parallel by Ising modeling the millenary human Go game on strategic thinking for territory preeminence is remarkable impressive. Newly the Go gaming formalization by Ising model has been applied for modeling the complex dynamics of cancer metastasis [17]. Alongside, AlphaGo Go gaming automation using DNN is impressive for recognition in complex scenarios. But it lacks on proper Go gaming understanding. This understanding is better approached by means of the proposed Ising model based method.

5 Conclusions

Phenomenology of Go gaming as dichotomy variables interaction process is clarified by Ising model. Experimental computer simulations allow conclusions that black – white stones' interaction during Go gaming is traced by means of the proposed Ising model energy function. Strength of any Go stones pattern is precisely calculated as a result of the relative positions among ally stones as well as with respect to adversaries that dynamically change during the match evolving. Evolution in Go gaming patterns eventually yields to phase-transition-like phenomena occurring when one stone placement strength territory control at some board area that overrides adversaries. During a Go match any stone at board is affected from the global board state, which effect may be seen as the external field in the Ising model.

Acknowledgment. To Carlos Villarreal from Instituto de Física, Universidad Nacional Autónoma de México, who advised us on apply Ising model for displaying stochastic processes in physics. Arturo Yee' special thank to PROFAPI Programa de Fomento y Apoyo a Proyectos de Investigación, number PROFAPI2015/304.

References

1. McCarthy, J.: AI as sport. Science **276**, 1518–1519 (1997)
2. Chen, K., Chen, Z.: Static analysis of life and death in the game of Go. Inf. Sci. Inf. Comput. Sci. **121**, 113–134 (1999)
3. Benson, D.B.: Life in the game of Go. Inf. Sci. **10**, 17–29 (1976)
4. Allis, L.V.: Searching for Solutions in Games and Artificial Intelligence. University of Limburg, The Netherlands (1994)
5. Richards, N., Moriarty, D.E., Miikkulainen, R.: Evolving neural networks to play Go. Appl. Intell. **8**, 85–96 (1998)
6. van der Werf, E.C.D., van den Herik, H.J., Uiterwijk, J.W.H.M.: Learning to estimate potential territory in the game of Go. In: van den Herik, H.J., Björnsson, Y., Netanyahu, N.S. (eds.) CG 2004. LNCS, vol. 3846, pp. 81–96. Springer, Heidelberg (2006). https://doi.org/10.1007/11674399_6
7. Yee, A., Alvarado, M.: Well-time pattern recognition in Go gaming automation. Math. Methods Comput. Tech. Sci. Eng. 174–181 (2014)

8. Browne, C.B., Powley, E., Whitehouse, D., Lucas, S.M., Cowling, P.I., Rohlfshagen, P., Tavener, S., Perez, D., Samothrakis, S., Colton, S.: A survey of Monte Carlo tree search methods. IEEE Trans. Comput. Intell. AI Games **4**, 1–43 (2012)

9. Silver, D., Guang, A., Guez, A., Sifre, L., van den Driessche, G., Schrittwieser, J., Antonoglou, I., Panneershelvam, V., Lanctot, M., Dieleman, S., Grewe, D., Nham, J., Kalchbrenner, N., Sutskever, I., Lillicrap, T., Leach, M., Kavukcuoglu, K., Graepel, T., Hassabis, D.: Mastering the game of Go with deep neural networks and tree search. Nature **529**, 484–489 (2016)

10. Bonaccorsi, E., Merlino, S., Pasero, M., Macedonio, G.: Microsommite: crystal chemistry, phase transitions, Ising model and Monte Carlo simulations. Phys. Chem. Miner. **28**, 509–522 (2001)

11. Matsuda, H.: The Ising model for population biology. Prog. Theoret. Phys. **66**, 1078–1080 (1981)

12. Tkacik, G., Schneidman, E., Berry, M.J.I., Bialek, W.: Ising models for networks of real neurons (2006)

13. Hue, M., Riffle, M., Vert, J.-P., Noble, W.: Large-scale prediction of protein-protein interactions from structures. BMC Bioinform. **11**, 1–9 (2010)

14. Peter, J., Freyer, R., Smith, M.F., Scarfone, C., Coleman, R.F., Jaszczak, R.J.: Nuclear medicine image segmentation using a connective network. In: Nuclear Science Symposium, Conference Record, pp. 1782–1786. IEEE (1996)

15. Aoki, M.: New Approaches to Macroeconomic Modeling: Evolutionary Stochastic Dynamics, Multiple Equilibria, and Externalities as Field Effects. Cambridge University Press, Cambridge (1998)

16. Wolkenhauer, O., Fell, D., De Meyts, P., Bluthgen, N., Herzel, H., Le Novere, N., Hofer, T., Schurrle, K., van Leeuwen, I.: SysBioMed report: advancing systems biology for medical applications. IET Syst. Biol. **3**, 131–136 (2009)

17. Barradas-Bautista, D., Alvarado-Mentado, M., Agostino, M., Cocho, G.: Cancer growth and metastasis as a metaphor of Go gaming: an Ising model approach. PLOS ONE (2018)

A Novel Criterion to Obtain the Best Feature Subset from Filter Ranking Methods

Lauro Vargas-Ruíz[1,2]([✉]), Anilu Franco-Arcega[2],
and María-de-los-Ángeles Alonso-Lavernia[2]

[1] Instituto Tecnológico Superior del Oriente del Estado de Hidalgo,
43900 Apan, Hidalgo, Mexico
lvargas@itesa.edu.mx
[2] Instituto de Ciencias Básicas e Ingenierías,
Universidad Autónoma del Estado de Hidalgo,
42184 Mineral de la Reforma, Hidalgo, Mexico
{afranco,marial}@uaeh.edu.mx

Abstract. The amount of data available in any field is permanently increasing, including high dimensionalities in the datasets that describe them. This high dimensionality makes the treatment of a dataset more complicated since algorithms require complex internal processes. To address the problem of dimensionality reduction, multiple Feature Selection techniques have been developed. However, most of these techniques just offer as result an ordered list of features according to their relevance (ranking), but they do not indicate which one is the optimal feature subset for representing the data. Therefore, it is necessary to design additional strategies for finding this best feature subset. This paper proposes a novel criterion based on sequential search methods to choose feature subsets automatically, without having to exhaustively evaluate rankings derived from filter selectors. The experimental results on 27 real datasets, applying eight selectors and six classifiers for evaluating their results, show that the best feature subset are reached.

Keywords: Feature selection · Filter · Ranking · Evaluation criterion

1 Introduction

Nowadays, large amount of data from different environments are generated and stored. In some cases, high dimensionality for representing the data can be presented and this supposes diverse problems for processing them, i.e. slowness in the process or complexity in the interpretation of results. To minimize these aspects, a reduction of the feature subset can be done using Feature Selection (FS) techniques, to obtain optimal feature subset.

In literature, there are two kinds of FS approaches, called Filter and Wrapper. Basically, the difference between them consists in the inclusion of a classification

© Springer International Publishing AG, part of Springer Nature 2018
J. F. Martínez-Trinidad et al. (Eds.): MCPR 2018, LNCS 10880, pp. 12–22, 2018.
https://doi.org/10.1007/978-3-319-92198-3_2

algorithm in the evaluation process. In the case of Filters, commonly they process the features one by one and get an ordered list of the features or variables, which is known as ranking and represents a descending order depending on the importance of the features; whereas Wrappers process feature subsets evaluating them with a classifier, the best subset according this algorithm is returned.

Since filters only produce a ranking, the owner of the data have to manually choose the feature subset that adequately represents the problem. Therefore, several methods have been developed for automatically obtaining the optimal feature subset for the dataset. In the literature has reported works that propose different alternatives. Among the most common are (*i*) use the first k-features in the ranking [1], or (*ii*) choose those that reach a previously defined threshold [2].

Choosing the first k-features does not necessarily ensures that such selection represents the optimal subset. On the other hand, establishing the threshold value requires knowing the instances nature under study on the other hand, if mathematical tools are used, the complexity of the method is increased. Therefore, if a criterion for choosing features is not used, it is necessary to exhaustively evaluate all the possible subsets that can be derived from that ranking, in order to find the optimal one.

Considering the disadvantages of the alternatives mentioned, it is proposed a criterion for evaluating a feature filter ranking, which do not evaluate it in an exhaustive way.

This article includes a section referring to the description of Filter methods for FS, then the proposed ranking evaluation criterion is presented, as well as the obtained experimental results. Finally, conclusions and future work are shown.

2   Filter Methods for FS

One of the objectives pursued by the FS algorithms is to determine the importance of the existing features in a dataset whose classification is previously known. Frequently, this is achieved by identifying the relevance and redundancy of the features, allowing the factibility to eliminate some of them without affecting the definition and classification rates of the dataset under study.

Filter algorithms can be classified as Univariate or Multivariate depending on the quantity of features studied at the same time, in the first case the features are studied one by one and in the second, subsets of them are included. This work considers only univariate algorithms, where the output produced by them is a features list, ordered by their relevance.

From a given ranking, it is possible to determine which features can be eliminated from the original data set. However, in order to carry out this process, the criterion of an expert person in the scope of the problem context is often required, so as to determine which features are considered useful and which are not.

This way of choosing features is not the most adequate because (*i*) there is not always an expert knowledge in the domain of the data, (*ii*) human participation can include errors or deviations that affect the validity of the results, causing subjectivity and (*iii*) manual processing is slower.

When an expert in the subject domain is not available, it can be performed an exhaustive evaluation of the ranking. In the literature, it is common to evaluate feature subsets by a classification algorithm, considering its precision to determine which subset is the one that best represents the data. However, this exhaustiveness entails a high computational cost.

There are some algorithms for automate the search process based on sequential methods. Greedy stepwise is one that is implemented on Weka platform [3]. However other authors have reported that this search method presents some problems produced by noise in local data, in consequence global maxima is not reached [4]. This algorithm can be configured with the features quantity to select, so the human intervention is required.

For the above reasons, it is useful to have a procedure to choose a feature subset automatically, this situation justify the development of new methods.

3   Proposed Criterion for Evaluating Rankings

The proposed algorithm has the fundamental purpose of determining a feature subset by means of a ranking evaluation derived from a filter type selector based on the classifier performance, so it takes as input a features ranking generated by an univariate filter algorithm. Then a search method is used in order to evaluate the classifier behavior, finally, a feature subset that satisfied a criterion for detention of evaluation is produced.

This work uses the search method Sequential Forward Search (SFS) [5], which evaluates first the most important feature, using a classification method, i.e. SFS applies the classifier considering the objects description of a set using only that feature. Subsequently, it is added the next most important feature and evaluates in the same way. This process is repeated until all the features are included in the evaluation.

SFS evaluates the features one by one, however not all them must be evaluated since, at any time during the evaluation process, the proposed criterion can identify a feature subset that produces the best performance for a given classifier. When the whole feature subset has been evaluated, it is said that an exhaustive search has been carried out.

In order to avoid exhaustive searches, the criterion uses a parameter called *window* (*w*), whose purpose is to define the tests quantity that have to be performed consecutively so as to identify a decreasing behavior in the classifier performance. When this behavior is identified, the criterion returns the selected features subset up to that moment.

The identification of the positive or negative trend in the behavior of a classifier, is reflected in obtaining consecutive values, either ascending or descending respectively. As it is presented in Sect. 4, considering a percentage of tests based on the included features quantity in a dataset, it is possible to determine the optimal subset.

This criterion considers to find that negative trend in the precision rate of the classifier that evaluates the possible feature subsets. Analyzing the exhaustive results from a ranking, it was observed that if the classifier performance decreases, there is a strong chance to continue with this behavior. The experimental design is focused on identifying the tests quantity that effectively indicates the negative tendency of classifier. This amount of tests is indicated by the parameter w.

Figure 1 presents the algorithm of the proposed criterion to choose the features subset that best represents a dataset. The process begins with a ranking where the features will be processed using a SFS strategy, some control parameters are initialized with value 0, among them there is one that will assume the count of the selected features and one more to store the iterations number. In another hand, the w parameter is initialized with a percentage of all features of whole dataset. Later, an iterative process evaluates the classifier accuracy registering the best value. If a maximum value is identified, from this moment the times quantity where the precision does not increase is counted while this

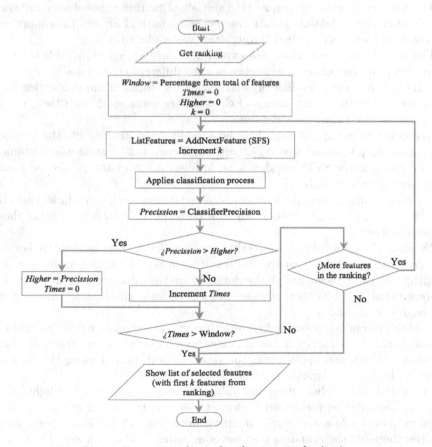

Fig. 1. Process performs by the proposed criterion

number does not exceed w value. The process ends when a maximum value was found or when the ranking was fully evaluated, thus the feature subset is established.

4   Experimental Results

Several filter algorithms were used in order to show the efficiency of the proposed criterion: Chi Squared (CS) [6], Gain Ratio (GR) [7], Info Gain (IG) [8], Laplacian Score (LS) [9], One R (O) [10], Relief (R) [11], SVM [12] and Symmetrical Uncertainty (Sy) [13]. These algorithms were selected because they are the most used in the literature, due to their strengths.

In addition to these FS algorithms, to validate the ranking lists of features issued by them, several methods of supervised classification were used, in order to verify the relevance of the criterion use with different algorithms.

The used classifiers to evaluate the feature subsets are: SMO (Sequential Minimal Optimization) [14], Naive Bayes [15], two neighborhood-based algorithms [16,17], C4.5 supported by graphs [18] and an algorithm created over instance filter combination - classifier [3]. All the methods, both of FS and the supervised classification have been applied through the Weka platform [3].

The used datasets to perform the experiments are described in Table 1, where it can seen that the examples were chosen with different characteristics. Some of them include numeric, nominal or mixed features. In addition, properties such as the total of features, instances and classes were considered, even there is one case with balanced class (*Iris* dataset).

According to all of datasets, FS and classification algorithms, the number of experiments performed were 1272, although only 1123 results were obtained because the selector SVM could not be applied in 16 of the 27 datasets and Laplacian Score in 9 of them.

For study convenience, the features nomenclature was changed in all cases by $X = \{x_1, x_2, x_3, x_4, \ldots, x_n, class\}$, where n corresponds to the quantity of them in each dataset.

To show the detailed procedure that was applied to the datasets, it is used the *Messidor* set. Table 2 shows the resulting features ranking from each FS algorithm. As can be seen, not all the rankings are the same and it is precisely this difference that suggests their evaluation to determine the best features subset that represent the data.

Table 3 presents the obtained results through an exhaustive SFS search process to obtain the accuracy of the six classifiers included in the study. To show the proposed criterion application, the results are displayed using the ranking generated by the FS algorithm *One R*.

In Table 3, the highest precision value for each classifier is highlighted. In addition, the criterion results are observed, defining the size of w with a corresponding value to 20% of features quantity, in the case of *Messidor* there are 19 features, therefore the rounding parameter acquires a value of w equal to 4. The subsets are evaluated adding one by one the features, until in the iteration "i" a

Table 1. Description of used datasets

Datasets	Instances	Features	Classes
1 Abalone	4,177	8	28
2 Adults	48,842	14	2
3 Cylinder bands	539	39	2
4 Breast cancer	286	9	2
5 Car evolution	1,728	6	4
6 Chess	3,196	36	2
7 Congressional voting records	435	16	2
8 Dermatology	366	34	6
9 Ecoli	336	7	8
10 Geographical music chromatic	1,059	116	33
11 Geographical music simple	1,059	68	33
12 German credit	1,000	20	2
13 Glass	214	9	6
14 Hepatitis	155	19	2
15 Horse colic	300	27	2
16 Iris	150	4	3
17 Lymphography	148	18	4
18 Madelon	2,000	500	2
19 Messidor features	1151	19	2
20 Mushroom	8,124	22	2
21 Nursery	12,960	8	5
22 Primary tumor	339	17	21
23 Sensorless	58,509	48	11
24 Statlog - Australian credit	690	15	2
25 Tic tac toe	958	9	2
26 Wisconsin breast cancer	699	10	2
27 Zoo	101	17	7

decreasing performance in the classifier accuracy is identified. Once this behavior is detected, the precision value of iteration "$i-1$" is stored to be compared with the obtained precision values in the next w iterations. If the consecutive iterations quantity (equal to the size of w) presents a lower performance than the stored precision, the criterion stops and the feature subset of iteration "$i-1$" are returned as the best subset.

Similarly, the process was applied in each dataset. Figure 2 shows the results of the criterion application with the dataset *Adults* described by 14 features, using the ranking given by the Info Gain selector. In this figure, the criterion application is shown with a box, for the NB results, observing that with $w = 3$,

Table 2. Ranking for *Messidor* dataset, obtained from the FS algorithms

CS	GR	IG	LS	O	R	SVM	Sy
x_3	x_{15}	x_3	x_1	x_3	x_3	x_3	x_{15}
x_{15}	x_{16}	x_{16}	x_2	x_{15}	x_4	x_7	x_{16}
x_{16}	x_1	x_{15}	x_{19}	x_4	x_{19}	x_4	x_{14}
x_4	x_{14}	x_4	x_{14}	x_5	x_9	x_9	x_3
x_{14}	x_3	x_{14}	x_{15}	x_{16}	x_5	x_{15}	x_4
x_5	x_{13}	x_5	x_6	x_6	x_6	x_{10}	x_5
x_6	x_4	x_6	x_5	x_{14}	x_{10}	x_8	x_6
x_9	x_5	x_9	x_7	x_{13}	x_{15}	x_{16}	x_{13}
x_{13}	x_6	x_{13}	x_4	x_8	x_7	x_6	x_7
x_7	x_7	x_7	x_{13}	x_9	x_8	x_{13}	x_9
x_8	x_9	x_8	x_3	x_7	x_{11}	x_5	x_8
x_2	x_8	x_2	x_{16}	x_1	x_{12}	x_2	x_1
x_1	x_{12}	x_1	x_8	x_2	x_{16}	x_{14}	x_2
x_{19}	x_2	x_{19}	x_{12}	x_{12}	x_{14}	x_{11}	x_{19}
x_{12}	x_{19}	x_{12}	x_{11}	x_{17}	x_2	x_{18}	x_{12}
x_{18}	x_{18}	x_{18}	x_9	x_{19}	x_{13}	x_1	x_{18}
x_{17}	x_{17}	x_{17}	x_{10}	x_{11}	x_{18}	x_{12}	x_{17}
x_{11}	x_{11}	x_{11}	x_{17}	x_{10}	x_1	x_{17}	x_{11}
x_{10}	x_{10}	x_{10}	x_{18}	x_{18}	x_{17}	x_{19}	x_{10}

Table 3. Precision of classifiers through *SFS* with the ranking *One R*, dataset *Messidor*

Iteration	Features	SMO	Naive Bayes	Lazy KStar	J48 Graft	Lazy Ibk	Meta filtered
1	None	53.084	53.084	53.084	53.084	53.084	53.084
2	x_3	59.253	59.166	56.212	60.990	59.687	59.687
3	x_{15}	60.122	57.255	61.772	61.685	58.384	62.554
4	x_4	59.861	60.209	62.207	60.556	66.116	62.815
5	x_5	60.817	**61.946**	63.944	62.815	68.810	62.989
6	x_{16}	60.817	57.863	63.510	63.076	**68.897**	63.076
7	x_6	63.162	58.818	64.639	63.597	67.420	62.815
8	x_{14}	63.510	56.820	**64.987**	63.336	66.811	62.815
9	x_{13}	63.597	56.038	64.553	63.076	66.030	62.815
10	x_8	64.639	56.038	63.510	63.510	65.943	62.902
11	x_9	65.248	56.038	64.553	63.858	66.203	**63.249**
12	x_7	65.074	56.299	63.944	63.076	66.03	63.249
13	x_1	65.421	56.299	64.031	63.076	66.116	63.249
14	x_2	67.246	56.386	64.466	64.205	65.508	63.249
15	x_{12}	67.420	56.646	64.031	63.423	66.116	63.249
16	x_{17}	66.638	56.646	62.641	63.597	63.684	63.249
17	x_{19}	66.551	56.646	62.815	64.466	62.815	63.249
18	x_{11}	67.333	56.820	63.423	64.379	62.902	63.249
19	x_{10}	**67.941**	56.820	61.338	**65.074**	61.685	63.249
20	x_{18}	67.593	56.820	61.251	64.639	61.338	63.249

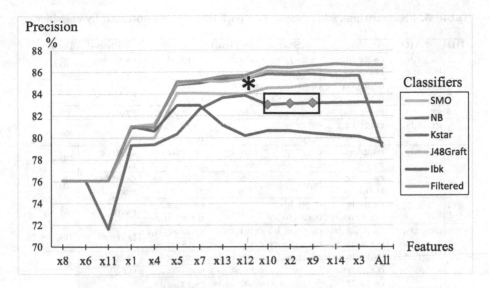

Fig. 2. Precision of classifiers through SFS with the ranking Info Gain, dataset Adults

which corresponds to rounding the 20% of features, it is possible to identify the features subset that produces the best behavior, in this case, it is integrated by nine features $\{x_8, x_6, x_{11}, x_1, x_4, x_5, x_7, x_{13}, x_{12}\}$, according to the established order by the ranking.

4.1 The w Parameter

In order to identify the appropriate value of the w parameter for the criterion operation, several experiments were carried out using four alternatives: 10%, 20%, 30% and 50% of the features number in the corresponding dataset.

The obtained results during the experiment are shown in Table 4, where the percentage indicates in how many of the 1123 experiments, the criterion chooses the features subset that achieve the best classification performance, with the respective w size. As it is observed, a w equivalent to 20% produces the best result. This comment responds to the fact that with this value it is found a

Table 4. Efficiency of the proposed criterion according to the w size.

w	Percentage of success cases	
	Individual	Accumulated
10%	8.01%	8.01%
20%	65.09%	73.10%
30%	7.46%	80.56%
50%	12.56%	93.12%
100%	6.88%	100%

Table 5. FS algorithms where maximum performance was obtained by classifier.

BD	SMO	NB	KStar	J48 Graft	Ibk	Filtered	Total
1	cs,gr,ig, ls,o,r,sy	cs,gr,ig, ls,o,r,sy	cs,gr,ig, ls,o,r,sy	cs,gr,ig, ls,o,r,sy	cs,gr,ig, o,r,sy	cs,gr,ig, o,r,sy	40
2	gr,ig,o, sy	cs,gr,ig, o,sy	cs,gr,ig, o,sy	cs,ig,o, r,sy	cs,ig,o, r,sy	gr,o,r,sy	30
3	gr	cs,ig	o	gr,o,r,sy	cs,ig,r,sy	gr,o,r,sy	16
4	gr,ig,ls, o	cs,gr,ig, sy	cs,gr,ig, o,sy	cs,gr,o	cs,gr,ig, r,sy	gr,o	23
5	cs,gr,ig, r,sy	cs,gr,ig, r,sy	cs,gr,ig, r,sy	cs,gr,ig, r,sy	cs,gr,ig, r,Sy	cs,gr,ig, r,sy	30
6	ls,r	cs,gr,ig, ls,o,r,sy	ls,r	cs,gr,ig ls,r,sy	cs,ig,ls, sy	cs,ig,ls, r,sy	26
7		cs,gr,ig, o,r,svm,sy	cs,gr,ig, o,r,svm,sy	svm	cs,gr,ig, o,r,svm,sy	svm	23
8	cs,gr,ls, o,svm,sy	cs,gr,ig,ls, o,r,svm,sy	cs,gr,ig,ls, o,r,svm,sy	cs,gr,ls, o,r,sy	cs,gr,ig,ls, o,r,svm,sy	ls,o,sy	39
9	cs,gr,ig,ls, o,r,sy	cs,gr,ig,ls, o,r,svm,sy	cs,gr,ig,ls, o,r,sy	cs,gr,ig,ls, o,r,svm,sy	cs,gr,ig,ls, o,r,svm,sy	cs,gr,ig,ls, o,r,sy	45
10	ls,o,r,sy	cs,gr,ig,ls, o,r,sy	ls,o,r,sy	cs,gr,ig,ls, o,r,sy	cs,gr,ig,ls, o,r,sy	o,r,sy	32
11	cs,gr,ig,ls, o,r,sy	cs,gr,ig, ls,sy	o,r	ig,ls,o,r, sy	cs,gr,ig,ls, o,r,sy	o,r	28
12	cs,gr,ig,ls, r,sy	o,r	cs,gr,ig,ls, r,sy	cs,gr,ig,ls, r,sy	cs,ig,r,sy	cs,ig,r,sy	28
13	cs,gr,ig,ls, o,r,svm,sy	cs,gr,ig,ls, o,r,svm,sy	cs,gr,ig,ls, o,r,sy	cs,gr,ig,ls, o,r,svm,sy	cs,gr,ig,ls, o,r,sy	cs,gr,ig,ls, o,r,sy	45
14		cs,ig,r,svm	cs,ig,r,sy	cs,gr,ig,o, svm,sy	cs,gr,ig,o, r,svm	cs,ig,o,r, svm	25
15		cs,gr,ig,o, r,svm,sy	cs,gr,ig,r, svm,sy	cs,gr,ig,sy	cs,gr,ig,o, r,svm,sy	cs,gr,ig, svm,sy	29
16	cs,gr,ig,ls, o,r,svm,sy	cs,gr,ig,ls, o,r,svm,sy	cs,gr,ig,ls, o,r,svm,sy	cs,gr,ig,ls, o,r,svm,sy	cs,gr,ig,ls, o,r,svm,sy	cs,gr,ig,ls, o,r,svm,sy	48
17	gr,ls	gr,ig	o,r	ls,r	gr,sy	ig,o,r	13
18	o,r,svm	cs,ig,ls,o, r,svm,sy	cs,gr,ig,ls, o,r,svm,sy	gr,ls,o,r, svm,sy	ls,o,r,svm	cs,gr,ig,ls, r,svm,sy	35
19	cs,gr,ig,o, r,sy	cs,gr,ig,o, r,sy	cs,gr,ig,o, r,sy	cs,gr,ig,o, r,sy	cs,gr,ig,o, r,sy	cs,gr,ig,o, r,sy	36
19	cs,gr,ig,o, r,sy	cs,gr,ig,o, r,sy	cs,gr,ig,o, r,sy	cs,gr,ig,o, r,sy	cs,gr,ig,o, r,sy	cs,gr,ig,o, r,sy	36
21	cs,gr,ig,r, sy	cs,gr,ig,o, r,sy	cs,gr,ig,o, r,sy	cs,gr,ig,r, sy	cs,gr,ig,o, sy	cs,gr,ig,r, sy	32
22	cs,gr,ig,o, r,sy	cs,ig,o,r, sy	sy	cs,gr,ig,o, r,sy	cs,gr,ig,o, r,sy	cs,gr,ig,o, r,sy	30
23	ls,svm	cs,gr,ig,ls, o,svm,sy	cs,gr,ig,ls, o,r,svm,sy		cs,ig,svm,sy	ls	22
24	cs,gr,ig,ls, o,r,svm,sy		ls,o,r,svm	ls,r,svm	ls,r,svm	cs,gr,ig,ls, o,r,svm,sy	26
25	cs,gr,ig,o, r	cs,gr,ig,o, r,svm	cs,gr,ig,ls, o,r,sy	cs,gr,ig,o, r,svm,sy	gr,ls,o,r, svm	cs,gr,ig,ls, o,r,svm,sy	38
26	ls,o,r	cs,ig,sy	gr,ls,o	gr,ls,o,r	gr,ls,o	cs,gr,ls,o, r,sy	22
27	cs,gr,ig, o,r,sy	cs,gr,ig, o,r,sy		cs,gr,ig, o,r,sy	cs,gr,ig, o,r,sy		24

Total : 821

Total of successful applications of the criterion ($w = 20\%$) : 73.10%

balance between the iterations number that have to be performed by the criterion and the search of the best feature subset.

According to the obtained results on 27 real datasets, the criterion shows a good performance, recognizing 821 of the 1123 performed experiments, what is equivalent to 73.10% with the maximum performance of the all used classifiers and considering w as the 20% of the features. The details of these experiments are presented in Table 5, where for each dataset is shown the FS algorithms that reach the best accuracy results according to the classifier methods.

With other values of w parameter, the criterion effectiveness increases, but the required tests quantity is greater and the difference does not justify the necessary processing time, the best results were obtained with $w = 20\%$. The experiments show that in several cases where $w = 30\%$ the tests quantity was approaching to the exhaustiveness. So, the larger the w value, the more tests are performed because the process requires more tests to determine if the behavior is decreasing for real.

5 Conclusions

The proposed selection criterion uses a sequential search method, where the w parameter helps to define the iterations quantity needed for finding a decreasing behavior of the classifier performance used to validate the ranking. With $w = 20\%$, it is possible identifying the feature subset that obtains the best classification performance, without evaluating exhaustively all feature subsets. If the w value increases, more success results could be recognized. This would imply making more iterations, however the difference is not as significant in the resulting precision.

Throughout the experimentation, it was found that the proposed criterion is able to reduce 58.67% of features, regardless of the characteristics of the included datasets.

The obtained results demonstrate that the application of the proposed criterion can process the derived ranking from any filter feature selection method and, based on that list, it can find the feature subset that produces the best classification performance, The criterion can be applied to the ranking derived from any filter feature selection method and combine it with either classification algorithm.

References

1. Sánchez-Maroño, N., Alonso-Betanzos, A., Tombilla-Sanromán, M.: Filter methods for feature selection – a comparative study. In: Yin, H., Tino, P., Corchado, E., Byrne, W., Yao, X. (eds.) IDEAL 2007. LNCS, vol. 4881, pp. 178–187. Springer, Heidelberg (2007). https://doi.org/10.1007/978-3-540-77226-2_19
2. Belanche, L.A., Gonzalez, F.F.: Review and evaluation of feature selection algorithms in synthetic problems. Technical report. Universitat Politecnica de Catalunya, Barcelona (2011). http://mawi.wide.ad.jp/mawi/

3. Hall, M., Frank, E., Holmes, G., Pfahringer, B., Reutmann, P., Witten, I.: The WEKA data mining software: an update. SIGKDD Explor. **11**, 10–18 (2009). http://www.cs.waikato.ac.nz/ml/weka/
4. Sadeghi, R., Zarkami, R., Sabetraftar, K., Van Damme, P.: Application of genetic algorithm and greedy stepwise to select input variables in classification tree models for the prediction of habitat requirements of *Azolla filiculoides* (Lam) in Anzali wetland, Iran. Ecol. Model. **215**, 44–53 (2013)
5. Pudil, P., Novovicova, J., Kittler, J.: Floating search methods in feature selection. Pattern Recognit. Lett. **15**, 1119–1125 (1994)
6. Dunning, T.: Accurate methods for the statistics of surprise and coincidence. Comput. Linguist. **19**, 61–74 (1993)
7. Quinlan, J.R.: C4.5: Programs for Machine Learning. Morgan Kaufmann Publishers Inc., San Francisco (1993)
8. Quinlan, J.R.: Induction of decision trees. Mach. Learn. **1**, 81–106 (1986)
9. He, X., Cai, D., Niyogi, P.: Laplacian score for feature selection. In: Advances in Neural Information Processing Systems, vol. 18, pp. 507–514. MIT Press, Cambridge (2005)
10. Holte, R.C.: Very simple classification rules perform well on most commonly used datasets. Mach. Learn. **11**, 63–91 (1993)
11. Kira, K., Rendell, L.A.: The feature selection problem: traditional methods and a new algorithm. In: Tenth National Conference on Artificial Intelligence, pp. 129–134. MIT Press, San Jose (1992)
12. Vapnik, V., Lerner, A.: Pattern recognition using generalized portrait method. Autom. Remote Control **24**, 774–780 (1963)
13. Press, W.H., Teukolsky, S.A., Vetterling, W.T., Flannery, B.P.: Numerical Recipes in C. Press Syndicate of the University of Cambridge, Cambridge (1988)
14. Singh, R., Kumar, H., Singla, R.K.: Analysis of feature selection techniques for network traffic dataset. In: IEEE (eds.) International Conference on Machine Intelligence and Research Advancement, pp. 42–46, Katra, India (2013)
15. Platt, J.C.: Sequential minimal optimization: a fast algorithm for training support vector machines. Technical report. Microsoft Co. (1998)
16. Titterington, D.M., Murray, G.D., Murray, L.S., Spiegelhalter, D.J., Skene, A.M., Habbema, J.D.F., Gelpke, G.J.: Comparison of discrimination techniques applied to a complex dataset of head injured. J. Roy. Stat. Soc. Ser. A **144**, 145–175 (1981)
17. Fix, E., Hodges Jr., J.L.: Discriminatory analysis nonparametric discrimination consistency properties, Project number 21-49-004. University of California, Berkeley (1951)
18. Cleary, J.G., Trigg, L.E.: K*: an instance-based learner using an entropic distance measure. In: 12th International Conference on Machine Learning, pp. 108–114. University of Waikato, New Zealand (1995)

Class-Specific Reducts vs. Classic Reducts in a Rule-Based Classifier: A Case Study

Manuel S. Lazo-Cortés[(✉)], José Fco. Martínez-Trinidad,
and Jesús Ariel Carrasco-Ochoa

Instituto Nacional de Astrofísica, Óptica y Electrónica, Puebla, Mexico
{mlazo,fmartine,ariel}@inaoep.mx

Abstract. In Rough Set Theory, reducts are minimal subsets of
attributes that retain the ability of the whole set of attributes to discern
objects belonging to different classes. On the other hand, class-specific
reducts allow discerning objects belonging to a specific class from all
other classes. This latest type of reduct has been little studied. Here
we show, through a case study, some advantages of using class-specific
reducts instead of classic ones in a rule-based classifier. Our results show
that it is worthwhile to deepen in the study of this issue.

1 Introduction

In many data analysis applications, information and knowledge are stored and
represented as a decision table which provides a convenient way to describe a
finite set of objects within a universe through a finite set of attributes. In a
decision table, rows represent objects, columns are attributes and each cell is
the value of an object on an attribute. A decision table is a special data table
such that the set of attributes is the union of a set of condition attributes and a
decision attribute.

The notion of reduct plays a fundamental role in rough set analysis. Pawlak
[11] defined a reduct of a decision table as a minimal subset of condition
attributes that has the same discernibiliy ability as the entire set of condition
attributes with respect to the decision attribute. Following this approach, most
studies have been focused on the classification-based definition of reduct. As
examples, see references [6–8,18,20,22].

In Rough Set Theory (RST)[10], the core idea is the so-called closed world
assumption. According to this maxim any two objects described by two identical
vectors of parameter values must be treated as equal in all subsequent analyses.
Formally, the main tool that ensures this property in data analysis is the relation
of indiscernibility between objects.

In some classification problems, it may be natural to consider different subsets
of attributes to differentiate objects, depending on the class they belong to. In
contrast to traditional feature selection methods where a single feature subset is
selected for all classes, class-specific methods choose a possibly different feature
subset for each class. In the literature, class-specific feature selection has received

© Springer International Publishing AG, part of Springer Nature 2018
J. F. Martínez-Trinidad et al. (Eds.): MCPR 2018, LNCS 10880, pp. 23–30, 2018.
https://doi.org/10.1007/978-3-319-92198-3_3

some attention [2,12,19,21,23], but it has not been not enough. That is why in this paper we focus on class-specific reducts.

The underlying idea of class-specific reducts is related to the widely used strategy of one-versus-rest that transforms a k-class classification problem into k two-class classification problems.

In RST, reducts are commonly used for building rule based classifiers. In this paper we study the effect of using class-specific reducts instead of classic ones for generating rules in a rule-based classifier.

The rest of the document is organized as follows. Section 2 provides the basic concepts. Section 3 presents and discusses the experimental results obtained in a comparison of the application of two variants of a rule-based classifiers over the same data set, considering in one case the rules generated from the classic reducts and, in the other case, the rules generated from class-specific reducts for every class. Finally Sect. 4 concludes this paper.

2   Basic Concepts

The type of datasets considered in this paper is a decision table, which is formally defined as

Definition 1 *(decision table). A decision table is a pair $S = (U, A_t = A_t^* \cup \{d\})$ where U is a finite set of objects, A_t is a set of attributes. A_t^* is a finite set of conditional attributes and d is a decision attribute indicating the decision class for each object in the universe. Each $a \in A_t$ corresponds to the function $I_a : U \to V_a$ called evaluation function, where V_a is called the value set of a. The decision attribute allows partitioning the universe into blocks (classes) determined by all possible decision values.*

Sometimes we will use D for denoting $\{d\}$, i.e. ($\{d\} = D$).

A *decision table* can be implemented as a two-dimensional array (matrix), in which one usually associates rows to objects, columns to attributes and cells to values of objects on attributes.

It is important to introduce the definition of the indiscernibility relation.

Definition 2 *(indiscernibility relation). Given a subset of conditional attributes $A \subseteq A_t^*$, the indiscernibility relation is defined as*
$$IND(A|D) = \{(u,v) \in U \times U : [I_d(u) = I_d(v)] \vee \forall a \in A, [I_a(u) = I_a(v)]\}.$$

We can find several formal definitions of reduct (see for example, [9]), nevertheless, according to the aim of this paper, we refer to reducts assuming the classical definition of discerning decision reduct as follows.

Definition 3 *(reduct for a decision table). Given a decision table S, an attribute subset $R \subseteq A_t^*$ is a reduct, if R satisfies the following two conditions:*

(i) $IND(R|D) = IND(A_t^*|D)$;
(ii) For any $a \in R, IND((R - \{a\})|D) \neq IND(A_t^*|D)$.

This definition ensures that a reduct has the same ability to distinguish objects belonging to different classes as the whole set of attributes, being minimal with regard to inclusion, i.e. a reduct does not contain redundant attributes or, equivalently, a reduct does not include other reducts. The original idea of reduct is based on inter-class discernment.

We will denote the set of all reducts of a decision table S as $RED(S)$.

Notice that, when defining a reduct, all classes ar collectively considered. As a result, although a reduct is a minimal set for the entire inter-class differentiation, it may not be minimal for each pairwise inter-class differentiation. Looking at a specific class independently from the other classes, we can review the notion of class-specific reduct, but first let us re-visit the indiscernibility relation.

Definition 4 *(indiscernibility relation with respect to a specific class). Given a decision table S, partitioned into c classes $K_1, K_2, ..., K_c$ and a subset of conditional attributes $A \subseteq A_t^*$, the indiscernibility relation with respect to the class K_i is defined as*
$$IND(A|K_i) = \{(u,v) \in U \times U : [I_d(u) = I_d(v) = K_i] \vee [I_d(u) \neq K_i \wedge I_d(v) \neq K_i] \vee \forall a \in A, [I_a(u) = I_a(v)]\}.$$

Taking into account this indiscernibility relation, a class-specific reduct can be formally defined as follows.

Definition 5 *(class-specific reduct for a decision table). Given a decision table S, partitioned into c classes $K_1, K_2, ..., K_c$, an attribute subset $R \subseteq A_t^*$ is a class-specific reduct of S with respect to the class K_i, if R satisfies the following two conditions:*

(i) $IND(R|K_i) = IND(A_t^*|K_i)$;
(ii) For any $a \in R, IND((R - \{a\})|K_i) \neq IND(A_t^*|K_i)$.

We will denote the set of all class-specific reducts of a decision table S with respect to the class K_i as $RED(S_{|K_i})$.

When considering this class-specific reduct definition, the focus is on a particular class considering all the remaining classes as if they were just one class. Following this line of thought it is easy to see that class-specific reducts can be computed as classic reducts but considering several two class decision tables instead of the original decision table for the c classes, i.e., if S is a decision table partitioned into c classes $K_1, K_2, ..., K_c$, and $S|K_i$ the decision table that results from considering in S only two classes, K_i and its complement $U - K_i$, we have that:

Proposition 1. $RED(S|K_i) = RED(S_{|K_i})$.

This proposition [21] is very important and has consequences, for example from the algorithmic point of view. Since class-specific reducts are classic reducts of a modified decision table, no new algorithms for computing class-specific reducts are needed. It is enough modifying the original decision table and then applying any available algorithm for classic reduct computation.

As a classic reduct is a subset of attributes jointly sufficient and individually necessary to discern between any pair of objects belonging to different classes; we can assure that if $R \subseteq A_t^*$ is a classic reduct of a decision table, i. e. $R \in RED(\mathcal{S})$, then R satisfies condition (i) in Definition 5 with respect to every class K_i. As a consequence we have the following result.

Proposition 2 [21]. *For any classic reduct $R \in RED(\mathcal{S})$ and for any class K_i in $\mathcal{S}$ there exists a class-specific reduct $R' \in RED(\mathcal{S}_{|K_i})$ such that $R' \subseteq R$.*

From this property we can arrive at an interesting result, related to the length of the shortest reducts and it is the following.

Corollary 1. *Let $\mathcal{S}$ be a decision table, and let $\mathbf{m}$ be the length of the shortest classic reducts related to $\mathcal{S}$. Let $\mathbf{m_i}$ be the length of the shortest class-specific reducts of $\mathcal{S}$ with respect to the class K_i. Then for every class K_i it follows that $\mathbf{m_i} \leq \mathbf{m}$.*

In this paper, we will use a set of reducts as a support for creating decision rules. So, Corollary 1 allows us to affirm that decision rules based on class-specific reducts are usually shorter than those rules based on classic reducts.

Let us take a look about how to obtain a set of decision rules supported on a set of reducts for classifying unseen objects. We will use the procedures included in the software tool RSES ver. 2.2.2, which has been widely used in the literature [3,14,15].

In RSES, once the reducts of a decision table have been computed, each object in the training sample is matched against each reduct. This matching gives as result a rule having in its conditional part, the attributes of the reduct, each one associated with the values of the currently considered object, and in its decision part it has the class for this training object.

When we attempt to classify an unseen object using the generated rule set, it may happen that several rules suggest different decision values. In such conflict situations a strategy to reach a final result (decision) is needed. RSES provides a conflict resolution strategy based on voting. In this method, each rule that its antecedent matches the object under consideration casts a vote in favor of the decision value of its consequent. Votes are counted and the decision value reaching the majority of the votes is chosen as the class for the object.

This simple method may be extended by assigning weights to rules. In RSES this method (also known as Standard Voting) assigns as weight for a rule the number of training objects supported by this rule. Then, each rule votes with its weight and the decision value reaching the highest weight sum is considered as the class for the object.

3   Experimental Results

In this section, through a case study, we will show how the use of class-specific reducts can improve a rule-based classifier. We will consider the lymphography dataset, taken from the UCI Machine Learning Repository [1]. In fact, we consider the original lymphography dataset and four datasets generated by the one-versus-the-rest approach. We randomly generate two folds in order to perform two-fold cross validation. Characteristics of the lymphography dataset and the folds can be seen in Table 1.

The computation of reducts and rules were performed by using RSES [16].

Table 1. Characteristics of the lymphography dataset

Attributes	Classes	Objects	Objects per class			
			K_1	K_2	K_3	K_4
18	4	148	2	81	61	4
	Fold 1	74	1	40	31	2
	Fold 2	74	1	41	30	2

First, for each fold, we calculate classic reducts and class-specific reducts for each class. Table 2 shows the number of reducts calculated for each fold.

Table 2. Number of classic and class-specific reducts for the lymphography dataset (two folds)

Fold	Classic	Class-specific			
		K_1	K_2	K_3	K_4
1	530	42	457	494	206
2	317	46	307	317	143

As a corroboration of Corollary 1, with respect to the length of classic and class-specific reducts, in Table 3, it can be seen, for both folds, that the shortest classic reducts have length 5 while class-specific reducts get shorter lengths (lengths 1 and 2 for classes K_1 and K_4, respectively, in fold 1, and length 1 for classes K_1 and K_4 in fold 2).

Likewise, with respect to the maximum length, for classic reducts it is 10 for the first fold and 9 for the second one, however when calculating class-specific reducts, for the classes K_1 and K_4, shorter lengths are obtained (lengths 4 and 6 for classes K_1 and K_4, respectively, in the first fold, and length 5 for classes K_1 and K_4 in the second one).

Later, we generate a set of reduct-based rules for the set of classic reducts, then we apply, over the two folds, the RSES rule based classifier Standard Voting and compute the average of the classification accuracy obtained in each fold.

Table 4 shows, in the first row, the results obtained in terms of accuracy for each fold and in average when classic reducts were used in the rule based classifier Standard Voting. Additionally, in the remaining rows of Table 4, we

Table 3. Length of classic and class-specific reducts for the lymphography dataset

Fold	Length	Classic	Class-specific			
			K_1	K_2	K_3	K_4
1	Minimum	5	1	5	5	2
	Maximum	10	4	10	9	6
2	Minimum	5	1	5	5	1
	Maximum	9	5	9	9	5

show the accuracy obtained by the rule based classifier Standard Voting in the respective class. On average, the rule based classifier Standard Voting obtained an accuracy of 0.73.

Table 4. Accuracy of the rule based classifier Standard Voting for the lymphography dataset using classic reducts

Class	Fold 1	Fold 2	Average
All	0.70	0.76	0.73
K_1	0.00	0.00	0.00
K_2	0.68	0.85	0.77
K_3	0.80	0.71	0.75
K_4	0.00	0.00	0.00

We performed another experiment by gathering all class-specific reducts computed in each class, and we calculated the set of rules based on this new set of reducts, then we performed the classification of the two folds and obtained the results that appear in Table 5.

Table 5. Accuracy of the rule based classifier Standard Voting for the lymphography dataset using all the class specific reducts gathered from each class

Class	Fold 1	Fold 2	Average
All	0.78	0.84	0.81
K_1	1.00	1.00	1.00
K_2	0.76	0.93	0.84
K_3	0.83	0.71	0.77
K_4	0.5	1.00	0.75

As we can see from Table 5, when considering rules generated from joining all class-specific reducts instead of all classic reducts, the classification accuracy heightened for every class. Therefore, global accuracy, considering rules generated from joining all class-specific reducts, was 0.81 in contrast with 0.73 when classic reducts were used.

Finally, taking into account that we are evaluating the practical utility of using class-specific reducts for a rule-based classifier, we wanted to compare the results obtained to those obtained with other well-known rule-based classifiers widely used in the literature. We select C4.5 [13], RIPPER [4] and SLIPPER [5]. These classifiers were run using the KEEL Software Suite [17].

Table 6 shows the results obtained by each compared classifier in ascending order. As we can see class-specific reduct based classifier got the best result.

Table 6. Accuracy of five rule-based classifiers for the lymphography dataset

Algorithm	Accuracy
RIPPER	0.69
Classic-reducts	0.73
SLIPPER	0.76
C4.5	0.78
Class-specific reducts	**0.81**

4   Conclusions

The main purpose of the research reported in this paper has been to discuss through a case study the possible advantages that we can obtain when using class-specific reducts instead of classic reducts, particularly when we use attribute subsets for generating rule-based classifiers. Experimental results allows concluding that class-specific reducts can generate shorter rules and, what is more important, they can improve classification accuracy.

The results achieved in this case study motivate to delve into the advantages of using class-specific reducts instead of classic ones, especially it may be interesting to study the effect of some reduct selection methods to generate the rules instead of considering the rules generated by the whole set of reducts.

References

1. Bache, K., Lichman, M.: UCI machine learning repository. School of Information and Computer Science, University of California, Irvine, CA (2013). http://archive.ics.uci.edu/ml
2. Baggenstoss, P.M.: Class-specific feature sets in classification. IEEE Trans. Signal Process. **47**, 3428–3432 (1999)
3. Barman, T., Rajesh, G., Archana, R.: Rough set based segmentation and classification model for ECG. In: Conference on Advances in Signal Processing (CASP), pp. 18–23. IEEE (2016)
4. Cohen, W.W.: Fast effective rule induction. In: Machine Learning: Proceedings of the Twelfth International Conference, Lake Tahoe California, USA, pp. 1–10 (1995)

5. Cohen, W.W., Singer, Y.: A simple, fast, and effective rule learner. In: Proceedings of the Sixteenth National Conference on Artificial Intelligence, Orlando Florida, USA, pp. 335–342 (1999)

6. Gao, C., Yao, Y.: An addition strategy for reduct construction. In: Miao, D., Pedrycz, W., Ślęzak, D., Peters, G., Hu, Q., Wang, R. (eds.) RSKT 2014. LNCS (LNAI), vol. 8818, pp. 535–546. Springer, Cham (2014). https://doi.org/10.1007/978-3-319-11740-9_49

7. Jia, X.Y., Shang, L., Zhou, B., Yao, Y.Y.: Generalized attribute reduct in rough set theory Knowl. Based Syst. **91**, 204–218 (2016)

8. Liang, J.Y., Wang, F., Dang, C.Y., Qian, Y.H.: A group incremental approach to feature selection applying rough set technique. IEEE Trans. Knowl. Data Eng. **26**, 294–308 (2014)

9. Miao, D.Q., Zhao, Y., Yao, Y.Y., Li, H.X., Xu, F.F.: Reducts in consistent and inconsistent decision tables of the Pawlak rough set model. Inf. Sci. **179**(24), 4140–4150 (2009)

10. Pawlak, Z.: Rough sets. Int. J. Comput. Inf. Sci. **11**, 341–356 (1982)

11. Pawlak, Z.: Rough Sets, Theoretical Aspects of Reasoning About Data, pp. 315–330. Kluwer Academic Publishers, Dordrecht (1992)

12. Pineda-Bautista, B.B., Carrasco-Ochoa, J.A., Martínez-Trinidad, J.F.: General framework for class-specific feature selection. Expert Syst. Appl. **38**, 10018–10024 (2011)

13. Quinlan, J.R.: MDL and categorical theories (continued). In: Machine Learning: Proceedings of the Twelfth International Conference, Lake Tahoe California, USA, pp. 464–470 (1995)

14. Rana, H., Lal, M.: A rough set theory approach for rule generation and validation using RSES. Int. J. Rough Sets Data Anal. **3**(1), 55–70 (2016)

15. Rana, H., Lal, M.: A comparative study based on rough set and classification via clustering approaches to handle incomplete data to predict learning styles. Int. J. Decis. Supp. Syst. Technol. **9**(2), 1–20 (2017)

16. Skowron, A., Bazan, J., Szczuka, M., Wroblewski, J.: Rough set exploration system (version 2.2.2). http://logic.mimuw.edu.pl/~rses/

17. Triguero, I., Gonzlez, S., Moyano, J.M., Garca, S., Alcal-Fdez, J., Luengo, J., Fernndez, A., del Jesus, M.J., Snchez, L., Herrera, F.: KEEL 3.0: an open source software for multi-stage analysis in data mining. Int. J. Comput. Intell. Syst. **10**, 1238–1249 (2017)

18. Wang, G.Y., Ma, X.A., Yu, H.: Monotonic uncertainty measures for attribute reduction in probabilistic rough set model. Int. J. Approx. Reason. **59**, 41–67 (2015)

19. Wang, L.P., Wang, Y.L., Chang, Q.: Feature selection methods for big data bioinformatics: a survey from the search perspective. Methods **111**, 21–31 (2016)

20. Yao, Y., Fu, R.: The concept of reducts in Pawlak three-step rough set analysis. In: Peters, J.F., Skowron, A., Ramanna, S., Suraj, Z., Wang, X. (eds.) Transactions on Rough Sets XVI. LNCS, vol. 7736, pp. 53–72. Springer, Heidelberg (2013). https://doi.org/10.1007/978-3-642-36505-8_4

21. Yao, Y.Y., Zhang, X.: Class-specific attribute reducts in rough set theory. Inf. Sci. **418**(419), 601–618 (2017)

22. Zhang, X.Y., Miao, D.Q.: Double-quantitative fusion of accuracy and importance: systematic measure mining, benign integration construction, hierarchical attribute reduction. Knowl. Based Syst. **91**, 219–240 (2016)

23. Zhang, M.L., Wu, L.: LIFT: multi-label learning with label-specific features. IEEE Trans. Pattern Anal. Mach. Intell. **37**, 107–120 (2015)

On the Construction of a Specific Algebra for Composing Tonal Counterpoint

Erick G. G. de Paz[1]($\boxtimes$), Malaquías Quintero-Flores[1],
and Xavier Quiñones-Solís[2]

[1] Tecnológico Nacional de México,
Av. Instituto Tecnológico s/n, 90300 Apizaco, Mexico
erickggdepaz@yandex.com
[2] Escuela de Música del Estado de Tlaxcala,
Av. Fernando Solana s/n, 90401 Apizaco, Mexico

Abstract. Polyphonic music involves the manipulation of harmonic principles to get that several melodies concur gracefully. This paper describes a specific algebraic structure to compose tonal polyphonic music. The model has been carefully designed according to music theory principles for tonal composition. And, it consists of considering operands to the two-notes chords; and operators to the techniques of melodic conduction. The algebraic paradigm introduced in this paper produces chord progressions in accord with reconfigurable constrains which allow to drive the structural coherence of automatic compositions. As illustrative results, instances of polyphonic phrases have been designed by means of this algebraic model.

Keywords: Group theory · Music composition
Structural patterns modelling

1 Introduction

The automatic composition research is widely dominated by stochastic approaches which naturally focus on the problem of chords-transition [9]. Other authors concentrate on the structure and coherence that music has to keep, and tackle this problem by evolutionary algorithms [7], generative grammars [16] or the simple study of finite-state machines supported by artificial intelligence methods [3,11]. Some other approaches may be considered as improved derivations of these.

This paper introduces a new perspective based on an algebraic structure called magma which, by definition, requires two factors [2]:

1. **A set M:** For this case, represented by a set of two-voices chords and some directions.

We would like to thank Evelyn Groesch, principal of the EMET, for all the given facilities.

2. **A function** F such that maps M^2 into M, useful to describe composition laws.

In this context, thematic successions of chords are constructed gradually based on some initial chords and their harmonic relations; factor which is easily modelled by a family of functions. On the one hand, each part of the model has been carefully designed according to music theory laws. On the other, however, music composition is a huge field, specially the polyphony; reason why this first attempt is restricted to the most basic form of academic polyphony, named, **first specie counterpoint**. For not musicians, this term, *first specie* stands for a two-voices composition such that both melodies got the same rhythm. The last description and the word basic do not have to discredit this approach; because, against common sense, some rules get relaxed or lifted for counterpoint with more than two-voices [5].

In the next section the set for representing chords is induced and formally defined. The third section describes a family of functions which lets model, by a rule-based way, the relations between two chords. And, the last section shows how to use the chords and operators to produce polyphonic phrases; some of them are analysed through a musical perspective.

2   Numerical Model

2.1   Pitch Representation

Pitch is the quality of a sound governed by the rate of produced vibrations in the environment [4]. These vibrations are measured in Hertz, unit of frequency, defined as $Hz = vibrations/s$. The most of musical instruments are designed to emit a standard range of frequencies; these are divisible into discrete units called semitones. Hence, the relation between a given semitone $p \in \mathbb{Z}$ and its frequency Hz is stated as:

$$Hz = 440 \sqrt[12]{2^{p-9}} \tag{1}$$

Regard that $p = 0$ is equivalent to the piano middle C. Thus, forwards $p = 1$ stands for $C\#$, $p = 2$ for D, ...; and, backwards $p = -1$ stands for B, and so on. This equivalence is illustrated in Fig. 1.

Fig. 1. A partial chromatic scale, the corresponding value of p is above

Musical instruments have got a finite range of frequencies limited by their physical characteristics and the human ear capability to perceive sounds. Therefore, let replace the infinite set of integers $\mathbb{Z}$ by a subset $\mathbb{P} \subset \mathbb{Z}$. For subsequent practical implementations in this paper, this set is defined as

$$\mathbb{P} = [-17, +17] \cap \mathbb{Z} \tag{2}$$

2.2   Tonality Limits

The set $\mathbb{P}$ contains all the possibles semitones that a certain instrument be able to emit. However, the most of western music avoids developing a melody with semitones lacking of relation to the first semitone of the melody. This first semitone is called tonic and determines which other semitones are proper or lacking for belonging to the melody. The sorted collection of proper semitones constitutes the called diatonic scale. The two most important distributions of proper semitones for a given tonic are the major and minor modes.

Both modes are easy to identify in a piano keyboard for specific cases. The semitones corresponding to white keys of piano belong to the major mode of C ($p = 0$), and simultaneously, belong to the minor mode of A ($p = 9$). Hence, it is possible to model the distribution of proper semitones by means of relative distances from each white key to their corresponding tonics.

The Fig. 2 shows the relative differences for both modes. Regard that the keyboard pattern is periodic each 12 semitones. Thus, the subset $\mathbb{P}_+$ of proper semitones for the major mode with tonic $p = 0$ is formally defined by $\mathbb{P}_+ \subset \mathbb{P} | \forall p \in \mathbb{P}_+ \exists s \in \mathbb{S}_+ : [12|p - s]^1$, where $\mathbb{S}_+ = \{-10, -8, -7 - 5, -3, 0, 2, 4, 5, 7, 9, 11\}$ (Observe the Fig. 2). The subset $\mathbb{P}_-$ of proper semitones for the minor mode with tonic $p = 0$ is given by an analogous expression, replacing $\mathbb{S}_+$ by $\mathbb{S}_- = \{-10, -9, 7, -5, -4 - 2, 0, 2, 3, 5, 7, 8, 10\}$.

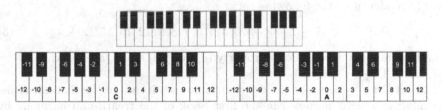

Fig. 2. Relative distances of diatonic scale for both modes major (C, $p = 0$) and minor (A, $p = 9$)

2.3   Harmonic Space

Counterpoint is the technique of setting two melodies simultaneously. As a consequence, two different semitones $(p_x, p_y) \in \mathbb{P}^2$ are played simultaneously. In music theory, harmony is the field which states the proper semitone-distances between p_x and p_y.

In order to introduce some important concepts, the Fig. 3 shows three plots. The initial pair of plotted frequencies corresponds to two semitones p_x and p_y, respectively, such that $(p_x, p_y) \in \mathbb{P}^2$ and for this particular example $p_x - p_y = 12$. The third plot is the addition of the two last plots and corresponds to the same pair (p_x, p_y) played simultaneously. Regard that the frequency of p_x is periodic

---

[1] Inside brackets, $[a|b]$ means a divides b.

each line, the frequency of p_y is periodic each two lines (dotted lines). Then, the addition of the two last frequencies is also periodic each two lines. Hence, it is possible to state that (p_x, p_y) sounds like p_y. In musical terms, the pair of semitones (p_x, p_y) is called **consonant**; and p_y (the resulting semitone) is called **fundamental** [1]. A pair (p_x, p_y) is dissonant if the addition of their frequencies does not correspond to any other pitch $p \in \mathbb{P}$. For each pair of consonant pitches, an unique fundamental pitch exists; so the fundamental of a consonant pair can always be represented by a function g. For the last example of Fig. 3: $g(p_x, p_y) = p_y$.

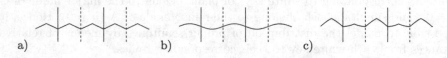

Fig. 3. Illustrative frequencies of two independent semitones p_x (a) and p_y (b). The third plot(c) is the addition of the two last plots and corresponds to the same pair (p_x, p_y) played together

The last plotting technique can be used to find a set $\mathbb{D} \subset \mathbb{P}$ such that every $d \in \mathbb{D}$ creates consonant pairs $(p + d, p) \forall p \in \mathbb{P}$. This subject is exposed in deep by Schoenberg [14] and Rameau [12] treatises on Harmony. The theoreticians of music have identified the following set:

$$\mathbb{D} = \{\dots, -7, -5, -4, -3, 0, 3, 4, 5, 7, 8, 9, 12, 15, 16, \dots\}, \qquad (3)$$

and an important periodicity property $(d \bmod 12) \in \mathbb{D}^* \ \forall d \in \mathbb{D}$, where $\mathbb{D}^* = \{0, 3, 4, 5, 7, 8, 9\}$.

The set $\mathbb{D}$ also originates the distribution of semitones in the diatonic scale. This affair is widely discussed in the first book of the treatise on harmony by Rameau [12].

Hence regard that there are two important restrictions to create a set $\mathbb{H}$ containing pleasant pairs of semitones:

1. The tonality, which is represented by limiting the original set of semitones $\mathbb{P}$ to $\mathbb{P}_+$ or $\mathbb{P}_-$.
2. The harmony (consonances), which limits the Cartesian product $\mathbb{P}_+{}^2 = \mathbb{P}_+ \times \mathbb{P}_+$ to $\mathbb{H}_+ \subset \mathbb{P}_+{}^2 | \forall h = (p_{+x}, p_{+y}) \in \mathbb{H}_+ \exists d^* \in \mathbb{D}^* : [abs(p_{+x} - p_{+y}) \bmod 12] = d^*$. And analogously for $\mathbb{H}_- \subset \mathbb{P}_-{}^2$.

The Fig. 4 shows the items of $\mathbb{H}_-$ and $\mathbb{H}_+$ like points. Both axis represents the set P. This illustration lets us observe the relation between the pitch and the harmony. Hence, a tonal two voices counterpoint melody may be represented as a variable $h \in \mathbb{H}_+ (\text{or } \mathbb{H}_-)$ which takes different values in n discrete time units $[h_1, h_2, \dots, h_n \in \mathbb{H}_+]$. Naturally, attentive readers guess a Markov model; an approach that is useful to create a trainable model. However, for this paper, the approach is to create music by means of rules belonging to music theory.

In the next section, we describe a basic algebra to compose melodies.

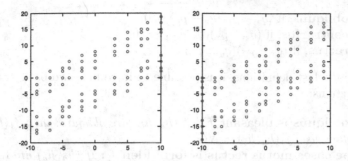

Fig. 4. Harmonic sets $\mathbb{H}_-$ (minor) and $\mathbb{H}_+$ (major) respectively

3 Functional Space

Hereafter, $\mathbb{H}$ stands for whichever selected set $\mathbb{H}_-$ (minor mode) or $\mathbb{H}_+$ (major mode); and $h \in \mathbb{H}$ be called **chord** according to Rimsky-Korsakov's definition [13]

3.1 A Family of Functions $\mathbb{F} : \mathbb{M}^2 \rightarrow \mathbb{M}$

Let $\mathbb{F}$ be a family of functions which describes the relation between a given pair $(h_x, h_y) \in \mathbb{H}^2$ according to several composition principles. The collection of possible relations is:

1. **YES:** It is agreeable to emit h_y after h_x during a melody.
2. **NO:** It is not agreeable to emit h_y after h_x during a melody; or well, it is forbidden.
3. **A value** $h_z \in \mathbb{H}$: It is agreeable to emit the following sequence: h_x, h_z, h_y.

In order to reduce this scheme to a set, let define $\mathbb{M} = \{YES, NO\} \cup \mathbb{H}$. Over this set, two operators are defined in the Table 1. The set $\mathbb{M}$ and both operators constitute an algebraic structure called *magma* [10].

Table 1. Definition of two magma operators over $\mathbb{M}$

m_a	m_b	$m_a \vee m_b$	$m_a \wedge m_b$	m_a	m_b	$m_a \vee m_b$	$m_a \wedge m_b$	m_a	m_b	$m_a \vee m_b$	$m_a \wedge m_b$
YES	YES	YES	YES	NO	YES	YES	NO	h_a	YES	YES	h_a
YES	NO	YES	NO	NO	NO	NO	NO	h_a	NO	h_a	NO
YES	h_b	YES	YES	NO	h_b	h_b	NO	h_a	h_b	h_a	h_a

3.2 Conduction Rules

The harmonic conduction of voices identifies three basic motions [17]. To define them, let $(h_a, h_b) \in \mathbb{H}^2$ be two chords consecutively emitted; for practicality $h_a = (p_x, p_y)$ and $h_b = (q_x, q_y)$. Then, the motion is classified as [18]:

1. **Motus obliquus**, if $(q_x - p_x)(q_y - p_y) = 0$.
2. **Motus contrarius**, if $(q_x - p_x)(q_y - p_y) < 0$.
3. **Motus rectus**, if $(q_x - p_x)(q_y - p_y) > 0$.

Exposed the last definitions, it is possible to introduce two basic conduction rules as functions:

- **Motus obliquus is pleasant** f_1: If (h_a, h_b) *are obliquus, then* $f_1(h_a, h_b) = YES$. *Otherwise,* $f_1(h_a, h_b) = NO$.
- **For some cases motus rectus is forbidden** f_2: If (h_a, h_b) *are rectus and* $[abs(q_y - q_x) \bmod 12] \in \{0, 7\}$, *then* $f_2(h_a, h_b) = NO$. *Otherwise,* $f_2(h_a, h_b) = YES$.

These conduction functions map only to two values YES, NO. The next class of functions, called bridge functions map to values of the set $\mathbb{H}$.

3.3 Bridge Function

A bridge function $f*(h_a, h_b)$ returns, if it is possible, an optimal h^* to be emitted within the sequence $\{h_a, h^*, h_b\}$. The optimal criterion c is given by the musical principle of the shortest motion of voices [14], or well, the minimal Manhattan distance in the corresponding plane of the Fig. 4.

Formally, a **bridge function** f^* is a derivation of an original function f such that $f, f^* \in \mathbb{F}$. In order to define f^* on basis of f, firstly consider the following auxiliary set $\mathbb{H}'$:

For a given pair of values (h_a, h_b), let $\mathbb{H}'(h_a, h_b)$ be the collection of chords $\mathbb{H}'(h_a, h_b) \subset \mathbb{H} | f(h_a, h) \neq NO, f(h, h_b) \neq NO \; \forall h \in \mathbb{H}'(h_a, h_b)$.

Then, with the corresponding set $\mathbb{H}'$ for each possible pair, f^* is defined as:

- $f^*(h_a, h_b) = NO$, if $\mathbb{H}'(h_a, h_b) = \emptyset$
- $f^*(h_a, h_b) = h^* \in \mathbb{H}'(h_a, h_b) | c(h_a, h^*, h_b) \leq c(h_a, h, h_b) \forall h \in \mathbb{H}'(h_a, h_b)$, where:
  - $c((x_a, y_a), (x, y), (x_b, y_b)) = [abs(x_a - x) + abs(y_a - y) + abs(x_b - x) + abs(y_b - y)]$.

3.4 Absolute Function

A function $f \in \mathbb{F}$ is an absolute function if $f(k) \in \mathbb{H} \forall k \in \mathbb{H}^2$. This behaviour defines a magma over $\mathbb{H}$. In the next section, an absolute function is used as an operator for composing music. In order to find the absolute, let continue with the definitions of functions:

- *Limited bridge function:* $f_3 = f_1^* \wedge f_2$
- *Several motions function:* $f_4 = f_1 \vee f_3$
- *Absolute function:* $f_5 = f_4^*$.

The conveniently reduced set $\mathbb{H}$ has been explored (means of brute force) by the operator $(\circ = f_5)$. The results let conclude that for all possible given chords (X, Y), there is a way to connect them by a middle chord $h \in \mathbb{H}$. Therefore, the operator $(\circ)$ may be considered as a magma over $\mathbb{H}$. Another interesting point is that $(* = f_4)$ helps to identify the middle conduction from X to Y (Details in the following section).

4   Pseudorandom Music Generation

4.1   Theme Creation

A musical theme is the chief idea of a piece. During the piece, the theme is repeated several times as originally and latter with some variations.

In order to produce example themes structurally proper, it is necessary to:

1. Start and finish a theme with a random-selected tonic chord (Δ), defined as $\Delta = h \in \mathbb{H}|g(h) \bmod 12 - 0$. Remember that g determines the fundamental.
2. Use a random-selected subdominant chord (∇), defined $\nabla = h \in \mathbb{H}|g(h) \bmod 12 - 5$, as the penultimate chord of the theme.
3. Conduct properly the middle chords, fact ensured by $(\circ)$ and $(*)$.

The Algorithm 1 produces a phrase composed by a theme, two variations and a modulation (process to change the tonic).

Algorithm 1. Example of pseudocode for composing a musical phrase.

For two random-selected chords $(X, Y) = (h_a, h_b) \in \mathbb{H}^2$

1. $T = \Delta$
2. $S = \nabla$
3. $A = T \circ X$
4. $B = X \circ Y$
5. $C = Y \circ S$
6. $Theme = \{T, T * A, A, A * X, X, X * B, B, B * Y, Y, Y * C, C, C * S, S, T\}$
7. $ThemeVariationI = \{T, A, X, B, Y, C, T, A, X, B, Y, C, S, T\}$
8. $ThemeVariationII = \{T, C, Y, B, X, A, T, C, Y, B, X, A, S, T\}$
9. $Modulation = \{T, A, X, B, Y, C, S, T, S\}$
10. $Phrase = \{Theme, ThemeVariationI, ThemeVariationII, Modulation\}$
11. $EMIT(t = 0, Phrase)$
12. $EMIT(t = 5, Phrase)$

In the Algorithm 1, the variable A is equivalent to a chord within a succession from T to X. The magma property ensures that for any pair (T, X), $A = T \circ X$ exists. However, the operator $(* = f_4)$ does not have this property; this means that some pairs $(X, Y) \in \mathbb{H}^2$ cannot be successfully connected. The operator $(*)$ always depends on a result from $(\circ)$. For instance, $A = T \circ X$ ensures that

38   E. G. G. de Paz et al.

A can appear after T, so the operator $(*)$ just determinate whether is a direct connection or it depends on a auxiliary middle chord (aux) such that (T, aux, A) be a good succession. If the connection is not directed $T*A$ returns the auxiliary chord; otherwise a *empty* value.

The phrase involves a modulation; what implies that the phrase have to be emitted for the first time with $t = 0$ as tonic, and then with $t = 5$. Regard that a tonic $t \neq 0$ affects each harmony belonging to the phrase: Let (p_x, p_y) be the corresponding pitches for each chord $h \in \mathbb{H}$ of the phrase, then the modified pitches to emit are $(t + p_x, t + p_y)$.

The Algorithm 1 just describes one of many possibilities of phrase-structure. The Figs. 5 and 6 show examples of phrases produced by that algorithm. In the next subsection, the aesthetic and musical aspects of these results are analysed.

Fig. 5. Example of a *C major* phrase generated automatically

Fig. 6. Example of a *A minor* phrase generated automatically

4.2 Discussion

From a musical perspective, the harmony and counterpoint are technologies which set formal principles on how to utilize tones simultaneously and successively in a composition. The counterpoint student learns structures (chords) and ornaments in order to create a successful conduction of the concurring melodies. Directions just avoid known ways to get a displeasant-conduction, reducing the set of possible options for continuing a melody; but naturally, directions do not ensure beauty. All the grace in music comes from the design of motifs, tiny parts of melody, which may be repeated, altered and easily remembered. The design of motifs originates the identity of a melody.

The exposed approach is absolutely and exclusively based on harmonic and polyphonic rules. The most criticizable aesthetic point is that the creation of motifs seems to be an accidental result, which comes from the conduction rules that have set up. This problem is shared by the most of automatic composition systems; except for them which tackle the affaire directly and as a priority. The most of the literature which deals the motifs construction and analysis is based in grammars, for example [6,8].

Looking back on the got instances of phrases, Figs. 5 and 6, the melodies have got a good level of independence; however, the melodic sense may be broken by long jumps. And, another important aesthetic factor is the iteration of the same pair of voices, or well, the same two-voices chord structure in succession; situation that is not usual in *first specie counterpoint*.

Although these problems, the model originates acceptable short phrases. In addition, it lets select and handle the tonality and even the degrees of the scale to visit (For last subsection examples, these parameters have been randomly selected). According to Schubart and Schubart [15], the control over just these two factors is sufficient to create a clear emotional conduction. Thus, the model can be extended by the taste of the user creating algorithmic-like schemes which describe properties relatives to tonality and rhythm; just like the Algorithm 1.

4.3   Future Work

The paradigm introduced in this paper opens a perspective to produce music automatically according to configurable constrains. Some of the branches to continue the present field of research are:

1. Introducing more operators, with special attention to operators for producing musical ornaments. These additions will let produce other forms of academic counterpoint (still limited to *species*).
2. Extending the model for producing counterpoint with more than two-voices; taken also basis from the geometrical Tymoczko's theory [18].
3. Developing a *programming language* to code this specific class of algorithms (phrase-structures) as input for producing music sheets as output.

Finally, the authors would have to declare that it is absolutely necessary continuing with elementary tests of *species* in order to introduce properly more complex forms of counterpoint. Although this, they consider that this paper settles basis for the subsequent research.

References

1. Benade, A.: Fundamentals of Musical Acoustics: Second, Revised Edition. Dover Books on Music. Dover Publications, New York (2012). https://books.google.com.mx/books?id=0E0LHSXU0foC
2. Bourbaki, N.: Algebra I: Chapters 1–3. Springer, Heidelberg (1989). Actualités scientifiques et industrielles

3. Dean, R., McLean, A.: The Oxford Handbook of Algorithmic Music. Oxford Handbooks. Oxford University Press, Oxford (2018). https://books.google.com.mx/books?id=mA5EDwAAQBAJ
4. Encyclopaedia Britannica, Inc.: Britannica Enciclopedia Moderna. Encyclopaedia Britannica, Incorporated, Chicago (2011)
5. Gago, J.: Tratado de contrapunto: tonal y atonal. Clivis, Barcelona (1998)
6. Hsu, J.L., Liu, C.C., Chen, A.L.P.: Discovering nontrivial repeating patterns in music data. IEEE Trans. Multimed. 3(3), 311–325 (2001)
7. Martin, C.P., Ellefsen, K.O., Torresen, J.: Deep predictive models in interactive music. ArXiv e-prints, January 2018
8. McCormack, J.: Grammar based music composition. Complex Syst. 96, 321–336 (1996)
9. Merwe, A.V.D., Schulze, W.: Music generation with Markov models. IEEE Multimed. 18(3), 78–85 (2011)
10. Agustín-Aquino, O.A., Janine du Plessis, E.L.P.M.M.: Una introducción a la Teoría de Grupos con aplicaciones en la Teoría Matemática de la Música. Textos, vol. 10, Sociedad Matemática Mexicana (2009)
11. Oliwa, T., Wagner, M.: Composing music with neural networks and probabilistic finite-state machines. In: Giacobini, M., et al. (eds.) EvoWorkshops 2008. LNCS, vol. 4974, pp. 503–508. Springer, Heidelberg (2008). https://doi.org/10.1007/978-3-540-78761-7_55
12. Rameau, J.: Treatise on Harmony. Dover Books on Music. Dover Publications, Mineola (2012)
13. Rimsky-Korsakov, N., Achron, J., Hopkins, N.: Practical Manual of Harmony. Carl Fischer, New York (2005)
14. Schoenberg, A.: Theory of Harmony. California Library Reprint Series. University of California Press, Berkeley (1983)
15. Schubart, C., Schubart, L.: C. F. D. Schubart's Ideen zu einer Aesthetik der Tonkunst. C. F. D. Schubart's, des Patrioten, gesammelte Schriften und Schicksale, Scheible (1839)
16. Smaill, A.: Music informatics. School of Informatics, The University of Edinburg, Lecture, January 2018
17. Tchaikovsky, P.: Guide to the Practical Study of Harmony. Dover Books on Music. Dover Publications, Mineola (2013)
18. Tymoczko, D.: A Geometry of Music: Harmony and Counterpoint in the Extended Common Practice. Oxford University Press, Oxford (2011)

The Impact of Basic Matrix Dimension on the Performance of Algorithms for Computing Typical Testors

Vladímir Rodríguez-Diez[1,2]([✉]), José Fco. Martínez-Trinidad[1],
Jesús Ariel Carrasco-Ochoa[1], and Manuel S. Lazo-Cortés[1]

[1] Coordinación de Ciencias Computacionales, Instituto Nacional de Astrofísica,
Óptica y Electrónica, Luis Enrique Erro # 1, Tonantzintla, Puebla, Mexico
vladimir.rodriguez@inaoep.mx
[2] Universidad de Camagüey, Circunvalación Nte. km 51/2, Camagüey, Cuba

Abstract. Within Testor Theory, typical testors are irreducible subsets
of attributes preserving the object discernibility ability of the original
set of attributes. Computing all typical testors from a dataset has exponential complexity regarding its number of attributes, however there are
other properties of a dataset that have some influence on the performance of different algorithms. Previous studies have determined that a
significant runtime reduction can be obtained from selecting the appropriate algorithm for a given dataset. In this work, we present an experimental study evaluating the effect of basic matrix dimensionality on the
performance of the algorithms for typical testor computation. Our experiments are carried out over synthetic and real–world datasets. Finally,
some guidelines obtained from the experiments, for helping to select the
best algorithm for a given dataset, are summarised.

Keywords: Typical testor · Reduct · Basic matrix

1 Introduction

Testors were originally created by Cheguis and Yablonskii [3] as a tool for analysis
of problems connected with control and diagnosis of faults in electronic circuits.
Within Testor Theory, typical testors are irreducible subsets of attributes preserving the object discernibility ability of the original set of attributes. Thus,
typical testors have been used for feature selection as shown in [5,16]. Typical
testors are needed for solving some real–world applications. For instance, in [23]
the informational weight is used to identify risk factors on transfusion, related
to acute lung injury; and to establish an assessment for each attribute.

Unfortunately, computing all typical testors from a dataset has exponential
complexity regarding its number of attributes. Thus, the development of fast
algorithms for typical testor computation have been an active research topic
for more than three decades. One of the first algorithms for finding all typical

© Springer International Publishing AG, part of Springer Nature 2018
J. F. Martínez-Trinidad et al. (Eds.): MCPR 2018, LNCS 10880, pp. 41–50, 2018.
https://doi.org/10.1007/978-3-319-92198-3_5

testors, was proposed in [17] and modified in [20]. This algorithm, called BT, codifies a subset of attributes as a binary word, and evaluates candidate subsets in the natural ascending order induced by the binary numbers. In [18] the REC algorithm was presented. REC works directly over the dataset, handling a huge amount of superfluous information. Then, the CER algorithm [1], overcomes this drawback and uses a different traversing order. Later, a new algorithm called LEX [22] was introduced. The key point of LEX was its new traversing order of candidates that resembles the lexicographical order in which character strings are compared. This traversing order was also followed by the subsequent reported algorithms: CT_EXT [19] and BR [9]. The most recent algorithms reported for typical testor computation are the newest versions of these two algorithms: fast–CT_EXT [21] and fast–BR [10].

Recently, reducts from the Rough Set Theory (RST) have been related to typical testors [4]. RST was proposed by Pawlak in 1981 [11] as a mathematical theory to deal with imperfect knowledge, in particular with vague concepts. In [8], it was proven that algorithms for reduct computation can be applied to typical testor computation, since these two concepts are equivalent for consistent datasets. In [14], the GCreduct algorithm for reduct computation was presented and it was evaluated against fast–CT_EXT and fast–BR. In this work, it was concluded that GCreduct outperforms fast–CT_EXT in all cases.

It is a well known fact that there is not one unique algorithm for computing typical testors having the best performance for every given problem. Most algorithms for computing typical testors operate over the basic matrix. The basic matrix is a reduced binary matrix representing the discernibility information of the dataset. Former studies [10,15], have performed experiments by categorizing the basic matrices according to their density of 1's; i.e. the number of ones divided by the total number of cells of the matrix. In [6] it was concluded that the performance of the algorithms for computing typical testors is related to the number of rows, the density of 1's and the number of typical testors of the basic matrix. In [13] it was detailed a procedure for evaluating these algorithms over a synthetic sample of basic matrices with the same dimension and different density of 1's. This procedure was also followed in [14]. As a next step, in this work, we present an experimental study on the effects of the basic matrix dimensions on the performance of the algorithms for typical testor computation. For our experiments we have selected fast–BR and GCreduct, since these algorithms are the most recent and fastest algorithms reported for typical testor (reduct) computation. The selected algorithms are first executed over a sample of synthetic basic matrices, and the conclusions drawn from this experiment are corroborated over real–world datasets taken from the UCI machine learning repository [2].

The rest of this paper is structured in the following way. In Sect. 2, some basic concepts from Testor Theory are introduced and the pruning properties for typical testor computation are presented. In Sect. 3, we describe both algorithms: GCreduct and fast–BR. Then, in Sect. 4, we present our experimental study and we discuss the results. Finally, our conclusions appear in Sect. 5.

2 Theoretical Background

In this section, we introduce the main concepts of Testor Theory, as well as the definitions and propositions supporting the pruning strategies used in GCreduct and fast–BR.

2.1 Basic Concepts

Let DS be a dataset with k objects described by n attributes and grouped into r classes. Every attribute in the set of attributes $R = \{x_1, ..., x_n\}$, has a predefined Boolean comparison criterion. Let DM be the binary comparison matrix obtained from comparing every pair of objects in DS belonging to different classes. Every comparison of a pair of objects adds a row to DM with $0 =$ equal, $1 =$ different in the corresponding attribute position (column). DM has m rows and n columns. Comparisons generating a row with only 0's, hereinafter referred to as empty row, imply that two objects from different classes are equal according to their attribute values.

Definition 1. *Let $T \subseteq R$ be a subset of attributes from DS. T is a testor of DS (or DM) if in the sub-matrix of DM formed by the columns corresponding to attributes in T, there is not any empty row.*

Usually the number of rows in DM (m) is large. In [7] a reduction of DM without loss of relevant information was proposed, and in [12] it was proved that this reduced matrix, called *basic matrix* (BM), and DM; have the same set of testors. Then, we can substitute DM by BM in the Definition 1 without any loss of generality.

Definition 2. *A subset of attributes $T \subseteq R$ is a typical testor in BM iff T is a testor and $\forall x_i \in T, T \setminus x_i$ is not a testor.*

2.2 Pruning Properties for Typical Testor Computation

The concept of contribution presented in Definition 3 is a key aspect for both algorithms: GCreduct and fast–BR.

Definition 3. *Given $T \subseteq R$ and $x_i \in R$ such that $x_i \notin T$. x_i contributes to T iff the sub-matrix of BM formed with only those attributes in T has more empty rows than that matrix formed with attributes in $T \cup \{x_i\}$.*

First introduced for the CT_EXT algorithm, Proposition 1 was stated and proved in [21].

Proposition 1. *Given $T \subseteq R$ and $x_i \in R$ such that $x_i \notin T$. If x_i does not contribute to T, then $T \cup \{x_i\}$ cannot be a subset of any typical testor.*

The following propositions are stated and proved in [10].

Definition 4. *Given $T \subseteq R$. The compatibility mask of T, denoted as cm_T, is the binary word in which the jth bit is 1 if the jth row of BM has a 1 in only one of the columns corresponding to attributes in T, and otherwise it is 0.*

Proposition 2. *Given $T \subseteq R$ and $x_i \in R$ such that $x_i \notin T$. We denote as c_{x_k} to the binary word in which the jth bit is 1 if the jth row of BM has a 1 in the column corresponding to x_k. If $\exists x_k \in T$ such that $cm_{T \cup \{x_i\}} \wedge c_{x_k} = (0, ..., 0)$, then, $T \cup \{x_i\}$ cannot be a subset of any typical testor, and we will say that x_i is exclusionary with T.*

Proposition 3. *Given $T \subseteq R$ and $x_i \in R$ such that $x_i \notin T$. The subset $T \cup \{x_i\}$ is a typical testor iff it is a testor and x_i is not exclusionary with T.*

We will refer to Proposition 2 as exclusion evaluation. Proposition 3 expresses how to apply the exclusion evaluation for determining whether or not a subset T of attributes is a typical testor.

The propositions presented in this section constitute the basis for understanding the differences between fast–BR and GCreduct.

3   Fast-BR and GCreduct Algorithms

In this section, we present a comparison of the candidate evaluation process of fast–BR and GCreduct. We aim to provide enough elements to understand the different performance of these two algorithms for a given dataset. It is important to highlight that both algorithms operate over the basic matrix. Thus, when referring to characteristics of the basic matrix, we are indeed referring also to characteristics of the dataset from which the basic matrix was computed.

In GCreduct, a new candidate is generated by including a new attribute to the previous candidate. First, this new attribute is tested for contribution by using Definition 3. This process has a time complexity $\Theta(m)$, where m is the number of rows in the basic matrix. By Proposition 1, if the new attribute does not contribute to the candidate, this attribute is rejected. Otherwise, the candidate is evaluated for the testor condition by using Definition 1. This operation has also a time complexity $\Theta(m)$ as it was stated in [14]. Then, for those candidates satisfying the testor condition, the exclusion evaluation is performed to determine whether or not they are typical testors. This final verification is accomplished by means of Proposition 3, and its time complexity is $\Theta(mn)$; where n is the number of columns in the basic matrix.

In fast–BR, a new candidate is also generated by including a new attribute to the previous candidate. In the same way, the first evaluation step for the candidate is the test for contribution of the new attribute, which has a time complexity $\Theta(m)$. However, for contributing candidates, the next step is the exclusion evaluation. This process is accomplished by means of Proposition 2 and it has a time complexity $\Theta(mn)$. If the new attribute is exclusionary with the previous candidate, the attribute is rejected. Otherwise, the testor condition is verified by using Definition 1. This final process has a time complexity $\Theta(m)$.

Those candidates evaluated as testors, in this candidate evaluation process, are also typical testors because of the order followed in this algorithm.

In both algorithms, the candidate evaluation has a time complexity $\Theta(mn)$. Also, the total number of evaluated candidates has an exponential relation to the number of attributes in the dataset, for both algorithms. Thus, for both algorithms, the time complexity for typical testor computation is exponential. However, there are significant differences in the runtime of fast–BR and GCreduct for a given dataset.

The exclusion evaluation is the step with the highest time complexity in the candidate evaluation process for both algorithms. In GCreduct, this step is only executed for those candidates satisfying the testor condition, which are usually a small fraction of the total contributing candidates. In fast-BR, the exclusion evaluation is performed for every contributing candidate, which makes its candidate evaluation process more computationally expensive than GCreduct's. However, fast-BR takes advantage of this costly evaluation by discarding all the supersets of an exclusionary candidate by applying Proposition 2. This advantage is more effective for basic matrices with a higher density of 1's, as it was shown in [14].

4   Experimental Study

In [14], GCreduct was evaluated against fast–BR over a set of 500 randomly generated basic matrices with 2000 rows and 30 columns. The basic matrices were generated with densities of 1's uniformly distributed in the range (0.20–0.80). From this experiment it is followed that for matrices with density under 0.36 the fastest algorithm was GCreduct, fast–BR was the fastest for matrices with density between 0.36 and 0.66, and both algorithms showed similar performance for matrices with density above 0.66. However, in [14], it is concluded that the density of 1's is not the only factor affecting the performance of these algorithms, and they proposed a wider study of other factors as future work.

In this paper, we propose the exploration of the influence of basic matrix dimension on the performance of GCreduct and fast–BR. For this purpose, we present two experiments over synthetic datasets controlling both the density of the matrices as well as their size in rows and columns. In the first experiment, the number of rows of the basic matrices is varied while keeping constant the number of columns. In the second experiment, the number of columns of the basic matrices is varied while keeping constant the number of rows. In a last experiment, we corroborate the results obtained in the first experiments, over 10 real–world datasets taken from the UCI machine learning repository [2].

For our experiments we used a Java implementation of both algorithms. All experiments were run on a Celeron G1620 Intel processor at 2.70 GHz, with 4 GB in RAM, running GNU/Linux. The source code for the algorithms as well as all the datasets taken from UCI and synthetic basic matrices used in these experiments, can be downloaded from http://ccc.inaoep.mx/~ariel/Dimensions.

For the first experiment, we present 4 sets of 500 synthetic basic matrices each. All the basic matrices have 30 columns and their number of rows is 250

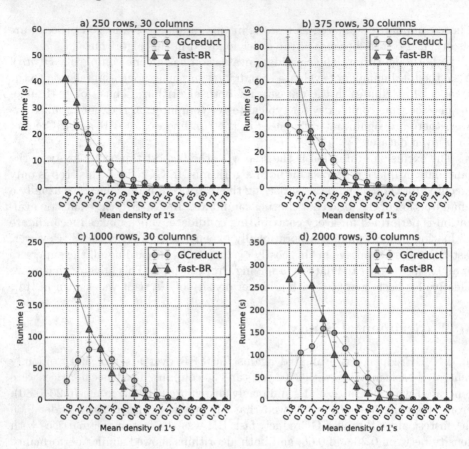

Fig. 1. Average runtime vs. density of 1's for GCreduct and fastBR. The number of columns of the basic matrices is 30, while the number of rows in each set is: (a) 250, (b) 375, (c) 1000 and (d) 2000.

for the first set, 375 for the second one, 1000 for the third one, and 2000 for the last one. The number of columns and the maximum number of rows in this experiment were selected to keep the algorithm's runtime within reasonable boundaries. The basic matrices in each set were generated with densities of 1's uniformly distributed in the range (0.20–0.80) using a step of 0.04.

The runtime for the execution of GCreduct and fast–BR over each set of basic matrices is shown in Fig. 1, as a function of the density of 1's. For clarity purposes, the 500 matrices in each set were split into 15 bins by discretizing the range of densities. Each bin has approximately 33 basic matrices. In Fig. 1 each vertical bar shows the standard deviation of each bin.

From Figs. 1–a to d, we noticed that there is a density value delimiting the basic matrices for which each algorithm is faster. This boundary value of density increases from 0.25 in Fig. 1–a to 0.32 in Fig. 1–d. It is important to notice that the time complexity of the candidate evaluation process of both algorithms is

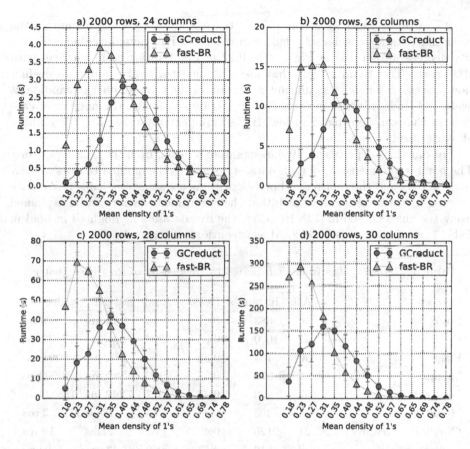

Fig. 2. Average runtime vs. density of 1's for GCreduct and fastBR. The number of rows of basic matrices is 2000, while the number of columns in each set is: (a) 24, (b) 26, (c) 28 and (d) 30.

proportional to the number of rows. Fast–BR takes advantage of making a costly candidate evaluation to evaluate a lower number of candidates in relation to GCreduct. From this experiment, we can infer that the increase in the number of rows of the basic matrix, makes the candidate evaluation process more significant regarding the number of evaluated candidates. Thus, a higher number of rows in the basic matrix is convenient for GCreduct.

For our second experiment, we used 4 sets of 500 synthetic basic matrices with 2000 rows and their number of columns is 24 for the first set, 26 for the second one, 28 for the third one, and 30 for the last one. The number of rows and the maximum number of columns in this experiment were selected to keep the algorithm's runtime within reasonable boundaries. The basic matrices in each set were generated with densities of 1's uniformly distributed in the range (0.20–0.80) again. The results from this experiment are shown in Fig. 2.

It can be seen in Figs. 2–a to d, that there is a density value delimiting the basic matrices for which each algorithm is faster. This boundary value of density decreases from 0.41 in Fig. 2–a to 0.32 in Fig. 1–d, for basic matrices with 2000 rows. This trend reveals that fast–BR, using a costly candidate evaluation process, can make a significant reduction in the total number of candidates evaluated. Indeed, when an exclusionary attribute is found, the number of candidates that can be avoided in fast–BR is exponentially related to the number of attributes in the dataset.

For our third experiment, 10 datasets were selected from the UCI repository. The name and dimensions of each dataset, as well as the number of rows in their basic matrix and the runtime of both algorithms are shown in Table 1. We have selected five of these datasets such that their runtime behavior can be explained using the rule exposed in [14]. However, the five datasets highlighted in bold in Table 1, were intensionally selected as exceptions of that rule.

Table 1. Datasets taken from UCI. Sorted by the density of their basic matrix.

Dataset	Atts	Instances	Density	Rows	fast–BR	GCreduct
Soybean	36	683	0.21	33	**256 ms**	697 ms
Credit-g	21	1000	0.35	223	81 ms	**32 ms**
Flags	30	194	0.35	390	1633 ms	**1098 ms**
Sponge	46	76	0.39	109	**359 ms**	59902 ms
Lung cancer	57	32	0.47	327	**7342 ms**	133434 ms
Heart-c	14	303	0.49	58	15 ms	**2 ms**
Cardiotocography	21	2126	0.49	81	24 ms	**18 ms**
Cylinder-bands	40	512	0.53	2062	**533 ms**	4594 ms
Chronic kidney disease	25	400	0.54	187	38 ms	**11 ms**
Colic	23	368	0.61	562	72 ms	**37 ms**

According to [14], GCreduct should be the fastest for basic matrices with density under 0.36, and fast–BR should be the fastest otherwise, for the datasets shown in Table 1. **Soybean**, which have a density of 0.21, is a clear exception of the results shown in [14]. However, under the new results obtained in this paper, we can infer that the density frontier for 36 attributes should be drastically below 0.36. Another contradiction with [14] is observed for **Heart-c**, **Cardiotocography**, **Chronic Kidney Disease** and **Colic**. For these datasets, the reduced number of columns of their basic matrix produces an increment in the boundary density value, as it was concluded from Fig. 2.

5   Conclusions

In this paper, we have explored the relation between the dimensions of the basic matrix associated to a dataset and the performance of fast-BR and GCreduct.

These are the most recent and fastest algorithms reported for typical testor (reduct) computation. Previous studies found that the density of 1's in the basic matrix can be used to determine a priori the fastest algorithm for a given dataset. In addition, we have found in this work, that basic matrices with a high number of rows are favorable for GCreduct, in the same manner that a high number of attributes makes a dataset better suited for fast–BR. Thus, the boundary density dividing the datasets for which each algorithm has the best performance should be computed taking into account the basic matrix dimensions.

Finally, we corroborated our results obtained from synthetic datasets over a set of real–world datasets taken from the UCI machine learning repository. These results allowed explaining the behavior of the two algorithms better than just using the density of 1's in the basic matrix.

For future work, we propose performing a deeper and wider experimentation in order to define a rule to determine which algorithm would be the best for a specific dataset.

Acknowledgments. This work was partly supported by National Council of Science and Technology of Mexico under the scholarship grant 399547.

References

1. Ayaquica, I.O.: A new external scale algorithm for typical testor computation. Memories of the II Iberoamerican Worshop on Pattern Recognition, pp. 141–148 (1997). (in Spanish)
2. Bache, K., Lichman, M.: UCI machine learning repository (2013)
3. Cheguis, I.A., Yablonskii, S.V.: About testors for electrical outlines. Uspieji Matematicheskij Nauk **4**(66), 182–184 (1955). (in Russian)
4. Chikalov, I., Lozin, V.V., Lozina, I., Moshkov, M., Nguyen, H.S., Slowron, A., Zielosko, B.: Three Approaches to Data Analysis. Springer Science & Business Media, Heidelberg (2013). https://doi.org/10.1007/978-3-642-28667-4
5. Dmitriev, A., Zhuravlev, I., Krendeliev, F.: About mathematical principles and phenomena classification. Diskretni Analiz **7**, 3–15 (1966). (in Russian)
6. González-Guevara, V.I., Godoy-Calderon, S., Alba-Cabrera, E., Ibarra-Fiallo, J.: A mixed learning strategy for finding typical testors in large datasets. Progress in Pattern Recognition, Image Analysis, Computer Vision, and Applications. LNCS, vol. 9423, pp. 716–723. Springer, Cham (2015). https://doi.org/10.1007/978-3-319-25751-8_86
7. Lazo-Cortés, M., Ruiz-Shulcloper, J., Alba-Cabrera, E.: An overview of the evolution of the concept of testor. Pattern Recogn. **34**(4), 753–762 (2001)
8. Lazo-Cortés, M.S., Martínez-Trinidad, J.F., Carrasco-Ochoa, J.A., Sánchez-Díaz, G.: On the relation between rough set reducts and typical testors. Inf. Sci. **294**, 152–163 (2015)
9. Lias-Rodríguez, A., Pons-Porrata, A.: BR: a new method for computing all typical testors. In: Bayro-Corrochano, E., Eklundh, J.-O. (eds.) CIARP 2009. LNCS, vol. 5856, pp. 433–440. Springer, Heidelberg (2009). https://doi.org/10.1007/978-3-642-10268-4_50
10. Lias-Rodríguez, A., Sánchez-Díaz, G.: An algorithm for computing typical testors based on elimination of gaps and reduction of columns. Int. J. Pattern Recogn. Artif. Intell. **27**(08), 1350022 (2013)

11. Pawlak, Z.: Classification of objects by means of attributes. Institute of Computer Science, Polish Academy of Sciences [PAS] (1981)
12. Piza-Davila, I., Sanchez-Diaz, G., Lazo-Cortes, M.S., Rizo-Dominguez, L.: A CUDA-based hill-climbing algorithm to find irreducible testors from a training matrix. Pattern Recogn. Lett. **95**, 22–28 (2017). https://doi.org/10.1016/j.patrec.2017.05.026
13. Rodríguez-Diez, V., Martínez-Trinidad, J.F., Carrasco-Ochoa, J.A., Lazo-Cortés, M.S.: Fast-BR vs. Fast-CT_EXT: an empirical performance study. In: Carrasco-Ochoa, J.A., Martínez-Trinidad, J.F., Olvera-López, J.A. (eds.) MCPR 2017. LNCS, vol. 10267, pp. 127–136. Springer, Cham (2017). https://doi.org/10.1007/978-3-319-59226-8_13
14. Rodríguez-Diez, V., Martínez-Trinidad, J.F., Carrasco-Ochoa, J.A., Lazo-Cortés, M.S.: A new algorithm for reduct computation based on gap elimination and attribute contribution. Inf. Sci. **435**, 111–123 (2018)
15. Rodríguez-Diez, V., Martínez-Trinidad, J.F., Carrasco-Ochoa, J.A., Lazo-Cortés, M., Feregrino-Uribe, C., Cumplido, R.: A fast hardware software platform for computing irreducible testors. Expert Syst. Appl. **42**(24), 9612–9619 (2015)
16. Ruiz-Shulcloper, J.: Pattern recognition with mixed and incomplete data. Pattern Recogn. Image Anal. **18**(4), 563–576 (2008)
17. Ruiz-Shulcloper, J., Aguila, L., Bravo, A.: BT and TB algorithms for computing all irreducible testors. Rev.cienc. matemáticas **2**, 11–18 (1985). (in Spanish)
18. Ruiz-Shulcloper, J., Alba-Cabrera, E., Lazo-Cortés, M.: Introduction to typical testor theory. Green Series No. 50. CINVESTAV-IPN, México (1995). (in Spanish)
19. Sanchez-Díaz, G., Lazo-Cortés, M.: CT-EXT: an algorithm for computing typical testor set. In: Rueda, L., Mery, D., Kittler, J. (eds.) CIARP 2007. LNCS, vol. 4756, pp. 506–514. Springer, Heidelberg (2007). https://doi.org/10.1007/978-3-540-76725-1_53
20. Sánchez-Díaz, G., Lazo-Cortés, M.: Modifications to the BT algorithm for reducing its runtime. Rev. cienc. matemáticas **20**(2), 129–136 (2002). (in Spanish)
21. Sanchez-Diaz, G., Piza-Davila, I., Lazo-Cortes, M., Mora-Gonzalez, M., Salinas-Luna, J.: A fast implementation of the CT-EXT algorithm for the testor property. In: Sidorov, G., Hernández Aguirre, A., Reyes García, C.A. (eds.) MICAI 2010. LNCS (LNAI), vol. 6438, pp. 92–103. Springer, Heidelberg (2010). https://doi.org/10.1007/978-3-642-16773-7_8
22. Santiesteban, Y., Pons-Porrata, A.: LEX: a new algorithm for the calculus of typical testors. Rev. cienc. matemáticas **21**(1), 85–95 (2003). (in Spanish)
23. Torres, M.D., Torres, A., Cuellar, F., Torres, M.D.L.L., Ponce De León, E., Pinales, F.: Evolutionary computation in the identification of risk factors. Case of TRALI. Expert Syst. Appl. **41**(3), 831–840 (2014)

Fast Convex Hull by a Geometric Approach

Alberto Beltrán-Herrera and Sonia Mendoza[✉]

Department of Computer Science - CINVESTAV-IPN, Av. IPN 2508 San Pedro
Zacatenco, Gustavo A. Madero, 07360 Mexico City, Mexico
abeltran@computacion.cs.cinvestav.mx, smendoza@cs.cinvestav.mx

Abstract. Advances in sensors and cameras allow current research in convex hull algorithms to focus on defining methods capable of processing a big set of points. Typically, in most of these algorithms, the orientation function needs around five sums and two multiplications. In this paper, we propose SymmetricHull, a novel algorithm that, unlike the related ones, only performs two comparisons per point, discarding points with a low probability of belonging to the convex hull. Our algorithm takes advantage of the symmetric geometry of convex hulls in 2D spaces and relies on the convexity principle to get convex hulls, without needing further calculations. Our experiments show that SymmetricHull achieves good results, in terms of time and number of necessary operations, resulting especially efficient with sets of points between 10^4 and 10^7. Given that our datasets are organized by quadrants, the features of our algorithm can be summarized as follows: (1) a fast point discard based on known points with a good chance to be part of the convex hull, (2) a lexicographic sort of points with a high probability of belonging to the convex hull, and (3) a simple slope analysis to verify whether a point is within the convex hull or not.

Keywords: Convex hull · Point cloud · 2D spaces · Symmetry · Slope

1 Introduction

The convex hull problem consists in calculating, given a set D of points, the smallest convex set that contains D [5]. Since the convex hull problem has repercussions in many fields, there are different ways to solve it. Many solutions based on sorting algorithms have been proposed, from the former approach by Chand and Kapur with $O(n^2)$ complexity [4] to other classic approaches with $O(nlogn)$ complexity, such as Graham's Scan [6], Monotone Chain [1], Ultimate Planar Convex Hull [7], QuickHull [2], and Chan's algorithm [3].

As convex hull algorithms represent a tool for other research areas, they might not be a final process, and other processes would need to be executed at the same time. Hence, new algorithms have been proposed, such as Liu and Chen's algorithm [8] that takes advantage of the geometry of every quadrant

© Springer International Publishing AG, part of Springer Nature 2018
J. F. Martínez-Trinidad et al. (Eds.): MCPR 2018, LNCS 10880, pp. 51–61, 2018.
https://doi.org/10.1007/978-3-319-92198-3_6

in 2D spaces, or QuiGran [10] that combines two popular techniques, Graham's Scan and QuickHull, to get better results than those obtained from these two algorithms separately. The hardware capacity for processing points continues increasing [12], that is why research in convex hull goes on, focusing on finding how to efficiently compute a big quantity of points.

A low cost optimization over many convex hull algorithms is the maximum inscribed parallelogram, usually represented by four extreme points: top (the maximum ordinate), bottom (the minimum ordinate), leftmost (the minimum abscissa), and rightmost (the maximum abscissa) [8]. This optimization is useful, since all points inside the maximum inscribed parallelogram are not part of the convex hull, so it is possible to eliminate a big quantity of them. In this paper, we take the results of this optimization process to get convex hulls in 2D spaces, without needing other calculations.

Our main contribution is a novel algorithm, called SymmetricHull, which can be viewed as an improvement of Monotone Chain [1] that follows a geometrical approach similar to Liu & Chen's algorithm [8]. Our approach takes advantage of the geometric features (symmetry and convexity) of every quadrant, so the convex hull can be found by just performing one comparison per point, decreasing the computational cost of our algorithm dramatically.

The rest of this paper is organized as follows. In Sect. 2, we define the properties of the four quadrants in 2D spaces. In Sect. 3, we describe the SymmetricHull algorithm, using the lemmas presented in the previous section. Experimental results and comparisons between our proposal and the main related algorithms are shown in Sect. 4. Finally, conclusions and future work are discussed in Sect. 5.

2   Geometric Context

It is usual to try eliminating many points before applying a convex hull algorithm. One of the simplest ideas is the *maximum inscribed parallelogram*, so it is necessary to identify the four extreme points in the four main directions of the 2D space.

Let D denote the dataset of points, and U be a point of D. Let P_{Top}, P_{Bottom}, $P_{MostRight}$, and $P_{MostLeft}$ denote points in D, and R be the maximum inscribed parallelogram, whose extreme points in the four main directions of the 2D space are described by such points (see Fig. 1). Thus, if U is inside R, then no further check is necessary to assess that U does not belong to the convex hull of D [5].

Many algorithms allow determining whether a point U is into R. However, we select a method based on the slope of the extreme points, which is explained by two lemmas:

Lemma 1. Let CHS be an array, sorted by the Y coordinate, of all points in the convex hull, and P, P_A, and P_B denote points in CHS. Let y_a, y, and y_b be the Y coordinate value, and x_a, x, and x_b denote the X coordinate value for P_A, P, and P_B, respectively. If $y_a \leq y \leq y_b$, and P, P_A, and P_B are in the same quadrant, then P can only exist into the rectangle described by P_A and P_B.

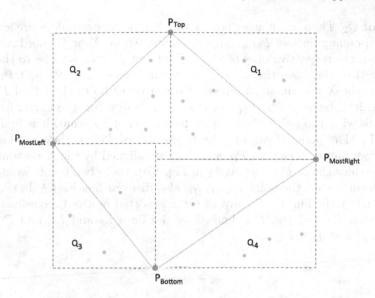

Fig. 1. Dataset partition by extreme points (red points), where continuous blue lines represent the *maximum inscribed parallelogram* (Color figure online)

This lemma means that the following rules apply for every quadrant: (1) Q_1: $x_b \leq x \leq x_a$ and $y_a \leq y \leq y_b$, (2) Q_2: $x_a \leq x \leq x_b$ and $y_a \leq y \leq y_b$, (3) Q_3: $x_b \leq x \leq x_a$ and $y_a \leq y \leq y_b$, and (4) Q_4: $x_a \leq x \leq x_b$ and $y_a \leq y \leq y_b$.

Proof. There are two facts for this demonstration: (1) a curve is convex if and only if every point in the curve is convex with respect to any other points in such a curve; and (2) there are four points that are unequivocally part of the convex hull: P_{Top}, P_{Bottom}, $P_{MostRight}$, $P_{MostLeft}$. Using these two facts, we can proof the rules for every quadrant:

Quadrant Q_1. There are neither points, whose Y coordinate is less than the one of $P_{MostRight}$ nor points, whose Y coordinate is bigger than the one of P_{Top}. Moreover, there are neither points, whose X coordinate is less then the one of P_{Top} nor points, whose X coordinate is bigger than the one of $P_{MostRight}$. The point P_B needs to be to the left of P_A, or they can have the same X coordinate when P_A, P_B, and P_{Top} are aligned by the X coordinate. In fact, P_B can never be to the right of P_A, such as P_1 in Fig. 2(a), because P_A, P_1, and $P_{MostRight}$ form a concave curve, breaking Fact 1. In the same way, the point P cannot be to the right of P_A, since it is limited by the line L_1. The point P can only be to the right of P_B, or they can have the same X coordinate, in case P, P_B, and P_{Top} are aligned by the X coordinate. If P were to the left of P_B, as P_2 in Fig. 2(a), these two points would form a concave curve with $P_{MostRight}$, also breaking Fact 1. In this case, P is limited by the line L_2. Finally, since CHS is sorted by the Y coordinate, and P is between P_A and P_B, P is limited by the lines L_3 and L_4, so P achieves $x_b \leq x \leq x_a$ and $y_a \leq y \leq y_b$.

Quadrant Q_2. There are neither points, whose Y or X coordinates are less than the corresponding ones of $P_{MostLeft}$ nor points, whose X or Y coordinates are bigger than the respective ones of P_{Top}. The point P_B needs to be to the right of P_A, or they can have the same X coordinate, when P_A, P_B and P_{Top} are aligned by the X coordinate. However, P_B can never be to the left of P_A, like P_1 in Fig. 2(b), because P_A, P_1, and $P_{MostLeft}$ form a concave curve, breaking Fact 1. Likewise, the point P cannot be to the left of P_A, since it is limited by the line L_1. The point P can only be to the left of P_B, or they can have the same X coordinate, in case P, P_B, and P_{Top} are aligned by the X coordinate. If P were to the right of P_B, such as P_2 in Fig. 2(b), these two points would form a concave curve with the point $P_{MostLeft}$, also disregarding Fact 1. In this case, P is limited by the line L_2. Finally, as CHS is sorted by the Y coordinate, and P is between P_A and P_B, P is limited by the lines L_3 and L_4, and P fulfills $x_a \leq x \leq x_b$ and $y_a \leq y \leq y_b$.

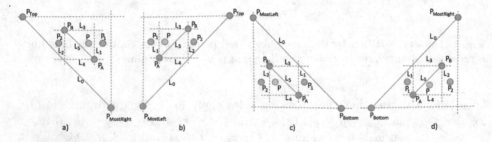

Fig. 2. Rectangles for every quadrant that can contain the points of a convex hull

Quadrant Q_3. There are neither points, whose Y coordinate is less than the one of P_{Bottom} nor points, whose Y coordinate is bigger than the one of $P_{MostLeft}$. Moreover, there are neither points, whose X coordinate is less than the one of $P_{MostLeft}$ nor points, whose X coordinate is bigger than the one of P_{Bottom}. The point P_B needs to be to the left of P_A, or they can have the same X coordinate, when P_A, P_B, and $P_{MostLeft}$ are aligned by their X coordinate. Nevertheless, P_B can never be to the right of P_A, such as P_1 in Fig. 2(c), because P_A, P_1 and $P_{MostLeft}$ form a concave curve, going against Fact 1. In a similar way, the point P cannot be to the right of P_A, as it is limited by the line L_1. The point P can only be to the right of P_B, or they can have the same X coordinate in case P, P_B, and $P_{MostLeft}$ are aligned by the X coordinate. If P were to the left of P_B, such as P_2 in Fig. 2(c), these two points would form a concave curve with the point $P_{MostLeft}$, also infringing Fact 1. In this case, P is limited by the line L_2. Finally, since CHS is sorted by the Y coordinate, and P is between P_A and P_B, P is limited by the lines L_3 and L_4, and P accomplishes $x_b \leq x \leq x_a$ and $y_a \leq y \leq y_b$.

Quadrant Q_4. There are neither points, whose Y or X coordinates are less than the correponding ones of P_{Bottom} nor points, whose X or Y coordinates are bigger than the respective ones of $P_{MostRight}$. The point P_B needs to be to the right of P_A, or they can have the same X coordinate when P_A, P_B and $P_{MostRight}$ are aligned by the X coordinate. However, P_B can never be to the left of P_A, like P_1 in Fig. 2(d), because P_A, P_1 and $P_{MostRight}$ form a concave curve, failing to observe Fact 1. Likewise, the point P cannot be to the left of P_A, as it is limited by the line L_1. The point P can only be to the left of P_B, or to have the same X coordinate, in case P, P_B and $P_{MostRight}$ are aligned by the X coordinate. If P were to the right of P_B, like P_2 in Fig. 2(d), these two points would form a concave curve with the point $P_{MostRight}$, also disobeying Fact 1. In this case, P is limited by the line L_2. Finally, as CHS is sorted by the Y coordinate, and P is between P_A and P_B, P is limited by the lines L_3 and L_4, and P satisfies $x_a \leq x \leq x_b$ and $y_a \leq y \leq y_b$.

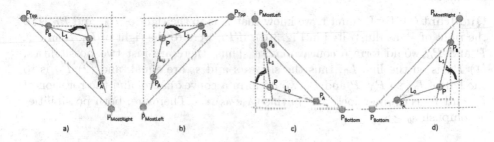

Fig. 3. Slope rotation of the lines L_0 and L_1 in every quadrant

Lemma 2. Let x and y denote the X and Y coordinates of the point $P \in CHS$ and s represent the slope between P and the previous point in CHS in the same quadrant. Let y_a and y_b be the Y coordinates of the points P_A and $P_B \in CHS$, respectively, and s and s_b denote the slopes of P and P_B, respectively. If $y_a \leq y \leq y_b$, and the points P_A, P, and P_B are in the same quadrant, the following rules apply for two points P and P_B in the same quadrant: (1) Q_1: $s_b \geq s$, (2) Q_2: $s_b \leq s$, (3) Q_3: $s_b \leq s$, and (4) Q_4: $s_b \geq s$.

Proof. We know that the general slope behavior consists in decreasing its value in clockwise and increasing its value in counterclockwise. Thus, taking into account two lines formed by three points: L_0 (described by P_A and P) and L_1 (described by P and P_B), we can demonstrate for each quadrant the aforementioned inequations as follows:

Quadrant Q_1. We know by Lemma 1 that P is to the left of P_A, and P_B is to the left of P, as shown in Fig. 3(a). If P_B were to the right of L_0, then P_A, P and P_B would form a concave curve. Hence, the only two possibilities are: (1) P_B is on the line L_0, so the slopes s and s_b are the same, and (2) P_B is to the left of L_0, so P_A, P, and P_B would form a convex curve, and the rotation of L_0 and L_1 is counterclockwise; in this case $s_b > s$. Then, by joining both possibilities, we have that $s_b \geq s$ is satisfied.

Quadrant Q_2. By Lemma 1, we know that P is to the right of P_A, and P_B is to the right of P, as shown in Fig. 3(b). If P_B were to the left of L_0, then P_A, P and P_B would form a concave curve. Hence, there are just two possibilities: (1) P_B is on the line L_0, thus the slopes s and s_b are equal, and (2) P_B is to the right of L_0, so P_A, P, and P_B would form a convex curve, and the rotation of L_0 and L_1 is clockwise; in this case $s_b < s$. Thus, both possibilities fulfill $s_b \le s$.

Quadrant Q_3. We know by Lemma 1 that P is to the left of P_A, and P_B is to the left of P, as shown in Fig. 3(c). If P_B were to the left of L_0, then P_A, P and P_B would form a concave curve. Consequently, the only two possibilities are: (1) P_B is on the line L_0, so the slopes s and s_b are the same, and (2) P_B is to the right of L_0, then P_A, P and P_B would form a convex curve, and the rotation of L_0 and L_1 is clockwise; in this case $s_b < s$. By joining both possibilities, $s_b \le s$ is achieved.

Quadrant Q_4. By Lemma 1, we know that P is to the right of P_A, and P_B is to the right of P, as illustrated in Fig. 3(d). If P_B were to the right of L_0, then P_A, P and P_B would form a concave curve. Thus, there are just two possibilities: (1) P_B is on the line L_0, thus the slopes s and s_b are equal, and (2) P_B is to the left of L_0, so P_A, P and P_B would form a convex curve, and the rotation of L_0 and L_1 is counterclockwise; in this case $s_b > s$. Therefore, both possibilities accomplish $s_b \ge s$.

3   SymmetricHull Algorithm

The proposed algorithm aims at reducing, around one hundred, the number of algebraic operations. To achieve this goal, it is necessary to have a good knowledge about the slope behavior in every quadrant and to substitute the basic operations in the Monotone Chain algorithm [1] for operations based on the slope between consecutive points.

Monotone Chain uses, as a basic operation, the orientation function, which is useful to determine whether a point is part or not of the convex hull. Monotone Chain works under the premise that all points take part of the convex hull and uses this function to discard those points that do not follow a convex way. This function requires five subtractions and two multiplications for each point of the dataset; these operations can be used many times to eliminate many nonconvex points. Thus, a lot of both algebraic and stack operations are performed, increasing the algorithm runtime.

An alternative to the orientation function is the slope, but it is often discarded because it is necessary to calculate two slopes and compare their results. Hence, four subtractions and two divisions are required, besides a control to avoid zeros in the denominator. Moreover, the logic of Monotone Chain still applies this comparison to every point in the dataset. Thus, the times used by the orientation function and the slope comparison are very close. To improve the algorithm runtime, it is necessary to algebraically operate over a little set of points that has a high probability of being part of the convex hull, and to add only a part of this set to the stack, to decrease the number of stack operations. To reduce both algebraic and stack operations, we propose a change in the point description. Usually, a point is described by its (x, y) coordinates, but in our proposal, points are described by (x, y, s), where s is the the slope between the current point and the previous one in the stack of the convex hull candidates.

Algorithms, like Monotone Chain, usually are divided in two parts, sorting and search, taking into account that sorting is needed to begin the search process. Many algorithms sort the complete dataset or discard points by methods, such as the maximum inscribed parallelogram or the maximum inscribed circle. However, to discard points, a lot of operations need to be performed, e.g., those needed by the orientation function. At this point, two important questions arise: Is it possible to sort just a subset of the points? Is there a method that uses few simple operations to determine whether a point is part of the convex hull? For both questions, the answer is affirmative, so we need to use the *convexity principle* (see Lemmas 1 and 2).

According to Lemma 1, a point can be excluded from the convex hull, given certain rules for every quadrant. We can deduce the points having a good chance of being part of the convex hull, by correctly choosing the relation operators for every quadrant.

Let DS be a dataset sorted by the Y coordinate (considering descending order for quadrants Q_1 and Q_2, and ascending order for quadrants Q_3 and Q_4) and P_I represent a two-dimensional point, such that $P_I \in DS$, whose X coordinate is denoted by x_i. Given the convexity property and the fact that DS is sorted, we can determine whether a point has a good probability of belonging to the convex hull, reducing Lemma 1 to the rules:

$$Q_1 \text{ and } Q_4 : x_{i-1} \le x_i \le x_{i+1}, Q_2 \text{ and } Q_3 : x_{i+1} \le x_i \le x_{i-1} \qquad (1)$$

However, the dataset is not sorted, so it is necessary to sort it lexicographically, although the time will not be improved. To solve this question, we can construct, for every quadrant, a double linked list, which only contains the highly probable candidate points to be part of the convex hull, following a lexicographic order. These double linked lists are initialized with the extreme points for every quadrant, considering a descending order for quadrants Q_1 and Q_2 (*SSL1* and *SSL2*), and an ascending order for quadrants Q_3 and Q_4 (*SSL3* and *SSL4*):

$$\begin{aligned} SSL1 = P_{Top}, P_{MostRight}, SSL2 = P_{Top}, P_{MostLeft} \\ SSL3 = P_{Bottom}, P_{MostLeft}, SSL4 = P_{Bottom}, P_{MostRight} \end{aligned} \qquad (2)$$

We are sure that any point in the convex hull does not have coordinates that exceed the extremes of its respective quadrant. Then, the SSL lists are sorted by the Y coordinate, and we can proceed to iterate over the D unsorted dataset, where we decide the corresponding quadrant for every point (i.e., we know the four extremes, so we only need to compare the coordinates of a point with the ones of the extremes). Thus, we find the position of the point P_I, given its Y coordinate, in the respective SSL list, and we insert such a point in the correct position, always preserving a sorting based on the Y coordinate. The point is inserted only if Inequation 1 has a positive result, and we then eliminate the points that do not belong to the convex hull, with the following cycle:

$$Q_1: while(x_{i+1} > x_i) : delete(SSL1_{i+1}), Q_2 : while(x_{i+1} < x_i) : delete(SSL2_{i+1})$$
$$Q_3: while(x_{i+1} < x_i) : delete(SSL3_{i+1}), Q_4 : while(x_{i+1} > x_i) : delete(SSL4_{i+1})$$
$$(3)$$

where a delete operation only consists in changing the reference between the previous point and the next one.

The saved time is owing to the lists, since the insertion and deletion operations consume $O(1)$ time. However, we have another problem concerning the search of the correct position of a point into the respective list. We can carry out a binary search or some similar technique since a dynamic list does not have an index. In fact we can put an index, but it is then necessary to refresh all the indexes in every push and pop movement. This situation is undesirable and would probably take more time than a normal sort process. To avoid this situation, we can define an auxiliary array for every SSL list ($SSLA1$, $SSLA2$, $SSLA3$, $SSLA4$) that stores references to points in the SSL lists, every N points, where N is a number defined by $m/log(m)$, and m is the number of points in the D dataset. Thus, every certain number of processed points (N would be a good number), we refresh the auxiliary array by going through the list and taking references to every $N - th$ point. In this way, we have a list of addresses of every $N - th$ point in the SSL lists. Using this auxiliary array, we can first find a good approach to the final location of a point that will be sorted by a binary search or a similar technique, and we can then go through the array to find the final location of such a point.

This process would seem to require many operations, but the SSL lists do not work over a m size, but over a h size, where h is the number of points in the convex hull. In a real scene, this process results in a big saving in time and operations.

At this point, we have a sort list for every quadrant (SSL lists). These lists only contain the points having high probabilities of belonging to the convex hull, and every point in the SSL lists satisfies Lemma 1. The next part of the SymmetricHull algorithm consists in discarding all the points that do not take part of such a convex hull. There are some points that satisfy Lemma 1 but do not belong to the convex hull. To determine whether a point is or not part of the convex hull, we need to operate on every point in the SSL lists, in order to calcuate the corresponding slope. Recalling Lemma 2, we can discard a point, according to its slope, by means of different rules for every quadrant. However, to apply Lemma 2, it is necessary to know the adjacent lower point, so an ordered dataset is required. Once this condition has been satisfied, we apply Lemma 2 recursively to discard the points that do not take part of the convex hull, by calculating the slope of every point in the SSL lists as the slope between the current point and the immediately preceding point. Let s_i denote the slope between the point P_I and the point P_{I-1}, then the discard process is carried out in the following way (see Eq. 4):

$$Q_1 : while(s_i < s_{i-1}) : delete(SSL1_{i-1}, RefreshSlope(s_i))$$
$$Q_2 : while(s_i > s_{i-1}) : delete(SSL2_{i-1}, RefreshSlope(s_i))$$
$$Q_3 : while(s_i > s_{i-1}) : delete(SSL3_{i-1}, RefreshSlope(s_i))$$
$$Q_4 : while(s_i < s_{i-1}) : delete(SSL4_{i-1}, RefreshSlope(s_i))$$

$$(4)$$

To avoid the overflow of the *SSL* lists, due to the cycles in Eq. 4, we initialize the slope value for the first element of every *SSL* list with a value that never satisfies the cycle conditions of Eq. 4. These values are:

$$SSL1 : s_0 = -\infty, SSL2 : s_0 = \infty, SSL3 : s_0 = \infty, SSL4 : s_0 = -\infty \quad (5)$$

This means that the SymmmetryHull algorithm needs to calculate the slope one time per point on the *SSL* lists and refresh it for every deleted point. This algorithm just implies two subtractions and one division for each point in such lists, and the same calculation for every deleted point. On the contrary, applying the orientation function, such as Monotone Chain, it is required five subtractions and two multiplication per point, and the same calculation for every deleted point. In addition, in the search phase, Monotone Chain (like many other algorithms) operates over the whole dataset, while our algorithm only operates over a dataset of h length approximately, where h is the number of points in the convex hull.

After performing the cycles of Eq. 4, we have four lists that just contain the points being part of the convex hull, and we only need to connect the lists (with a $O(1)$ cost) in order to create a unique list with all points of the convex hull.

4   Experimental Results

To test our algorithm, we compare our results with the ones of popular algorithms, such as Scan [6], Monotone Chain [1], and QuickHull [2]. We use the datasets proposed by Liu et al. [9] and Changyuan et al. [11], which include the following distributions generated in Matlab 8.4: mu = [2 3], SIGMA = [1 0.5; 0.5 10], D1 = mvnrnd (mu, SIGMA, N), D2 = unifrnd (0, 1, N, 2), D3 = exprnd (5, N, 2), D4 = evrnd (1, 2, N, 2), D5 = lognrnd (3, 2, N, 2), and D6 = johnsrnd ([−1.7 −.5.5 1.7], N, 2), where N represents the amount of points in the dataset.

By the characteristics of SymmetricHull, we suspect that its performance might be less, when using a set of points that falls in the perimeter of the convex hull than when using a set of points distributed in a space. Hence, we have generated three datasets, in order to test the algorithms in extreme conditions. These datasets are: D7 = circle (1, N), D8 = circlePerimeter (1, N), and D9 = rectangularPerimeter (1, 1, N), where the circle (1, N) function generates random points in a circle of radius 1; the circlePerimeter (1, N) function produces random points that fall into the boundary of a circle of radius 1; and rectangularPerimeter (1, 1, N) has the same function but takes into account a rectangle described by the given width and height.

Table 1 shows the average time of the Scan, Monotone Chain, QuickHull, and SymmetricHull algorithms after 100 executions for different amounts of points.

Table 1. Average time in milliseconds of convex hull algorithms after 100 executions.

Amount of points	Algorithm	D1	D2	D3	D4	D5	D6	Circle	Circle perimeter	Rectangular perimeter
10^4	Scan	1	2	1	2	1	2	0.9	2	1
	Monotone chain	3	3	3	2	3	3	3	3	3
	QuickHull	0.3	0.01	1	0.3	0.3	0.3	0.01	0.01	0.3
	SymmetricHull	**0.01**	**0.01**	**0.03**	**0.01**	**0.01**	**0.01**	**0.01**	**0.01**	**0.01**
10^5	Scan	10	8	8	8	7	8	8	8	8
	Monotone chain	12	12	13	13	12	12	12	12	13
	QuickHull	5	3	3	3	2	2	3	2	3
	SymmetricHull	**0.8**	**1**	**1**	**0.9**	**1**	**0.9**	**1**	**0.9**	**1**
10^6	Scan	79	79	81	79	79	82	80	80	79
	Monotone chain	112	111	109	112	111	114	112	111	113
	QuickHull	30	29	32	29	79	29	29	29	29
	SymmetricHull	**14**	**14**	**11**	**14**	**14**	**9**	**14**	**14**	**12**
10^7	Scan	789	705	771	788	702	821	732	760	778
	Monotone chain	801	1275	1050	1175	1046	1164	1085	1016	1038
	QuickHull	256	252	268	288	256	289	277	310	262
	SymmetricHull	**142**	**164**	**164**	**153**	**142**	**161**	**151**	**149**	**141**

These times were obtained from optimal implementations of the algorithms in C++, using a computer Intel i7 3.4 GHz with 8 GB of RAM and Windows 8.1.

As we can see, in all the cases, our algorithm has a good performance using sets of points between 10^4 and 10^5 points, specially in the 10^4 case, where the difference is about three hundred times with respect to Monotone Chain, and thirty times with respect to QuickHull. However, the difference is less in the datasets of 10^6 and 10^7 points, where in general the time of SymmetricHull is half the time of QuickHull. This fact is attributed to the management of big auxiliary lists (*SSLA*). SymmetricHull has not been tested using small sets of points since, in those cases, we expect a bad performance due to the need of creating auxiliary lists.

5   Conclusion and Future Work

We have proposed a new algorithm, called SymmetricHull, which is able to determinate the convex hull of a dataset of points in 2D spaces. Based on the convex principle, the geometry of every quadrant, and the slope behavior in an unsorted set of points, our algorithm is capable of optimizing its performance, while discarding and sorting points. By making simple decisions about the coordinates of a point and the ones of neighbor points, SymmetricHull can easily deduce whether a point has a chance to be part of the convex hull and, by relying on the convex principle to compare their slopes, it can determine whether such a point actually belongs to the convex hull. In this way, the proposed algorithm saves a lot of complex operations and easily discards many points. Moreover, the use of the two-dimensional points represented by the triplet (x, y, s) allows

SymmetricHull to compare the slopes among three points but only calculating half the operations required by the orientation function.

Our proposal showed good results in datasets, whose size varies from 10^4 to 10^7. In this range, we obtained the best comparative results. However, it is clear that SymmetricHull and QuickHull tend to converge. The good performance of our algorithm has a price: the use of the SSL lists and auxiliary SSL lists since they consume an important space in memory. The SSL lists are only composed of pointers to the points in the original dataset, preserving their size as small as the size in memory of said dataset.

Although the results of SymmetricHull are good, we found that the main operation and time expense concerns the search process for every point position even with the proposed optimizations. Then, as part of the improvements of our algorithm, we plan to create new methods to determine the position of a particular point in the SSL lists.

References

1. Andrew, A.: Another efficient algorithm for convex hulls in two dimensions. Inf. Process. Lett. **9**(5), 216–219 (1979)
2. Barber, C.B., Dobkin, D.P., Huhdanpaa, H.: The quickhull algorithm for convex hulls. ACM Trans. Math. Softw. **22**(4), 469–483 (1996)
3. Chan, T.: Optimal output-sensitive convex hull algorithms in two and three dimensions. Discrete Computat. Geom. **16**(4), 361–368 (1996)
4. Chand, D.R., Kapur, S.S.: An algorithm for convex polytopes. J. ACM (JACM) **17**(1), 78–86 (1970)
5. de Berg, M., Cheong, O., van Kreveld, M., Overmars, M.: Computational Geometry: Algorithms and Applications, 3rd edn. Springer, Heidelberg (2008). https://doi.org/10.1007/978-3-540-77974-2
6. Graham, R.L.: An efficient algorithm for determining the convex hull of a finite planar set. Inf. Process. Lett. **1**(4), 132–133 (1972)
7. Kirkpatrick, D.G., Seidel, R.: The ultimate planar convex hull algorithm. SIAM J. Comput. Cornell Univ. **15**(1), 287–299 (1986)
8. Liu, G.H., Chen, C.B.: A new algorithm for computing the convex hull of a planar point set. J. Zhejiang Univ. Sci. A **8**(8), 1210–1217 (2007)
9. Liu, R., Fang, B., Tang, Y.Y., Wen, J., Qian, J.: A fast convex hull algorithm with maximum inscribed circle affine transformation. Neurocomput. **77**(1), 212–221 (2012)
10. Sharif, M.: A new approach to compute convex hull. Innov. Syst. Des. Eng. **2**(3), 186–192 (2011)
11. Changyuan, X., Zhongyang, X., Yufang, Z., Xuegang, W., Jingpei, D., Tingping, Z.: An efficient convex hull algorithm using affine transformation in planar point set. Arab. J. Sci. Eng. **39**(11), 7785–7793 (2014)
12. Zavala, J.P., Anaya, E.K., Isaza, C., Castillo, E.: 3D measuring surface topography of agglomerated particles using a laser sensor. IEEE Lat. Am. Trans. **14**(8), 3516–3521 (2016)

An Experimental Study on Ant Colony Optimization Hyper-Heuristics for Solving the Knapsack Problem

Bronson Duhart, Fernando Camarena, José Carlos Ortiz-Bayliss[✉],
Ivan Amaya, and Hugo Terashima-Marín

Tecnologico de Monterrey, Escuela de Ingeniería y Ciencias, Monterrey, Mexico
b_duhart@live.com.mx, fernando@camarenat.com,
{jcobayliss,iamaya2,terashima}@itesm.mx

Abstract. The knapsack problem is a fundamental problem that has been extensively studied in combinatorial optimization. The reason is that such a problem has many practical applications. Several solution techniques have been proposed in the past, but their performance is usually limited by the complexity of the problem. Hence, this paper studies a novel hyper-heuristic approach based on the ant colony optimization algorithm to solve the knapsack problem. The hyper-heuristic is used to produce rules that decide which heuristic to apply given the current problem state of the instance being solved. We test the hyper-heuristic model on sets with a variety of knapsack problem instances. Our resulting data seems promising.

1 Introduction

Imagine you are given a bag in a store. The owner says you are free to grab as many items as you wish, as long as they all fit together in the bag. Each product in the store has a specific value and weight. But, the bag has limited capacity (represented by the maximum total weight it can hold). Obviously, you would want to pack the products that maximize the overall monetary value. How would you decide such a combination of items? This is a very simple example of what the literature refers to as the knapsack problem.

The knapsack problem is nothing but a simplification of more complicated real-life optimization problems. But, they all have a distinctive feature: Select an item subset that maximizes the total profit. Of course, there is an imposed constraint on the items that can be selected. Also, each item within the set has an associated weight and profit.

Given a set of n items, 2^n possible subsets can be formed. Therefore, an enumerating approach is unpractical for most cases. In fact, this is one of the features that make the knapsack problem a well known NP-complete problem. This means that no exact solving method has been found that runs in polynomial time. Moreover, should one ever be found, it could also be used to solve any other NP problem [1, 2]. Hence, its importance.

© Springer International Publishing AG, part of Springer Nature 2018
J. F. Martínez-Trinidad et al. (Eds.): MCPR 2018, LNCS 10880, pp. 62–71, 2018.
https://doi.org/10.1007/978-3-319-92198-3_7

Exact methods guarantee finding the optimal solution. But, they require that a solution exists and that enough run time is given. Dynamic programming and branch and bound are included in this category. Unfortunately, these methods can only solve small instances because of the exponential growth in the solution space.

Aside from exact methods, literature also describes approximated ones. These are known as heuristics. With them, finding the optimal solution is not guaranteed. But, it is feasible to find one acceptable enough, according to some specific performance metric. Heuristics select the next item to pack following the best evaluation of one or more criterion. Despite their success, some major drawbacks prevent heuristics from becoming the definite solver. First, they behave inconsistently across a wide range of instances. Thus, a heuristic that performs exceptionally well on some instances can be easily outperformed by others on different ones. Hence, the performance of heuristics changes from instance to instance. Because of that, there is no single heuristic that best solves all instances of the knapsack problem.

A potential solution to this problem is to try and learn the patterns that characterize specific 'classes' of instances. This knowledge can then be applied for automatically switching heuristics as the search progresses, attempting to improve the solution process. Such an approach is known as a hyper-heuristic. The idea is to find a set of rules for deciding when to apply each particular heuristic. Hence, they are usually referred to as "heuristics to choose heuristics" [3]. In this work, we propose using the ant colony optimization (ACO) algorithm to search the space of heuristics. We strive to find a combination that remains steadily competent on a wider range of instances.

The remainder of this document is organized as follows. Section 2 presents a review of some important concepts related to this work. The solution model proposed herein is described in Sect. 3. Section 4 presents the experiments we conducted, their results and analysis. Finally, Sect. 5 presents the conclusion and future work derived from this investigation.

2 Background and Related Work

In this work, we aim at exploring how ACO can be used to produce hyper-heuristics for solving the knapsack problem. The ACO algorithm is a meta-heuristic based on swarm intelligence. Such swarm intelligence relates to the fact that there is no centralized control of the search. Instead, the algorithm discovers the best solutions in a way similar to ants finding the most convenient paths to food sources in nature [4]. In the past, ACO has been already used to solve the knapsack problem in its different variants [1,5–9]. Some works have even combined ACO with other techniques, such as fuzzy logic [10].

Regarding hyper-heuristics, ACO was used as a hyper-heuristic on the traveling salesman problem (TSP) and compared against other seven meta-heuristics that operated at the problem level [11]. The results presented in that work show that ACO, when used within a hyper-heuristic, generally achieves a better performance than isolated heuristics. Other problem domains where ACO has been used with a hyper-heuristic include the traveling tournament problem (TTP) [12], the set covering problem (SCP) [13] and the 2D bin packing problem (2DBPP) [14]. In all the cases, these hyper-heuristics have obtained competent results.

2.1 Heuristics for the Knapsack Problem

In this work, we have taken four commonly used heuristic from literature. Each one of them selects an item following a particular criterion, whilst only three focus on a greedy strategy. They can be briefly described as:

Default (DF). Items are packed in the same order they are initially presented in the problem.

Maximum profit (MP). Items are sorted decreasingly by their profit. Afterwards, MP begins packing objects in this order as long as there is space for them. This strategy attempts to gain as much profit as possible and as quickly as it can, by going for the most valuable elements first.

Minimum weight (MW). Items are sorted increasingly by their weight. Then, items are selected one by one until filling the knapsack. The rationale behind this heuristic is that taking more items results in higher profits.

Maximum profit per weight (MPW). Items are sorted decreasingly by the quotient of profit over weight.

3   Solution Model

In this section, we proceed to explain our solution. First, we present how we defined a suitable representation for the problem state, which makes it possible to extract knowledge about the best heuristics for a particular instance. Afterwards, we describe the ACO algorithm that we applied for the generation of hyper-heuristics in the form of state-action rules.

3.1   Problem Representation

We closely followed the selection of features used in [15], due to the similarity of the problems. Our representation describes the state of the items available to pick from, as well as the state of the knapsack, since some problems may share the same set of items and only differ in their knapsacks. The representation we define also takes into account the progress of a solution.

In this way, the eight features considered for our proposal are the following: normalized median weight of the objects ($\tilde{w}/\max w_i$), normalized mean weight of the objects ($\bar{w}/\max w_i$), normalized standard deviation of the weight of the objects ($\sigma_w/\max w_i$), normalized median profit of the objects ($\tilde{p}/\max p_i$), normalized mean profit of the objects ($\bar{p}/\max p_i$), normalized standard deviation of the profit of the objects ($\sigma_p/\max p_i$), normalized pearson correlation between the profit and the weight of the objects ($\text{corr}(w,p)/2 + 0.5$) and normalized remaining capacity of the knapsack ($\frac{C-\sum w_i x_i}{C}$), where $\tilde{w}$, $\bar{w}$, $\tilde{p}$ and $\bar{p}$ denote the mean weight, median weight, mean profit and median profit, respectively. All features were normalized to the interval $[0, 1]$ to set a uniform scale for the training phase.

3.2   The Hyper-heuristic Generation Algorithm

The solution we developed is based on the original ACO algorithm [4]. The general idea is to gradually build a population of candidate hyper-heuristics (the 'solutions' found by the ants) and select the best among them. At the beginning of each iteration, each ant is assigned a problem instance from the training set. Then, each ant selects one of the available heuristics and applies such a heuristic to solve its respective problem instance, which results in a new point in the problem space according to our representation (defined by the eight features described in Sect. 3.1). Each iteration ends when all of the ants have finished solving their respective problem instances. When one iteration ends, the pheromone trace is updated, proportional to the quality of the solution found by each ant. In this way, each ant constructs a set of state-heuristic pairs by the end of each iteration. Such set of rules constitutes a potential hyper-heuristic. Thus, the result of the process, when the termination criterion is met, is the hyper-heuristic that performed the best across all the iterations, among all ants. This hyper-heuristic can then be applied to both seen and unseen instances.

The complete hyper-heuristic generation algorithm is shown in Fig. 1. It should be noted that the sampling of problems for initializing the ants is done with repetition and that we discretized the problem space through multiplying every feature by 10 and dropping the fractional part. In order to measure the quality of the solutions obtained by the ants, we employed the normalized profit of the knapsack, relative to the original total profit of the items: $\hat{P} = \sum p_i x_i / \sum p_i$.

Regarding the specific parameters for the ACO algorithm, we can mention the following. The probability of selecting a heuristic H to apply in state s is given by Eq. 1.

$$p(s, H) = \frac{(\tau_{s,H})^\alpha (\eta_{s,H})^\beta}{\sum_h (\tau_{s,h})^\alpha (\eta_{s,h})^\beta} \tag{1}$$

where $\tau_{s,h}$ is the pheromone level of the edge (s, h), and $\eta_{s,h}$ is the attractiveness of this edge, that corresponds to applying heuristic h to the problem at state s. The attractiveness is a user defined function, which in our case was chosen to be the same as the solution evaluation, i.e. the normalized profit that we would obtain if the problem was solved by only using h to solve it from state s onward. If the result returned by some heuristic at a given state is that no object can be packed, then we set $\eta_{s,h} = 0$, which gives zero probability of selecting it.

For parameters α and β, which balance the importance given to exploration and exploitation of solutions, we tried several different values but the ones suggested in literature provided the best results [16,17]. We also found $Q = 10$

repeat
    Randomly assign a problem from the training set to k ants
    $i \leftarrow 0$
    while some ant can pack more items **do**
      for all ants **do**
        $s_i \leftarrow$ state representation of the problem
        Solve the problem with each heuristic and compute $\eta_{s_i,H}$
        Compute $p(s_i, H)$ for all heuristics
        $h^* \leftarrow$ heuristic with the highest probability $p(s_i, H)$
        Add the edge (s_i, h^*) to the ant's path and apply h^* to the problem
      end for
    end while
    $i \leftarrow i + 1$
    Update pheromone levels of all edges (s, h) accordingly
    Save the hyper-heuristic (path) with the highest profit
until a termination criterion is met
return the best hyper-heuristic (best path)

Fig. 1. Hyper-heuristic generation process through ACO.

and $\tau_{s,h}(0) = 1$ to be suitable values for the purpose of generating a hyper-heuristic with the desired features. The number of ants was selected as to have a probability of selecting a problem for solution construction equal to 80%.

The pheromone for the next iteration is updated with the expression: $\tau_{s,h}(i + 1) = \rho\tau_{s,h}(i) + \Delta\tau_{s,h}$, where $\Delta\tau_{s,h}$ is the total amount of pheromone left by all ants that walked over edge (s, h). The pheromone update of ant k is obtained from a pheromone supply Q and the normalized profit $\hat{P}$ according to Eq. 2

$$\Delta\tau_{s,h}^k = \begin{cases} \hat{P}Q & (s, h) \text{ is in the ant's path} \\ 0 & \text{otherwise} \end{cases} \tag{2}$$

4   Experiments and Results

In order to evaluate the performance of our proposed strategies, we have classified a total of 1000 problem instances under four different instance sets. The sets S1 and S2 correspond to synthetic instances, while problems in P20 and P50 correspond to a subset of hard instances described by Pisinger [18]. S1, S2 and P50 contain instances with 50 items, while P20 contains instances with 20 items. The knapsack capacity for sets S1 and S2 is fixed to 50, while in P20 and P50 the capacity varies from instance to instance. In the case of synthetic problems —S1 and S2—, the sets were assembled in such a way that they contained a balanced number of favorable instances for each individual heuristic. Therefore, DF was the best performer on 22.25% of the instances; MP, on 25%; MPW, on 28.5%, and MW, on 25.25%.

For training, we designed two different schemes. In the first of them, we used set S1 as training set for the hyper-heuristics. On the second scheme, we also wanted to evaluate the effect of extending training with instances from other sources. Therefore, we added 60% of P20 and of P50 to the training set. In both schemes, the test set was composed by S2 and the remaining 40% of P20 and P50. Thus, two hyper-heuristics were produced and tested: ACO-HHS and ACO-HHSP (hyper-heuristics trained with the first and the second scheme, respectively).

Since the ACO-based hyper-heuristic incorporates stochastic components in the decision phase, we averaged the profits of the model over various runs. Because the number of different outcomes was finite and small, with little variance among the respective profits, we used 10 repetitions of the testing phase to provide an adequate trade off between uncertainty and calculation time. In the following section, we only report the results that correspond to the best performing ACO-HH and ACO-HHSP out of the five trained for each training scheme.

4.1   Analysis of Hyper-heuristics

The first part of our analysis involves the evaluation of the quality of the solutions obtained by all the methods considered for this investigation. To compare the methods, we define four metrics. The first two metrics are related to the profit error (the difference between the method's profit and a profit reference value). We used two different reference values to obtain the first two metrics: (1) F_B, the difference between the solution of the method and the best known solution from any of the methods under study (four heuristics and two hyper-heuristics) and E_O, (2) the difference between the solution of the method and the optimal solution (obtained in this case by using dynamic programming). The third and fourth metrics, the success rates, are defined as the percentage of instances where each method obtains a profit error equal to zero. Following the rationale behind the first two metrics, two versions are also obtained for the success rate: (1) SR_B, the percentage of instances where the method is as good as the best known solution from any of the methods under study and SR_O, (2) the percentage of instances where the method finds the optimal solution. The results of this comparison are shown in Table 1.

Based on the results from Table 1 we can observe that the individual results of the heuristics degrade due to the results obtained by the hyper-heuristics. We also observe that ACO-HHSP obtains better success rates than any heuristic. Regarding the learning strategies, we can state two important claims. First, training with a mixture of instances improves the performance of ACO-based hyper-heuristics, as we can observe in Table 1.

4.2   Selection of Heuristics Throughout the Search

Aiming at a better understanding of the behavior of the ACO-based hyper-heuristics proposed, we analyzed the frequency of use of each particular heuristic

Table 1. Analysis of heuristics and hyper-heuristics with respect to the optimal and best solutions. Best results for each set and metric are highlighted in bold.

Set	Method	SR_B (%)	$\bar{E}_B$	SR_O (%)	$\bar{E}_O$
S2	DF	19.25	593.41	5.75	598.81
	MP	24.75	336.44	22.25	341.84
	MPW	27.75	**28.25**	19.75	**33.65**
	MW	25.00	255.75	12.50	261.15
	ACO-HHS	18.25	59.05	11.25	64.45
	ACO-HHSP	**34.50**	111.92	**28.25**	117.32
P20	DF	16.66	333.60	2.50	424.45
	MP	27.08	536.28	**14.16**	627.13
	MPW	**36.25**	158.64	12.50	249.49
	MW	15.00	420.85	3.33	511.70
	ACO-HHS	26.25	196.49	9.58	287.34
	ACO-HHSP	35.00	**157.19**	12.08	**248.04**
P50	DF	9.58	803.95	1.66	913.96
	MP	18.75	1658.30	9.58	1768.32
	MPW	49.16	108.98	**22.08**	219.00
	MW	16.66	574.68	2.08	684.69
	ACO-HHS	26.25	430.20	15.41	540.21
	ACO-HHSP	**51.25**	**108.24**	20.00	**218.25**

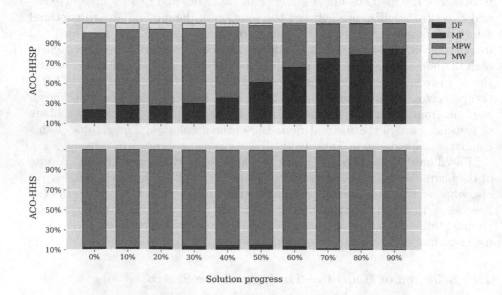

Fig. 2. Average heuristic selection through the different stages of solutions for set S2.

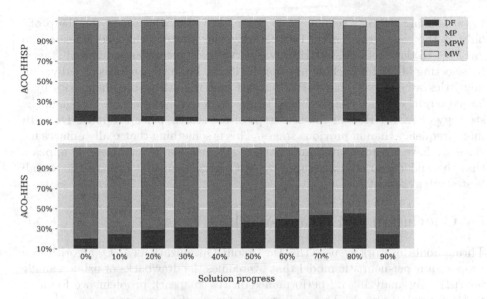

Fig. 3. Average heuristic selection through the different stages of solutions for set P20.

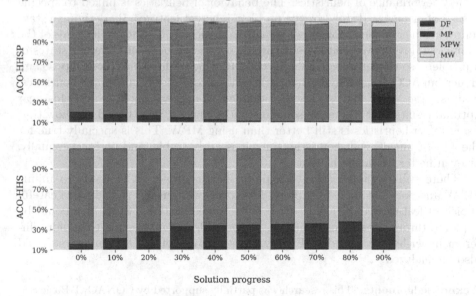

Fig. 4. Average heuristic selection through the different stages of solutions for set P50.

across different stages of the solution process. This information is shown in Figs. 2, 3 and 4. Based on these results, we can explain why ACO-HHS behaved so poorly in comparison to ACO-HHSP. In the three sets, it indistinctly selected MPW, with a slight preference for MP. ACO-HHSP shows a peculiar behavior. In set S2, it starts using MPW most of the times and it progressively moves towards using MP on a regular basis. Then, ACO-HHSP is greedy on the profit only at the end of the search. Interestingly, this strategy changed for sets P20 anf P50. In these sets, ACO-HHSP was very consistent through different stages, by selecting MPW for packing most of the items. From the analysis of individual heuristics we observed that MPW outperforms the other three heuristics by a large margin, especially in set P50. There is, however, a noticeable change in the strategy of ACO-HHSP in the last steps of the search, since it applies DF with more frequency than in previous stages. This is something that really amazes us, since we have already stated how naïvely DF behaves. Nonetheless, it appears that this sudden variety introduced by ACO-HHSP helped it become the overall best strategy for set P50.

5   Conclusion and Future Work

Throughout this work we used the Ant Colony Optimization (ACO) algorithm to propose a hyper-heuristic model that overcomes the drawbacks of using a single heuristic. By analyzing its performance on the knapsack problem, we found it to be a good approach. The main reason for its effectiveness comes from the varied performance of heuristics. The behavior of heuristics is linked to specific classes of instances, defined by the problem inherent features. By deriving a state representation of the problem, we were able to identify distinctive features of the problem. This allowed the hyper-heuristic to discern between different states of a problem, so that it selected the method that best suited the current problem. Hence, an ACO-trained hyper-heuristic generalizes better than simple heuristics. Even so, the MPW heuristic is very difficult to outperform since it yields near optimal results. But, there are some instances where it fails. Our data show that using hyper-heuristics is still better than using MPW. This is specially true for the ACO-trained hyper-heuristic, since it is fairly stable, and performs equally, or even better, than the heuristics.

There still remains paths to explore. For example, ACO tends to mimic MPW and does not tend to explore. Moreover, we consider that a more careful choice of features could yield better state representations. Such idea could be explored through statistical analysis. It would also be interesting to explore different hyper-heuristic models. Finally, the sensitivity of ACO parameters should also be analyzed.

Acknowledgements. This research was partially supported by CONACyT Basic Science Projects under grants 241461, 221551 and 287479, and ITESM Research Group with Strategic Focus in Intelligent Systems.

References

1. Schiff, K.: Ant colony optimization algorithm for the 0–1 knapsack problem. Technical Transactions. Autom. Control **R 110**(AC-3), 39–52 (2013)
2. Sahni, S.: Approximate algorithms for the 0/1 knapsack problem. J. ACM **22**(1), 115–124 (1975)

3. Burke, E.K., Gendreau, M., Hyde, M., Kendall, G., Ochoa, G., Özcan, E., Qu, R.: Hyper-heuristics: a survey of the state of the art. J. Oper. Res. Soc. **64**(12), 1695–1724 (2013)
4. Dorigo, M., Stützle, T.: Ant Colony Optimization. Bradford Company, Scituate (2004)
5. Zhang, J.: Comparative study of several intelligent algorithms for knapsack problem. Procedia Environ. Sci. **11**, 163–168 (2011)
6. Ke, L., Feng, Z., Ren, Z., Wei, X.: An ant colony optimization approach for the multidimensional knapsack problem. J. Heuristics **16**(1), 65–83 (2010)
7. Ren, Z., Feng, Z.: An ant colony optimization approach to the multiple-choice multidimensional knapsack problem. In: Proceedings of the 12th Annual Conference on Genetic and Evolutionary Computation, GECCO 2010, pp. 281–288. ACM (2010)
8. Du, D., Zu, Y.: Greedy strategy based self-adaption ant colony algorithm for 0/1 knapsack problem. In: Park, J.J.J.H., Pan, Y., Chao, H.-C., Yi, G. (eds.) Ubiquitous Computing Application and Wireless Sensor. LNEE, vol. 331, pp. 663–670. Springer, Dordrecht (2015). https://doi.org/10.1007/978-94-017-9618-7_70
9. He, L., Huang, Y.: Research of ant colony algorithm and the application of 0/1 knapsack. In: 2011 6th International Conference on Computer Science Education (ICCSE), pp. 464–467 (2011)
10. Changdar, C., Mahapatra, G.S., Pal, R.K.: An ant colony optimization approach for binary knapsack problem under fuzziness. Appl. Math. Comput. **223**, 243 253 (2013)
11. Aziz, Z.A.: Ant colony hyper-heuristics for travelling salesman problem. Procedia Comput. Sci. **76**, 534–538 (2015)
12. Chen, P.C., Kendall, G., Berghe, G.V.: An ant based hyper-heuristic for the travelling tournament problem. In: 2007 IEEE Symposium on Computational Intelligence in Scheduling, pp. 19–26 (2007)
13. Ferreira, A.S., Pozo, A., Gonçalves, R.A.: An ant colony based hyper-heuristic approach for the set covering problem. Adv. Distrib. Comput. Artif. Intell. J. **4**, 1–21 (2015)
14. Cuesta-Cañada, A., Garrido, L., Terashima-Marín, H.: Building hyper-heuristics through ant colony optimization for the 2D bin packing problem. In: Khosla, R., Howlett, R.J., Jain, L.C. (eds.) KES 2005. LNCS (LNAI), vol. 3684, pp. 654–660. Springer, Heidelberg (2005). https://doi.org/10.1007/11554028_91
15. López-Camacho, E., Terashima-Marin, H., Ross, P., Ochoa, G.: A unified hyper-heuristic framework for solving bin packing problems. Expert Syst. Appl. **41**(15), 6876–6889 (2014)
16. Gaertner, D., Clark, K.: On optimal parameters for ant colony optimization algorithms. In: Proceedings of the International Conference on Artificial Intelligence 2005, pp. 83–89. CSREA Press (2005)
17. Wei, X.: Parameters analysis for basic ant colony optimization algorithm in TSP. Int. J. u- e-Serv. Sci. Technol. **7**(4), 159–170 (2014)
18. Pisinger, D.: Where are the hard knapsack problems? Comput. Opera. Res. **32**(9), 2271–2284 (2005)

A Linear Time Algorithm for Computing #2SAT for Outerplanar 2-CNF Formulas

Marco A. López[1], J. Raymundo Marcial-Romero[1]([⊠]), Guillermo De Ita[2], and Yolanda Moyao[2]

[1] Facultad de Ingeniería, UAEM, Toluca, Mexico
mlopezm158@alumno.uaemex.mx, jrmarcialr@uaemex.mx
[2] Facultad de Ciencias de la Computación, BUAP, Puebla, Mexico
{deita,ymoyao}@cs.buap.mx

Abstract. Although the satisfiability problem for two Conjunctive Normal Form formulas (2SAT) is polynomial time solvable, it is well known that #2SAT, the counting version of 2SAT is #P-Complete. However, it has been shown that for certain classes of formulas, #2SAT can be computed in polynomial time. In this paper we show another class of formulas for which #2SAT can also be computed in lineal time, the so called outerplanar formulas, e.g. formulas whose signed primal graph is outerplanar. Our algorithm's time complexity is given by $O(n+m)$ where n is the number of variables and m the number of clauses of the formula.

1 Introduction

#SAT (the problem of counting models for a Boolean formula) is of special concern to Artificial Intelligence (AI), and it has a direct relationship to Automated Theorem Proving, as well as to approximate reasoning [1–3]. #SAT can be reduced to several different problems in approximate reasoning. For example, in the cases of: estimating the degree of belief in propositional theories, the generation of explanations to propositional queries, repairing inconsistent databases, in Bayesian inference, in a truth maintenance systems [2–4]. The previous problems come from several AI applications such as planning, expert systems, approximate reasoning, etc.

#SAT is #P-complete, even for formulas in two conjunctive normal form, so for complete methods, only exponential-time algorithms are known. The exact algorithm with the best bound until now was presented by Wahlström [5], who provides an $O(1.2377^n)$-time algorithm, where n is the number of variables of the formula. There are also randomized algorithms, in this direction, the algorithm of Dantsin and Wolpert [6] has the best bound $O(1.3238^n)$. #SAT appears to be harder than SAT since 2SAT is polynomial time solvable while #2SAT is #P-complete. However, it has been shown that for some classes of formulas, #2SAT can be computed in polynomial time [1]. The most relevant cases are monotone formulas and cactus formulas [7].

In this paper we present a new class of formulas for which #2SAT can be computed in polynomial time. We call these formulas outerplanar since their

© Springer International Publishing AG, part of Springer Nature 2018
J. F. Martínez-Trinidad et al. (Eds.): MCPR 2018, LNCS 10880, pp. 72–81, 2018.
https://doi.org/10.1007/978-3-319-92198-3_8

representation via primal graphs provide outerplanar graphs. A graph is outerplanar if it has a crossing-free embedding in the plane such that all vertices
are on the same face. The outerplanar graphs contain as subsets to the cactus
graphs which are used in the theory of condensation in statistical mechanics and
as simplified models of real lattices. Cactus graphs have also found applications
in the theory of electrical and communication networks [7,8].

Another special class of graphs contained into outerplanar graphs is the class
of polygonal array graphs that has been widely used in mathematical chemistry,
since they are molecular graphs used to represent the structural formula of chemical compounds. In particular, hexagonal arrays are the graph representations of
an important subclass of benzenoid molecules, unbranched catacondensed benzenoid molecules, which play a distinguished role in the theoretical chemistry of
benzenoid hydrocarbons [9,10].

In our case, we are more interested in the application of counting models on
conjunctive normal form formulas as a medium to develop methods for approximate reasoning. For example, for computing the degree of belief on propositional
formulas, or for building Bayesian models. It is relevant to know how many
models are maintained while input conjunctive normal form formulas are being
updating [2,4,6].

Our method firstly decompose the input conjunctive normal form formula to
its signed primal graph, secondly a treewidth decomposition of the graph is computed, outerplanar graphs have treewidth at most 2 so a linear time algorithm
can be used. Finally, a procedure that uses macros (cumulative basic operations)
is applied on the nodes of the treewidth.

The paper is organized as follows, in Sect. 2 the preliminaries are established.
In Sect. 3 a treewidth decomposition of outerplanar formulas is presented. In
Sect. 4, our main procedure is presented and finally, the Conclusion.

2   Preliminaries

Let $X = \{x_1, \ldots, x_n\}$ be a set of n Boolean variables. A literal is either a variable
x_i or a negated variable $\overline{x}_i$. As usual, for each $x_i \in X$, we write $x_i^0 = \overline{x}_i$ and
$x_i^1 = x_i$. A clause is a disjunction of different literals (sometimes, we also consider
a clause as a set of literals). For $k \in N$, a k-clause is a clause consisting of exactly
k literals and, a ($\leq k$)-clause is a clause with at most k literals. A variable $x \in X$
appears in a clause c if either the literal x^1 or x^0 is an element of c.

A Conjunctive Normal Form (CNF) F is a conjunction of clauses (we also
call F a Conjunctive Form). A k-CNF is a CNF containing clauses with at most
k literals.

We use $\nu(Y)$ to express the set of variables involved in the object Y, where Y
could be a literal, a clause or a Boolean formula. $Lit(F)$ is the set of literals which
appear in a CNF F, i.e. if $X = \nu(F)$, then $Lit(F) = X \cup \overline{X} = \{x_1^1, x_1^0, \ldots, x_n^1, x_n^0\}$.
We also denote $\{1, 2, \ldots, n\}$ by $[[n]]$.

An assignment s for F is a Boolean function $s : \nu(F) \to \{0, 1\}$. An assignment
can be also considered as a set which does not contain complementary literals.

If $x^\epsilon \in s$, being s an assignment, then s turns x^ϵ true and $x^{1-\epsilon}$ false, $\epsilon \in \{0,1\}$. Considering a clause c and assignment s as a set of literals, c is satisfied by s if and only if $c \cap s \neq \emptyset$, and if for all $x^\epsilon \in c$, $x^{1-\epsilon} \in s$ then s falsifies c.

If $F_1 \subset F$ is a formula consisting of some clauses of F, then $\nu(F_1) \subset \nu(F)$, and an assignment over $\nu(F_1)$ is a partial assignment over $\nu(F)$.

Let F be a Boolean formula in CNF, F is satisfied by an assignment s if each clause in F is satisfied by s. F is contradicted by s if any clause in F is contradicted by s. A model of F is an assignment for $\nu(F)$ that satisfies F. We will denote as $SAT(F)$ the set of models for the formula F.

Given a CNF F, the SAT problem consists on determining if F has a model. The #SAT problem consists of counting the number of models of F defined over $\nu(F)$. #2-SAT denotes #SAT for formulas in 2-CNF.

2.1   The Signed Primal Graph of a 2-CF

There are some graphical representations of a CNF (see e.g. [11]), we use here the signed primal graph of a two conjunctive normal form.

Let F be a 2-CNF, its signed primal graph (constraint graph) is denoted by $G_F = (V(F), E(F))$, with $V(F) = \nu(F)$ and $E(F) = \{\{\nu(x), \nu(y)\} : \{x,y\} \in F\}$, that is, the vertices of G_F are the variables of F, and for each clause $\{x,y\}$ in F there is an edge $\{\nu(x), \nu(y)\} \in E(F)$. For $x \in V(F)$, $\delta(x)$ denotes its degree, i.e. the number of incident edges to x. Each edge $c = \{\nu(x), \nu(y)\} \in E$ is associated with an ordered pair (s_1, s_2) of signs, assigned as labels of the edge connecting the literals appearing in the clause. The signs s_1 and s_2 are related to the literals x^ϵ and y^δ, respectively. For example, the clause $\{x^0, y^1\}$ determines the labelled edge: "$x \overset{-}{\underset{+}{}} y$" which is equivalent to the edge "$y \overset{-}{\underset{+}{}} x$".

Formally, let $S = \{+, -\}$ be a set of signs. A graph with labelled edges on a set S is a pair (G, ψ), where $G = (V, E)$ is a graph, and ψ is a function with domain E and range S. $\psi(e)$ is called the label of the edge $e \in E$. Let $G = (V, E, \psi)$ be a signed primal graph with labelled edges on SxS. Let x and y be vertices in V, if $e = \{x, y\}$ is an edge and $\psi(e) = (s, s')$, then $s(resp.s')$ is called the adjacent sign to $x(resp.y)$. We say that a 2-CNF F is a path, cycle, a tree, or an outerplanar graph, if its signed constraint graph G_F represents a path, cycle, a tree, an outerplanar graph, respectively. We will omit the signs on the graph if all of them are $+$.

Notice that a signed primal graph of a 2-CNF can be a multigraph since two fixed variables can be involved in more than one clause of the formula forming so parallel edges. Furthermore, a unitary clause is represented by a loop (an edge to join a vertex to itself). A polynomial time algorithm to process parallel edges and loops to solve #SAT has been shown in [1].

Let $\rho : \text{2-CNF} \to G_F$ be the function whose domain is the space of Boolean formulas in 2-CNF and codomain the set of multi-graphs, ρ is a bijection. So any 2-CNF formula has a unique signed constraint graph associated via ρ and viceversa, any signed constraint graph G_F has a unique formula associated.

3 Outerplanar 2-CNF Formulas

An outerplanar 2-CNF formula is one whose signed primal graph is outerplanar e.g the graph has a planar drawing for which all vertices belong to the outer face of the drawing. Outerplanar graphs may be characterized (analogously to Wagner's theorem for planar graphs) by the two forbidden minors K_4 and $K_{2,3}$, or by their Colin de Verdière graph invariants. They have Hamiltonian cycles if and only if they are biconnected, in which case the outer face forms the unique Hamiltonian cycle. Every outerplanar graph is 3-colorable, and has degeneracy and treewidth at most 2 [12]. The outerplanar graphs are a subset of the planar graphs, of the serial-parallel graphs, and of the circle graphs.

3.1 Tree Decomposition

Many hard problems can even be solved efficiently on graphs that might not be trees, but are in some sense still sufficiently treelike. A formal parameter that is widely accepted to measure this likeliness is the treewidth of a graph [13].

Treewidth is one of the most basic parameters in graph algorithms. There is a well established theory on the design of polynomial (or even linear) time algorithms for many intractable problems where their input is restricted to graphs of bounded treewidth. More importantly, there are problems on graphs with n vertices and treewidth at most k that can be solved in time $O(c^k \cdot n^{O(1)})$, where c is a problem dependent constant [14].

For example, a maximum independent set (a MIS) of a graph can be found in time $O(2^k \cdot n)$, given a tree decomposition of width at most k. Therefore, a quite natural approach to compute $i(G)$ would be to find a treewidth T_G of G, and to determine how to join the partial results on the nodes of T_G. However, for any general graph G, finding its minimum treewidth is a NP-complete problem.

A tree decomposition of a graph $G = (V, E)$ is a pair $(\{X_i \mid i \in I\}, T = (I, F))$ with $\{X_i \mid i \in I\}$ a collection of subsets of V, called bags, and $T = (I, F)$ a tree, such that for all $v \in V$ there exists an $i \in I$ with $v \in X_i$, for all $\{v, w\} \in E$ there exists and $i \in I$ with $v, w \in X_i$, and for all $v \in V$, the set $I_v = \{i \in I \mid v \in X_i\}$ forms a connected subgraph (subtree of T).

The width of a tree decomposition $(\{X_i \mid i \in I\}, T = (I, F))$ is defined as $\max_{i \in I} |X_i| - 1$. The treewidth of a graph G is the minimum width of a tree decomposition of G. It is NP-complete to decide whether the treewidth of a graph is at most k (if k is part of the input) [15]. But, for every fixed k, there is a linear-time algorithm deciding whether the treewidth is at most k, and when that is the case, producing a corresponding tree decomposition [12]. Algorithm 1 computes the 2-treewidth decomposition of an outerplanar graph [16].

Algorithm 1 keeps the structure of a tree, and then, we can combine the algorithms to be presented in the following section, in order to compute $i(T)$.

Algorithm 1. Procedure that computes the treewidth decomposition ($\{X_i \mid i \in I^*\}, T^*$) of and outerplanar graph $G = (V, E)$.

1: **procedure** TREEWIDTH(G)
2:   **if** $|V| <= 3$ **then**
3:     $X_i = G$
4:     I={i}
5:     **return** ($\{X_i\}, T = (I, \emptyset)$)
6:   **else**
7:     **let** ($v \in V$ such that $\delta(v) = 2$ or $\delta(v) = 1$)
8:     ($\{X_i\}, T = (I, F)$)=Treewidth(($V - \{v\}, (E - \{(v, w), (v, x)\}) \cup \{(w, x)\}$)
9:     **let** ($i \in I$ with $w \in X_i \wedge x \in X_i$ for some bag X_i)
10:    **let** ($i^* \notin I$)
11:    $I^* = I \cup \{i^*\}$
12:    $X_{i^*} = \{v, w, x\}$
13:    $T^* = (I^*, F \cup \{(i, i^*)\})$
14:    **return** ($\{X_i \mid i \in I^*\}, T^*$)
15: **end if**

---

4   Computing #2SAT on Outerplanar 2-CNF Formulas

If F consists of disconnected sub-formulas then $\#2SAT(F) = \prod_{i=1}^{k} \#2SAT(F_i)$ where $F_i, i = 1, \ldots, k$, are the disconnected sub-formulas of F [3]. The time complexity for computing $\#2SAT(F)$, denoted as $T(\#2SAT(F))$, is given by the rule $T(\#2SAT(F)) = max\{T(\#2SAT(F_i)) : F_i$ is a disconnected subformula of $F\}$. Thus, a first decomposition of the formula is done via its connected components, and from here on, we consider only outerplanar connected formulas.

Our algorithm is based on the following Theorem.

Theorem 1. *If the treewidth of a graph G is of size k, G has a tree decomposition where each bag is of size at most $k + 1$ [17].*

Due to the fact that the treewidth of outerplanar graphs is 2, there is a tree decomposition of outerplanar graphs where each bag has at most 3 vertices forming so trees, simple cycles or disconnected components. Additionally each node (bag) is connected to its descedents or ancestor via a common edge or vertices.

We built a pair of linear equations whose solution represents the values (α, β) on each node of the tree decomposition.

Let B_1 and B_2 be two nodes in the tree decomposition of an outerplanar graph. Assume that B_2 is a child of B_1 in the tree decomposition. By definition of a tree decomposition, B_1 and B_2 share: a common edge or, a common vertex or, two non-adjacent vertices (either connected by a path or disconnected).

We present a procedure for computing $\#2SAT(F)$ traversing in postorder by the nodes B_i $1 \leq i \leq j$ of the tree decomposition. We begin computing the values (α, β) on the leaves, and later on, for interior nodes and finally, for the root node.

Fig. 1. On the left a constrained graph representing the Formula $\{\{x_1, x_2\}, \{x_1, x_3\},$ $\{x_2, x_4\}, \{x_2, x_3\}, \{x_3, x_4\}\}$. On the right, its tree decomposition.

The computation of $\#2SAT(B_j)$ when B_j is a leaf node can be done according to the procedures presented at [7], since it contains a path, a tree, a simple cycle or disconnected subgraphs. In case that a node contains disconnected subgraphs, the number of models is the product of the models of each subgraph.

The pair (α, β) for each leaf node is not represented by single numbers, instead this pair is represented by a pair of linear equations. Hence, the order of the computation is important since the pair of linear equations has to be associated to the vertex or edge that is joined to its father's node.

Let us show an example, consider the formula $F = \{\{x_1, x_2\}, \{x_1, x_3\}, \{x_2, x_4\},$ $\{x_2, x_3\}, \{x_3, x_4\}\}$ whose signed primal graph is shown on the left of Fig. 1. A tree decomposition is shown on the right of Fig. 1.

The leaf node B_2 contains a cycle, so according to the procedure presented at [7] two computing threads have to be computed. Since the edge (x_2, x_3) is the joint to its father's node. The computation should begins at one joint vertex and ends on the other. Lets us assume the computation begins at x_2. The two computing threads: L_p, L_c, and its associated pairs are expressed as basic operations between the symbolic variables: α and β, in the following way:

$$
\begin{array}{ccccc}
 & x_2 & x_1 & x_3 & x_3 \to x_2 \\
L_p : & (\alpha, \beta) \to & (\alpha+\beta, \alpha) \to & (2\alpha + \beta, \alpha + \beta) \Rightarrow & (2\alpha + \beta, \alpha + \beta) \\
L_c : & (0, \beta) \to & (\beta, 0) \to & (\beta, \beta) \Rightarrow & \text{- } (0, \beta) \\
\hline
 & & & & (2\alpha + \beta, \alpha)
\end{array}
\tag{1}
$$

The symbol $\Rightarrow$ is used to establish that the first component of L_c is set to 0 since we are counting the assignments were both x_2^0 and x_3^0 do not appear.

Instead of evaluating the pair to get the models of B_2 we will associate to the edge (x_2, x_3) the pair of linear equations $(2\alpha+\beta, \alpha)$ which we call, the macro M_1.

A relevant property of a macro, as defined in this paper, is the possibility to represent cumulative operations via symbolic variables, making macros indistinguishable from individual operators. If subsequences of operators are repeated, a hierarchy of macros can represent a more compactly plan than a simple operator sequence, replacing each occurrence of a repeating subsequence with a macro [18].

When the computation of $\#2SAT(B_1)$ starts, for example at vertex x_4, two new threads are created (since the bag contains a simple cycle too) $L_P = (\alpha, \beta)$

and $L_c = (0, \beta)$. When the vertex x_3 is reached, $L_P = (\alpha+\beta, \alpha)$ and $L_c = (\beta, 0)$. When (x_2, x_3) is visited, it implies the substitution of α and β in the macro M_1 by the values given at L_P, and L_c pairwise. In our example $L_P = (2(\alpha + \beta) + \alpha, \alpha + \beta) = (3\alpha + 2\beta, \alpha + \beta)$ and $L_c = (2\beta, \beta)$. The simple cycle is then closed so the last pair of equation is $(3\alpha + 2\beta, \alpha + \beta) - (0, \beta) = (3\alpha + 2\beta, \alpha)$. Finally $\#2SAT(F) = 3\alpha + 2\beta + \alpha$. With the initial values $\alpha = \beta = 1$ we have that $\#2SAT(F) = 6$.

M_1 indicates that it does not matter the values for α and β, the values for those variables can be substituted by a current pair of values in order to obtain a final pair of linear equations and such that in those new equations, the value for $\#2SAT(B_2)$ has been considered as part of its cumulative operations.

In our case, the *expansion* of a macro consists in the substitution of the symbolic variables α and β, appearing in its pair of equations, by the current values already computed when the common edge is reached. This process of expansion is well-defined since no macro appears in its own expansion.

The correctness of our method is based in the following Theorem.

Theorem 2. *Let F_1 and F_2 be two formulas in 2-CNF. If $F_1 \cap F_2 = \{x_1^\epsilon, x_2^\delta\}$, e.g. a single clause then*

$$\#2SAT(F_1 \cup F_2) = \#2SAT(F_1 |_{\{x_1^\epsilon, x_2^\delta\} \subseteq s}) \times \#2SAT(F_2 |_{\{x_1^\epsilon, x_2^\delta\} \subseteq s})$$
$$+ \#2SAT(F_1 |_{\{x_1^\epsilon, x_2^{\delta-1}\} \subseteq s}) \times \#2SAT(F_2 |_{\{x_1^\epsilon, x_2^{\delta-1}\} \subseteq s})$$
$$+ \#2SAT(F_1 |_{\{x_1^{\epsilon-1}, x_2^\delta\} \subseteq s}) \times \#2SAT(F_2 |_{\{x_1^{\epsilon-1}, x_2^\delta\} \subseteq s})$$

Proof. In order to satisfy $F_1 \cup F_2$ the clause $\{x_1^\epsilon, x_2^\delta\}$ has to be satisfied, so either $\{x_1^\epsilon, x_2^\delta\} \subseteq s$ or $\{x_1^\epsilon, x_2^{\delta-1}\} \subseteq s$ or $\{x_1^{\epsilon-1}, x_2^\delta\} \subseteq s$. The computation of the satisfying assignments of $F_1 \cup F_2$ is given by

$$\#2SAT(F_1 \cup F_2) = \#2SAT(F_1 \cup F_2 |_{\{x_1^\epsilon, x_2^\delta\} \subseteq s})$$
$$+ \#2SAT(F_1 \cup F_2 |_{\{x_1^\epsilon, x_2^{\delta-1}\} \subseteq s})$$
$$+ \#2SAT(F_1 \cup F_2 |_{\{x_1^{\epsilon-1}, x_2^\delta\} \subseteq s})$$

Assigning truth values to the variables x_1 and x_2 to satisfy $\{x_1^\epsilon, x_2^\delta\}$ in $F_1 \cup F_2$ gives two disconnected formula, by the hypothesis that $F_1 \cap F_2 = \{x_1^\epsilon, x_2^\delta\}$, so the conclusion holds.   □

The previous theorem states that if we know the models of F_1 where the truth values of the variables x_1 and x_2 which joint F_1 to another formula F_2 via a clause $\{x_1^\epsilon, x_2^\delta\}$ are known, then we can substitute the models where x_1^ϵ and x_2^δ appears in F_1 into those of F_2 considering the truth values of x_1 and x_2 in F_2.

Algorithm 2 presents the computation of $\#2SAT(F)$ when F is an outerplanar formula.

Algorithm 2. Procedure that computes a pair of linear equations $(A\alpha, B\beta)$ such that when substituting $\alpha = \beta = 1$ gives $\#2SAT(F) = A + B$. F is an outer planar formula based whose tree decomposition is denoted by T computed by its signed constrained graph G.

1: **procedure** #2SAT(T)
2: **if** $T = NULL$ **then**
3:    **return**
4: **end if**
5: **for** each child C of T **do**
6:    #2SAT(C){Postorder traversal of T}
7: **end for**
8: **if** T is a leaf **then**
9:    **switch** (in case the joint of T and its fathers is)
10:    **(a vertex** x**)**: compute the pairs of T using x as the root node{e.g leaving the pair (α_x, β_x) as a partial result}
11:    **(an edge:** (x,y)**)** compute the macro M of T using either x as the root vertex {e.g leaving the macro M as a partial result on x, y}
12:    **end switch**
13: **end if**
14: **if** T is an interior node **then**
15:    let $((\alpha_i, \beta_i)$ the pair associated to each child of T){A macro or a pair (α, β)}
16:    **switch** (in case the joint of T and its fathers is)
17:    **(a vertex** x**)**: Traverse the vertices of T in postorder using as root the vertex x
18:    **(an edge:** (x,y)**)** compute the macro M of T using either x or y as the root node{e.g leaving the macro M as a partial result}
19:    **end switch**
20:    Substitute M or (α_i, β_i) when the child of T is reached in the traversal {according to the procedures of [1]}
21: **end if**
22: **if** T is the root **then**
23:    let $((\alpha_i, \beta_i)$ the pair associated to each child of T) {A macro M or a pair (α, β)}
24:    Choose a vertex x of T as the root node
25:    Traverse the vertices of T in postorder
26:    Substitute M or (α_i, β_i) when the child of T is reached in the traversal {According to the procedures of Section [1]}
27: **end if**
28: **return** (α_x, β_x).

---

5 Results

We implement our proposal and compare its runtime against sharpSAT which to the best of our knowledge is the leading sequential implementation. Our outer-planar formulas represent polygonal chain graphs where each polygon has three or four sides. Table 1 shows the running time of our proposal against sharpSAT. It is work to said that both implementations are sound and complete hence the exact number of models is computed in both of them.

Table 1. Formulas whose signed constraint graphs is outerplanar.

Instance	Variables	Clauses	Time in seconds	
			markSAT	sharpSAT
1	102	201	0.002	0.028
2	202	401	0.005	0.035
3	502	1001	0.021	0.083
4	1002	2001	0.076	0.230
5	2,002	4,001	0.295	0.822
6	3,002	6,001	0.649	1.792
7	4,002	8,001	1.134	3.176
8	5,002	10,001	1.726	4.898
9	10,002	20,001	6.927	19.335
10	15,002	30,001	21.821	43.411
11	20,002	40,001	47.379	77.283
12	25,002	50,001	83.371	121.271
13	30,002	60,001	129.012	174.213
14	35,002	70,001	186.094	237.553
15	40,002	80,001	249.291	310.091

6   Conclusion

We present a new class of conjunctive form formulas where counting their number of models can be computed in linear time. These formulas are the logical expressions of outerplanar graphs via two conjunctive normal forms.

Our procedure requires the construction of the tree decomposition of the outerplanar graphs, which in this case it is done in time $O(n)$ on the number of vertices of the input formula. Once a tree decomposition has been built a postorder traversal of both the tree and their bags is done in time complexity $O(m)$, where m is the number of edges in the graph.

References

1. De Ita, G., Bello, P., Contreras, P.: New polynomial classes for #2SAT established via graph-topological structure. Eng. Lett. **15**(2), 250–258 (2007)
2. Darwiche, A.: On the tractability of counting theory models and its application to belief revision and truth maintenance. J. Appl. Non-classical Logics **11**(1–2), 11–34 (2001)
3. Roth, D.: On the hardness of approximate reasoning. Artif. Intell. **82**(1–2), 273–302 (1996)
4. Ita Luna, G.: Polynomial classes of Boolean formulas for computing the degree of belief. In: Lemaître, C., Reyes, C.A., González, J.A. (eds.) IBERAMIA 2004. LNCS (LNAI), vol. 3315, pp. 430–440. Springer, Heidelberg (2004). https://doi.org/10.1007/978-3-540-30498-2_43

5. Wahlström, M.: A tighter bound for counting max-weight solutions to 2SAT instances. In: Grohe, M., Niedermeier, R. (eds.) IWPEC 2008. LNCS, vol. 5018, pp. 202–213. Springer, Heidelberg (2008). https://doi.org/10.1007/978-3-540-79723-4_19

6. Dantsin, E., Wolpert, A.: An improved upper bound for SAT. In: Bacchus, F., Walsh, T. (eds.) SAT 2005. LNCS, vol. 3569, pp. 400–407. Springer, Heidelberg (2005). https://doi.org/10.1007/11499107_31

7. López, M.A., Marcial-Romero, J.R., De Ita Luna, G., Montes Venegas, H.A., Alejo, R.: A linear time algorithm for solving #2SAT on cactus formulas. CoRR, abs/1702.08581 (2017)

8. Zmazek, B., Zerovnik, J.: Estimating the traffic on weighted cactus networks in linear time. In: Ninth International Conference on Information Visualisation (IV 2005), pp. 536–541 (2005). https://doi.org/10.1109/IV.2005.48

9. Shiu, W.C.: Extremal Hosoya index and Merrifield-Simmons index of hexagonal spiders. Discret. Appl. Math. **156**, 2978–2985 (2008)

10. Wagner, S., Gutman, I.: Maxima and minima of the Hosoya index and the Merrifield-Simmons index. Acta Appl. Math. **112**(3), 323–346 (2010)

11. Szeider, S.: On fixed-parameter tractable parameterizations of SAT. In: Giunchiglia, E., Tacchella, A. (eds.) SAT 2003. LNCS, vol. 2919, pp. 188–202. Springer, Heidelberg (2004). https://doi.org/10.1007/978-3-540-24605-3_15

12. Bodlaender, H.L.: A linear time algorithm for finding tree-decompositions of small treewidth. SIAM J. Comput. **25**(6), 1305–1317 (1996)

13. Kneis, J., Langer, A.: A practical approach to Courcelle's theorem. Electron. Not. Theor. Comput. Sci. **251**(Supplement C), 65–81 (2009). Proceedings of the International Doctoral Workshop on Mathematical and Engineering Methods in Computer Science (MEMICS 2008)

14. Fomin, F.V., Gaspers, S., Saurabh, S., Stepanov, A.A.: On two techniques of combining branching and treewidth. Algorithmica **54**(2), 181–207 (2009)

15. Stefan, A., Corneil, D.G., Proskurowski, A.: Complexity of finding embeddings in a k-tree. SIAM J. Algebraic Discret. Methods **8**(2), 277–284 (1987)

16. Bodlaender, H.L.: Classes of graphs with bounded tree-width. Technical report, Utrecht University (1986)

17. Bodlaender, H.L.: A partial k-arboretum of graphs with bounded treewidth. Theor. Comput. Sci. **209**(1), 1–45 (1998)

18. Bäckström, C., Jonsson, A., Jonsson, P.: Automaton plans. J. Artif. Intell. Res. **51**, 255–291 (2014)

Improving the List of Clustered Permutation on Metric Spaces for Similarity Searching on Secondary Memory

Karina Figueroa[1]($\boxtimes$), Nora Reyes[2], Antonio Camarena-Ibarrola[1], and L. Valero-Elizondo[1]

[1] Facultad de Ciencias Físico-Matemáticas and Facultad de Ing. Eléctrica,
Universidad Michoacana, Morelia, Mexico
{karina,lvalero}@fismat.umich.mx, camarena@umich.mx
[2] Departamento de Informática, Universidad Nacional de San Luis, San Luis,
Argentina
nreyes@unsl.edu.ar

Abstract. The similarity search is a central problem to many applications, such as multimedia databases and repositories containing complex non-structured objects. The metric space model is very useful in these scenarios, because metric indexes support efficient similarity search but most of them are designed for main memory. In this article we introduce an *improved* version of the *List of Clustered Permutations* (*iLCP*), a competitive index for approximate similarity search. Our proposal is specially adapted for secondary memory and performs well in several scenarios, especially on spaces of medium and high dimensionality. We assessed this new structure with several real-life metric spaces from SISAP, the results show that this new version keeps the rewarding characteristics of *LCP*, while obtaining a very good performance in terms of number of pages read per search.

1 Introduction

Similarity approaching is needed in several modern applications such as pattern recognition and multimedia retrieval, to mention a few [15]. In this scenario, the goal is to retrieve the most similar objects to a given query object. This problem can be mapped into a metric space in this way.

A metric space is defined as a tuple $(\mathbb{X}, d)$, where $\mathbb{X}$ is the universe of objects and d the metric distance between each element in $\mathbb{X}$; that is $d : \mathbb{X} \times \mathbb{X} \longmapsto \mathbb{R}^+$. The metric d must satisfy the following properties for $x, y, z \in \mathbb{X}$: *positiveness* $(d(x, y) \geq 0)$, $d(x, x) = 0$, *symmetry* $(d(x, y) = d(y, x))$, and *triangle inequality* $(d(x, y) \leq d(x, z) + d(z, y))$. Given a dataset $\mathbb{U} \subset \mathbb{X}$, with $|\mathbb{U}| = n$, the basic kind of queries that can be required are:

© Springer International Publishing AG, part of Springer Nature 2018
J. F. Martínez-Trinidad et al. (Eds.): MCPR 2018, LNCS 10880, pp. 82–92, 2018.
https://doi.org/10.1007/978-3-319-92198-3_9

- *range query*: given $q \in \mathbb{X}$ and $r \in \mathbb{R}^+$, a range query in defined as $R(q, r) = \{u, u \in \mathbb{U} \wedge d(u, q) \leq r\}$.
- *k-Nearest Neighbor query*: given $q \in \mathbb{X}$ and $k \in \mathbb{N}$, the *k-nearest neighbor query* retrieves the k closest elements to q from the database $\mathbb{U}$. Formally, $k - NN(q) = A \subseteq \mathbb{U}$ such that $|A| = k$ and $\forall x \in A \wedge \forall y \in \mathbb{U} - A, d(q, x) \leq d(q, y)$.

It is important to highlight that the distance function is the only way to compare similarity between objects and is usually expensive to compute.

Clearly, any query can be solved by comparing the query object q with each element $x \in \mathbb{U}$. However, as n grows it may be extremely expensive to solve a query this way would require n distance evaluations, therefore, we need to use a proximity index avoiding many distance computations. Nowadays, huge databases are common, so primary memory may not be enough to store the index, the database or both. Hence, an alternative is to use the following level in the memory hierarchy; that is secondary memory. However, if we consider using secondary memory to store the index, searches will involve not only distance computations but also I/O operations on disk. In this case, in order to solve queries efficiently we need to consider how to save both distance computations and I/O operations.

There are several indexes for general metric spaces, that allow reducing the cost of searching [13,15]. Most of them are only aimed to reduce the number of distance computations. Only few indexes are specially designed for secondary memory, where the I/O operations are very significant in the search cost [8,11]. Some might think that a good design for secondary-memory indexes is not needed because of the great capacity increase of main memory, however the volume of data grows even faster [9].

In high dimensional metric spaces, where queries are intrinsically hard, even with a good secondary-memory index the number of distance evaluations and I/O operations may be too high to be useful for most applications where real-time queries must be answered over large databases. In this case different strategies to reduce search costs have to be considered. A good strategy in this situation consists in accepting that queries can be answered faster at the cost of losing accuracy in the responses. This approach is used in the *Permutation Based Algorithm* (PBA) [4], and particularly in the *LCP* [6], and *(LCP*)* [12] where it was implemented for secondary memory. Hence, we want to answer approximate similarity queries on large volumes of data, working in secondary memory.

In this article, we introduce an *improvement* to the *List of Clustered Permutations (iLCP)* with a way to implement it on disk efficiently while keeping its good characteristics of its main-memory version. The rest of paper is organized as follow: In Sect. 2 we explain the previous work in this topic, then, in Sect. 3 we give details about our proposed technique to improve *LCP*. We show evidence of the improvement achieved in Sect. 4. Finally, conclusions and future work are given in Sect. 5.

2   Previous Work

There are several techniques for solving proximity queries using metric spaces either exactly or approximately. An exact answer to a query contains all the objects that satisfy the query, but exact query answers can be very expensive to compute [2]. An alternative is using approximate proximity searching, which consists of finding most of the objects that satisfies the proximity query with high probability, this is known as the approximate answer to a proximity query. For exact proximity searching the family of the so called partition-based algorithms work very well in low dimensions, see [3,14]. For approximate proximity searching in high dimensions the permutation-based algorithms [4] have the best performance. An important survey can be found in [13].

The partition-based algorithms [3,14] perform well for medium intrinsical dimensions. Particularly, the *List of Clusters (LC)* [3] is a very good representative of this family and it was shown that it is very competitive. Moreover, the best search performance on high dimensional metric spaces is obtained with the permutation-based algorithms [4], which are used for approximate similarity searching. The *LCP* [6] is a method that combines partition-based algorithms with permutation-based algorithms keeping the best of two worlds. We will briefly describe these two kinds of algorithms, then we will explain *LC*, and *LCP* indexes.

2.1   Partitions-Based Algorithms

This kind of algorithms divide the space in zones as compact as possible, this division is usually made in a recursive way. For each zone, a representative object (a *center*) c_i is stored along with some extra data that allows to quickly discard the whole zone at querying time. The general idea is to have coherent clusters of objects. During search, entire zones can be discarded depending on the distance from their cluster center c_i to the query q.

Two criteria can be used to delimit a zone. The first one discards objects by using the *Dirichlet Domains*, where a collection of centers are selected to arrange the objects in the database assigning them to the closest center. Each pair of centers is divided by an hyperplane and the intersection of all those hyperplanes is the cell of all the objects in the database closer to the respective center. Hence, the cells are delimited by hyperplanes and the zones are analogous to Voronoi regions in vector spaces. If $\{c_1, \ldots, c_m\}$ is the set of centers, at query time we evaluate $(d(q, c_1), \ldots, d(q, c_m))$, then we can choose the closest center c and discard every zone whose center c_i satisfies $d(q, c_i) > d(q, c) + 2r$, as its Dirichlet Domain cannot intersect with the query ball centered at q with radius r. Centers are usually selected in a random way. The second criterion is the *covering radius* $cr(c_i)$, which is the maximum distance between c_i and an element belonging to its zone. In this case, if we search $R(q, r)$ it is not necessary to consider the zone of the center c_i If $d(q, c_i) - r > cr(c_i)$, because this zone will not contain relevant elements to this query.

2.2 Permutation-Based Algorithms

In [4] the authors introduced a permutation-based algorithm. First, a set of permutants $\mathbb{P} = \{p_1, \ldots, p_s\} \subset \mathbb{U}$ are chosen from the database. Then, $\forall u \in \{\mathbb{U} - \mathbb{P}\}$ the distance to $\mathbb{P}$ are computed and sorted by proximity increasingly (i.e. from the closest to the farthest permutant). For each u the order of the permutants with respect to their distance to u, which is one of all the possible permutations of the permutants, and referred to as Π_u has to be stored, in fact the set of Π_u for all u conform the index. The authors compare permutations using the well-known metric *Spearman footrule* which computes how many positions apart each permutant is in one permutation with respect to the other permutation.

$$S_F(\Pi_u, \Pi_q) = \sum_{i=1}^{s} |\Pi_u^{-1}(i) - \Pi_q^{-1}(i)| \tag{1}$$

where $\Pi^{-1}(i)$ denotes the position of permutant i. For example, in $\Pi_u = (2,1,4,3,5)$, permutant p_1 is in position 2, and in $\Pi_q = (1,2,3,4,5)$ permutant p_1 is in position 1, so the difference is $|1 - 2|$. The Spearman footrule computes the sum of the differences of the positions for all the permutants so $S_F(\Pi_u, \Pi_q) = |1 - 2| + |2 - 1| + |3 - 4| + |4 - 3| + |5 - 5| = 4$. In [1,5] authors used the same idea of PeBA but they sacrificed precision with a small part of the permutation.

2.3 List of Clusters

An efficient way to organize a dataset is using a partition-based algorithm. In [3] an economical index called *List of Clusters* (LC) was introduced, it uses $O(n)$ space and has a competitive performance in high dimensions. However, its construction needs $O(n^2)$ distance evaluations, which means, this index is expensive to build. For LC the clusters are compact zones with respect to a center, and there are two ways to define the zones. Let c be a center, a zone can be determined with *fixed radius* r^* or with *bounded number of elements* b. In the first case each element at a distance from c less or equal to r^* will belong to its zone. In the other case, only the b-closest elements to c will belong to its zone. For this work we use the option of having clusters with fixed number of b of elements, so b is the only parameter of this index.

The build process of LC is as follows: first, a center $c \in \mathbb{U}$ is randomly selected. The center c selects its b-closest elements from the dataset and forms the set I. So, the first *cluster* of the list is a tuple (c, I, cr_d), where I contains the b-nearest neighbors of c, and cr_d is the covering radius of c. The covering radius $cr_d = \max_{u \in I}\{d(c, u)\}$; that is, the distance between c and its farthest neighbor in I. The process continues recursively with the rest of the non-clustered elements E, i.e. $E = \mathbb{U} - (\{c\} \cup I)$.

It is important to mention that there are no intersections between clusters, and they are visited in the same order in which the index was built. Therefore, when a query $R(q, r)$ is given, q is compared with the first center c_1 of the list.

Let be $dist = d(q, c_1)$, if $dist < r$ then c_1 is reported to the answer. Then if $dist - r \leq cr_d$ it is necessary to search exhaustively in I. Next, we have to consider the rest of the list, but it has to be revised only if $dist + r > cr_d$. The search process continues recursively until we find a center c_i that satisfies $d(q, c_i) + r > cr_d$, since then the following clusters will not contain any relevant element, or we reached the last cluster in the list.

2.4 List of Clustered Permutations

In [6] the authors introduced a smart combination of *List of Clusters* and a *permutation-based algorithm*. This new data structure is called as *List of Clustered Permutations*. Basically, they proposed choosing a set of centers $\mathbb{P} = \{c_1, c_2, \ldots, c_s\} \subset \mathbb{U}$ and compute the permutations of every element u (Π_u) in the database $\mathbb{U}$. Then, they clustered the elements in zones centered at each permutation Π_{c_i}, they selected the b most similar objects (excluding cluster centers, so that no center would be inside the bucket of another one). By using the Spearman footrule metric to estimate similarity, the elements in the cluster of a center c_i can be considered elements that have similar permutations to Π_{c_i}. However, it is important to mention that each cluster is also a tuple (c, Π_c, I, cr_d), where cr_d is the covering radius as in LC, that is $cr_d = \max_{u \in I} \{d(c, u)\}$. Elements in the cluster are grouped by similarity of the permutations but the covering radius of the cluster is kept using the distance between elements. Therefore, all permutations calculated for the elements of the same cluster are discarded when the cluster is already determined because in the cluster the real objects are stored. The process is iterative the first cluster is built for Π_{c_1}, then for Π_{c_2}, and so on. Hence, it can be noticed that b have to be $\frac{|\mathbb{U}| - |\mathbb{P}|}{|\mathbb{P}|} = \frac{n}{|\mathbb{P}|} - 1$.

During the search of $R(q, r)$, q is compared with all the centers to obtain Π_q. Every center that is at distance less or equal than r from q is reported. Then, they decided by two criteria if a cluster will be revised using the distance $d(q, c)$ and the cr_d as the original technique; and the second criterion is using a *computingShift* proposal, which computes just the shift of some permutants at the center's permutation.

In [12] authors implemented LCP in secondary memory, they called LCP^*. Basically they stored each cluster in the same (or contiguous) disk-page and, during the query time, they sorted the non-discarded clusters and just review a fraction f of them.

2.5 Secondary Memory

Since the index will be stored in secondary memory, we took into account that each I/O operation on disk will consume: *access time* and *transfer time*. Access time is the time between a request of an I/O operation and the moment the transference of data begins; that is the time needed to move the arm (that supports the read/write heads) to the corresponding *track* plus the time of rotational delay to wait for the requested *sector* in this track. A *disk page* is a fixed-size portion of data on the disk that can be transferred in a single access, usually is considered the amount of data that fits in a sector of a disk cylinder.

For simplicity, we considered the I/O time as the number of disk pages read and/or written. We call B the size of the disk page in bytes. Given a dataset of $|\mathbb{U}| = n$ objects of N bytes and a disk page size B, queries can be trivially answered by performing n distance evaluations and N/B I/Os. Therefore, the main goal of a secondary-memory index is to preprocess the dataset so as to answer queries with as few distance evaluations and I/Os as possible.

In order to take advantage of each I/O operation, we must manage that all the recovered data in the reading of a disk page are really useful. We also have to consider that the access time is more relevant when we read/write random pages on disk, but it is less significative when sequential pages are read/written. Besides, the access time for any page of a file is lower, even making random access, if this file is located over as few disk cylinders as possible; Access time in a smaller file is lower than within a larger file.

3   Our Proposal

In a similar way as described in [6] for LCP, the build process begins selecting the centers $\mathbb{P} = \{c_1, c_2, \ldots, c_s\} \subset \mathbb{U}$, that will also act as permutants. Then, we compute permutation Π_u for each element u in the database $\mathbb{U}$, with respect to the centers. As we mentioned previously, it is convenient that similar objects in a cluster are stored in the same disk page in order to minimize the number of I/O operations. Besides, to exploit the use of all data retrieved/stored in each read/write operation, it is important to take advantage of all available space in a disk page. Therefore, parameter b must be chosen according to the size of a disk page; (i. e. we select b as the maximum number of elements that can fit in a disk page, excluding the necessary space for other information maintained in a cluster). Hence, the number of centers s can not be some arbitrary number, it has to be $s = \lceil \frac{n}{b+1} \rceil$.

After we have all permutations we may start building the clusters. This building process is similar to original LCP. For a cluster with center c_i, we select the b-nearest neighbors c_i. We compute the Spearman footrule between the permutation of each database element and Π_{c_i} and store S_F between Π_{c_i} and the most dissimilar permutation of an element in that cluster as its covering radius (cr_{S_F}). It should be noticed that the original LCP maintains the covering radius by using the real distance d. Our $iLCP$ version for disk stores the covering radius using the Spearman footrule metric between permutations (cr_{S_F}). Hence, for each cluster we have a tuple that is stored in a disk page (c, Π_c, I, cr_{S_F}). Therefore, only s write operations on disk are needed to store all the list of clusters. Algorithm 1 illustrates a simplified version of the building process of our improved version of LCP for disk (build-$iLCP$). It should be noticed that in line 4, when we set B as a leaf, this implies a write operation of this cluster on a disk page. As it may be seen, each node of the list have two pointers: $child_1$ links the real cluster and $child_2$ links the following node into the list. Besides, at line 9, when set O_t selects the most similar objects according to S_F, we have to register the distance to the farthest element included as its covering radius cr_{S_F}.

Algorithm 1. build-$iLCP(node,\ Centers,\ O)$

1: Let O the set of objects
2: **if** $|O| \leq bucketSize$ **then**
3:     createBucket B with the set O
4:     $node.leaf \leftarrow B$
5: **else**
6:     Let c be a center picked from the set $Centers$
7:     $\forall\ u \in O$, we compute $S_F(\Pi_u, \Pi_c)$
8:     sort by S_F value
9:     Let O_t the most similar objects according to S_F
10:     $node.child_1 \leftarrow$ build($list,\ Centers,\ O_t$)
11:     $node.child_2 \leftarrow$ build($list,\ Centers,\ O - O_t$)
12: **end if**
13: **return** $node$

Since the list will be allocated on disk and as we know, retrieving any information from disk is costly, we decided to maintain some basic information from the list of clusters in main memory. In this way, we will not have to read a cluster from disk unless it is unavailable in memory. We maintain for each cluster $(c, \Pi_c, cr_{S_F}, \#P)$, where c is the cluster center, Π_c is its permutation, cr is its covering radius using Spearman footrule, and $\#P$ is the page number where this cluster is stored on disk. Therefore, we need to store s tuples in main memory containing each one an object and $s + 2$ integer numbers; that is $O(s^2)$ space in main memory, plus s disk pages.

For a search, first we compare q with all the centers in main memory to determine Π_q and report as part of the answer each center c_i whose distance $d(q, c_i) \leq r$. Then, with the information available in main memory, we traverse the list and when we consider a tuple $(c_i, \Pi_{c_i}, cr_{S_F}, \#P)$, if it is true that $S_F(\Pi_q, \Pi_{c_i}) \leq \alpha \leq cr_{S_F}$, where α is a parameter, we read the cluster from disk (located on disk page $\#P$). Once we read the disk page of a relevant cluster, we exhaustively search on it to determine the elements to report. Hence, at line 2 we report the elements whose distance from q is $\leq r$. A simplified version of range search process is shown in Algorithm 2.

We may improve the search cost of Algorithm 2 if instead of reading each cluster directly at line 2, we include this cluster in a set of candidate clusters that have to be read from disk. Then, we sort all candidate clusters (belonging to this set) by their disk page number before starting reading them one by one. Finally, we perform a sequential pass on the disk when reading the candidate clusters, and we reduce access time avoiding unnecessary seeks.

Algorithm 2. Search($node\ t,\ q,\ r,\ \alpha$)

1: **if** t is a leaf **then**
2:     load a disk page, and compare all elements against q
3: **else**
4:     let c_t be the center of node t and cr_{S_F} its covering radius
5:     let $d_p = S_F(\Pi_q, \Pi_{c_t})$
6:     **if** $d_p - \alpha \leq cr_{S_F}$ **then**
7:         return Search($t.child_1, q, r, \alpha$)
8:     **end if**
9:     **if** $d_p + \alpha \geq rc_{S_F}$ **then**
10:         return Search($t.child_2, q, r, \alpha$)
11:     **end if**
12: **end if**

---

4   Experimental Results

In this section we evaluate and compare the performance of our technique for different metric spaces. For lack of space, we only show the results obtained with three real world datasets (English dictionary, Colors Database, and NASA Database). All this datasets are available from the SISAP project's metric space benchmark set [7]. The experiments were run on an Intel Xeon workstation with 2.4 GHz CPU and 32 GB of RAM with Centos Linux distribution, running kernel 2.6.18-419. We evaluated our proposal both in distance evaluations and in number of pages read when the new parameter α is changing.

Colors Database. This real-life database has 112,682 objects, which are color histograms, represented as 112-dimensional feature vectors, we used the Euclidean distance. From the database, we selected 500 histograms randomly as test set, obviously this subset was not indexed. In this space we used range searches with a radii that retrieves 0.01%, 0.1%, and 1% of the database. Figure 1 illustrates the average of search performance among all elements searched. Notice that lines in horizontal is the original LC (just in a comparative way) because it does not have α parameter. Our results show that our $iLCP$ just need to review less than 10% of pages to retrieve the 100% of the answers.

NASA Database. This database is from NASA, it contains 40,150 objects. Again, we randomly chose 500 vectors and searched for k-nearest neighbors using $k = 1, 2, 4,$ and 8. Figure 2 shows the performance of our proposal. In this case, notice that we need to read just 1% of pages to retrieve all answers. The original LC needs to read almost 8% of disk pages and LCP^* needs almost 7% to retrieve 100% of nearest neighbor.

English Dictionary. Finally, the last real-life database is an English Dictionary with 69,069 words. Once again, 500 strings were chosen as test set. In this case we searched the k-nearest neighbors for $k = 1, 2, 4,$ and 8. Figure 3 depicts our results. As the other results, in this dataset we need to review just almost 0.2%

90   K. Figueroa et al.

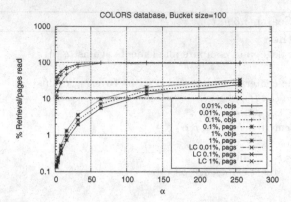

Fig. 1. Performance of our proposal *(iLCP)* using 100 elements per bucket

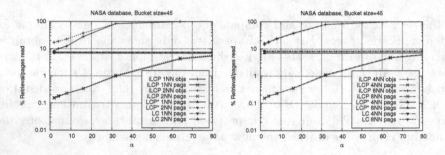

Fig. 2. Performance of our proposal *(iLCP)* vs *LC* and *LCP** using a bucket size of 45 elements.

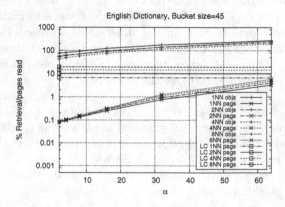

Fig. 3. Performance of our proposal *(iLCP)* using a bucket size of 45 elements.

to retrieve at least the 100%. In this case, retrieval is more than 100% because there are more objects at the same distance.

5 Conclusions and Future Work

We have shown a new secondary-memory version of a competitive in-memory index for approximate similarity $iLCP$. This new proposal offers a good balance between construction and search time. Besides, it supports approximate searches by calculating few distances and reading very few disk pages. We transformed LCP into a more practical index that keeps its rewarding characteristics, but now it can be applied on massive datasets that require secondary-memory storage.

For future work we will analyze how the disk page size affects the search performance and validate our results over huge databases. We will also study the way how new elements may be inserted in an already built index without degrading searching performance. Also we will evaluate the benefit of storing short permutations of objects in the clusters, in order to filter out elements that are not relevant, avoiding unnecessary calculations of distances, in this case, we hope to trade off space for time. Finally, we will use the same strategy of LCP^*, that is, sorting the promissory clusters. Besides, we will also analyze the application of "cut-regions" [10] to LCP, in order to improve its filtering capacity.

References

1. Amato, G., Savino, P.: Approximate similarity search in metric spaces using inverted files. In: 3rd International ICST Conference on Scalable Information Systems, INFOSCALE 2008, Vico Equense, Italy, 4–6 June 2008, p. 28 (2008). https://doi.org/10.4108/ICST.INFOSCALE2008.3486
2. Chávez, E., Navarro, G.: Probabilistic proximity search: fighting the curse of dimensionality in metric spaces. Inf. Process. Lett. **85**(1), 39–46 (2003)
3. Chávez, E., Navarro, G.: A compact space decomposition for effective metric indexing. Pattern Recogn. Lett. **26**(9), 1363–1376 (2005)
4. Chavez, E., Figueroa, K., Navarro, G.: Effective proximity retrieval by ordering permutations. IEEE Trans. Pattern Anal. Mach. Intell. **30**(9), 1647–1658 (2008)
5. Esuli, A.: Use of permutation prefixes for efficient and scalable approximate similarity search. Inf. Process. Manag. **48**(5), 889–902 (2012). https://doi.org/10.1016/j.ipm.2010.11.011
6. Figueroa, K., Paredes, R.: List of clustered permutations for proximity searching. In: Brisaboa, N., Pedreira, O., Zezula, P. (eds.) SISAP 2013. LNCS, vol. 8199, pp. 50–58. Springer, Heidelberg (2013). https://doi.org/10.1007/978-3-642-41062-8_6
7. Figueroa, K., Navarro, G., Chávez, E.: Metric spaces library (2007). http://www.sisap.org/Metric_Space_Library.html
8. Jin, S., Kim, O., Feng, W.: M^X-tree: a double hierarchical metric index with overlap reduction. In: Murgante, B., Misra, S., Carlini, M., Torre, C.M., Nguyen, H.-Q., Taniar, D., Apduhan, B.O., Gervasi, O. (eds.) ICCSA 2013. LNCS, vol. 7975, pp. 574–589. Springer, Heidelberg (2013). https://doi.org/10.1007/978-3-642-39640-3_42

9. Leskovec, J., Rajaraman, A., Ullman, J.D.: Mining of Massive Datasets, 2nd edn. Cambridge University Press, New York (2014)
10. Lokoč, J., Moško, J., Čech, P., Skopal, T.: On indexing metric spaces using cut-regions. Inf. Syst. **43**, 1–19 (2014). http://www.sciencedirect.com/science/article/pii/S0306437914000258
11. Navarro, G., Reyes, N.: New dynamic metric indices for secondary memory. Inf. Syst. **59**, 48–78 (2016)
12. Roggero, P., Reyes, N., Figueroa, K., Paredes, R.: List of clustered permutations in secondary memory for proximity searching. J. Comput. Sci. Technol. **15**(02), 107–113 (2015)
13. Samet, H.: Foundations of Multidimensional and Metric Data Structures, 1st edn. The Morgan Kaufman Series in Computer Graphics and Geometic Modeling, Morgan Kaufmann Publishers, University of Maryland at College Park (2006)
14. Uhlmann, J.: Satisfying general proximity/similarity queries with metric trees. Inf. Process. Lett. **40**(4), 175–179 (1991)
15. Zezula, P., Amato, G., Dohnal, V., Batko, M.: Similarity Search: The Metric Space Approach. Advances in Database Systems, vol. 32. Springer, Heidelberg (2006). https://doi.org/10.1007/0-387-29151-2

Modelling 3-Coloring of Polygonal Trees via Incremental Satisfiability

Cristina López-Ramírez[✉], Guillermo De Ita, and Alfredo Neri

Facultad de Ciencias de la Computación, BUAP, Puebla, Mexico
cristyna2001@hotmail.com, anerjas@hotmail.com, deita@cs.buap.mx

Abstract. A novel method to model the 3-coloring on polygonal tree graphs is presented. This proposal is based on the logical specification of the constraints generated for a valid 3-coloring on polygonal graphs. In order to maintain a polynomial time procedure, the logical constraints are formed in a dinaymic way. At the same time, the graph is traversing in postorder, resulting in a polynomial time instance of the incremental satisfiability problem. This proposal can be extended for considering other polynomial time instances of the 3-coloring problem.

Keywords: Incremental satisfiability problem · Graph coloring
Polygonal tree graphs · 3-coloring

1 Introduction

The graph vertex coloring problem consists of coloring the vertices of the graph with the smallest possible number of colors, so that two adjacent vertices can not receive the same color. If such a coloring with k colors exists, the graph is k-colorable. The chromatic number of a graph G, denoted as $\chi(G)$, represents the minimum number of colors for proper coloring G. The k-colorability problem consists of determining whether an input graph is k-colorable.

The inherent computational complexity, associated with solving NP-hard problems, has motivated the search for alternative methods, which allow in polynomial time the solution of special instances of NP-hard problems. For example, in the case of the vertex coloring problem, 2-coloring is solvable in polynomial time. Also, in polynomial time has been solved the 3-colorability for some graph's topologies, such as: AT-free graphs and perfect graphs, as well as to determine $\chi(G)$ for some classes of graphs such as: interval graphs, chordal graphs, and comparability graphs [7]. In all those cases, special structures (patterns) have been found to characterize the classes of graphs that are colorable in polynomial time complexity.

Graph vertex coloring is an active field of research with many interesting subproblems. The graph coloring problem has many applications in areas such as: scheduling problems, frequency allocation, planning, etc. [1,4,5].

In particular, hexagonal chains are the graph representations of an important subclass of benzenoid molecules, unbranched catacondensed benzenoid

© Springer International Publishing AG, part of Springer Nature 2018
J. F. Martínez-Trinidad et al. (Eds.): MCPR 2018, LNCS 10880, pp. 93–102, 2018.
https://doi.org/10.1007/978-3-319-92198-3_10

molecules, which play a distinguished role in the theoretical chemistry of benzenoid hydrocarbons [8]. The propensity of carbon atoms to form compounds,
made of hexagonal arrays fused along the edges, motivated the study of chemical
properties of hydrocarbons via hexagonal chains. Those graphs have been widely
investigated and represent a relevant area of interest in mathematical chemistry,
since they are used for quantifying relevant details of the molecular structure of
the benzenoid hydrocarbons [3,8,9].

If the array of polygons follows the structure of a tree where instead of nodes
we have polygons, and any two consecutive polygons share exactly one edge, then
we called that graph a *polygonal tree* [2]. We consider here a logical procedure
to color a polygonal tree. Polygonal tree graphs have been widely investigated,
and they represent a relevant area of interest in mathematical chemistry, since
they are molecular graphs used to represent the structural formula of chemical
compound. We show in this article, the relevance to recognize structural patterns
on graphs, that allows to design efficient algorithms for coloring those patterns.

On the other hand, the satisfiability propositional problem (SAT) is an important theoretical problem representing the computational difficulty of the NP-
complete class. Despite the theoretical hardness of SAT, current state-of-the-art
decision procedures, known as SAT solvers, have become surprisingly efficient.
Subsequently, these solvers have been used for industrial applications. These
applications are rarely limited to solving just one decision problem, instead, an
application typically solves a sequence of related problems. Modern SAT solvers
handle such problem sequences as an instance of the incremental satisfiability
problem (ISAT) [10].

The ISAT problem is considered a dynamic incremental satisfiability problem, starting with an initial satisfiable formula F_0, and adding later on, new
set of clauses: $F_1, \ldots, F_n$. Each F_i results from a change in the preceding F_{i-1}
imposed by the 'outside world'. Although the change can be a restriction (add
clauses) or a relaxation (remove clauses), we will focus in the restriction case.
The process of adding new clauses is finished when F_i is unsatisfiable or there
are no more clauses to be added.

ISAT is of interest to a large variety of applications that need to be processed
in an evolutive environment, such as: applications in reactive scheduling and
planning, dynamic combinatorial optimization, reviewing faults in combinatorial
circuits, designing algorithms to coloring graphs, dynamic constraint satisfaction,
and machine learning in dynamic environments [6].

Both, SAT and 3-coloring have been shown to be hard problems (NP-
complete problems). We propose a novel greedy algorithm for the 3-coloring
on polygonal tree graphs. Our proposal is based on the logical specification of
the constraints given by a 3-coloring of an polygonal array, forming in this way,
a polynomial time instance of the incremental satisfiability problem.

2   Preliminaries

Let $G = (V, E)$ be an undirected simple graph (i.e. finite, loop-less and without
multiple edges) with vertex set V (or $V(G)$) and set of edges E (or $E(G)$).

Two vertices v and w are called *adjacent*, if there is an edge $\{v, w\} \in E$ joining them. The *Neighborhood* of $x \in V$ is $N(x) = \{y \in V : \{x, y\} \in E\}$ and its *closed neighborhood* is $N(x) \cup \{x\}$, which is denoted by $N[x]$. Note that v is not in $N(v)$, but it is in $N[v]$. We denote the cardinality of a set A by $|A|$. The degree of a vertex $x \in V$, denoted by $\delta(x)$, is $|N(x)|$. The maximum degree of G, or just the degree of G, is $\Delta(G) = max\{\delta(x) : x \in V\}$.

A path from a vertex v to w is a sequence of edges: $v_0v_1, v_1v_2, \ldots, v_{n-1}v_n$ such that $v = v_0$, $v_n = w$, v_k is adjacent to v_{k+1} and the length of the path is n. A simple path is a path such that $v_0, v_1, \ldots, v_{n-1}, v_n$ are all different. A cycle is just a nonempty path in which the first and last vertices are identical; and a simple cycle is a cycle in which no vertex is repeated, except the first and last vertices. A k-cycle is a cycle of length k (it has k edges). A cycle of odd length is called an odd cycle, while a cycle of even length is called an even cycle. A graph without cycles is called acyclic.

Given a subset of vertices $S \subseteq V$, the subgraph of G where S is the set of vertices and the set of edges is $\{\{u, v\} \in E : u, v \in S\}$, is called the *subgraph of G induced by S* and it is denoted by $G|S$. $G - S$ denotes the graph $G|(V - S)$. The subgraph induced by $N(v)$ is denoted as $H(v) = G|N(v)$, which contains all the nodes of $N(v)$ and all the edges that connect them.

A connected component of G is a maximal induced subgraph of G, that is, a connected subgraph which is not a proper subgraph of any other connected subgraph of G. Note that, in a connected component, for every pair of vertices x, y, there is a path from x to y. If an acyclic graph is also connected, then it is called a *tree*. When a vertex is identified as the root of the tree, it is called a *rooted tree*.

The coloring of a graph $G = (V, E)$ is an assignment of colors to its vertices. The coloring is *proper* if adjacent vertices always have different colors. A k-coloring of G is a mapping from V into the set $\{1, 2, \ldots, k\}$ of k "colors". The k-colorability problem consists of deciding whether an input graph is k-colorable. The chromatic number of G denoted by $\chi(G)$ is the minimum value k such that G has a proper k-coloring. If $\chi(G) = k$, then G is said to be k-chromatic or k-colorable. When $k = 2$, it is polynomially solvable to determine if a graph is k-colorable. However, for $k > 2$ the problem is NP-complete, even for graphs G with degree $\Delta(G) \geq 3$.

Let $G = (V, E)$ be a graph. G is a *bipartite graph* if V can be partitioned into two subsets U_1 and U_2, called *partite sets*, such that every edge of G joins a vertex of U_1 to a vertex of U_2. If $G = (V, E)$ is a k-chromatic graph, then it is possible to partition V into k independent sets $V_1, V_2, \ldots, V_k$, called *color classes*, but it is not possible to partition V into $k - 1$ independent sets.

3   Polygonal Tree Graphs

Given an undirected simple connected graph $G = (V, E)$, applying a depth-first search on G produces a tree graph T_G, where $V(T_G) = V(G)$. The edges in T_G are called *tree edges*, whereas the edges in $E(G) \backslash E(T_G)$ are called *frond edges*.

Let $e \in E(G)\backslash E(T_G)$ be a given frond edge. The union of the path in T_G, between the endpoints of e with the edge e itself, forms a simple cycle, such cycle is called a basic (or fundamental) cycle of G with respect to T_G. Each frond edge holds the maximum path contained in the basic cycle, which is part of. We define the *end-points* of a cycle as the vertices that are part of the frond edge of the cycle.

Let $\mathcal{C} = \{C_1, C_2, \ldots, C_k\}$ be the set of fundamental cycles found during the depth-first search on G. Given any pair of basic cycles C_i and C_j from $\mathcal{C}$, if C_i and C_j share any edges, then they are called *intersected* cycles, otherwise they are called *independent* cycles. In particular, if two cycles share just one edge, they are called *adjacent*.

For two intersected cycles C_i and C_j, the new cycle formed by the symmetric difference between its set of edges (denoted as $C_{ij} = C_i \triangle C_j$) is a composed cycle of G and C_i and C_j are called the component cycles of C_{ij}. A form to compute the composed cycle C_{ij} is $C_{ij} = (E(C_i) \cup E(C_j)) - (E(C_i) \cap E(C_j))$. Notice that the set $E(C_{ij})$ is independent of the order of edges considered in its component cycles, since the common edges between C_i and C_j are always the same.

Let C_k be a simple cycle graph of size k. C_k is also called a polygon of size k. A polygonal chain $P_{k,t}$ is a graph obtained by identifying a finite number of t polygons of size at least k, such that each polygon, except the first and the last one, is adjacent to exactly two polygons. When each polygon in $P_{k,t}$ has the same number of k vertices, then $P_{k,t}$ is a linear array of t k-gons, denoted as P_t.

The way that two adjacent polygons are joined, via a common vertex or a common edge, defines different classes of graphs, that are knowing as molecular graphs [8]. Let $G = (V, E)$ be a molecular graph, which is a representation of the structural formula of a chemical compound in tems of graph theory. Let $P_t = h_1 h_2 \cdots h_t$ be a polygonal chain with t polygons, where each h_i and h_{i+1} have exactly one common edge $e_i, i = 1, 2, \ldots, t - 1$. A polygonal chain with at least two polygons has two end-polygons: h_1 and h_t. Meanwhile $h_2, \ldots, h_{t-1}$ are the internal polygons of the chain. In a polygonal chain, each vertex has degree either 2 or 3. The vertices of degree 3 are exactly the end points of the common edges between two consecutive polygons.

The recognition of repetitive structures 'patterns' in graphs is essential for the design of efficient combinatorial algorithms. For example, the basic patterns of the graphs to be studied here are polygons following a tree structure.

Many hard problems can be solved efficiently on graphs that might not be trees, but they are in some sense still sufficiently treelike. Since the graphs to be considered have a tree topology, it allows the design of an efficient algorithm for its 3-coloring vertices. For this, we extend the definition of *polygonal trees* introduced in [2] with the following characterization of a polygonal tree $G_T = (V, E)$, see e.g. Figure 1.

Characterization of Polygonal Trees

i. All acyclic component in G_T is left outside of the internal faces of the polygons.

ii. Two polygons are adjacents if they share a common edge, a common vertex, or they are joined by just one edge linking a vertex of each polygon.

iii. Any chain of adjacent polygons does not form a cycle of polygons. It means that the way of adjacent polygons follows the structure of a tree where a polygon could sustitute a single vertex of the tree.

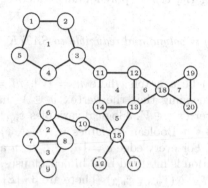

Fig. 1. A polygonal tree graph

The fact that a polygonal tree has a characterization, allow us to propose an efficient algorithm for recognizing the graph, as well as to propose an order on the vertices for their 3-coloring. We show in the following chapter how to build, in polynomial time on the size of the input graph, a valid 3-coloring for polygonal trees.

4   Coloring a Polygonal Tree

Let K be a conjunctive normal form (CNF) and l be a literal, the reduction of K by l, denoted by $K[l]$, is the formula generated by removing the clauses containing l from K (subsumption), and by removing $\bar{l}$ from the remaining clauses (unit resolution). The reduction $K[s]$, where s is set of literals $s = \{l_1, l_2, \ldots, l_k\}$, is defined by successively applying $K[l_i]$, l_i, $i = 1, \ldots, k$. The reduction of K by l_1 gives the formula $K[l_1]$, following a reduction of $K[l_1]$ by l_2, gives the result of $K[l_1, l_2]$, and so on. The process continues until $K[s] = K[l_1, \ldots, l_k]$ is reached. In case that $s = \emptyset$, then $K[s] = K$.

Let K be a CNF and s a partial assignment of K. If a pair of contradictory unitary clauses is obtained, while $K[s]$ is being computed, then K is falsified by the assignment s. Furthermore, during the computation of $K[s]$, new unitary clauses can be generated. Thus, the partial assignment s is extended by adding the already found unitary clauses, that is, $s = s \cup \{u\}$ where $\{u\}$ is a unitary clause. So, $K[s]$ can be again reduced using the new unitary clauses. The above iterative process is called $Unit\_Propagation(K, s)$. For simplicity we abbreviate $Unit\_Propagation(K, s)$ as $UP(K, s)$.

Applying $UP(K, s)$ generates a new assignment s' that extends to s, and a new subformula K' formed by the clauses from K that are not satisfied by s'. We denote the previous formula as $K' = UP(K, s)$. Notice that if s falsifies K, then K' contains the null clause and s' could have complementary literals. And when s satisfies K, then K' is empty.

We present the codification of the 3-coloring of a graph as a satisfiability problem by considering the classic polynomial reduction from 3-coloring to a 3-SAT instance.

Lemma 1. *3-Coloring is polynomial reducible to* $SAT(K \land \phi)$, *K a 2-CNF, ϕ a 3-CNF.*

Proof. Let $G = (V, E)$ be a graph where $n = |V|$, $m = |E|$. We define the logical variables $x_{v,c}$ meaning that the vertex $v \in V$ has assigned the color $c \in \{1, 2, 3\}$. For each vertex $v \in V$, 3 logical variables $x_{v,1}, x_{v,2}, x_{v,3}$ are created. Therefore, there are $3 * n$ Boolean variables in $(K \land \phi)$. We define first the constraints forming K. For every edge $e = \{u, v\} \in E$, u and v must be colored differently. This restriction is modeled by 3 binary clauses, in the following way: $(\overline{x}_{u,1} \lor \overline{x}_{v,1}) \land (\overline{x}_{u,2} \lor \overline{x}_{v,2}) \land (\overline{x}_{u,3} \lor \overline{x}_{v,3})$. There are $3 * |E|$ binary clauses of this class.

The other class of binary constraints allows to define the restriction that every vertex must not have more than one color. This restriction is modeled by 3 binary clauses in the following way. For each vertex $v \in V$: $(\overline{x}_{v,1} \lor \overline{x}_{v,2}) \land (\overline{x}_{v,2} \lor \overline{x}_{v,3}) \land (\overline{x}_{v,3} \lor \overline{x}_{v,1})$. There are $3 * |V|$ binary clauses for this class. Both sets of $3 * (|V| + |E|)$ binary clauses form the 2-CNF K.

Notice that in this case, $SAT(K)$ is not enough to determine a 3-coloring of G, since although K would be satisfiable, there is not a 3-coloring deducible from $SAT(K)$. In order to build such 3-coloring instance, a 3-CNF ϕ has to be formed by the clauses that model the restriction that every vertex must be assigned at least one color. Then, for each vertex $v \in V$ the following clause is generated: $(x_{v,1} \lor x_{v,2} \lor x_{v,3})$. ϕ has $|V|$ 3-clauses. Furthermore, each of the $3 * n$ variables of $v(K)$ has only one occurrence in ϕ.

This reduction can be performed in polynomial time on the size $n = |V|$ and $m = |E(G)|$, since it consists of creating $3 * (n + m)$ binary clauses and (n) 3-clauses for ϕ. We also have that G has a 3-Coloring if and only if $(K \land \phi)$ is satisfiable.

Given the set of contraints $(K \land \phi)$, any 3-SAT solver needs (until now), an exponential time on the size $|K \cup \phi|$ to determine a 3-coloring of G. The non-deterministic character in the process of assigning a color to each vertex of G is reflected in the exponential time requested to solve its respective 3-SAT instance. However, for special graph topologies, as it is the case of outerplanar graphs and polygonal trees, new constraints added to $(K \land \phi)$ are helpful to solve the new incremental satisfiable instance in polynomial time.

Let us assume as an input, a connected graph $G = (V, E)$, with $n = |V|$ and $m = |E|$. We fix a unique depth-first search on G, starting the search with a vertex $v \in V$ of minimum degree and visiting the vertex of lowest degree whenever there are multiple possible vertices to visit. We denote this depth first search as $dfs(G)$. Let $G' = dfs(G)$ be the new graph generated by the depth-first search. dfs allows us to detect if G has cycles or not, and whether these cycles are even or odd in time $O(m \cdot n)$.

Given $G' = dfs(G)$, let T_G be the spanning tree of G'. Notice that $V(T_G) = V(G)$. Let $\mathcal{C} = \{C_1, C_2, \ldots, C_k\}$ be the set of fundamental cycles found during the $dfs(G)$. If G is an acyclic graph, then $T_G = G'$ and $\mathcal{C} = \emptyset$.

Lemma 2. *If $G' = dfs(G)$ is acyclic or G' is bipartite, then G' is 2-colorable.*

Proof. If G' is acyclic or it contains only even fundamental cycles (G is bipartite), then G' is proper colorable with only two basic colors, because the vertices in G' can be colored by levels. This means that all nodes in the same level have the same color, and the nodes of two sequential levels are colored with two alternating colors.

Let us consider now a polygonal tree graph G_P whose specification for any 3-coloring has been codified by $\phi_0 = (K \wedge \phi)$, a 3-CNF. We present an order to perform the 3-coloring of the vertices of G_P. This is strategic to find a valid 3-coloring. Let Fr be the set of strategic vertices to be colored first. Fr is formed in the following way:

1. All end-points from the common edges between adjacents polygons must be in Fr.
2. Also, the common vertices between adjacent polygons joined by one vertex are aggregated to Fr.
3. And, the end-points that are the bridges between two adjacent polygons are aggregated to Fr.
4. Finally, all element in Fr is sorted in such way to form maximal paths among vertices in Fr.

Let $x_{v,c}$ be the logical variable that denotes that the vertex v has the color $c \in \{1, 2, 3\}$. Let $Three = \{1, 2, 3\}$ be the set containing the three possible colors. To each vertex $v \in V(G_P)$ a set $Taboo(v)$ is associated. $Taboo(v)$ indicates the prohibited colors for the vertex v. In fact, $Taboo(v)$ contains the variables associated to the vertex v that has a false value, i.e. $Taboo(v) = \{c : (x_{u,c} = True), \text{ and } \{u, v\} \in E(G)\}$. Notice that $|Taboo(v)| < 2, \forall v \in V$, because when $|Taboo(v)| = 2$ the clause $(x_{v,1} \vee x_{v,2} \vee x_{v,3})$ assigns a color to the vertex v.

From Fr, new unitary clauses will be added to $(K \wedge \phi)$. These unitary clauses fix a color for the vertices of G_P. The elements in Fr are sorted in order to form maximal paths. We show now the process for assigning a color to the current element of Fr of the Fig. 1 (see Figs. 2, 3 and 4).

$F_r = \{\{14, 13\}, \{12, 13\}, \{7, 8\}, \{18\}, \{3, 11\}\}$

Sorting the vertices in F_r in order to form maximal paths:

$13 - 18 - 12 - 13 - 14 - 11 - 3, 7 - 8$

$\{13, 18\} \rightarrow (x_{13,1}), (x_{18,2}) \rightarrow (\overline{x}_{12,1}), (\overline{x}_{12,2}), (\overline{x}_{14,1}), (\overline{x}_{15,1}) \rightarrow (x_{12,3}) \rightarrow (\overline{x}_{11,3})$

$\{18, 12\} \rightarrow \emptyset$

Algorithm 1. $3\text{-}coloring(T_G)$

Remove any vertex of degree at most two, as well as any acyclic subgraph from G
{these subgraphs can be colored at the end of the process}
while $((Fr \neq \emptyset)\text{and}(\Phi_0 \neq \emptyset))$ **do**
  Let $e = push(Fr)$;
  $e = u$ OR $e = \{u, v\}$
  if u (and v when $e == \{u, v\}$) has already been colored **then**
    Continue {consider next element of Fr}
  else
    if $e = \{u\}$ **then**
      for $v \in N(x)$ and $a \in Taboo(v) - Taboo(u)$ **do**
        $s = \{(x_{u,a})\}$
      end for
    else
      if u has already been colored **then**
        $b = min\{Tres - Taboo(v)\}$
      end if
    else
      if v has already been colored **then**
        $a = min\{Tres - Taboo(u)\}$
      end if
    else
      if $(Taboo(v) == Taboo(u)) == \emptyset$ **then**
        $a = 1; b = 2$;
      end if
    else
      if $Taboo(u) \neq \emptyset$ **then**
        $a = min\{Tres - Taboo(u)\}; Taboo(v) = Taboo(v) \cup \{a\}$;
      end if
    else
      if $Taboo(v) \neq \emptyset$ **then**
        $b = min\{Tres - Taboo(v)\}; Taboo(u) = Taboo(u) \cup \{b\}; a = min\{Tres - Taboo(u)\}$
      end if
    end if
    end if
  end if
  Let $s = \{(x_{u,a}), (x_{v,b})\}$ be an assignment that determines color to u, v
  Apply $\Phi_0 = UP(\Phi_0, s)$
end while
Go back vertices removed in step 1;
Apply 2-coloring assigning them a different color to that of their neighbours

---

$\{12, 13\} \rightarrow \emptyset$
$\{13, 14\} \rightarrow (x_{14,2}) \rightarrow (\overline{x}_{11,2}), (\overline{x}_{15,2}) \rightarrow (x_{11,1}), (x_{15,3}) \rightarrow (\overline{x}_{3,1})$
$\{14, 11\} \rightarrow \emptyset$
$\{11, 3\} \rightarrow (x_{3,2})$
$\{7, 8\} \rightarrow (x_{7,1}), (x_{8,2}) \rightarrow (\overline{x}_{6,1}), (\overline{x}_{6,2}) \rightarrow (x_{6,3}), (x_{9,3})$

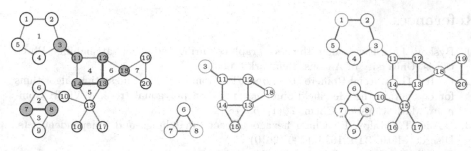

Fig. 2. The elements of Fr

Fig. 3. The first part of the coloring (Color figure online)

Fig. 4. The final 3-coloring of the polygonal graph (Color figure online)

The correctness of our proposal is supported by the following Lemmas.

Lemma 3. *A triangular array is 3-colorable.*

Proof. Given two triangles t_i, t_j joined by a common edge $e = \{i, j\}$, the satisfiability of the contraints: $(x_{i,1} \lor x_{i,2} \lor x_{i,3})$, $(x_{j,1} \lor x_{j,2} \lor x_{j,3})$, $(\overline{x}_{i,1} \lor \overline{x}_{i,2})$, $(\overline{x}_{i,3} \lor \overline{x}_{i,2})$, $(\overline{x}_{i,1} \lor \overline{x}_{i,3})$, $(\overline{x}_{j,1} \lor \overline{x}_{j,2})$, $(\overline{x}_{j,3} \lor \overline{x}_{j,2})$, $(\overline{x}_{j,1} \lor \overline{x}_{j,3})$, and $s = \{(x_{i,1}), (x_{j,2})\}$ determines a 3-coloring.

Lemma 4. *Every polygonal array where the polygons has more than 4 sides, is 3-colorable.*

Proof. If we delete all 2-degree vertex from the array, then we obtain the edges of Fr. The previous algorithm determines a 3-coloring to all vertex involved in the set Fr. After that, the 2-degree vertices removed are come back, and they are 3-colorable since their nighborhoods vertices have used just two colors.

Lemma 5. *Every polygonal array where the polygons have an even number of sides is 3-colorable.*

Proof. The procedure is based on Lemma 2, since the subgraph formed by consecutive even polygons is bipartite.

Thus, for any pattern used to join polygons in a polygonal tree, our proposal give us a polynomial time procedure for 3-coloring such polygonal tree.

5   Conclusions

We propose a novel method to model the problem of 3-coloring on polygonal tree graphs. Our proposal is based on the specification of the logical constraints generated for a greedy 3-coloring on basic patterns: polygons and subtrees that appear in the polygonal tree graph. It results in a polynomial time algorithm that solves specific instances of the incremental satisfiability problem. Our method can be extended to 3-color graphs containing more patterns subgraphs, for example, polygons and outerplanar subgraphs.

References

1. Byskov, J.M.: Exact algorithms for graph colouring and exact satisfiability. Ph.D. thesis, University of Aarbus, Denmark (2005)
2. De Ita, G., Marcial-Romero, R., Lopez, P., Gonzalez, M.: Linear-time algorithms for computing the Merrifield-Simmons index on polygonal trees. MATCH Commun. Math. Comput. Chem. **79**(1), 55–78 (2018)
3. Došlić, T., Måløy, F.: Chain hexagonal cacti: matchings and independent sets. Discret. Math. **310**, 1676–1690 (2010)
4. Dvořák, Z., Král, D., Thomas, R.: Three-coloring triangle-free graphs on surfaces. In: Proceedings of 20th ACM-SIAM Symposium on Discrete Algorithms, pp. 120–129 (2009)
5. Mertzios, G.B., Spirakis, P.G.: Algorithms and almost tight results for 3-colorability of small diameter graphs. Technical report (2012). arxiv.org/pdf/1202.4665v2.pdf
6. Mouhoub, M., Sadaoui, S.: Systematic versus non systematic methods for solving incremental satisifiability. Int. J. Artif. Intell. Tools **16**(1), 543–551 (2007)
7. Stacho, J.: 3-colouring AT-free graphs in polynomial time. In: Cheong, O., Chwa, K.-Y., Park, K. (eds.) ISAAC 2010. LNCS, vol. 6507, pp. 144–155. Springer, Heidelberg (2010). https://doi.org/10.1007/978-3-642-17514-5_13
8. Shiu, W.C.: Extremal Hosoya index and Merrifield-Simmons index of hexagonal spiders. Discret. Appl. Math. **156**, 2978–2985 (2008)
9. Wagner, S., Gutman, I.: Maxima and minima of the Hosoya index and the Merrifield-Simmons index. Acta Applicandae Mathematicae **112**(3), 323–346 (2010)
10. Wieringa, S.: Incremental satisfiability solving and its applications. Ph.D. thesis, Department of Computer Science and Engineering, Alto University (2014)

Deep Learning, Neural Networks and Associative Memories

Performance Analysis of Deep Neural Networks for Classification of Gene-Expression Microarrays

A. Reyes-Nava[1]([✉]), J. S. Sánchez[2], R. Alejo[3], A. A. Flores-Fuentes[1],
and E. Rendón-Lara[3]

[1] Universidad Autónoma del Estado de México,
Toluca-Atlacomulco KM. 60, 50000 Atlacomulco, Mexico
adriananava0@gmail.com
[2] Department Computer Languages and Systems,
Institute of New Imaging Technologies, Universitat Jaume I,
Av. Sos Baynat s/n, 12071 Castelló de la Plana, Spain
[3] Division of Studies of Postgrade and Research, Instituto Tecnológico de Toluca,
Tecnológico Nacional de México, Av. Tecnológico s/n, Col. Agrícola Bellavista,
52140 Metepec, Mexico

Abstract. In recent years, researchers have increased their interest in deep learning for data mining and pattern recognition applications. This is mainly due to its high processing capability and good performance in feature selection, prediction and classification tasks. In general, deep learning algorithms have demonstrated their great potential in handling large scale data sets in image recognition and natural language processing applications, which are characterized by a very large number of samples coupled with a high dimensionality. In this work, we aim at analyzing the performance of deep neural networks for classification of gene-expression microarrays, in which the number of genes is of the order of thousands while the number of samples is typically less than a hundred. The experimental results show that in some of these challenging situations, the use of deep neural networks and traditional machine learning algorithms does not always lead to high performance results. This finding suggests that deep learning needs a very large number of both samples and features to achieve high performance.

Keywords: Deep learning · Gene-expression microarray
Curse of dimensionality

1 Introduction

Traditional neural networks generally consist of three layers: the first indicates the data entries, the second is the hidden layer, and the third corresponds to the output layer. When the architecture of the neural network has more than three layers, it is commonly referred to as deep neural network. The most representative example of this architecture is the multi-layer perceptron with many hidden

J. F. Martínez-Trinidad et al. (Eds.): MCPR 2018, LNCS 10880, pp. 105–115, 2018.
https://doi.org/10.1007/978-3-319-92198-3_11

layers, where each layer trains a different set of features based on the output of the previous layer [1,2].

Deep learning algorithms have usually been applied to problems whose complexity is high due to the amount of data stored, that is, there is a large number of features and samples. They have been used extensively in various scientific areas to tackle very different problems [3,4]. The main advantages of this type of neural networks are three-fold: high performance, robustness to overfitting, and high processing capability.

In this work, we analyze the performance of several deep neural networks and other machine learning models in the classification of gene-expression microarrays, which are characterized by a very large number of features coupled with a small number of samples. This could represent a challenging situation because typical applications with deep neural networks refer to problems in which both the dimensionality and the number of samples are high. Therefore, the purpose of this paper is to investigate the efficiency of deep learning algorithms when applied to data sets with those especial characteristics, thus checking whether or not they perform as good as in those applications where they have demonstrated to behave significantly better than state-of-the-art algorithms.

2   Related Works

Nowadays, the use of deep learning to solve a variety of real-life problems has attracted the interest of many researchers because these algorithms allow to obtain generally better results than traditional machine learning methods [5]. As already mentioned, deep neural networks consist of a very large number of hidden layers, which lead to high computational cost when processing data of large size and high dimension.

The areas in which deep neural networks have been most applied are image recognition and natural language processing. For instance, Cho et al. [6] employed a recurrent neural network (RNN) encoder-decoder to detect semantic and syntactic representations of language when translating from English into French, thus obtaining a better translation in the analyzed sentences. The analysis of information to recognize translations, dialogues, text summaries and text produced in social networks was studied using techniques such as the convolutional neural network (CNN) and the RNN [7]. Nene [8] reviewed the developments and applications of deep neural networks in natural language processing.

In image processing, the use of deep neural networks makes tasks faster and allows to obtain better results. Dong et al. [9] proposed a CNN approach to learn an end-to-end mapping between low- and high-resolution images, performing better than the state-of-the-art methods. On the other hand, Wen et al. [10] combined a new loss function with the softmax loss to jointly supervise the learning of a CNN for robust face recognition. Gatys et al. [11] showed how the generic feature representations learned by high-performing CNNs can be used to independently process and manipulate the content and the style of natural images. A deep neural network based on bag-of-words for image retrieval tasks was proposed by Bai et al. [12]. A novel maximum margin multimodal deep neural network was introduced to take advantage of the multiple local descriptors of an image [13].

Apart from image and natural language processing, deep neural networks have also been applied to some other practical domains. For instance, Langkvist et al. [14] reviewed the use of deep learning for time-series modeling and prediction. Hinton et al. [15] presented an overview of the application of deep neural networks to acoustic modeling in speech recognition. Noda et al. [16] utilized a deep denoising autoencoder for acquiring noise-robust audio features and a CNN to extract visual features from raw mouth area images. Wang and Shang [17] employed deep belief networks to extract features from raw physiological data. Kraus and Feuerriegel [18] studied the use of deep neural networks for predicting stock market movements subsequent to the disclosure of financial materials. Heaton et al. [19] introduced an autoencoder-based hierarchical decision model for problems in financial prediction and classification.

The biomedical domain is another scientific area where the use of deep learning is gaining much attention in last years. For instance, Maqlin et al. [20] proposed the application of the deep belief neural network to determine the nuclear pleomorphism score of breast cancer tissues. Danaee [21] used a stacked denoising autoencoder for the identification of genes critical for the diagnosis of breast cancer. Abdel-Zaher and Eldeib [22] presented an automatic diagnosis system for detecting breast cancer based on deep belief network unsupervised pre-training phase followed by a supervised back-propagation neural network phase. Hanson et al. [23] implemented deep bidirectional long short-term memory recurrent neural networks for protein intrinsic disorder prediction. Salaken et al. [24] designed an autoencoder for the classification of pathological types of lung cancers. Geman et al. [25] proposed the application of deep neural networks for the analysis of large amounts of data produced by the human microbiome. Chen et al. [26] developed an incremental RNN to discriminate between benign and malignant breast cancers.

3   Deep Learning Methods

In this section, the deep neural networks that will be further used in the experiments are briefly described.

3.1   Multilayer Perceptron

The multilayer perceptron (MLP) constitutes the most conventional neural network architectures. These are commonly based on three layers: input, output, and one hidden layer. Nevertheless, the MLPs can also be translated into deep neural networks by incorporating more than two hidden layers in its architecture; this allows to reduce the number of nodes per layer and use less parameters, but in turn this leads to a more complex optimization problem [1, 25].

In deep MLP networks, each layer trains with a different set of features, which are based on the output of the previous layer. It is possible to select features in a first layer and the outputs of this will be used in the training of the next layer.

3.2   Recurrent Neural Network

Recurrent neural networks are a type of network for sequential data processing, allowing to scale very long and variable length sequences [1]. In this type of network, a neuron is connected to the neurons of the next layer, to those of the previous layer and to it by means of the weights, values that change in each time step.

The recurrent neural networks can adopt different forms depending on the particular design:

– Networks that produce an output in each time step with recurring connections between the hidden units.
– Networks that produce an output and have recurring connections only from the output to the hidden unit of the next step.
– Networks with recurring connections between hidden units that read the complete sequence of data and produce a simple output.

A design that improves the use of recurrent neural networks is based on LSTM units, thus giving solution to the problem of the vanishing gradient that occurs in a conventional recurrent network. This means that the gradient changes the weights with respect to the change of the error. If the gradient is not known, then it is not possible to adjust the weights in the direction of decreasing the error, which causes the network to stop learning; this happens because the processed data go through many stages of multiplication.

Figure 1 shows the structure of the recurrent neural network working with LSTM cells, where x are the inputs, y are the outputs, and s consists of the values that the cells take. Unlike the bidirectional recurrent neural network, which works with both forward and backward propagation (see Fig. 2), the recurrent neural network works only with forward propagation.

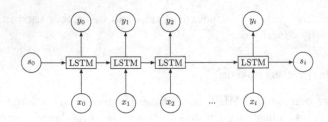

Fig. 1. Recurrent neural network with LSTM

An LSTM contains information in a closed cell independent of the flow of the neural network. This information can be stored, written or read, which helps to preserve the error that can be propagated back to the passage of the layers. If the error remains constant, this allows the network to continue learning over time. The cell of the LSTM decides when to store, write or erase by means of gates that open and close analogically, which act by signals; this allows to adjust the weights by decreasing the gradient or to propagate the error again [27].

The basic idea of the LSTM is very simple: some of the units are called constant error carousels, which are used as an activation function (an identity function) and have a connection to itself with a fixed weight of 1.0 [2].

3.3 Bidirectional Recurrent Neural Network

Bidirectional recurrent neural networks are a type of network where a recurrent network is used with forward propagation and another with backward propagation. This type of network is used for input data sequences where it is known its beginning and end (e.g., spoken sentences and protein structures). To know the past and future of each sequence element, a recurrent network processes the sequence of data from the beginning to the end, and another processes backing up from the end to the beginning [2].

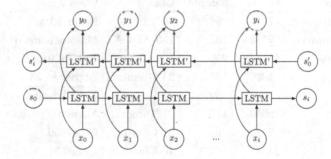

Fig. 2. Bidirectional recurrent neural network with LSTM

3.4 Autoencoder

An autoencoder is a type of neural network that copies the input to the output. It consists of an encoder that does the training task and a decoder that obtains the same inputs as outputs. In general, it can be used for feature selection, dimensionality reduction and classification [1].

There are different types of autoencoders, which can make different tasks depending on the structure of them:

- Incomplete autoencoder: wait for the results of the training, from where it takes useful features that result from restricting h less to x, where h are the nodes of the encoder and x are the inputs.
- Regularized autoencoder: this type uses a loss function that allows to have other properties in addition to copying the input to the output.

- Dispersed autoencoder: a training dispersion penalty is applied; it is used to learn functions used in classification tasks.
- Autoencoder for elimination of noise: it obtains useful characteristics minimizing the reconstruction error, this receives a damaged data set and is trained to predict the original data set not damaged as an output.

4   Experimental Set-Up

The purpose of the experiments in this work is to compare some state-of-the-art machine learning algorithms with deep learning for the classification of gene-expression microarrays. To this end, a collection of publicly available microarray cancer data sets taken from the Kent Ridge Biomedical Data Set Repository (http://datam.i2r.a-star.edu.sg/datasets/krbd) were used (see Table 1).

Table 1. Description of the data sets. The imbalance ratio (IR), which corresponds to the ratio of the majority class size to the minority class size is reported in the last column

Database	Features	Samples	Class 1	Class 2	IR
Lung-Michigan	7129	96	86 Tumor	Normal 10	8.60
Lung-Ontario	12533	182	150 ADCA	Mesothelioma 31	4.84
Ovarian	15154	253	162 Cancer	Normal 91	1.78
DLBCL	4026	47	24 Germinal	Activated 23	1.04
Colon	2000	62	22 Positive	Negative 40	1.82
Prostate	12600	136	77 Tumor	Normal 59	1.31
CNS	7129	60	21 Class1	Class0 39	1.86
Breast	24481	97	46 Class1	Class0 51	1.11

For the experimental design, we adopted the holdout method 10 times was adopted, with 70% of the samples for training and 30% for testing. The traditional machine learning methods used in these experiments were the radial basis function (RBF) neural network, the random forest (RNDF), the nearest neighbor (1NN) rule, the C4.5 decision tree, and a support vector machine (SVM) using a linear kernel function with the soft-margin constant $C = 1.0$ and a tolerance of 0.001. The deep learning models analyzed in this work were recurrent neural network (RNN), bidirectional recurrent neural network (BRNN) and autoencoder (AE). In addition, we included two versions of MLP: one with two hidden layers (MLP2) and one with three hidden layers (MLP3). The main parameters of the deep neural networks are listed in Table 2.

The state-of-the-art machine learning methods were applied using the default parameters as defined in the WEKA data mining toolkit [28].

Table 2. Parameters of the deep neural networks

Method	Parameters
MLP2	Sigmoidal activation function; learning rate = 0.3; Adam optimizer; hidden layers = 2
MLP3	Rectified linear unit (ReLU) activation function; learning rate = 0.1; Adagrad optimizer; hidden layers = 3
RNN	Hyperbolic tangent (tanh) activation function; learning rate = 0.1; gradient descendent optimizer; hidden layers = 1
BRNN	tanh activation function; learning rate = 0.1; gradient descendent optimizer; hidden layers = 1
AE	Autoencoders = 2; hidden size = 10; weight regularization = 0.1; sparsity proportion = 0.05; linear decoder transfer function; cross entropy loss function; softmax activation function; hidden layers = 1

5   Results

Table 3 reports the accuracy results and standard deviations for each classifier and each database. In addition, the Friedman's average rankings are also included. Bold values indicate the best model for each data set.

From the Friedman's rankings, one can see that the best algorithms were MLP2 and AE followed by the classical random forest, whereas the two versions of recurrent neural networks (RNN and BRNN) performed the worst in average. When focusing on the accuracy results on each particular database, it was found that the autoencoder was the best method in four out of the eight problems (Lung-Michigan, Lung-Ontario, Ovarian, and Colon), and the MLP2 model was the best performing algorithm in two cases (Prostate and Breast).

It is worth noting that Lung-Michigan, Lung-Ontario and Ovarian, which correspond to three of the databases where the AE method performed the best, are the cases with the highest imbalance ratio as reported in Table 1. On the other hand, the only problem where a state-of-the-art machine learning method achieved the best accuracy was CNS, which is one of the databases with the smallest number of samples and features.

To check the results of the classifiers and to determine whether or not there exist significant differences between each pair of algorithms, the Wilcoxon's paired signed-rank test at a significance level of $\alpha = 0.05$ was employed. This statistic ranks the differences in performance of two algorithms for each data set, ignoring the signs, and compares the ranks for the positive and the negative differences. In Table 4, one can see the results of this test where the symbol "•" represents that the classifier in the column was significantly better than the

Table 3. Accuracy results (and standard deviation) for the classifiers

	MLP2	AE	RNDF	C4.5	1NN	MLP3	RBF	SVM	RNN	BRNN
Lung-Michigan	0.990	**0.997**	0.931	0.993	0.993	0.972	0.914	0.883	0.852	0.841
	(0.01)	(0.01)	(0.06)	(0.01)	(0.01)	(0.04)	(0.05)	(0.04)	(0.03)	(0.05)
Lung-Ontario	0.993	**0.998**	0.969	0.931	0.935	0.947	0.976	0.838	0.810	0.790
	(0.01)	(0.005)	(0.03)	(0.02)	(0.02)	(0.08)	(0.02)	(0.03)	(0.16)	(0.15)
Ovarian	0.970	**0.987**	0.949	0.952	0.941	0.632	0.859	0.775	0.543	0.564
	(0.02)	(0.01)	(0.02)	(0.02)	(0.03)	(0.03)	(0.05)	(0.08)	(0.07)	(0.08)
DLBCL	0.859	0.886	0.819	0.684	0.725	**0.899**	0.772	0.812	0.696	0.784
	(0.09)	(0.10)	(0.10)	(0.12)	(0.06)	(0.09)	(0.14)	(0.06)	(0.17)	(0.10)
Colon	0.821	**0.832**	0.779	0.790	0.753	0.779	0.737	0.668	0.616	0.537
	(0.06)	(0.06)	(0.08)	(0.05)	(0.08)	(0.05)	(0.07)	(0.07)	(0.14)	(0.13)
Prostate	**0.885**	0.871	0.849	0.837	0.763	0.744	0.622	0.529	0.603	0.591
	(0.05)	(0.06)	(0.06)	(0.05)	(0.07)	(0.11)	(0.07)	(0.05)	(0.05)	(0.04)
CNS	0.650	0.567	0.589	0.578	0.600	0.517	0.628	**0.667**	0.639	0.620
	(0.07)	(0.08)	(0.06)	(0.16)	(0.08)	(0.12)	(0.07)	(0.07)	(0.03)	(0.12)
Breast	**0.578**	0.570	0.647	0.577	0.557	0.547	0.517	0.490	0.426	0.410
	(0.08)	(0.11)	(0.08)	(0.06)	(0.05)	(0.09)	(0.07)	(0.06)	(0.07)	(0.07)
Average	0.843	0.838	0.816	0.793	0.783	0.755	0.753	0.708	0.648	0.642
Rank	2.250	2.625	4.187	5.062	5.437	5.687	6.000	6.875	8.250	8.625

Table 4. Wilcoxon's paired signed-rank test ($\alpha = 0.05$)

	MLP3	MLP2	RNN	BRNN	AE	RBF	RNDF	1NN	C4.5	SVM
MLP3	-	•	○	•	•	○	○	○	○	○
MLP2		-	•	•	○	•	○	•	•	•
RNN			-	○	•	•	•	•	•	○
BRNN				-	•	•	•	•	•	•
AE					-	•	○	•	○	•
RBF						-	○	○	○	○
RNDF							-	○	○	•
1NN								-	○	○
C4.5									-	○
SVM										-

classifier in the row, whereas the symbol "∘" indicates that the classifier in the row performed significantly better than the classifier in the column.

6 Conclusions

In this paper, we have carried out an empirical comparison between several deep neural networks and some traditional machine learning methods for the classification of gene-expression microarray data, which characterize by a large number of samples and a very small number of features. While deep learning has demonstrated to be a powerful tool in applications with a huge amount of both samples and features, there is no study in problems that suffer from the "curse of dimensionality" phenomenon, such as is the case of gene-expression microarray analysis.

The experimental results have shown that the autoencoder and an MLP with two hidden layers were the best performing deep neural networks. On the other hand, it has also observed that there is no single method with the highest accuracy on all databases, and even the SVM (a traditional machine learning algorithm) was superior to the remaining models on one problem. Another interesting finding is that the recurrent neural networks were the worst techniques in average.

Acknowledgment. This work has partially been supported by the Spanish Ministry of Education and Science and the Generalitat Valenciana under grants TIN2009–14205 and PROMETEO/2010/028, respectively.

References

1. Goodfellow, I., Bengio, Y., Courville, A.: Deep Learning. MIT Press, Cambridge (2016)
2. Schmidhuber, J.: Deep learning in neural networks: an overview. Neural Netw. **61**, 85–117 (2015)
3. LeCun, Y., Bengio, Y., Hinton, G.: Deep learning. Nature **521**, 436–444 (2015)
4. Liu, W., Wang, Z., Liu, X., Zeng, N., Liu, Y., Alsaadi, F.E.: A survey of deep neural network architectures and their applications. Neurocomputing **234**, 11–26 (2017)
5. Guo, Y., Liu, Y., Oerlemans, A., Lao, S., Wu, S., Lew, M.S.: Deep learning for visual understanding: a review. Neurocomputing **187**, 27–48 (2016)
6. Cho, K., Merrienboer, B.V., Gulcehre, C., Bougares, F., Schwenk, H., Bengio, Y.: Learning phrase representations using RNN encoder-decoder for statistical machine translation. CoRR abs/1406.1078 (2014)
7. Young, T., Hazarika, D., Poria, S., Cambria, E.: Recent trends in deep learning based natural language processing. CoRR abs/1708.02709 (2017)
8. Nene, S.: Deep learning for natural language processing. Int. Res. J. Eng. Technol. **4**, 930–933 (2017)
9. Dong, C., Loy, C.C., He, K., Tang, X.: Learning a deep convolutional network for image super-resolution. In: Fleet, D., Pajdla, T., Schiele, B., Tuytelaars, T. (eds.) ECCV 2014. LNCS, vol. 8692, pp. 184–199. Springer, Cham (2014). https://doi.org/10.1007/978-3-319-10593-2_13

10. Wen, Y., Zhang, K., Li, Z., Qiao, Y.: A discriminative feature learning approach for deep face recognition. In: Leibe, B., Matas, J., Sebe, N., Welling, M. (eds.) ECCV 2016. LNCS, vol. 9911, pp. 499–515. Springer, Cham (2016). https://doi.org/10.1007/978-3-319-46478-7_31
11. Gatys, L.A., Ecker, A.S., Bethge, M.: Image style transfer using convolutional neural networks. In: IEEE Conference on Computer Vision and Pattern Recognition, Las Vegas, NV, pp. 2414–2423 (2016)
12. Bai, Y., Yu, W., Xiao, T., Xu, C., Yang, K., Ma, W.Y., Zhao, T.: Bag-of-words based deep neural network for image retrieval. In: 22nd ACM International Conference on Multimedia, Orlando, FL, pp. 229–232 (2014)
13. Ren, Z., Deng, Y., Dai, Q.: Local visual feature fusion via maximum margin multimodal deep neural network. Neurocomputing 175, 427–432 (2016)
14. Langkvist, M., Karlsson, L., Loutfi, A.: A review of unsupervised feature learning and deep learning for time-series modeling. Pattern Recogn. Lett. 42, 11–24 (2014)
15. Hinton, G., Deng, L., Yu, D., Dahl, G.E., Mohamed, A., Jaitly, N., Senior, A., Vanhoucke, V., Nguyen, P., Sainath, T.N., Kingsbury, B.: Deep neural networks for acoustic modeling in speech recognition: the shared views of four research groups. IEEE Sig. Process. Mag. 29(6), 82–97 (2012)
16. Noda, K., Yamaguchi, Y., Nakadai, K., Okuno, H.G., Ogata, T.: Audio-visual speech recognition using deep learning. Appl. Intell. 42(4), 722–737 (2015)
17. Wang, D., Shang, Y.: Modeling physiological data with deep belief networks. Int. J. Inf. Educ. Technol. 3(5), 505–511 (2013)
18. Kraus, M., Feuerriegel, S.: Decision support from financial disclosures with deep neural networks and transfer learning. Decis. Support Syst. 104, 38–48 (2017)
19. Heaton, J.B., Polson, N.G., Witte, J.H.: Deep learning for finance: deep portfolios. Appl. Stochast. Models Bus. Ind. 33(1), 3–12 (2017)
20. Maqlin, P., Thamburaj, R., Mammen, J.J., Manipadam, M.T.: Automated nuclear pleomorphism scoring in breast cancer histopathology images using deep neural networks. In: Prasath, R., Vuppala, A.K., Kathirvalavakumar, T. (eds.) MIKE 2015. LNCS (LNAI), vol. 9468, pp. 269–276. Springer, Cham (2015). https://doi.org/10.1007/978-3-319-26832-3_26
21. Danaee, P., Reza, G., Hendrix, D.A.: A deep learning approach for cancer detection and relevant gene identification. In: Pacific Symposium on Biocomputing, Honolulu, HI, pp. 219–229 (2016)
22. Abdel-Zaher, A.M., Eldeib, A.M.: Breast cancer classification using deep belief networks. Expert Syst. Appl. 46, 139–144 (2016)
23. Hanson, J., Yang, Y., Paliwal, K., Zhou, Y.: Improving protein disorder prediction by deep bidirectional long short-term memory recurrent neural networks. Bioinformatics 33, 685–692 (2016)
24. Salaken, S.M., Khosravi, A., Khatami, A., Nahavandi, S., Hosen, M.A.: Lung cancer classification using deep learned features on low population dataset. In: IEEE 30th Canadian Conference on Electrical and Computer Engineering, Windsor, Canada, pp. 1–5 (2017)
25. Geman, O., Chiuchisan, I., Covasa, M., Doloc, C., Milici, M.-R., Milici, L.-D.: Deep learning tools for human microbiome big data. In: Balas, V.E., Jain, L.C., Balas, M.M. (eds.) SOFA 2016. AISC, vol. 633, pp. 265–275. Springer, Cham (2018). https://doi.org/10.1007/978-3-319-62521-8_21
26. Chen, D., Qian, G., Shi, C., Pan, Q.: Breast cancer malignancy prediction using incremental combination of multiple recurrent neural networks. In: Liu, D., Xie, S., Li, Y., Zhao, D., El-Alfy, E.S. (eds.) ICONIP 2017. LNCS, vol. 10635, pp. 43–52. Springer, Cham (2017). https://doi.org/10.1007/978-3-319-70096-0_5

27. Greff, K., Srivastava, R.K., Koutník, J., Steunebrink, B.R., Schmidhuber, J.: LSTM: a search space odyssey. IEEE Trans. Neural Netw. Learn. Syst. **28**(10), 2222–2232 (2017)
28. Hall, M., Frank, E., Holmes, G., Pfahringer, B., Reutemann, P., Witten, I.H.: The WEKA data mining software: an update. ACM SIGKDD Explor. Newsl. **11**(1), 10–18 (2009)

Extreme Points of Convex Polytopes Derived from Lattice Autoassociative Memories

Gerhard X. Ritter[1] and Gonzalo Urcid[2]([✉])

[1] CISE Department, University of Florida, Gainesville, FL 32611–6120, USA
ritter@cise.ufl.edu
[2] Optics Department, INAOE, 72840 Tonantzintla, Puebla, Mexico
gurcid@inaoep.mx

Abstract. This paper presents a new algorithm to find several types of extreme points of higher dimensional lattice polytopes enclosing a given finite set as derived from the canonical min/max lattice autoassociative memories. The algorithm first computes the basic extreme points that include the corners of the hyperbox containing the data together with the translated min/max points. Then, the algorithm computes additional extreme points such as entry or exit line points from the basic ones. Using convex geometry and lattice algebra, we discuss the rationale of the proposed technique with simple illustrative examples.

1 Introduction

Various concepts of convex analysis and lattice neural networks are being employed in such diverse fields as pattern recognition, optimization theory, image analysis, computational geometry, and general data analysis. Here, we combine elements of convex geometry [1–4] and lattice algebra [5,6] to find other extreme points in lattice polytopes generated from the min and max lattice autoassociative memories. Thus, our purpose is to enrich the lattice computing approach towards new ways of solving real-world problems [7–9]. Section 2 provides basic material on convex geometry concepts and Sect. 3 gives the mathematical background on lattice polytopes. Section 4 presents the main discussion concerning extreme points of lattice polytopes including a new algorithm to find them. Numerical examples are provided to illustrate our technique.

2 Convex Hulls and Extremal Points

Data sets as commonly used in computer science are finite subsets of Euclidean spaces and, therefore, not convex sets. One strategy is to consider the smallest convex set containing the data and extrapolating unknown values from the

---

G. Urcid thanks SNI-CONACYT for partial financial support, grant # 22036.

J. F. Martínez Trinidad et al. (Eds.): MCPR 2018, LNCS 10880, pp. 116–125, 2018.
https://doi.org/10.1007/978-3-319-92198-3_12

data. Recall that a subset X of $\mathbb{R}^n$ is convex if $\boldsymbol{x}, \boldsymbol{y} \in X \Rightarrow \langle \boldsymbol{x}, \boldsymbol{y} \rangle \subset X$ where $\langle \boldsymbol{x}, \boldsymbol{y} \rangle$ denotes the line segment joining $\boldsymbol{x}$ with $\boldsymbol{y}$. We write $\mathbb{N}_k$ for the index set of integers $\{1, \ldots, k\}$ and from now on X will stand for a finite real-valued subset with $k > 1$ elements. Using induction, one can verify that if X is convex and $\{\boldsymbol{x}^1, \ldots, \boldsymbol{x}^k\} \subset X$, then given $\boldsymbol{x} \in \mathbb{R}^n$ with $\boldsymbol{x} = \sum_{i=1}^{k} \lambda_i \boldsymbol{x}^i$ and $\sum_{i=1}^{k} \lambda_i = 1$ where $\lambda_i \geq 0 \ \forall i \in \mathbb{N}_k$, it follows that $\boldsymbol{x} \in X$. Let $\mathcal{K} = \{C \subset \mathbb{R}^n : C$ is convex and $X \subset C\}$, then the *convex hull* of X defined as $\mathrm{ch}(X) = \bigcap_{C \in \mathcal{K}} C$ means that $\mathrm{ch}(X)$ is the smallest convex set containing X. Next, consider the two sets, X (finite) and $\mathfrak{X} = \{\boldsymbol{x} \in \mathbb{R}^n : \boldsymbol{x} = \sum_{i=1}^{k} \lambda_i \boldsymbol{x}^i$ and $\sum_{i=1}^{k} \lambda_i = 1$ where $\lambda_i \geq 0 \ \forall i \in \mathbb{N}_k\}$. Using the corresponding definitions of convexity it is not difficult to prove that $\mathrm{ch}(X) = \mathfrak{X}$ and this *finitely generated* convex hull is a polytope. The notion of corner or vertex points (vertices) associated with polytopes can be defined in terms of extreme points. A point $\boldsymbol{z}$ in a convex set $C \subset \mathbb{R}^n$ is called an *extreme* point if and only if $\boldsymbol{z} \in \langle \boldsymbol{x}, \boldsymbol{y} \rangle \subset C$ implies that $\boldsymbol{z} = \boldsymbol{x}$ or $\boldsymbol{z} = \boldsymbol{y}$. The set of extreme points of C will be denoted by $\mathrm{ext}(C)$. Furthermore, $\mathrm{ch}(X) = \mathrm{ch}(\mathrm{ext}(\mathrm{ch}(X)))$, and it is possible that there exists a strict subset Y of X such that $\mathrm{ch}(Y) = \mathrm{ch}(X)$. However, in most applications of convex analysis, the case $\mathrm{ext}(\mathrm{ch}(X)) \neq X$ rules and the determination of extremal points of the polytope $\mathrm{ch}(X)$ is generally very laborious.

3 Lattice Polytopes

A *lattice polytope* is a polytope that is also a complete lattice. In this paper we are interested in finding the *smallest lattice polytope* containing a given data set X. The *hyperbox*, $[\boldsymbol{v}, \boldsymbol{u}] = \{\boldsymbol{x} \in \mathbb{R}^n : v_i \leq x_i \leq u_i, i \in \mathbb{N}_n\}$ with $\boldsymbol{v} < \boldsymbol{u}$ is the smallest interval with the property $X \subset [\boldsymbol{v}, \boldsymbol{u}]$ and is the simplest n-dimensional lattice polytope with 2^n vertices (corner points) since $|\mathrm{ext}([\boldsymbol{v}, \boldsymbol{u}])| = 2^n$. Given X, the minimum and maximum (corner) points $\boldsymbol{v}$ and $\boldsymbol{u}$, respectively, can be computed using the formulae

$$\boldsymbol{v} = \bigwedge_{j=1}^{k} \boldsymbol{x}^j \quad \text{and} \quad \boldsymbol{u} = \bigvee_{j=1}^{k} \boldsymbol{x}^j. \tag{1}$$

The j-th coordinates of $\boldsymbol{v}$ and $\boldsymbol{u}$ will be denoted by v_j and u_j. The transpose of vector $\boldsymbol{x}$ will be denoted by $\boldsymbol{x}^t$. Let $S(X)$ be the *linear minimax span* of X defined by

$$\mathbf{x} = \bigvee_{k \in K} \bigwedge_{j \in J} (a_{jk_j} + \mathbf{x}^j), \tag{2}$$

where $\mathbf{x}^j \in X$ and K is a finite set of indices with k_j denoting that the index depends on the value $j \in J$. Since $X \subset [\boldsymbol{v}, \boldsymbol{u}]$ and $X \subset S(X)$, where the polytope $\mathcal{P}(X)$ defined by $\mathcal{P}(X) = [\boldsymbol{v}, \boldsymbol{u}] \cap S(X)$ has the property that $X \subset \mathrm{ch}(X) \subset \mathcal{P}(X)$ [6,8]. Furthermore, since both $[\boldsymbol{v}, \boldsymbol{u}]$ and $S(X)$ are convex, $\mathcal{P}(X)$ is also convex. Moreover, $\mathcal{P}(X)$ is a polytope as well as the smallest complete lattice containing X with universal bounds $\boldsymbol{v}$ and $\boldsymbol{u}$.

Hyperplanes, intersections of hyperplanes, and lines are affine subspaces of $\mathbb{R}^n$ that play a vital role in describing the shape of $S(X)$. For points $x \in \mathbb{R}^n$, the lines defined by, $L(x) = \{y \in \mathbb{R}^n : y = \lambda + x, \lambda \in \mathbb{R}\}$, are of particular interest in studying the geometry of $S(X)$. The connection between $L(x)$ and $S(X)$ is due to the fact if $x \in S(X)$, then $\lambda + x \in S(X)$ for any λ. Therefore, $L(x) \subset S(X)$. Another set of affine subspaces associated with $S(X)$ consists of specific types of hyperplanes. A *hyperplane* E in $\mathbb{R}^n$ is defined as the set of all points $x \in \mathbb{R}^n$ satisfying the equation, $\sum_{i=1}^{n} a_i x = b$, where the a_i's and b are constants. It follows that E is an $(n-1)$-dimensional affine subspace of $\mathbb{R}^n$. Any hyperplane E separates $\mathbb{R}^n$ into two open half-spaces E^+ and E^- whose common boundary is E which is also expressed in terms of the function $f(x) = \sum_{i=1}^{n} a_i x - b = 0$. We follow the convention of identifying the half-spaces E^+ and E^- with $\{x \in \mathbb{R}^n : f(x) > 0\}$ and $\{x \in \mathbb{R}^n : f(x) < 0\}$, respectively. The *closure* of E^+ is the convex set $\bar{E}^+ = \{x \in \mathbb{R}^n : f(x) \geq 0\}$. Similarly, $\bar{E}^- = \{x \in \mathbb{R}^n : f(x) \leq 0\}$. Suppose X is a subset of $\mathbb{R}^n$ and E is a hyperplane, then E is called a *support hyperplane* of X if and only if the following two conditions are satisfied: (a) either $X \subset \bar{E}^+$ or $X \subset \bar{E}^-$ and (b) $\exists x \in E$ such that $x \in \partial X$ (boundary of X). A nonempty subset $K \subset \mathbb{R}^n$ is called a *polyhedron* if it is the intersection of a finite number of closed half-spaces. Thus, if $E_1, \ldots, E_k$ are the hyperplanes of K, then $K = \bigcap_{i=1}^{k} \bar{E}_i^{\pm}$. If K is bounded set, then K is a *polytope*. If $\{e^1, \ldots, e^n\}$ is the standard basis of $\mathbb{R}^n$ let the scalars $\varepsilon = \| \sum_{j=1}^{n} e^j \|$ and $\delta_{ij} = \| e^i - e^j \|$ stand for the Euclidean norm use to define two directional vectors pertinent to our discussion, i.e., $e = \sum_{j=1}^{n} e^j / \varepsilon$ and $d_{ij} = (e^i - e^j)/\delta_{ij}$ where $i < j$, $1 \leq i < n$, and $1 < j \leq n$. An *oriented hyperplane* E with *orientation* d, denoted by $E(d)$, is a hyperplane with an associated directional unit vector d that is perpendicular to E. For a given point $y \in \mathbb{R}^n$, there are $n(n-1)/2$ distinct hyperplanes with orientation d_{ij} containing the point y. Since $E_y(d_{ij}) = \{x \in \mathbb{R}^n : x_i - x_j = y_i - y_j\}$, each of the hyperplanes contains the line $L(y)$ and the equality $\bigcap_{i<j} E_y(d_{ij}) = L(y)$ holds in general.

Our current focus will be on finite subsets of $\mathbb{R}^n$ with the property that if $X \subset \mathbb{R}^n$ and $x \in X$, then $x_i \geq 0$ for $i \in \mathbb{N}_n$. We recall that the canonical lattice autoassociative memory matrices, $\mathfrak{W} = (\mathfrak{w}_{ij})$ and $\mathfrak{M} = (\mathfrak{m}_{ij})$ obtained from X, as well as their corresponding $\mathbf{W} = (w^j)$ and $\mathbf{M} = (m^j)$ translate matrices are defined by [5, 9],

$$\mathfrak{w}_{ij} = \bigwedge_{\xi=1}^{k} (x_i^\xi - x_j^\xi) \quad \text{and} \quad w^j = u_j + \mathfrak{w}^j, \tag{3}$$

$$\mathfrak{m}_{ij} = \bigvee_{\xi=1}^{k} (x_i^\xi - x_j^\xi) \quad \text{and} \quad m^j = v_j + \mathfrak{m}^j. \tag{4}$$

In (3) and (4), vectors w^j and m^j are just translates of the respective basis vectors $\mathfrak{w}^j$ and $\mathfrak{m}^j$ in the direction e so that, $L(w^j) = L(\mathfrak{w}^j)$ and $L(m^j) = L(\mathfrak{m}^j)$. Notice that the number of columns of $\mathbf{W}$ and $\mathbf{M}$ may be less than n

since it is possible that $w^j = w^\ell$ or $m^j = m^\ell$ with $j \neq \ell$. The sets of columns $\{w^j\}$ and $\{m^j\}$ (possible reduced) will be denoted by W and M. We end this section with a list of various theoretical propositions relevant in the analysis of the lattice polytope $\mathcal{P}(X)$ and its extreme points. Detailed proofs of the given results can be found elsewhere [6,8].

(a) - $u = \bigvee_{j=1}^n w^j$ and $v = \bigwedge_{j=1}^n m^j$.
(b) - $L(w^\ell) = L(w^j) \Leftrightarrow w^\ell = w^j$, and $L(m^\ell) = L(m^j) \Leftrightarrow m^\ell = m^j$.
(c) - $W \cup M \subset \partial[v, u] \cap \bigcup_{i=1}^n [L(w^i) \cup L(m^i)]$.
(d) - For $i \in \mathbb{N}_n$, $E_{w^i}(e^i) \cap E_{m^i}(e^i) = \varnothing \Leftrightarrow v_i < u_i$.
(e) - For $i, j \in \mathbb{N}_n$ with $i \neq j$, $m^j \in E_{w^i}(e^i) \Leftrightarrow m_i^j = u_i$ and $w_j^i = v_j$.
(f) - $m^j \in E_{w^i}(e^i) \Leftrightarrow \langle m^j, w^i \rangle \subset E_{m^j}(e^j) \cap E_{w^i}(e^i)$.
(g) - $E_{w^j}(d_{ij}) = E_{w^i}(d_{ij}) \Leftrightarrow w_i^j = p + m_i^j$ where $p = u_j - v_j$.
(h) - $S(X) = \bigcap_{i=1}^{n-1} \bigcap_{j=i+1}^n [\bar{E}_{m^i}^+(d_{ij}) \cap \bar{E}_{w^i}^-(d_{ij})]$.

Proposition (b) plays a role in data reduction. Any two equal column vectors are just duplicates of the same information and it makes sense to discard one of them. It may happen that $[v, u] \subset \mathbb{R}^n$, but $\dim[v, u] < n$. For instance, if $u_i = v_i$ for some $i \in \mathbb{N}_n$, then $[v, u] \subset E_x(e^i)\ \forall x \in [v, u]$, and the dimension of $[v, u]$ is reduced accordingly. Proposition (e) implies that if $m^j \in E_{w^i}(e^i)$, then $\langle m^j, w^i \rangle$ is an edge of $\mathcal{P}(X)$ with $w^i, m^j \in \text{ext}(\mathcal{P}(X))$ as will be seen in Figs. 2 and 3. Proposition (g) shares some similarities with Proposition (e). A consequence of both (e) and (g) is that if $u_j = v_j$ and $w_i^j = m_i^j$, then $E_{w^j}(e^j) = E_{m^j}(e^j)$ and $E_{w^j}(d_{ij}) = E_{w^i}(d_{ij})$. Also, since $[v, u]$ is the intersection of half-spaces, i.e., $[v, u] = \bigcap_{i=1}^n [\bar{E}_v^+(e^i) \cap \bar{E}_u^-(e^i)]$, then $E_v(e^i) = E_{m^i}(e^i)$ and $E_u(e^i) = E_{w^i}(e^i)$ with $E_{m^i}(e^i) \parallel E_{w^i}(e^i)$.

4 The Geometry of $\mathcal{P}(X)$

The geometry of the lattice polytope $\mathcal{P}(X)$ is determined by $\text{ext}(\mathcal{P}(X))$ since $\text{ch}(\text{ext}(\mathcal{P}(X))) = \mathcal{P}(X)$. It follows from the definitions of extreme point and polytope $\mathcal{P}(X)$ that the elements of the set $V = W \cup M \cup \{v, u\}$ are vertices of $\mathcal{P}(X)$. More explicitly, since

$$L(w^\ell) = \begin{cases} \partial S(X) \cap \bigcap_{j=2}^n E_{w^1}(d_{1j}) & \text{if } \ell = 1 \\ \partial S(X) \cap \left(\bigcap_{i=1}^{\ell-1} E_{w^\ell}(d_{i\ell}) \right) \cap \left(\bigcap_{j=\ell+1}^n E_{w^\ell}(d_{\ell j}) \right) & \text{if } 1 < \ell < n \\ \partial S(X) \cap \bigcap_{i=1}^{n-1} E_{w^n}(d_{in}) & \text{if } \ell = n, \end{cases} \quad (5)$$

then $L(w^\ell)$ is an edge of $S(X)$. Furthermore $w_\ell^\ell = u_\ell$ so that $\{w^\ell\} = L(w^\ell) \cap E_u(e^\ell)$. Thus, the edge $L(w^\ell)$ of $S(X)$ is being cut by $E_u(e^\ell)$ at the edge point w^ℓ of $S(X)$. A similar argument applies to $\{m^\ell\} = L(m^\ell) \cap E_v(e^\ell)$ and it can be verified that w^ℓ and m^ℓ are vertex points of $\mathcal{P}(X)$. Finally, since v and u are vertices of the hyperbox $[v, u]$ and since $v, u \in S(X)$, they are also vertices of $\mathcal{P}(X)$. Therefore, $V \subset \text{ext}(\mathcal{P}(X))$ and $\text{ch}(V) \subset \mathcal{P}(X)$.

120   G. X. Ritter and G. Urcid

Example 1. Let $X = \{x^1, \ldots, x^{12}\} \subset \mathbb{R}^2$ be given as the data matrix (x^j) for $j \in \mathbb{N}_{12}$ where point x^j is the j-th column of X. Thus, from (1)

$$X = \begin{pmatrix} 2.5 & 2 & 2.5 & 4 & 5 & 4.5 & 4 & 4.5 & 3.5 & 3.5 & 4 & 2.5 \\ 3.5 & 2 & 1 & 2 & 4 & 5 & 3 & 3.5 & 2 & 3.5 & 2.5 & 2.5 \end{pmatrix} \Rightarrow v = \begin{pmatrix} 2 \\ 1 \end{pmatrix}, u = \begin{pmatrix} 5 \\ 5 \end{pmatrix}.$$

Equations (3) and (4) yield the following matrices,

$$\mathfrak{W} = \begin{pmatrix} 0 & -1 \\ -2 & 0 \end{pmatrix}, \mathfrak{M} = \begin{pmatrix} 0 & 2 \\ 1 & 0 \end{pmatrix}, \mathbf{W} = \begin{pmatrix} 5 & 4 \\ 3 & 5 \end{pmatrix}, \mathbf{M} = \begin{pmatrix} 2 & 3 \\ 3 & 1 \end{pmatrix}.$$

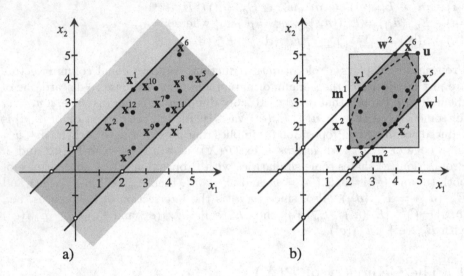

a)   b)

Fig. 1. (a) Data set X, the associated half-spaces $\bar{E}_{\mathfrak{w}1}^-(d_{12})$, $\bar{E}_{\mathfrak{w}2}^+(d_{12})$, and the dark shaded set $S(X) = \bar{E}_{\mathfrak{w}1}^-(d_{12}) \cap \bar{E}_{\mathfrak{w}2}^+(d_{12})$. The base points $\mathfrak{w}^1, \mathfrak{w}^2, \mathfrak{m}^1, \mathfrak{m}^2$ are shown as open circles on the x_1, x_2 axes. In (b), the dark shaded region represents the lattice polytope $\mathcal{P}(X)$ and the extremal points in V. The dotted lines form $\partial \operatorname{ch}(X)$.

Figure 1 illustrates the subset relationship $X \subset \operatorname{ch}(X) \subset \mathcal{P}(X)$. If $X \subset \mathbb{R}^2$ is as in Example 1 then $V = \operatorname{ext}(\mathcal{P}(X))$ so that $\operatorname{ch}(V) = \mathcal{P}(X)$. The next example answers the question as to wether or not the equality $V = \operatorname{ext}(\mathcal{P}(X))$ holds for $n > 2$.

Example 2. Let $X \subset \mathbb{R}^3$ be given as the data matrix (x^j) for $j \in \mathbb{N}_3$. Then, applying (1) to (4), we first get the minimum and maximum vectors,

$$X = \begin{pmatrix} 6 & 1 & 5 \\ 1 & 6 & 5 \\ 14 & 14 & 20 \end{pmatrix} \Rightarrow v = \begin{pmatrix} 1 \\ 1 \\ 14 \end{pmatrix}, u = \begin{pmatrix} 6 \\ 6 \\ 20 \end{pmatrix}.$$

The base and translate matrices $\mathfrak{W}$ and $\mathbf{W}$, respectively, $\mathfrak{M}$ and $\mathbf{M}$,

$$\mathfrak{W} = \begin{pmatrix} 0 & -5 & -15 \\ -5 & 0 & -15 \\ 8 & 8 & 0 \end{pmatrix}, \mathbf{W} = \begin{pmatrix} 6 & 1 & 5 \\ 1 & 6 & 5 \\ 14 & 14 & 20 \end{pmatrix}, \mathfrak{M} = \begin{pmatrix} 0 & 5 & -8 \\ 5 & 0 & -8 \\ 15 & 15 & 0 \end{pmatrix}, \mathbf{M} = \begin{pmatrix} 1 & 6 & 6 \\ 6 & 1 & 6 \\ 16 & 16 & 14 \end{pmatrix}.$$

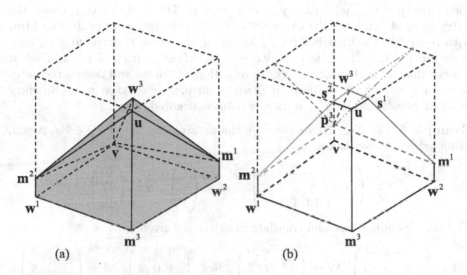

(a)   (b)

Fig. 2. In (a), the shaded region illustrates the polyhedron ch(V), (b) shows $[v, u] \cap S(X)$. The red lines indicate the intersections of $E_{w^1}(d_{13})$ and $E_{w^3}(d_{13})$ with the cube $[v, u]$, the blue lines correspond to the intersections of $E_{w^1}(d_{12})$ and $E_{w^2}(d_{12})$ with the cube, and the green lines mark the intersections of $E_{w^2}(d_{23})$ and $E_{w^3}(d_{23})$ with $[v, u]$. Here, ext($\mathcal{P}(X)$) = $V \cup \{s^1, s^2, p^3\}$ and $\mathcal{P}(X) \neq$ ch(V). (Color figure online)

Note that in set $V = W \cup M \cup \{v, u\}$, $W = X$. However, the polyhedron $\mathcal{P}(X)$ shown in Fig. 2 illustrates the fact that in dimensions $n > 2$ the equation $V = \text{ext}(\mathcal{P}(X))$ is not true in general. Clearly, $V \neq \text{ext}(\mathcal{P}(X))$ since the extreme points s^1, s^2, and p^3 of $\mathcal{P}(X)$ are not elements of V. Note that $|\text{ext}(\mathcal{P}(X))| = 11 > 8 = |V|$. Furthermore, ch(ext($\mathcal{P}(X)$)) = $\mathcal{P}(X)$. Thus, for a given data set $X \subset \mathbb{R}^n$, the geometry of $\mathcal{P}(X)$ is completely dependent on the set ext($\mathcal{P}(X)$). It is therefore imperative to establish a procedure able to produce additional extreme points of the lattice polytope $\mathcal{P}(X)$. To establish this goal we begin by examining Fig. 2(b) as it gives an example of a 3-dimensional lattice polytope. In constructing the polytope $\mathcal{P}(X)$ the three computed sets W, M, and $\{v, u\}$ make up the *basic extreme points*, used in deriving the additional extreme points s^1, s^2, and p^3. The basic extreme points are those used in finding the boundary pieces of $S(X) \cap [v, u]$. The corner point s^1 of $\mathcal{P}(X)$ is due to the intersection of $E_{w^3}(d_{13})$ with the line $E_{w^2}(e^2) \cap E_{w^3}(e^3)$. Similarly, $\{s^2\} = E_{w^3}(d_{23}) \cap (E_{w^1}(e^1) \cap E_{w^3}(e^2))$, and $\{p^3\} = E_{m^2}(d_{23}) \cap (E_{m^1}(e^1) \cap E_{m^2}(e^2))$. What can also be deduced from the drawing is that $s^1 = w^2 \vee w^3$, $s^2 = w^1 \vee w^3$, and

$p^3 = m^1 \wedge m^2$, where $s^1 = (5, 6, 20)^t$, $s^2 = (6, 5, 20)^t$, and $p^3 = (1, 1, 16)^t$. Another pertinent observation is that $p^3 \in E_{m^1}(d_{13}) \cap E_{m^2}(d_{23}) = L(w^3)$ and $p^3 = a + w^3$, where $a = -4$ so that $p^3 < w^3$. It follows that $\langle p^3, w^3 \rangle \subset L(w^3)$ is an edge of $\mathcal{P}(X)$ with endpoints $\{p^3, w^3\} = L(w^3) \cap \partial[v, u]$.

More generally, suppose X is a finite n-dimensional data set. If $w \in \mathbb{R}^n$ and $L(w) \cap \text{int}[v, u] \neq \varnothing$, then $|L(w) \cap \partial[v, u]| = 2$. Thus, if $\{p, q\} = L(w) \cap \partial[v, u]$, then since $p, q \in L(w)$, either $p < q$ or $q < p$. The lesser point is called the *entry point* of $L(w)$ and the larger point is called the *exit point* of the line $L(w)$ with respect to the hyperbox $[v, u]$. Assuming that $L(w^i) \cap \text{int}[v, u] \neq \varnothing$, then since $\{w^i\} = E_u(e^i) \cap L(w^i)$ and $\forall x \in [v, u] \cap L(w^i)$ with $x \neq w^i$, $x < w^i$, it follows that w^i is the exit point of $L(w^i)$. Henceforth we will denote the entry point of $L(w^i)$ by p^i. Similarly, if $L(m^j) \cap \text{int}[v, u] \neq \varnothing$, then m^j is an entry point of $L(m^j)$ into $[v, u]$ and its exit point is denoted by q^j.

Example 3. Let $X \subset \mathbb{R}^3$ be given by the data matrix (x^j) for $j \in \mathbb{N}_6$. Again, using (1) to (4), we have

$$X = \begin{pmatrix} 10 & 8 & 9 & 1 & 2 & 1 \\ 7 & 12 & 8 & 3 & 1 & 2 \\ 10 & 9 & 10 & 1 & 1 & 2 \end{pmatrix} \Rightarrow v = \begin{pmatrix} 1 \\ 1 \\ 1 \end{pmatrix}, u = \begin{pmatrix} 10 \\ 12 \\ 10 \end{pmatrix}.$$

The corresponding base and translate matrices are given by

$$\mathfrak{W} = \begin{pmatrix} 0 & -4 & -1 \\ -3 & 0 & -3 \\ -1 & -3 & 0 \end{pmatrix}, \mathbf{W} = \begin{pmatrix} 10 & 8 & 9 \\ 7 & 12 & 7 \\ 9 & 9 & 10 \end{pmatrix}, \mathfrak{M} = \begin{pmatrix} 0 & 3 & 1 \\ 4 & 0 & 3 \\ 1 & 3 & 0 \end{pmatrix}, \mathbf{M} = \begin{pmatrix} 1 & 4 & 2 \\ 5 & 1 & 4 \\ 2 & 4 & 1 \end{pmatrix}.$$

Following the rationale in Example 2 to find other extreme points not in V, we note that since $m^i \in E_{m^i}(e^i) = E_v(e^i)$ and $m^j \in E_{m^j}(e^j) = E_v(e^j)$, it follows that $m^i \wedge m^j \in E_v(e^i) \cap E_v(e^j)$. Thus, $m^i \wedge m^j$ is always an *edge point* of the hyperbox $[v, u]$ denoted by $r^\ell = m^i \wedge m^j$ and reminding that $i \neq \ell \neq j$. Similarly, $s^\ell = w^i \vee w^j \in E_u(e^i) \cap E_u(e^j)$. However, an edge point of $[v, u]$ *is not* necessarily an extremal point of $\mathcal{P}(X)$. That the points $w^i \vee w^j$ and $m^i \wedge m^j$ are indeed extremal points of $\mathcal{P}(X)$ is a consequence of the following equations:

$$s^1 = w^2 \vee w^3 = \left(E_u(e^2) \cap E_u(e^3)\right) \cap E_{w^3}(d_{13}) \tag{6}$$

$$s^2 = w^1 \vee w^3 = \left(E_u(e^1) \cap E_u(e^3)\right) \cap \left(E_{w^1}(d_{12}) \cap E_{w^3}(d_{23})\right) \tag{7}$$

$$s^3 = w^1 \vee w^2 = \left(E_u(e^1) \cap E_u(e^2)\right) \cap \left(E_{w^1}(d_{13}) \cap E_{w^2}(d_{23})\right) \tag{8}$$

$$r^1 = m^2 \wedge m^3 = \left(E_v(e^2) \cap E_v(e^3)\right) \cap E_{m^3}(d_{13}). \tag{9}$$

$$r^2 = m^1 \wedge m^3 = \left(E_v(e^1) \cap E_v(e^3)\right) \cap E_{m^3}(d_{23}) \tag{10}$$

$$r^3 = m^1 \wedge m^2 = \left(E_v(e^1) \cap E_v(e^2)\right) \cap E_{m^1}(d_{13}) \tag{11}$$

We collect in set S the column vectors s^j and in set R the vectors r^j both for $j = 1, 2, 3$. Here the resulting sets are given by,

$$S = \begin{Bmatrix} 9 & 10 & 10 \\ 12 & 7 & 12 \\ 10 & 10 & 9 \end{Bmatrix} \quad \text{and} \quad R = \begin{Bmatrix} 2 & 1 & 1 \\ 1 & 4 & 1 \\ 1 & 1 & 2 \end{Bmatrix}.$$

Accordingly, we now have a set $V \cup S \cup R$ of 14 easily computable extreme points of $\mathcal{P}(X)$. Other points in $\text{ext}(\mathcal{P}(X))$ such as the entry and exit points generated by the lines $L(\boldsymbol{w}^i)$ and $L(\boldsymbol{m}^j)$ must also be computed. Note that (7) and (8) represent the intersection of two lines while equations (6) and (9) through (11) represent the intersection of a line with a plane. Also, since

$$L(\boldsymbol{m}^2) = E_{\boldsymbol{w}^1}(\boldsymbol{d}_{12}) \cap E_{\boldsymbol{w}^3}(\boldsymbol{d}_{23}) = E_{\boldsymbol{m}^2}(\boldsymbol{d}_{12}) \cap E_{\boldsymbol{m}^2}(\boldsymbol{d}_{23}),$$
$$L(\boldsymbol{m}^3) = E_{\boldsymbol{w}^1}(\boldsymbol{d}_{13}) \cap E_{\boldsymbol{w}^2}(\boldsymbol{d}_{23}) = E_{\boldsymbol{m}^3}(\boldsymbol{d}_{13}) \cap E_{\boldsymbol{m}^3}(\boldsymbol{d}_{23}),$$

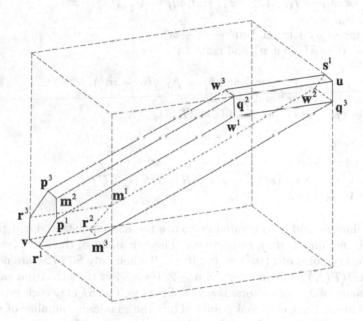

Fig. 3. The set $\mathcal{P}(X) \subset [\boldsymbol{v}, \boldsymbol{u}]$ and its extreme points.

it follows that $\boldsymbol{s}^3 = a + \boldsymbol{m}^3$ and $\boldsymbol{s}^2 = b + \boldsymbol{m}^2$ with $a = 8$ and $b = 6$. Since the two points $\boldsymbol{s}^3$ and $\boldsymbol{s}^2$ are just translates of $\boldsymbol{m}^3$ and $\boldsymbol{m}^2$, they correspond to the exit points $\boldsymbol{q}^3 = 8 + \boldsymbol{m}^3$ and $\boldsymbol{q}^2 = 6 + \boldsymbol{m}^2$. We also have $L(\boldsymbol{m}^1) \cap \partial[\boldsymbol{v}, \boldsymbol{u}] = \{\boldsymbol{m}^1, \boldsymbol{w}^2\}$ since $7 + \boldsymbol{m}^1 = \boldsymbol{w}^2$ so that $\boldsymbol{q}^1 = \boldsymbol{w}^2$ and $\boldsymbol{p}^2 = \boldsymbol{m}^1$. This holds whenever $L(\boldsymbol{m}^i) = L(\boldsymbol{w}^j)$. We now know the extreme points generated by $L(\boldsymbol{m}^i)$ for $i = 1, 2, 3$ and also $L(\boldsymbol{w}^2)$. For the line $L(\boldsymbol{w}^1)$ one tries to find the shortest distance from $\boldsymbol{w}^1$ (along $L(\boldsymbol{w}^1)$) to the set of planes $E_{\boldsymbol{v}}(\boldsymbol{e}^i)$ for $i = 1, 2, 3$. This can be achieved by setting $a = \bigvee_{i=1}^{3}(v_i - w_i^1)$ and computing $a + \boldsymbol{w}^1$. In this case one obtains $a = -6$ and $\boldsymbol{p}^1 = -6 + \boldsymbol{w}^1 = (4, 1, 3)^t$; similarly, $\boldsymbol{p}^3 = -6 + \boldsymbol{w}^3 = (3, 1, 4)^t$. This shows that $\text{ext}(\mathcal{P}(X)) = V \cup R \cup \{\boldsymbol{s}^1, \boldsymbol{p}^1, \boldsymbol{p}^3, \boldsymbol{q}^2, \boldsymbol{q}^3\}$ so that $|\text{ext}(\mathcal{P}(X))| = 16$. The region delimited by the solid and short dashed lines in Fig. 3 is the graph of the polyhedron $\mathcal{P}(X)$ together with the locations of its extreme points. The proposed method to determine additional extremal points of $\mathcal{P}(X)$ is given in Algorithm 1 using mathematical pseudocode. Assuming $k \gg n$ for most applications where

n satisfies $1 < n \le 100$, average computational complexity is $n^2 \mathcal{O}(\log k) = \mathcal{O}(\log k)$ since step S2 dominates the overall calculation effort.

Algorithm 1. [Extreme points of the lattice polytope $\mathcal{P}(X)$]

S0. input $X = \{x^1, \ldots, x^k\} \subset \mathbb{R}^n$
S1. for $i \in \mathbb{N}_n$
    let $u_i \leftarrow \bigvee_{j=1}^k x_i^j$ and $v_i \leftarrow \bigwedge_{j=1}^k x_i^j$
S2. for $i \in \mathbb{N}_n$
    for $j \in \mathbb{N}_n$
        let $\mathfrak{w}_{ij} \leftarrow \bigwedge_{\xi=1}^k (x_i^\xi - x_j^\xi)$ and $\mathfrak{m}_{ij} \leftarrow \bigvee_{\xi=1}^k (x_i^\xi - x_j^\xi)$
S3. for $j \in \mathbb{N}_n$
    let $w^j \leftarrow u_j + \mathfrak{w}^j$ and $m^j \leftarrow v_j + \mathfrak{m}^j$
S4. let $V \leftarrow W \cup M \cup \{v, u\}$ and reduce V
S5. for $j \in \mathbb{N}_n$
    let $a_j \leftarrow \bigvee_{i=1}^n (v_i - w_i^j)$ and $b_j \leftarrow \bigwedge_{i=1}^n (u_i - m_i^j)$
    let $p^j \leftarrow a_j + w^j$ and $q^j \leftarrow b_j + m^j$
S6. let $P \leftarrow \{p^j\}$, $Q \leftarrow \{q^j\}$ and $U \leftarrow (P \cup Q) \setminus V$
S7. for $i \in \mathbb{N}_n$
    for $j \in \mathbb{N}_n$
        let $r^j \leftarrow \bigwedge_{i \ne j} m^i$ and $s^j \leftarrow \bigvee_{i \ne j} w^i$
S8. let $R \leftarrow \{r^j\}$, $S \leftarrow \{s^j\}$ and $T \leftarrow (R \cup S) \setminus (V \cup U)$
S9. output $V \cup U \cup T$

The points p^j and q^j generated in S5 are the entry points and exit points of the lines $L(w^j)$ and $L(m^j)$, respectively. The exit point of the line $L(w^j)$ is w^j while the entry point of $L(m^j)$ is m^j. If $n = 2$, then only S0 to S4 are necessary and $V = \text{ext}(\mathcal{P}(X))$. Furthermore, if $n \ge 2$, then S4 of the algorithm can result in a maximum of $2n + 2$ vectors. If $n \ge 3$, S5 as well as S7 may each produce an additional $2n$ distinct extremal points. Thus the maximum number of extreme points (basic and additional) is $2(3n+1)$. The elements of T represent the points where the hyperplanes $E_{w^i}(d_{ij})$ or $E_{m^i}(d_{ij})$ cuts an edge of $[v, u]$. These points could also be exit or entry points of a line $L(w^i)$ or $L(m^i)$, while the elements of the set U obtained from S5 are all entry and/or exit points. Note that if for some j, $a_j = 0$ (or $b_j = 0$), then $p^j = w^j$ (or $q^j = m^j$). However, these points will not be members of U or T since by definition of U and T we have that $V \cap U = T \cap V = T \cap U = T \cap (V \cup U) = \varnothing$.

5   Conclusions

We give an algorithm to find several kinds of extremal points in any n-dimensional lattice polytope derived from the application of the min/max lattice autoassociative memories to a finite subset X of $\mathbb{R}^n$. Our rationale establishes a theoretical advancement concerning the geometrical structure of the linear minimax span $S(X)$. We sum up our findings in relation to Algorithm 1: (a) $V = \text{ext}(\mathcal{P}(X))$ if $n = 2$, (b) $V \cup T \cup U = \text{ext}(\mathcal{P}(X))$ if $n = 3$, and (c)

$V \cup T \cup U \subset \text{ext}(\mathcal{P}(X))$ if $n > 3$. In words, Algorithm 1 finds a large number of extreme points of $\mathcal{P}(X)$ for any n but not necessarily *all* of them for $n > 3$. However, the enlarged set of extremal points gives us the possibility of building adequate subsets whose points are affinely independent, which are fundamental to pursue new ways of processing multivariate data such as, for example, segmentation of color images [10] or endmember extraction in hyperspectral imagery [11,12].

References

1. Eggleston, H.G.: Convexity. Cambridge University Press, Cambridge (1977)
2. Kelly, P.J., Weiss, M.L.: Geometry and Convexity - A Study in Mathematical Methods. Wiley, New York (1979)
3. Brønsted, A.: An Introduction to Convex Polytopes. Springer, New York (1983)
4. De Berg, M., Van Kreveld, M., Overmars, M., Schwarzkopf, O.: Computational Geometry - Algorithms and Applications, 2nd edn. Springer, Heidelberg (2000). https://doi.org/10.1007/978-3-540-77974-2
5. Ritter, G.X., Urcid, G., Iancu, L.: Reconstruction of patterns from noisy inputs using morphological associative memories. J. Math. Imaging Vis. **19**(2), 95–111 (2003)
6. Ritter, G.X., Gader, P.: Fixed points of lattice transforms and lattice associative memories. In: Hawkes, P. (ed.) Advances in Imaging and Electron Physics, vol. 144, pp. 165–242. Academic Press, San Diego (2006)
7. Graña, M., Gallego, J., Torrealdea, F.J., D'Anjou, A.: On the application of associative morphological memories to hyperspectral image analysis. In: Mira, J., Álvarez, J.R. (eds.) IWANN 2003. LNCS, vol. 2687, pp. 567–574. Springer, Heidelberg (2003). https://doi.org/10.1007/3-540-44869-1_72
8. Ritter, G.X., Urcid, G.: Lattice algebra approach to endmember determination in hyperspectral imagery. In: Hawkes, P. (ed.) Advances in Imaging and Electron Physics, vol. 160, pp. 113–169. Academic Press, San Diego (2010)
9. Ritter, G.X., Urcid, G.: A lattice matrix method for hyperspectral image unmixing. Inf. Sci. **18**(10), 1787–1803 (2011)
10. Urcid, G., Valdiviezo, J.C., Ritter, G.X.: Lattice algebra approach to color image segmentation. J. Math. Imaging Vis. **42**(2–3), 150–162 (2011)
11. Valdiviezo, J.C., Urcid, G.: Convex set approaches for material quantification in hyperspectral imagery. In: Rustamov, R.B., Salahova, S.E. (eds.) Earth Observation, pp. 153–174. InTech, Rijeka (2012)
12. Lechuga, E., Valdiviezo, J.C., Urcid, G.: Multispectral image restoration of historical documents based on LAAMs and mathematical morphology. Proc. SPIE **9216**, 921604:1–10 (2014)

A Comparison of Deep Neural Network Algorithms for Recognition of EEG Motor Imagery Signals

Luis G. Hernández[✉] and Javier M. Antelis

Tecnológico de Monterrey en Guadalajara,
Av. Gral. Ramón Corona 2514, 45201 Zapopan, Jalisco, México
{luisg.hernandez,mauricio.antelis}@itesm.mx

Abstract. This study aims to compare classical and Deep Neural Networks (DNN) algorithms for the recognition of Motor Imagery (MI) tasks from electroencephalographic (EEG) signals. Four Artificial Neural Networks (ANNs) architectures were implemented and assessed to classify EEG motor imagery signals: (*i*) Single-Layer Perceptron (SLP), (*ii*) Fully connected Deep Neural Network (DNN), (*iii*) Deep Neural Network with Dropout (DNN+dropout) and (*iv*) Convolutional Neural Network (CNN). Real EEG signals recorded in a MI-based BCI experiment were used to evaluate the performance of the proposed algorithms in the classification of three classes (*relax, left MI* and *right MI*) using power spectral based features extracted from the EEG signals. The results of a systematic performance evaluation revealed not significant classification accuracies with SLP (averaged of 33.9% ± 0.0%), whereas DNN (59.7% ± 16.3%), DNN+dropout (58.4% ± 14.9%) and CNN (62.1% ± 15.2%) provided significant classification accuracies above chance level. The highest performances were obtained with DNN and CNN. This study indicates potential application of DNNs for the development of BCI systems in daily live activities with real users.

Keywords: Brain-computer interfaces · Motor imagery
Electroencephalogram · Deep neural networks
Convolutional neural networks

1 Introduction

Recognition of motor imagery (MI) mental tasks is an essential part of Brain-Computer Interfaces (BCI) based on non-invasive electroencephalographic (EEG) signals. The conventional way to classify such EEG signals is to employ classical supervised classifiers such as Linear Discriminant Analysis and Support Vector Machines or SVM [1]. This has provided satisfactory results in laboratory based settings. However, EEG-based BCIs require to give a step forward towards applications in real and daily live activities, which requires to detect with higher accuracy the MI mental tasks carried out by the user. To do so, it is necessary

© Springer International Publishing AG, part of Springer Nature 2018
J. F. Martínez-Trinidad et al. (Eds.): MCPR 2018, LNCS 10880, pp. 126–134, 2018.
https://doi.org/10.1007/978-3-319-92198-3_13

to explore novel classification models as those based on deep learning. Potentially, this could improve robustness and performance. Deep Neural Networks are a sort of machine learning algorithms that use multiples computational models with many processing layers to achieve learning representation of data [2]. DNNs have particularly strong power of discrimination and flexibility to represent data through multiple levels of abstraction [3]. Recently, Deep Learning approaches have been applied in BCI studies with satisfactory results [4]. Nevertheless, the number of studies in BCI with these algorithms is still reduced [5].

This work evaluates the performance of four ANNs: (*i*) Single-Layer Perceptron (SLP), (*ii*) Fully connected Deep Neural Network (DNN), (*iii*) Deep Neural Network with Dropout (DNN+dropout) and (*iv*) Convolutional Neural Network (CNN) in a three-class classification scenario using power spectral (PSD) based features extracted from the EEG signals during motor imagery mental tasks and presents a comparison of their performance. The results showed that DNN (59.7% ± 16.3%), DNN+dropout (58.4% ± 14.9%) and CNN (62.1% + 15.2%) obtained significant classification accuracies above chance level (33.60%). For SLP results, the accuracies were below chance level. This work shows that convolutional Neural Network can be an effective classification model to obtain highest confident classification accuracy in three different movements states of upper limbs. The rest of this paper is organized as follows. Section 2 describes details about how dataset was recorded and prepared, how attributes are calculated to extract relevant information from the EEG signals, the different ANNs architectures used and the performance evaluation process. Section 3 describes the results obtained for PSD analysis and the accuracies obtained to a three-class classification scenario.

2   Dataset Recording and Preparation

2.1   Data Recording

Eight healthy subjects voluntarily participated in this study. The experiment was conducted in accordance to the Helsinki declaration. All participants were duly informed about the goals of the research. During the execution of the experiment, EEG signals were recorded from 15 scalp locations according to the international 10/20 system (FC3, FC1, FCZ, FC2, FC4, C3, C1, CZ, C2, C4, CP3, CP1, CPZ, CP2 and CP4) using a g.USBamp with active electrodes (g.tec medical engineering GmbH, Austria). The reference and ground electrode were placed over left earlobe and AFZ, respectively. The EEG signals were acquired at a sampling frequency of 256 Hz and not filtering was applied.

2.2   Experiment Design

The experimental task consisted of many trials of imaging the movement of left or right hands. This was guided by visual cues presented on the screen (see Fig. 1a). A trial consisted of three visual cues (see Fig. 1b). The first cue was an image with the text "Relax" and the subjects were instructed to relax the body without performing any voluntary movement (relax phase). The second cue was an image with of an arrow pointing to the left or to the right and instructed to imagine the movement of the corresponding hand during three seconds (movement imagination phase). The last cue was an image with the text "rest" and indicated to rest, move voluntary or blink during three seconds (rest phase). 280 trials were recorded per participant, 140 trials for each condition (left or right hand).

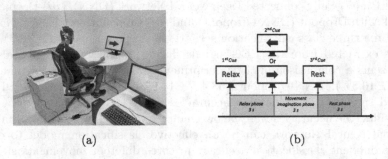

(a)   (b)

Fig. 1. (a) snapshot of the experimental setup and (b) time sequence of a trial during the execution of experiment.

2.3   Data Preprocessing

EEG signals were low-pass filtered at a cutoff frequency of 45 Hz using a 2nd-order Chebychev-type filter and then common average referenced (CAR). Afterwards, EEG signals were segmented in trials starting from the first visual cue and up to the second visual cue. For this research the time interval corresponding to third cue (rest phase) were not contemplated. Therefore, resulted trials had length of six seconds. The zero time reference was aligned with starting of second visual clue. Thus, the time intervals $[-3, 0)$ s and $[0, 3]$ s are rest and motor imagery, respectively. Finally, all the conditions were organized according to the experimental condition (*relax, left MI, right MI*) to construct the dataset.

2.4   Attributes

Power Spectral Density (PSD) of the EEG signals were used as feature to discriminate between three classes: Relax, left MI and right MI. The PSD is the Fourier Transform of the autocorrelation function of a signal and estimates how the average power is distributed as a function of frequency [6]. PSD is highly used in BCI due to the high correlation between the MI tasks and the spectral power changes [7]. In the case of brain activities related to MI, the spectral power changes are found over sensory-motor cortex areas in frequencies between [8–30] Hz, also known as α and β brain rhythms. For this reason, for each electrode, it was selected the frequency range between 8 and 27 Hz at a steps of 1 Hz to compute the PSD. Thus, the number of the PSD features for each electrode is 20. This yield to the dataset $\{\mathbf{X_i}, y_i\}_{i=1}^{N}$, where $\mathbf{X_i} \in \mathbb{R}^{300 \times 1}$ or $\mathbf{X_i} \in \mathbb{R}^{15 \times 20}$, y_i were labeled as $\{rest,\ left\ MI,\ right\ MI\}$ and $N = 560$.

2.5   Deep Neural Networks (DNNs)

In this research, 4 DNNs architectures were implemented and assessed to classify EEG motor imagery signals: (i) single layer perceptron (SLP), (ii) fully connected deep neural network (DNN), (iii) deep neural network with dropout (DNN+drop) and (iv) convolutional neural network (CNN). All of them were implemented with Tensorflow Library [8] and executed in a Geforce GTX Titan Xp GPU (Nvidia, USA).

Single Layer Perceptron (SLP). The single layer perceptron is the simplest model of neural network and consist of a single neuron with adaptable weights and bias. The importance of SLP lies in its ability to classify patterns there are linearly separable. This characteristic was demonstrated by Rosenblatt [9]. The perceptron model is described as:

$$y_k = \varphi \left(\sum_{j-1}^{p} w_{kj} x_j - \theta_k \right) \tag{1}$$

where w_{kj} is the k synaptic weight of the neuron, x is attribute j, θ_k is the bias and $\varphi(\cdot)$ is an activation function. For this research, SLP was implemented with 300 adjustable weights and as activation function was used soft-mask unit.

Fully Connected Deep Neural Network (DNN). DNN (also known as Multi-layer Perceptron) consists of a three-layer architecture: (i) an input layer that functions as an information receiver and has multiple sensory units, (ii) one o more hidden layers that makes a non-linear transformation of the input space into a high dimensional space and (iii) an output layer that gives the network response through an activation function. The aim of DNNs is to solve problems that cannot be separated linearly. This type of network is trained with the back-propagation learning algorithm [10]. In this research was employed a DNN with input layer of 300 nodes, 4 hidden layers, each one with 200, 100, 60, 30 nodes, respectively. For last, soft-mask unit was used as activation function.

Deep Neural Network with Dropout (DNN+dropout). One of the main problems in the previous DNN model is overfitting. To prevent this, it is used a technique called dropout. This technique allows to constrain the amount of nodes in a hidden layer without losing learning performance [11]. To identify which nodes must removed is random (all the dropped nodes has a fixed probability p independent of other units, where p can be chosen using a validation set or can simply be set at 0.5). Thus, the algorithm makes a lot of iterations trying to find the iteration with better accuracy during a validation phase. In this work, dropout technique was implemented for the DNN model above described with dropout rate was 10% of nodes.

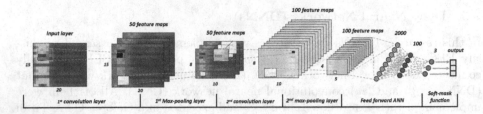

Fig. 2. Illustration of the CNN algorithm used in this work, which consisted of two pairs of convolution and pooling layers followed by a feed forward ANN.

Convolutional Neural Network (CNN). CNN is a sort of supervised deep learning algorithm [2,3] that have demonstrated notable results in the classification of data with grid-like topology [12]. CNN architecture is composed of: *(i)* a stack of building blocks with convolution kernels and pooling operators and *(ii)* a feed forward Artificial Neural Network (ANN). Each building block extracts relevant information from input map to its own significant feature maps. Finally, the feature maps feed the ANN to compute each class probabilities (using soft-mask function). The equation that describes the convolutional operation is:

$$S(i,j) = (I \times K)(i,j) = \sum_m \sum_n I(i+m, j+n) \cdot K(m,n) + b \qquad (2)$$

A building block consists of (i) a kernel K of size $m \times n$, which are convoluted (slided over the input map spatially) with input map to construct output feature map $S(i,j)$, (ii) an activation function that applied to each convoluted output feature map, (iii) a pooling layer that reduces the dimension of the convoluted maps trough operations as average or maximum. In a CNN, the number of building blocks, kernels, kernel's size, pooling's size and the structure of the feed forward ANN are adjustable hyperparameters, while the weights and bias in the kernels and in the feed forward ANN are parameters that are learned from a training set. Learning is typically carried out by the gradient descent method through the backpropagation algorithm [13]. The architecture of the CNN employed in this work is illustrated in Fig. 2. It consists of two pairs of building blocks followed by a feed forward ANN with a hidden layer. The first block consisted of 50 kernels of size 4×4, the rectified linear unit as activation function and maximum pooling with non-overlapping regions of size 2×2. This resulted in 50 feature maps of size 4×5. The second block consisted of $K = 100$ kernels of size 4×4 with the same characteristics of first convolution-pooling block. This resulted in 100 feature maps of size 2×3. The feed forward ANN consisted of 600 input neurons, one hidden layer with 100 neurons and 3 neurons in the output layer. The activation function in the hidden layer is the sigmoid while in the output layer is the soft-max.

Performance Evaluation. The total data was splitted in two mutually exclu-
sive sets. The training set consisted of 80% of the data and the rest 20% of
the data as evaluation set. The classifiers are trained using the training set and
final classification is performed on the evaluation set. In training, the algorithms
were trained in 400 steps. In each step, a batch data is sampled from training
data (20% of training data) with which classification model is fed and at final of
the training steps the model for evaluation is obtained. Performance metric was
classification accuracy which was computed as:

$$accuracy = \frac{TP+TN}{TP+TN+FP+FN} \tag{3}$$

where TP is the true positive rate, TN is the true negative rate, FP is the
false positive rate and FN is the false negative rate. This procedure is repeated
100 times and the distribution and *mean $\pm$ std* of the accuracy metric were
computed. The significant classification accuracy chance level was the computed
with the binomial distribution [14]. The significant classification *accuracy* chance
level is $accuracy_{chance} - 33.60\%$. To examine significant differences between
distribution of accuracy and $accuracy_{chance}$ the Wilcoxon signed-rank test was
applied, while to examine significant differences between three distributions of
accuracy the Wilcoxon rank-sum test was applied.

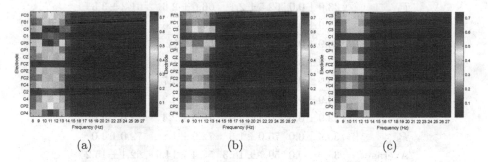

(a)   (b)   (c)

Fig. 3. (a), (b) and (c) shows a representation of average of all PSD values obtained
participant 3 in the three studied classes: (a) corresponds to *relax*, (b) to *left MI* and
(c) to *right MI*.

3   Experiments and Results

Figure 3a, b and c shows PSD averaged across all trials for participant 3 in the
three studied classes: *relax, left MI* and *right MI* respectively. It is observed
that in the three classes, the PSD values changes in the range of 8–13 Hz for all
electrodes except for FCZ, C1 and C2. This frequency range corresponds of μ
brain rhythms, where decreasing of PSD values are associated with activation
of motor imagery processes [15]. To find μ rhythms differences between classes,
PSD averaged values in electrodes of different brain locations were examined. For

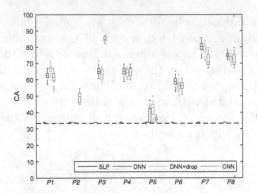

Fig. 4. Distribution of classification accuracy achieved with SLP, DNN, DNN+drop and CNN for each participant (P_1 to P_8)%. The horizontal dotted black line represents the significant chance level or $accuracy_{chance}$.

Table 1. Summary of classification accuracy results for each participant (P_1 to P_7) achieved with the SLP, DNN, DNN+drop and CNN. The lower row shows the grand-average across-all-participants.

% Mean ± std				
Participant	SLP	DNN	DNN+drop	CNN
P_1	33.9 ± 0.0	62.5 ± 2.1	66.6 ± 2.6	61.3 ± 3.5
P_2	33.9 ± 0.0	34.4 ± 2.8	34.3 ± 2.6	49.4 ± 3.4
P_3	33.9 ± 0.0	65.4 ± 2.4	58.3 ± 12.4	85.1 ± 1.8
P_4	33.9 ± 0.0	64.4 ± 4.9	59.2 ± 11.7	65.4 ± 2.7
P_5	33.9 ± 0.0	37.7 ± 4.8	41.3 ± 4.7	35.8 ± 1.3
P_6	33.9 ± 0.0	57.8 ± 6.1	56.0 ± 4.3	56.4 ± 3.4
P_7	33.9 ± 0.0	80.3 ± 2.6	78.5 ± 2.4	72.0 ± 4.0
P_8	33.9 ± 0.0	75.0 ± 1.6	72.9 ± 1.8	72.0 ± 4.0
Average	33.9 ± 0.0	59.7 ± 16.3	58.4 ± 14.9	62.1 ± 15.2

C4, CP4 and CP2 electrodes (placed above right side of brain) PSD averaged values of *left MI* are smaller than *relax* and *right MI*. PSD values decreasing in this electrodes are related to activation of motor imagery processes during a left-side limb movement [16]. For C3, CP3, CP1 electrodes (placed above left side of brain) PSD values are smaller in *right MI* class than *relax* and classes. This decreasing is associated to right-side limb movement. The four proposed architectures were evaluated in the three-class classification of *relax* versus *left MI* versus *right MI*. Figure 4 shows the distributions of accuracies computed for each participant and under every classification model. For all participants, the median of their distributions of accuracy are higher and significantly different than the $accuracy_{chance}(p < 0.05)$ except to SLP classification scenarios and

DNN and DNN+drop scenarios for participant 2. Participants 3, 7 and 8 shows the highest distributions of accuracy in range (70–90)% and participants 2 and 3 shows the lowest distributions of accuracy. Table 1 presents the summary of average accuracy for all participants. Also, the mean across all participants in each classification models are presented. Participant 3 in CNN scenario shows the highest mean value $(85.1 \pm 1.8)\%$. In the case of SLP, all the participants shows the lowest mean value $(33.9 \pm 0.0)\%$. For the average across all participants, CNN shows the highest average with $(62.1 \pm 15.2)\%$ followed by DNN with $(59.7 \pm 16.3)\%$, DNN+drop $(58.4 \pm 14.9)\%$ and last, SLP with $(33.9 \pm 0)\%$.

4 Conclusions

In this work, the performance of four Neural Networks was evaluated in a three-class classification scenario using of EEG motor imagery signals. For that, EEG signals were recorded during motor imagery mental task over eight healthy participants. On the one hand, power spectral were calculated for the three classes: *relax*, *left MI* and *right MI* and PSD values were used as attributes. The most PSD differences was observed in the motor-related μ frequency band. For *left MI*, the most PSD differences was observed in the electrodes around the right motor cortex and for *right MI* PSD differences was observed in the electrodes around the left motor cortex. On the other hand, for the classification and performance evaluation, a three-class classification scenario was followed to asses the classification accuracy with four different Network techniques. The results showed that the accuracy average obtain to CNN technique provides a classification accuracy superior than the other techniques implemented. The better results can be observed for participants 3 $(85.1\% \pm 1.8\%)$, 7 $(72.0\% \pm 4.0\%)$ and 9 $(72.0\% \pm 4.0\%)$. In addition, other notable result found is that DNN provides better results than DNN+drop. A possible reason could be that the dropout rate is high for the models. Note that Dropout rate is a adjustable hyperparameter. However, these results cannot be compared against the related state of the art due to there are several differences with others works [4,5], as experimental setup (execution of different movements), different state of participants (with some motor injury) and different attributes to classify (temporal features).

This work shows how the classification technique CNN allows to obtain a confident classification accuracy in three different movements states of upper limbs, particularly the accurate recognition for motor imagery task can be used in BCI area to control neurorehabilitation devices. This work can be a starting point in two ways; (*i*) to evaluate diverse CNN architectures that allow to improve the MI classification (*ii*) to explore the classification of motor imagery task using the CNN models in others classification contexts, such as on-line classification scenario or experiment execution with participants with neuromotor injuries to test the feasibility of CNN technique in a realistic neurorehabilitation BCI system.

134   L. G. Hernández and J. M. Antelis

Acknowledgments. This work was partially supported by the National Council of Science and Technology of Mexico (CONACyT) through grant PN2015-873 and scholarship 291197. We gratefully acknowledge the support of NVIDIA Corporation with the donation of the Titan X Pascal GPU used for this research.

References

1. Vega, R., et al.: Assessment of feature selection and classification methods for recognizing motor imagery tasks from electroencephalographic signals. Artif. Intell. Res. **6**(1), 37 (2017)
2. Goodfellow, I., et al.: Deep Learning. MIT Press, Cambridge (2016)
3. Lecun, Y., et al.: Deep learning. Nature **521**(7553), 436–444 (2015)
4. Plis, S.M., Hjelm, D.R., Salakhutdinov, R., Allen, E.A., Bockholt, H.J., Long, J.D., Johnson, H.J., Paulsen, J.S., Turner, J.A., Calhoun, V.D.: Deep learning for neuroimaging: a validation study. Front. Neurosci. **8**, 229 (2014). https://doi.org/10.3389/fnins.2014.00229
5. Tabar, Y.R., Halici, U.: A novel deep learning approach for classification of EEG motor imagery signals. J. Neural Eng. **14**(1), 016003 (2017)
6. Daubechies, I.: The wavelet transform, time-frequency localization and signal analysis. IEEE Trans. Inf. Theory **36**(5), 961–1005 (1990)
7. Subasi, A., et al.: Neural network classification of EEG signals by using AR with mle preprocessing for epileptic seizure detection. Math. Comput. Appl. **10**(1), 57–70 (2005)
8. Abadi, M., et al.: TensorFlow: large-scale machine learning on heterogeneous systems (2015). Software available from tensorflow.org
9. Rosenblatt, F.: The perceptron: a probabilistic model for information storage and organization in the brain. Psychol. Rev. **65**, 386–408 (1958)
10. Bishop, C.M.: Neural Networks for Pattern Recognition. Oxford University Press Inc., New York (1995)
11. Srivastava, N., et al.: Dropout: a simple way to prevent neural networks from overfitting. J. Mach. Learn. Res. **15**, 1929–1958 (2014)
12. Krizhevsky, A., et al.: Imagenet classification with deep convolutional neural networks. In: Advances in Neural Information Processing Systems, pp. 1097–1105 (2012)
13. LeCun, Y., Bengio, Y.: The Handbook of Brain Theory and Neural Networks, pp. 255–258. MIT Press, Cambridge (1998)
14. Combrisson, E., Jerbi, K.: Exceeding chance level by chance: the caveat of theoretical chance levels in brain signal classification and statistical assessment of decoding accuracy. J. Neurosci. Methods **250**, 126–136 (2015)
15. Pineda, J.A.: The functional significance of mu rhythms: translating "seeing" and "hearing" into "doing". Brain Res. Rev. **50**(1), 57–68 (2005)
16. Loosemore, R.: The inversion hypothesis: a novel explanation for the contralaterality of the human brain. Biosci. Hypotheses **2**(6), 375–382 (2009)

Learning Word and Sentence Embeddings Using a Generative Convolutional Network

Edgar Vargas-Ocampo[1] ⓘ, Edgar Roman-Rangel[2] ⓘ,
and Jorge Hermosillo-Valadez[1(✉)] ⓘ

[1] Centro de Investigación en Ciencias-(IICBA), UAEM, Cuernavaca, Morelos, México
egiovanni.vo@gmail.com, jhermosillo@uaem.mx
[2] Viper Group - CVM Lab, University of Geneva, Geneva, Switzerland
edgar.romanrangel@unige.ch

Abstract. In recent years, sentence modeling using dense vector representations has been a central concern in Natural Language Processing research. While many efforts are essentially focused on the quality of the embeddings in downstream classification tasks, our contribution focuses on the understanding of new forms of computing word representations using generative architectures based on 2D Convolutional Neural Networks. We treat a sentence as a $n \times m$ input image, such that it can be processed using 2D convolutional operations. In contrast to similar current approaches, where the input image remains untouched along the whole learning process, our contribution proposes the use of the learned 2D convolutional filters for modifying the input arrays in order to compute the corresponding word and sentence vector representations at once. We also propose to compute word dictionaries for local contexts and a global dictionary to fuse every word local meaning in a single representation. We call this proposed model a Word Embedding Generative Convolutional Network (WEGCN). Our experiments show that our method is capable of jointly estimating consistent word and sentence embeddings, thus opening pathways for future research in this vein.

Keywords: Generative models · Convolutional neural networks
Word embeddings · Rhetorical status classification

1 Introduction

In the last few years, research in Natural Language Processing (NLP) has focused on computing continuous vector representations of text, popularly known as *word embeddings* [1,2]. Recently, the development of methods for computing dense vector representations of sentences has gained momentum [3,4]. Indeed, sentence modeling is at the core of many NLP tasks, where it is used to represent semantic content with purposes of discrimination or generation. However, the debate about what is the best approach for sentences modeling is primarily driven by the application.

© Springer International Publishing AG, part of Springer Nature 2018
J. F. Martínez-Trinidad et al. (Eds.): MCPR 2018, LNCS 10880, pp. 135–144, 2018.
https://doi.org/10.1007/978-3-319-92198-3_14

We propose a method for computing vector representations of words and sentences in order to classify sentences on the basis of their rhetorical status. Concretely, this work introduces a Generative Convolutional Neural Network (GCN) trained to jointly: (a) estimate word and sentence embeddings; and (b) map such embeddings onto categorical labels, which reflect the rhetorical status of a sentence, as proposed by a method conceived for text summarization called *"Argumentative Zoning"* (AZ) [5]. We treat a sentence as a $n \times m$ input image as other related works have also proposed [3], such that it can be processed using convolutional operations. However, such and similar applications rely mostly on the use of 1D Convolutional Neural Networks (CNN), or the input image remains untouched along the whole learning process. In contrast, our contribution proposes the use of the learned 2D convolutional filters for modifying the input arrays in order to compute the corresponding word and sentence vector representations at once, and this for each class of rhetorical function. We also propose to compute word dictionaries, **one local dictionary** for each rhetorical class and **one common corpus-wide dictionary** that computes a single representation for all (rhetorical) meanings of each word. We call this proposed model a Word Embedding Generative Convolutional Network (WEGCN).

1.1 Related Work

A central class of sentence models are those related to neural networks. The paragraph vector model [6] is an adaptation of the `word2vec` method [2], to address sentence modeling and text classification by introducing a distributed sentence indicator as part of a neural language model. Nevertheless, this approach suffers of the inability to generalize sub-words, e.g., suffixes, but most importantly, it requires an *inference stage* to compute a vector for newly unseen paragraphs, which limits its generalization potential in classification tasks [7]. Although there exist works that have attempted to overcome these limitations [4,8], they suffer from the need to manually estimate *skipgrams* at character level [4], and require intermediate manual computations of word embeddings plus a later aggregation of them into a sentence representation before performing the actual classification task [8]. Here, we avoid both replacing them by the end-to-end automatic computation of embedding via the use of a GCN.

Recently, Recurrent Neural Networks (RNN's) and the Long Short-Term Memory (LSTM) have overtaken as the neural architectures best suited addressing sentence modeling tasks [9–11], achieving state-of-the-art results in text classification and language translation, mainly due to its cyclic feeding process between hidden layers specifically devised for sequential data [12]. However, only a few attempts have been made on the computation of word embeddings [13]. Furthermore, its is unclear how to extract embeddings for single tokens (i.e., words) from the output of a RNN which includes sequential data [14].

The extraction of word embeddings, however, seems more natural from Convolutional Neural Networks (CNNs) [15] that, even though exploit spatial relation between individual tokens, produce outputs that can be split into components, i.e., matrices into vectors. In view of this, CNNs have been used for text classification [3], translation [9], and sentence modeling [3,16], where embeddings are either represented via transfer learning with word2vec or neglected by directly processing the raw text as binary information [17].

Furthermore, the inclusion of generative models into deep learning architectures has successfully addressed problems like feature representation [18] and style transfer [19]. Therefore, it seems plausible to pair a generative estimator with a CNN for the purpose of jointly learning to classify sentences while estimating embeddings for their words. While those and similar approaches [7,20] are essentially focused on the quality of the embeddings in downstream classification tasks, our contribution focuses on the understanding of new forms of computing word representations using generative architectures based on 2D CNN.

The paper is organized as follows. In Sect. 2 we frame our proposal in the context of current CNN architectures. Section 3 describes the method proposed herein. Section 4 introduces the two datasets used for the validation of the method and the architecture utilized for the experiments. Experimental results are presented and discussed in Sect. 5. Conclusions are derived in Sect. 6.

2   Background

Convolutional Neural Networks. The base architecture of CNNs for image classification, commonly contains three types of layers: convolutional, fully connected, and softmax. The former type are usually the initial 3 to 5 layers, and they serve the purposes of down-sampling the size of the input image, while passing it through several convolutional kernels that filter out irrelevant information. Fully connected layers aggregate local information resulting from the several convolutional filters into a global representation, and weight its components to facilitate the target goal, e.g., classification. Finally, the softmax layer computes the probability that this global vector matches a target representation of the class corresponding to the image. Figure 1 shows the common architecture of a CNN used for classifying into five classes.

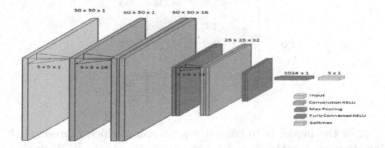

Fig. 1. The CGN used in this work, consisting of six layers: input, one embedding generator, two convolutional-pooling, one fully-connected, and one softmax.

Argumentative Zoning. *"Argumentative Zoning"* (AZ) [5] aimed at replacing manual summaries of texts by automatic, dynamic and flexible abstracts. It generates summaries by extracting sentences relevant to the searching needs of a user, as formulated by a query. For these purposes, rhetorical information, additional to the sentences extracted, is added manually in the form of fixed labels. The purpose of these labels is to represent the discourse function of a sentence or phrase, with respect to the overall rhetorical structure of the document.

3   Learning Word Embeddings for Sentences

We introduce now the proposed Word Embedding Generative Convolutional Network (WEGCN). Each sentence in natural language is a sequence $w_1, w_2, \cdots, w_T$ of words $w_i \in V$, where the vocabulary V is an arbitrarily large but finite set. We represent word w_i with a feature vector $x_i \in \mathbb{R}^m$, randomly initialized.

In our model, every sentence is represented as a matrix S, where the rows of the matrix represent words and columns represent features for each word. As sentences have a variable number of terms, we propose to build a matrix S as a concatenation of feature vectors x_i and padding vectors p_j.

A sentence therefore would look like a vertical concatenation of X and P:

$$S = \begin{bmatrix} X \\ P \end{bmatrix},$$

where X is a feature vector matrix of shape $[T \times m]$, P is a padding matrix of shape $[(n - T) \times m]$, and m is the dimensionality of the feature space.

Therefore, matrix S is of size $n \times m$, both being hyper-parameters of the model. The number of rows n may be fixed for all sentences based on criteria such as the maximum or average length of sentences in the corpus, and the size of the feature vector m may be equal to n so a to have a squared matrix.

Hence, for a sentence of T terms, the matrix S is required to be filled with $n - T$ padding vectors (p_j), which could contain any constant $d \in \mathbb{R}$:

$$S = \begin{bmatrix} x_{1,1} & x_{1,2} & \cdots & x_{1,m} \\ x_{2,1} & x_{2,2} & \cdots & x_{2,m} \\ \vdots & \vdots & \cdots & \vdots \\ x_{T,1} & x_{T,2} & \cdots & x_{T,m} \\ d & d & \cdots & d \\ \vdots & \vdots & \vdots & \vdots \\ d & d & \cdots & d \end{bmatrix} \begin{matrix} w_1 \\ w_2 \\ \vdots \\ w_T \\ p_1 \\ p_2 \\ p_{n-T} \end{matrix} \tag{1}$$

The goal of the model is to compute a mapping which represents the word embeddings that encode the rhetorical function of sentence S. With this goal in mind, the idea is to process S as if it was a $n \times m$ image.

In typical applications of Convolutional Neural Networks, the input image remains untouched along the whole learning process. However, in our case, we aim at modifying the input array (Eq. (1)) in order to compute the corresponding word vector representations of each sentence, and this for each class of rhetorical function. In this way, the CNN becomes a generative network.

To this end, we need a mapping $S^{t+1} = f(S^t, \Gamma^+)$, where Γ^+ are the mask weights updated within the back-propagation process, in order to modify the input "image" with new feature values. These new feature vectors would then account for the error between the predicted output and the actual rhetorical function class as given by the AZ labels. We propose to use the convolution operator to obtain this mapping:

$$S^{t+1} = S^t - S^t * \eta_e \Gamma^+, \tag{2}$$

where, η_e is a learning rate hyper-parameter that controls how much the training embeddings S are updated at each batch, and $*$ represents a convolutional operator. Note that this learning rate is additional to the standard one used to update the parameters Γ of the network.

In some possible interpretation of this model, one could think about k-means or Expectation Maximization (EM), where the characteristics of the data are estimated through an iterative process.

3.1 Word Embeddings Dictionaries

A key aspect of the model is the creation of dictionaries to store word embeddings, which are to be updated through the training process. In a first approach each class possesses its own dictionary. While this might seem counter-intuitive at a first glance, it is important to bear in mind that a same word might have different meanings in different contexts. It seems therefore reasonable to use one dictionary per class. Even if a same word would appear in the same class in different contexts, we expect that the word embedding would capture the essential information in order to make the sentence representation convey the meaning of its corresponding class.

Nevertheless, when a new sentence (never seen before) would have to be classified, it would be very difficult to decide from which class to assign a vector representation for each of its words. Hence, we propose a common (corpus-wide) dictionary. To this end, an aggregation of embeddings is computed as:

$$x_i^g = \sum_c \lambda^c x_i^c, \tag{3}$$

where, x_i^g is the global embedding for the i-th word (w_i), x_i^c is the local embedding for the same word in the c-th class, and λ^c is a parameter weighting the contribution of the c-th class in this aggregation, given by:

$$\lambda^c = \frac{|w_i|_c}{\sum_c |w_i|_c}, \tag{4}$$

where, $|w_i|_c$ denotes the cardinality of w_i in class c.

4   Experimental Setup

We designed two different scenarios to evaluate the capacity of our method for generating word embeddings from initial random representations. Namely, a **proof-of-concept** and a **sentence-based** scenario.

Proof-of-Concept. For this scenario we defined 5 categorical classes. For each class, we created 250 sentences, every one containing 100 words, each of them modeled by a vector of 100 random numbers[1]. All word vector representations were initialized at random following a uniform distribution. Therefore, each sentence is represented by a matrix S of shape $[100 \times 100]$ of real values.

In order to build the corpus of sentences, the following procedure was undertaken. For every class, a dictionary of 100 word entries is built: $(w_1, \cdots, w_{100})$. These entries work as row indices of matrix S. The association of dictionary entries and row indices is arbitrarily set at the beginning and remains fixed along the experiment. For instance, the first row may be indexed by entry w_1, and thus in every sentence, entry w_1 will always index row 1. However, in order to have multiple sentences ("expressing" different things about its corresponding class) every word entry in the dictionary has associated 10 different realizations, that represent a sort of synonyms. Therefore, the total vocabulary was 1000 words. In this way, for every word entry one of these 10 distinct realizations is chosen at random when building a sentence S.

It is important to bear in mind that for this scenario, sentences are meaningless in a natural language sense: they are but matrices of random numbers, where each row works as a placeholder indexed by a dictionary entry, and sentences are different insofar as placeholders are occupied by different word realizations.

Sentence-Based. This dataset is formed by 7 classes corresponding to the rhetorical labels of AZ [5]. The sentences in this scenario were obtained from scientific articles[2], and all seven classes were balanced by randomly choosing only 200 sentences for each of them. Moreover, selected sentences contain between 7 and 50 words, with neither numerical characters nor references. Since in this scenario matrices correspond to actual phrases in natural language, the same word might occur several times within a sentence, and in other sentences at different locations.

As before, a dictionary is created for each class. Every dictionary associates a word of the vocabulary to a 100-dimensional vector of random numbers. Therefore, a sentence in this case is represented by a matrix S of shape $[50 \times 100]$. However, contrary to the previous scenario, some sentences might need to be filled with padding vectors (see Eq. (1)).

The key difference between both scenarios is that, in the first one sentences are artificially created, the rows of a sentence are indexed by dictionary entries

---

[1] The number 100 is arbitrary. The reader must bear in mind that this number would correspond to the size of a sentence (number of words) or of the portion of the text to be represented.

[2] www.cl.cam.ac.uk/~sht25/AZ_corpus.html.

and work as placeholders for different embeddings; in the second scenario, every row is indexed by the position of the corresponding word in the natural language sentence and is filled with the corresponding embedding to which it was associated to in the dictionary.

4.1   Network Architecture

Our implementation of WEGCN consists of the following functional layers: one embedding generator, two convolutional-pooling, one fully-connected, and one softmax. Overall, this architecture contains six layers, including the input layer.

Embedding Generator Layer. The input layer in our network is a single convolutional filter that serves two purposes: (1) during the forward pass it maps the inputs onto an initial feature space; and (2) during the backward pass it generates the embedded representations by updating S accordingly to Eq. (2). Indeed, it is in this layer that the generative process for the estimation of the embeddings is computed. The weights of this filter are learned during the training of the WEGCN. In all of our experiments we used a single filter of size 5×5. This filter uses a ReLU activation function.

Convolutional-Pooling Layers. These are two layers, consisting of 16 and 32 convolutional filters of size 5×5, respectively. They are regular convolutional layers that processes image sections, and yield local image descriptors. All filters in these layers implement a ReLU activation function, and use *stride* = 1 and *zero-padding*. They also rely on a *max-pooling* step to down-size their outputs in half (i.e., *masksize* = 2×2), while retaining the most salient features.

Fully-Connected Layer. Following the standard CNN architecture, at the top of the convolutional layers, data is processed by a fully-connected layer of 1024 ReLU units that aggregates the local image descriptors into a single vector, and weights its components accordingly for the goal of classification.

Softmax Layer. The final layer is a standard softmax normalization operator that computes a probability distribution of the possible classes in the dataset. Here, classes are defined by the labels of the images or the AZ method [5].

Figure 1 shows a visual representation of this architecture. We used cross-entropy as loss function, and the Adam optimizer for training.

5   Experimental Results and Discussion

Figure 2 shows 2-D projections of the 100-D representations for the word embeddings in the proof-of-concept scenario. Contrary to the chaos exhibited by the initial random representations, once trained, the proposed WEGCN yields word embeddings that are consistent within each class, yet with the intra-class variation required to allow each class to span sections of the feature space and thus represent diverse concepts. This suggests that the proposed method adequately computes word embeddings from random initializations.

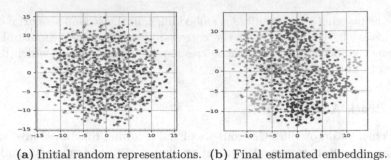

(a) Initial random representations.   (b) Final estimated embeddings.

Fig. 2. 2-D projection of the word embeddings of the five classes in the proof-of-concept scenario. (a) Initial random representation. (b) Embeddings after training the WEGCN. Each color represents a class. (Color figure online)

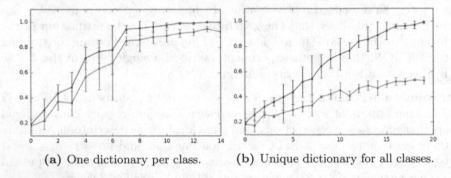

(a) One dictionary per class.   (b) Unique dictionary for all classes.

Fig. 3. Classification performance (y-axis) and training epochs (x-axis) on the sentence-based scenario, obtained using: (a) one dictionary per class; and (b) a unique dictionary common to all classes. Blue and green curves represent the training and test performance, respectively. (Color figure online)

Moreover, the classification of complete sentences exhibits very high performance on this scenario, which improves from random values (i.e., 0.22 ± 0.09) to almost perfect classification (i.e., 0.99 ± 0.01) in only 6 epochs of training.

Likewise, the evaluation on the sentence-based scenario demonstrates that the proposed approach correctly estimates word and sentence embeddings that are suitable for classification of sentences. Figure 3 shows the classification performance obtained in this scenario using different dictionaries in each class, and using a common single dictionary for all classes estimated as explained in Sect. 3. As shown by Fig. 3a, the method generalizes well for the test dataset when dictionaries are estimated independently for each class, as the curve on the test set is just below the curve of the training set. However, the generalization performance drops when using a unified dictionary for all classes, as it becomes harder to estimate word embeddings that are simultaneously common and discriminative. Notwithstanding the apparent low generalization performance when using a unified dictionary, this score is as three times as high than random performance (i.e., one on seven). Furthermore, note that only a few training epochs suffice to reach a plateau on the classification accuracy curve.

Figure 4 shows some of the filters obtained after training. These filters resemble visual patterns at different granularities, which might suggest that the WEGCN correctly captures semantic knowledge from the training instances.

(a) Embedding.   (b) Conv1.   (c) Conv2.

Fig. 4. Trained filters of the WEGCN. (a) Embedding layer; (b) 12 filters from the first conv layer; and (c) 25 filters from the second conv layer.

6 Conclusions

The method we propose in this work is a combination of CNNs and Generative Models, trained jointly to classify its input, as well as to learn to generate word embeddings in the process. Indeed, these word embeddings are both robust enough for classification of sentences, and consistent with semantic NLP definitions. Note that although we are not addressing the problem of generating synthetic data samples, our method could be used to explore this vein.

Our work constitutes a *proof-of-concept* and continues in progress. We stress that our aim was to explore the potential capability of CNNs for transforming a totally random input into a meaningful dense vector and matrix representation of words and sentences at once. In these respects, the results obtained in our experiments essentially show three things: the proposed network approach exploits spatial relationships between words within a sentence, thus providing structure to the embeddings; high classification rates are obtained when using one dictionary per class, yet the challenge remains in estimating a single dictionary common to the whole dataset; it seems plausible to design generative networks capable to operate in a single pipeline, in contrast to current similar approaches such as GAN's, which are based on parallel architectures and trickling exemplars.

References

1. Bengio, Y., Ducharme, R., Vincent, P., Janvin, C.: A neural probabilistic language model. J. Mach. Learn. Res. **3**, 1137–1155 (2003)
2. Mikolov, T., Sutskever, I., Chen, K., Corrado, G., Dean, J.: Distributed representations of words and phrases and their compositionality. In: Proceedings of the International Conference on Neural Information Processing Systems (NIPS) (2013)

3. Kim, Y.: Convolutional neural networks for sentence classification. In: Proceedings of the Conference on Empirical Methods in Natural Language Processing (EMNLP) (2014)
4. Bojanowski, P., Grave, E., Joulin, A., Mikolov, T.: Enriching word vectors with subword information. Trans. Assoc. Comput. Linguist. **5**, 135–146 (2017)
5. Teufel, S., Moens, M.: Summarizing scientific articles: experiments with relevance and rhetorical status. Comput. Linguist. **28**(4), 409–445 (2002)
6. Le, Q., Mikolov, T.: Distributed representations of sentences and documents. In: Proceedings of the International Conference on Machine Learning (ICML) (2014)
7. Hill, F., Cho, K., Korhonen, A.: Learning distributed representations of sentences from unlabelled data. In: Proceedings of the 15th Annual Conference of the North American Chapter of the Association for Computational Linguistics: Human Language Technologies (NAACL-HLT) (2016)
8. Joulin, A., Grave, E., Bojanowski, P., Mikolov, T.: Bag of tricks for efficient text classification. In: Proceedings of the Conference of the European Chapter of the Association for Computational Linguistics (2016)
9. Gehring, J., Auli, M., Grangier, D., Yarats, D., Dauphin, Y.: Convolutional sequence to sequence learning. In: Proceedings of the International Conference on Machine Learning (2017)
10. Socher, R., Huval, B., Manning, C.D., Ng, A.Y.: Semantic compositionality through recursive matrix-vector spaces. In: Proceedings of the Joint Conference on Empirical Methods in Natural Language Processing and Computational Natural Language Learning (EMNLP-CoNLL) (2012)
11. Tai, K.S., Socher, R., Manning, C.D.: Improved semantic representations from tree-structured long short-term memory networks. In: Proceedings of the Association of Computational Linguistics (ACL) (2015)
12. Goodfellow, I., Bengio, Y., Courville, A.: Deep Learning. MIT Press, Cambridge (2016)
13. Assawinjaipetch, P., Shirai, K., Sornlertlamvanich, V., Marukata, S.: Recurrent neural network with word embedding for complaint classification. In: Proceedings of the International Workshop on Worldwide Language Service Infrastructure (2016)
14. Goldberg, Y., Hirst, G.: Neural Network Methods in Natural Language Processing. Morgan & Claypool Publishers, San Rafael (2017)
15. LeCun, Y., Bottou, L., Bengio, Y., Haffner, P.: Gradient-based learning applied to document recognition. Proc. IEEE **86**(11), 2278–2324 (1998)
16. Kalchbrenner, N., Grefenstette, E., Blunsom, P.: A convolutional neural network for modelling sentences. In: Proceedings of the 52nd Annual Meeting of the Association for Computational Linguistics (2014)
17. Collobert, R., Weston, J., Bottou, L., Karlen, M., Kavukcuoglu, K., Kuksa, P.: Natural language processing (almost) from scratch. J. Mach. Learn. Res. **12**, 2493–2537 (2011)
18. Kingma, D.P., Welling, M.: Auto-encoding variational Bayes. In: Proceedings of the 2nd International Conference on Learning Representations (ICLR), arXiv:1312.6114 (2013)
19. Gatys, L.A., Ecker, A.S., Bethge, M.: Image style transfer using convolutional neural networks. In: Proceedings of the IEEE Conference on Computer Vision and Pattern Recognition (CVPR) (2016)
20. Kiros, R., Zhu, Y., Salakhutdinov, R., Zemel, R.S., Urtasun, R., Torralba, A., Fidler, S.: Skip-thought vectors. In: Advances in Neural Information Processing Systems (NIPS) (2015)

Dense Captioning of Natural Scenes
in Spanish

Alejandro Gomez-Garay[1], Bogdan Raducanu[2], and Joaquín Salas[1(✉)]

[1] Instituto Politécnico Nacional, Querétaro, Mexico
agomezg1600@alumno.ipn.mx, jsalasr@ipn.mx
[2] Centre de Visió per Computador, Barcelona, Spain
bogdan@cvc.uab.es

Abstract. The inclusion of visually impaired people to daily life is a challenging and active area of research. This work studies how to bring information about the surroundings to people delivered as verbal descriptions in Spanish using wearable devices. We use a neural network (Dense-Cap) for both identifying objects and generating phrases about them. DenseCap is running on a server to describe an image fed from a smartphone application, and its output is the text which a smartphone verbalizes. Our implementation achieves a mean Average Precision (mAP) of 5.0 in object recognition and quality of captions and takes an average of 7.5 s from the moment one grabs a picture until one receives the verbalization in Spanish.

Keywords: Computer vision · Deep learning · Image captioning
Spanish language

1 Introduction

Visual impairment makes it difficult for about 253 million people worldwide (grossly 36 million blind and 217 million with moderate to severe vision impairment) [31] to acquire information which potentially will facilitate them to navigate between places without colliding, access written information in their surroundings, and improve their social interaction. According to a report from the World Health Organization (WHO), in the region of the Americas (represented by ten countries), 0.35% of the population is blind and another 2.56% has low vision [30]. In the case of México [11], 10.84% of the population report visual impairment (nearly 13.5 million persons), including people using glasses and people with disabilities.

In general, visual impairment is a problem that tends to affect elderly, rural, ill and poor people. Creating equal conditions for everybody is a multidimensional problem where limited monetary resources, safety standards, and even aesthetic appearances collide to derive in what is accepted to be the best solution. In some contexts, guiding dogs, white canes, Braille signs, and sighted people contribute to providing visually impaired people with the support they need.

© Springer International Publishing AG, part of Springer Nature 2018
J. F. Martínez-Trinidad et al. (Eds.): MCPR 2018, LNCS 10880, pp. 145–154, 2018.
https://doi.org/10.1007/978-3-319-92198-3_15

In some others, researchers have explored the creation of technology to assist in way-finding, obstacle avoidance, object recognition and description of scenes. The reliable and efficient recognition of objects can help to visually impaired people to access by themselves unfamiliar environments and avoid risks [20,27]. In this document, we introduce a smartphone application which provides a verbal description of the scene in Spanish.

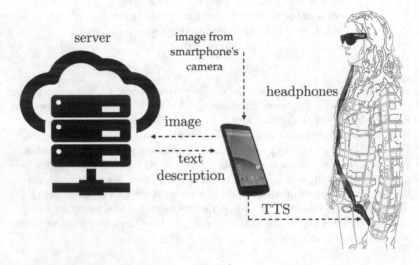

Fig. 1. System Architecture. Dense captioning of a scene in Spanish. A walking person obtains images using a smartphone equipped with a camera. In our design, the smartphone sends the images via a wi-fi connection to a server running a dense captioning system. The visual interpretation is sent back to the smartphone for it to verbalize it using Text-to-Speech (TTS) technology.

Assistive technology for visually impaired people tends to be bulky, makes the user seem weird, and it is difficult to use. Our approach aims to develop an easy to use, friendly-designed, and lightweight interface, making use of recent advances in voice recognition, speech synthesis, and wearable cameras (See Fig. 1). We use a smartphone to capture images of the surroundings via tapping commands. Afterward, the image is sent to a server for its analysis. The server returns to the smartphone a description of the scene as text, which is verbalized to the user.

Our contributions include: (i) a training dataset in Spanish for a dense captioning system, (ii) an application pipeline for the mobile use of a captioning system and (iii) insights obtained from experimental results of the usage of the application by users.

The visual description of a scene is a complex and challenging problem. Different people can describe the same image with different words, phrases, and stories [14,28]. Phrasing Eco [4], an image is a text from which we can say almost anything. In what follows, we describe in detail our system. Section 2 reviews the related literature. Then, in Sect. 3, we present a mobile image captioning system to verbally describe visual scenes in Spanish. Next, in Sect. 4, we show some experimental results we obtain when testing the system with normal sight users. Finally, we summarize our work, present our conclusion, and describe some lines for future research.

2   Related Work

In this section, we review topics related to the main components of our system, including image captioning, languages used for captioning, and scene description.

Image Captioning. Image captioning is the problem of assigning a caption to describe the content of an image. Yao *et al.* [32] generated captions for video using manual features operating over formal languages. Because of its lack of expressiveness, other efforts focused on reliable mechanisms, like object detection, and the use of templates of captions [7,22], or graphs to represent inference or syntactic analysis [17]. More recent approaches use a scheme encoder-decoder that encodes an image using a Convolutional Neural Network (CNN) and transforms the representation in a caption using a Recurrent Neural Network (RNN). While some authors consider as input to the RNN the features extracted just before the classification layer of the CNN [12,15,28], others take the features of the CNN and convert them to a hidden state of the RNN [23]. In the RNN, the next word is predicted using the previous words and the features of the CNN. A special case of Image Captioning is the concept of Dense Captioning by Johnson *et al.* [12], generating a phrase for each object that is recognized. This work relates the learning of visual features with the phrases associated with each object. With that, we have an object recognizer and a text associated [12,19,28] that requires some post-processing to generate plausible sentences. However, as it is the case for different people describing an image, the generation of descriptive text from a set of phrases may not be sufficient to explain an image properly [14].

Languages for Captioning. Jonhson *et al.* [12] constructed the first dense captioning system, and they did it in English. The main difficulty to extend it to other languages seems to be the considerable amount of work needed to associate reliable descriptions with objects in images. Some approaches to solving this problem include the use of machine translation from the English captions [9,10,18], the incremental semantic mapping of the labels from a base constructed manually and its expansion regarding context [29], and the generation of captions from scratch with crowd-sourcing [24,33]. Researchers face some difficulties including the asymmetry in the syntax of the languages and their different expressiveness, and the reduced number of images with captions or the reduced number of captions per image in datasets such as MS-COCO, and Flicker. Currently, we have been able to locate captioning systems in English [12,14,15,23,28], Japanese [24,33] Chinese [18,29], German [9,10] and French [9].

Scene Description. The human perception of a scene is highly structured, and its description has the same decomposition process. In the past, researchers approached the object recognition problem using handcrafted features, graphs of objects and attributes. Deep learning brought new techniques for image classification where each pixel is semantically segmented [5,8,21] and also the image captioning. This new line of research integrates vision, knowledge and natural language. However, the lack of *common sense* knowledge makes difficult to obtain a proper level of precision in the problem. Because one could extract knowledge from general texts, the major issues are now at the intersection of computer vision and natural language processing [1,13]. A long-term goal is *to see as humans do*, which implies the immediate comprehension of the scene meaning, including its global structure.

3   Automatic Description of Scenes

Johnson *et al.* [12] showed the feasibility to describe visual scenarios using dense captioning. We aim to develop a Spanish version of it for visually impaired people. The major issues we address include the creation of an appropriate description of the scenes in Spanish and the development of an application for a wearable device.

3.1   Dense Captioning in Spanish

The core of the system is its ability to recognize objects in the surroundings and to generate descriptions about them. We use DenseCap as our core dense captioning engine and make it operate on the Spanish translation of Visual Genome.

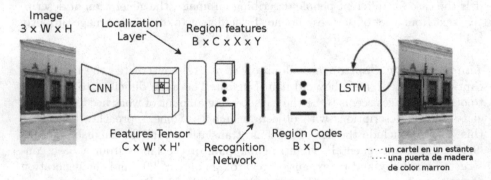

Fig. 2. DenseCap scheme architecture. With four principal components: A partial CNN generating convolutional features, a localization layer identifying and evaluating proposed regions, a recognition network classifying objects and a network of LSTM cells generating the phrases associated with each proposed region. Based on an image from [12].

On one hand, DenseCap [12] is a neural network architecture that generates phrases for objects in an image. Figure 2 shows a scheme of DenseCap. Its architecture includes a CNN for detection of objects and a RNN for their text description. The CNN includes a section for localization followed by a section for recognition. DenseCap takes as input images of 720×720 pixels (larger images are scaled down). The core of the recognition in DenseCap is VGG-16 [26], which is capable of recognizing 1,000 object categories (corresponding to the ImageNet challenge). On the other hand, Visual Genome [16] is an image database with annotations that associates each phrase with a Region of Interest (ROI). On average, an image has 50 ROIs, and there is one phrase for each ROI. We used the version of June 2016 with 108,077 images and 5,408,689 ROIs and associated phrases. We translate each phrase of Visual Genome into Spanish. For the translation, we used tools like Google Translate (a free web service) and *aspell* [2] (a GNU/Linux desktop dictionary). Even then, the data may still have mistranslated and misspelled words. Therefore, we apply the program *aspell* to detect these words and in subsequent cycles to detect phrases not in Spanish. We did not translate some terms, e g , proper names, established brands, origin denominations or iconic sites. Nonetheless, a variety of expressions from Google Translate appears like regionalisms of several Latin-American countries, so we changed those phrases to Mexican Spanish. The dataset is available at https://github.com/agomezgaray/spanish_captions.

3.2 System Architecture

Using our system, a person can query for verbal descriptions using pictures of their surroundings taken with the smartphone's camera. We developed an Android application to establish a dialogue-like process with the server. We require this distributed architecture in order to take advantage of the full computational power of the GPU on the server and thus to guarantee a near real-time response for the user.

Server Application. The application running on the server receives as input an image from the smartphone's camera, stores it and processes it using the DenseCap architecture to generate the scene description in Spanish which it sends back to the smartphone.

We use some directions of the *RESTful* web services, for stateless operations. The pipeline for the server includes the following steps. The image is sent in a compressed format using the HTTP POST protocol. Upon reception, the server assigns it a 16 digits URI, copies the image to disk and outputs the URI to the output folder. In case of success, the server generates an empty JSON file in the URI and sends to the smartphone a 302 HTTP code of redirection. The Android application downloads the empty JSON file and waits until the file changes as the server can take time to resolve the previous requests. Also, the JSON file is parsed to eliminate repeated phrases. Finally, the server returns the JSON file in the URI for verbalization in the smartphone.

System's Interface. We use an Android application for the communication with the server. Once the server makes available the file containing the text description, the smartphone downloads it, and verbalizes the phrases employing Text-To-Speech (TTS). The application has the following pipeline. It starts by tapping the smartphone's touchscreen (one touch verbalizes the message, two touches grab a picture). The picture is stored in the user space in the smartphone and then sent to the server. Upon processing it, the server returns a JSON file with a list with a maximum of 30 phrases sorted according to their relevance. The verbalization can take up to a minute, depending on its length. The application includes Network Connection (3G or Wi-Fi), Camera, Store File, and Talkback. We program this application for Android version 2.1 or later.

System Performance. To evaluate our system, we use a combination of Meteor, the Intersection over Union (IoU) and the mean Average Precision (mAP) to assess the relevance of the phrases regarding the objects identified in the ROI. Researchers designed the Meteor metric to assessing the automatic translation of texts, evaluating how similar are translations made by two entities, according to weights established by expert translators [3]. The IoU metric assesses to what extent a region covers another [6]. It is calculated as the ratio of the intersection area of two regions divided by their union. Meteor and IoU metrics are expressed in the interval between zero and one, inclusive. The mAP metric is used to assess the occurrence of objects in an image related to some thresholds. To consider the contribution of a phrase and a ROI, we had to modify the original metric [6]. To define precision, we consider a *positive* when the IoU and the Meteor metrics are both above a certain threshold. With the true and false positives, we calculated the precision for each ROI. Then, we compute the maximum precision for each combination of IoU and Meteor thresholds. Finally, we estimate the mAP by averaging over all the maximum precisions.

4   Experiment

We used an Exxact workstation with 128 GB RAM, 12 cores and 4 Titan X GPUs with CUDA 7.5 for training the neural network and a GNU/Linux Ubuntu server with 32 GB RAM, eight cores and a Tesla K40 GPU with CUDA 7.5 for dense captioning. For the Android application, we used an LG G3 smartphone with a camera of 2048×1536 pixels.

4.1   Training

We develop an Extract, Transform, Load (ETL) process [25] on the Visual Genome data, eliminating UTF-8 characters with no use in Spanish. For training, we used 108,077 images, from which we extract 5.4 million ROIs and its 5.4 million associated phrases. We have created two files: a HDF5 file with images, ROIs, and phrases and a JSON file with a dictionary of words (and their relation to numbers). Also, we modify the programs to make it possible to include the $\tilde{n}$

character. The final HDF5 file weights 128 GB and the JSON file 4.5 MB with 15,027 different words.

To train the network architecture, we use the Torch framework, version 7. Some parameters in the process include the minimum number of instances for the inclusion of a word (ten, below this number the words are substituted with the <UNK> word); a maximum generated phrase length (15); and the maximum number of generated phrases (299). We split the data into sets of 77,398 images for training, 5,000 for validation and 5,000 for testing (26,679 images are not used because they are considered as not representative of object distribution). The learning rate starts at 0.0001 and drops uniformly until 0.000001 during the 5 million iterations (corresponding to 64.6 epochs) of the training process. To compute the mAP, we considered five thresholds for the IoU (from 0.3 to 0.7 with increments of 0.1) and six thresholds for the Meteor (from −1 to 0.25 with increments of 0.25) and iterated over each pair of values. At the end, we obtain a mAP of 5.0 (versus a mAP of 5.7 for DenseCap [12])) and a loss of 19.25. During training, the processing of each epoch takes about 15 h. Meanwhile the Meteor evaluation over the validation set takes about 3 h.

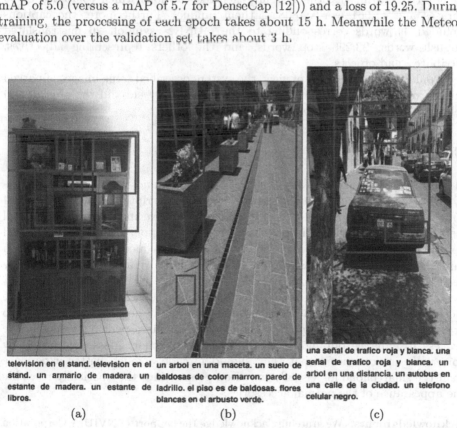

television en el stand. television en el stand. un armario de madera. un estante de madera. un estante de libros.

un arbol en una maceta. un suelo de baldosas de color marron. pared de ladrillo. el piso es de baldosas. flores blancas en el arbusto verde.

una señal de trafico roja y blanca. una señal de trafico roja y blanca. un arbol en una distancia. un autobus en una calle de la ciudad. un telefono celular negro.

(a)   (b)   (c)

Fig. 3. Visual Captioning in Spanish. The dense captioning web server generates dozens of captions in each image, but in the figure, we show only the first five captions and their bounding boxes. Figure best seen in color. (Color figure online)

4.2 Performance Evaluation

We provided this system to a person with normal sight who took pictures while walking the streets of the city of Querétaro's downtown and the installations of our university. The 317 pictures included 219 outdoors and 98 indoors, taken at different times of the day, and under different illumination conditions. Figure 3 shows three examples of these test images with only the first five captions.

Using 103 images out of these 317 pictures, we found that the neural network uses an average of 0.96 s for the description of an image. Then, we evaluated the response time of the smartphone application. For that, we use 32 pictures out of the 103 images. For an LG G3 smartphone quad-core 2.5 GHz, 2 GB internal memory, the performance is about 7.5 s, split into taking the picture (1.6 s), sending it to the server (2.4 s), downloading the description (2.5 s) and starting its verbalization (1.1 s).

For the 103 images, the system generated captions which contained 8,693 phrases and 47,061 words (838 of them unique). Furthermore, the captions included 44 words corresponding to the <UNK> symbol, 26 mistranslated English words, 23,296 stop words, and the others representing adjectives, attributes, and objects.

From a qualitative point of view, the system described some images of parked cars correctly, but the colonial architecture in the streets and the objects and colors in the phrases it generates are not precise.

Conclusion

In this work, we introduced a system to generate and verbalize descriptions of an image in Spanish. Our system provides a description based on a set of almost 5.5 million phrases. The user interface is intuitive and user-friendly. Initial tests showed its usability and potential to provide support to visually impaired persons in order to improve their quality of life and reduce their dependence on caretakers. Still, object recognition may need to improve and latency times may need to be reduced.

In future work, we will focus our research on constructing context-aware methods, which may take advantage of the previously acquired information to provide more pertinent support to the visually impaired person. We are in the process to enhance our interface with the use of smart glasses activated by voice. We are convinced that they should provide a much better experience than the smartphone for visually impaired people since they basically resemble the appearance of the normal accessories.

Acknowledgments. We gratefully acknowledge the support of NVIDIA Corporation with the donation of the GPU Tesla K40 used for this research. Rodrigo Carrillo, Miguel Torres, and Luis Sáenz developed the Android application. This work was partially funded by SIP-IPN 20180779 for Joaquín Salas. Bogdan Raducanu is supported by Grant No. TIN2016-79717-R, funded by MINECO, Spain. Alejandro Gomez-Garay is supported by Grant No. 434110/618827, funded by CONACyT.

References

1. Aditya, S., Yang, Y., Baral, C., Fermuller, C., Aloimonos, Y.: From images to sentences through scene description graphs using commonsense reasoning and knowledge. arXiv:1511.03292v1 (2015)
2. Atkinson, K.: GNU Aspell. http://aspell.net/. Accessed 08 Jan 2018
3. Denkowski, M., Lavie, A.: Meteor universal: language specific translation evaluation for any target language. In: Workshop on Statistical Machine Translation (2014)
4. Eco, U.: Tratado de semiótica General. Debolsillo, Madrid (2008)
5. Eslami, S., Heess, N., Weber, T., Tassa, Y., Szepesvari, D., Kavukcuoglu, K., Hinton, G.: Attend, infer, repeat: fast scene understanding with generative models. arXiv:1603.08575 (2016)
6. Everingham, M., Van Gool, L., Williams, C.K., Winn, J., Zisserman, A.: The Pascal visual object classes (VOC) challenge. Int. J. Comput. Vis. 88(2), 303–338 (2010)
7. Farhadi, A., Hejrati, M., Sadeghi, M.A., Young, P., Rashtchian, C., Hockenmaier, J., Forsyth, D.: Every picture tells a story: generating sentences from images. In: Daniilidis, K., Maragos, P., Paragios, N. (eds.) ECCV 2010, LNCS, vol. 6314, pp. 15–20. Springer, Heidelberg (2010). https://doi.org/10.1007/978-3-642-15561-1_2
8. Greene, M., Botros, A., Beck, D., Fei-Fei, L.: What you see is what you expect: rapid scene understanding benefits from prior experience. Attent. Percept. Psychophys. 77(4), 1239–1251 (2015)
9. Helcl, J., Libovický, J.: CUNI system for the WMT17 multimodal translation task. arXiv:1707.04550 (2017)
10. Hitschler, J., Schamoni, S., Riezler, S.: Multimodal pivots for image caption translation. arXiv:1601.03916v3 (2016)
11. Instituto Nacional de Estadística y Geografía: Estadísticas a propósito del día internacional de las personas con discapacidad. http://tinyurl.com/discapacidad. Accessed 15 Dec 2017
12. Johnson, J., Karpathy, A., Fei-Fei, L.: Densecap: fully convolutional localization networks for dense captioning. In: IEEE CVPR, pp. 4565–4574 (2016)
13. Johnson, J., Krishna, R., Stark, M., Li, L.J., Shamma, D., Bernstein, M., Fei-Fei, L.: Image retrieval using scene graphs. In: IEEE CVPR (2015)
14. Karpathy, A., Fei-Fei, L.: Deep visual-semantic alignments for generating image descriptions. In: IEEE CVPR (2015)
15. Kiros, J., Salakhutdinov, R., Zemel, R.: Unifying visual-semantic embeddings with multimodal neural language models. arXiv:1411.2539v1 (2014)
16. Krishna, R., Zhu, Y., Groth, O., Johnson, J., Hata, K., Kravitz, J., Chen, S., Kalantidis, Y., Jia-Li, L., Shamma, D., Bernstein, M., Fei-Fei, L.: Visual genome: connecting language and vision using crowdsourced dense image annotations. IJCV (2016)
17. Kulkarni, G., Premraj, V., Dhar, S., Li, S., Choi, Y., Berg, A., Berg, T.: Baby talk: understanding and generating simple image descriptions. In: IEEE CVPR (2011)
18. Lan, W., Li, X., Dong, J.: Fluency-guided cross-lingual image captioning. In: Proceedings of the 2017 ACM on Multimedia Conference, pp. 1549–1557 (2017)
19. LeCun, Y., Bengio, Y., Hinton, G.: Deep learning. Nature 521, 436–444 (2015)
20. Leo, M., Medioni, G., Trivedi, M., Kanade, T., Farinella, G.: Computer vision for assistive technologies. Comput. Vis. Image Underst. 154, 1–15 (2017)
21. Li, L.J., Socher, R., Fei-Fei, L.: Towards total scene understanding: classification, annotation and segmentation in an automatic framework. In: IEEE CVPR (2009)

22. Li, S., Kulkarni, G., Berg, T., Berg, A., Choi, Y.: Composing simple image descriptions using web-scale n-grams. In: Conference on Computational Natural Language Learning (2011)
23. Mao, J., Xu, W., Yang, Y., Wang, J., Huang, Z., Yuille, A.: Deep captioning with multimodal recurrent neural networks (M-RNN). In: ICLR (2015)
24. Miyazaki, T., Shimizu, N.: Cross-lingual image caption generation. In: Annual Meeting of the Association for Computational Linguistics, pp. 1780–1790 (2016)
25. Nisbet, R., Elder, J., Miner, G.: Handbook of Statistical Analysis and Data Mining Applications. Elsevier Inc., Amsterdam (2009)
26. Simonyan, K., Zisserman, A.: Very deep convolutional networks for large-scale image recognition. arXiv:1409.1556v6 (2015)
27. Tian, Y., Yang, X., Yi, C., Arditi, A.: Toward a computer vision-based wayfinding aid for blind persons to access unfamiliar indoor environments. Mach. Vis. Appl. **24**(3), 521–535 (2013)
28. Vinyals, O., Toshev, A., Bengio, S., Erhan, D.: Show and tell: a neural image caption generator. arXiv:1411.4555v2 (2014)
29. Wei, Q., Wang, X., Li, X.: Harvesting deep models for cross-lingual image annotation. In: Proceedings of the 15th International Workshop on Content-Based Multimedia Indexing (2017). http://doi.acm.org/10.1145/3095713.3095751
30. World Health Organization: global data on visual impairments 2010. https://tinyurl.com/globaldata2010. Accessed 29 Jan 2018
31. World Health Organization: visual impairment and blindness. http://tinyurl.com/impaired. Accessed 08 Dec 2017
32. Yao, B., Yang, X., Lin, L., Lee, M., Zhu, S.: I2T: image parsing to text description. Proc. IEEE **98**, 1485–1508 (2010)
33. Yoshikawa, Y., Shigeto, Y., Takeuchi, A.: Stair captions: constructing a large-scale japanese image caption dataset. arXiv:1705.00823v1 (2017)

Automated Detection of Hummingbirds in Images: A Deep Learning Approach

Sergio A. Serrano[1], Ricardo Benítez-Jimenez[1], Laura Nuñez-Rosas[2],
Ma del Coro Arizmendi[3], Harold Greeney[4], Veronica Reyes-Meza[2],
Eduardo Morales[1], and Hugo Jair Escalante[1]([✉])

[1] Instituto Nacional de Astrofísica, Óptica y Electrónica (INAOE), Puebla, Mexico
{sserrano,ricardo.benitez,emorales,hugojair}@inaoep.mx
[2] Centro Tlaxcala de Biología de la Conducta, Universidad Autónoma de Tlaxcala,
Tlaxcala, Mexico
lnunezr18@gmail.com, veronica.reyesm@uatx.mx
[3] Universidad Nacional Autónoma de México, Mexico City, Mexico
coro@unam.mx
[4] School of Natural Resources and the Environment, University of Arizona,
Tucson, USA
greeney@email.arizona.edu

Abstract. The analysis of natural images has been the topic of research in uncountable articles in computer vision and pattern recognition (e.g., natural images has been used as benchmarks for object recognition and image retrieval). However, despite the research progress in such field, there is a gap in the analysis of certain type of natural images, for instance, those in the context of animal behavior. In fact, biologists perform the analysis of natural images manually without the aid of techniques that were supposedly developed for this purpose. In this context, this paper presents a study on automated methods for the analysis of natural images of hummingbirds with the goal to assist biologists in the study of animal behavior. The automated analysis of hummingbird behavior is challenging mainly because of (1) the speed at which these birds move and interact; (2) the unpredictability of their trajectories; and (3) its camouflage skills. We report a comparative study of two deep learning approaches for the detection of hummingbirds in their nest. Two variants of transfer learning from convolutional neural networks (CNNs) are evaluated in real imagery for hummingbird behavior analysis. Transfer learning is adopted because not enough images are available for training a CNN from scratch, besides, transfer learning is less time consuming. Experimental results are encouraging, as acceptable classification performance is achieved with CNN-based features. Interestingly, a pretrained CNN without fine tunning and a standard classifier performed better in the considered data set.

Keywords: Image classification · Convolutional neural network
Transfer learning · Animal behavior analysis · Hummingbird detection

© Springer International Publishing AG, part of Springer Nature 2018
J. F. Martínez-Trinidad et al. (Eds.): MCPR 2018, LNCS 10880, pp. 155–166, 2018.
https://doi.org/10.1007/978-3-319-92198-3_16

1   Introduction

The analysis of natural images, and more specifically, of images depicting animals, has served as motivation and justification for many landmark papers in computer vision and pattern recognition, see e.g. [1–6], contributing to the development and establishment of fields such as image categorization, image retrieval and even object recognition. For instance, reference benchmarks depicting animals include: ImageNet [7][1], Caltech-101[2], VOC[3], Mammal animals [8], SAIAPRTC12 [9], among others. However, it is remarkable that related fields needing this sort of methods have not been benefited that much from this progress. This is the case of animal behavior analysis, in which biologist must be carefully trained and later manually analyze large amounts of images and videos in order to draw conclusions about the behavioral patterns of living organisms.

Among birds, the nesting behavior is complicated to analyze. Specially hummingbirds are difficult to analyze during nesting period because of their high speed movements, cryptic colors, and the trouble of accessing to the places where they build their nests. The aim of this paper is to develop tools that facilitate the analysis of hummingbirds nesting behavior. Specifically, the study focuses on methods for detecting the presence of hummingbirds in nests recorded in videos. Knowing the time spent in nests is important for studying maternal care and investment, and making accurate descriptions about breeding strategies and the relationship between mother and offspring. Additionally, this is the first time that image analysis methods are applied for the analysis of hummingbirds behavior.

The problem of detecting objects in images has been studied since the beginning of computer vision. Thanks to the achievements in this field, and those in related fields like machine learning, nowadays there are available methods that show outstanding performance in a number of tasks focusing on image and video analysis (e.g., face verification [10]). In recent years, these methods are converging to a single modeling methodology: deep learning [11]. Convolutional neural networks have rapidly established as reference methods in the analysis of spatio-temporal data. However, the success of this model depends on a number of aspects, most importantly the amount of data available for training the models: large amounts of labeled data are required for learning the huge number of parameters (commonly on the order of hundreds of millions).

For the problem approached in this paper, labeled data is scarce and difficult to obtain. In this scenario, transfer learning is a strategy that aims at alleviating the scarcity of data. Transfer learning aims to tailor models learned for related tasks to solve the problem at hand. In this regard, several variants have been proposed. In this paper, two transfer learning strategies are adopted for learning representations directly from raw pixels. We perform a comparative study between both methods using real imagery collected by biologists. Experimental

---

[1] http://www.image-net.org/.

[2] http://www.vision.caltech.edu/Image_Datasets/Caltech101/.

[3] http://host.robots.ox.ac.uk/pascal/VOC/.

results reveal that a straightforward pretraining formulation, results in a better performance when compared to another popular and more promising strategy.

The contributions of this paper can be summarized as follows:

- A comparative study between two transfer learning methodologies for image classification of natural images.
- The application of the considered methodologies for the detection of hummingbirds in videos with the goal of supporting animal behavior research, where one of the evaluated methods obtained acceptable performance in a real data set.
- Experimental results evidencing the usefulness of deep learning methods for approaching real problems in animal behavior analysis.

The remainder of this paper is organized as follows. In the next section we present background information on the application domain and on convolutional neural networks. In Sect. 3 we describe in detail the methodology followed in the development of our research. In Sect. 4 we present the performed experiments and the results we obtained. Finally, in Sect. 5 the conclusions and future work are presented.

2 Background and Related Work

In this section, we provide some background information about the analysis of hummingbird behavior and about convolutional neural networks and transfer learning.

2.1 Hummingbird Behavior Analysis

The hummingbirds (Aves: Trochilidae) are endemic to the American continent, there are 330 different species. Their distribution range is wide from sea level to 4500 m above sea level. These small birds, just weight from 2 to 22 grams, are responsible of pollinating more than 1300 different plants [12], they are the only birds that can fly sideways and backwards, flapping up to 60 wingbeats per second, this is the reason why they have the highest in-flight metabolism of any bird species. They eat principally nectar but, during breeding season, they also eat arthropods and small insects [13,14]. Males are polygynous, therefore, after mating they usually search for other females to mate [15]. The females build small nests in hidden places and care the nestlings until they fledge [16].

Although reproduction is a very important period for hummingbird survival, little is known about it [13,17–22]. Generating information about breeding sites preferences, reproductive success and maternal investment for incubation and fledged is important for describing the natural history of these animals and promote their conservation. However, studying this period is quite complicated because it is difficult to find the nest, to get visual access and avoid to be detected by the bird, additionally it implies very long observation periods. Such difficulties could be overcome using breakthrough technology for visual analysis. This paper presents a study in such direction.

2.2   Convolutional Neural Networks

Convolutional Neural Networks (CNN) are a special type of artificial neural network that are characterized, among other things, by applying convolutional operations. Unlike standard neural networks, CNNs retrieve input data in the form of a n-dimensional tensor (typically 2-dimensional) to which a set of convolutional operators is applied, also called kernels. Each kernel operates throughout the whole tensor and generates as a result a smaller tensor called feature map. For instance in Fig. 1, six different kernels are applied to the input matrix which generate six feature maps which are sub-sampled to create even smaller feature maps. Each set of kernels that share the same input data constitute a convolutional layer, and each step where tensors are sub-sampled is called a pooling layer.

In addition to the convolutional and pooling layers, usually one might incorporate to a CNN non-linear activation functions in order to transform the feature maps, *e.g.* the ReLU function [23]. Similarly, it is a common practice to attach at the end of a CNN a fully connected neural network to represent the network's output in the form of a vector of real values, such as *softmax* [24]. The output is a vector constituted by n elements, each of them represents the probability that the input belongs to the ith class.

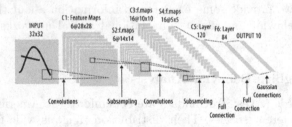

Fig. 1. General architecture of a CNN constituted by convolution, sampling and fully connected layers.

As previously mentioned, the performance of CNNs depends on the availability of a large enough data set from which CNNs' parameters can be adjusted. However, in many scenarios, including ours, labeled data is scarce and difficult to obtain. Hence, additional tricks or procedures must be performed to make CNNs work. In this context, a methodology that has been increasingly applied along with convolutional models is *transfer learning*, which was already being developed before CNN became a trend, for example, see [25–28]. In broad terms, transfer learning aims at approaching a target task A, by using as basis a model learned for task B that is often adjusted/modified to solve A. In the context of CNNs, transfer learning is a very popular solution for effectively using CNNs in tasks for which not enough labeled data is available.

3   Transfer Learning in CNNs for Detection of Hummingbirds in Images

In our study, labeled data is scarce: there are not enough labeled images depicting hummingbirds in nests, hence training a CNN from scratch is not an option. This particularity of the problem and the proved success of transfer learning in the context of CNNs inspired us for relying on transfer learning mechanisms for detecting hummingbirds in images with CNNs. In the remainder of this section we present fundamentals of CNNs, as well as on the two *transfer learning* methods compared in this paper: feature extraction with a pretrained CNN and fine tuning. Afterwards, we described the methodology followed in this research for the specific task we considered.

3.1   Transfer Learning Strategies

As previously mentioned, according to [27], transfer learning attempts to improve the learning of an objective function f_A that operates over a domain D_A, by using knowledge of another domain D_B, where $D_A \neq D_B$. What and how to transfer knowledge between different domains are the main research questions in its field, however, in the case of CNNs there are two transfer learning methods that have reported good results on image recognition tasks [29], features extraction along with a classifier and fine-tuning. Both strategies are considered in our study and described below.

Features Extraction from a Pretrained CNN

Usually, a CNN is constituted by several convolutional layers and their respective pooling layers, and at its end a fully connected neural network (see Fig. 1). This transfer learning approach uses the representation that a CNN, previously trained with millions of examples, generates for the instances retrieved in the input layer. The main idea behind this approach is to interpret the representations generated by the CNN as feature vectors, and use them to train a classifier, *e.g.* in [30] they show how effective this method can be. In Fig. 2 one may observe how the blue square encloses the CNN's layer from which the generated representation is taken and used for the classifier's training.

Fine-Tuning

We have previously mentioned the outstanding ability CNNs have in terms of large scale image classification. However, there are some tasks that do not require the recognition of a large amount of classes as in the ILSVRC challenge [6], and instead, few classes and a few number of training images are available. For this kind of smaller problems, the fine-tuning method is a good alternative. Fine-tuning is a form of transfer learning consisting of using a sub-set of parameters from a CNN that has already been trained over a general dataset, and compute the rest of the parameters by means of *back propagation*, training on a more specialized dataset, thus, the network will adjust itself to perform efficiently over the specialized task for which it was trained. The main advantage of using fine-tuning is that, unlike training a CNN from scratch, the training time decreases

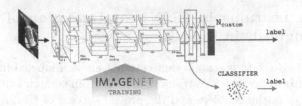

Fig. 2. The two transfer learning methods applied with CNNs: features extraction (blue) and fine-tuning (red). Figure from [31]. (Color figure online)

significantly and enables the usage of CNNs on problems with small datasets. In Fig. 2, the red square represents the section of layers that is re-trained using fine-tuning.

3.2 Detecting Hummingbirds with Transfered Learning from CNNs

The main goal of this paper is to determine the effectiveness of feature extraction and fine-tuning approaches along with an CNN, when applied to the task of detecting the presence of a hummingbird in an image. Our main motivation is to provide support tools for biologists that must manually analyze large amounts of videos. Implicitly, our aim is two-fold, (i) to prove the effectiveness of modern image classification algorithms in a real-world challenging domain and (ii) to verify whether either of the two transfer learning methods is significantly more effective than the other one on this specific problem. In the following we describe the considered data set and the adopted evaluation framework.

Data Collection and Division: The data set used in the development of our research was captured as follows. The videos were recorded in several places in Ecuador and Arizona, USA. The species recorded were *Aglaiocercus coelestis, Doryfera johannae, Heliangelus strophianus, Selaspherus platycercus* and *Topaza pyra*. First, the nest was located and then, videos were manually recorded with a camera for 45 min on average, making several recordings per day in the same nest.

The original data set is made up of 18 videos, this set was separated into 5 subsets, each formed by videos obtained from the same scene. One of these subsets was discarded due to its poor resolution and a lack of certainty when we manually attempted to label it. Figure 3 shows positive (hummingbird in nest) and negative (hummingbird not in nest) frames extracted form the four subsets retained; whereas Fig. 4 shows frames from the removed subset (for this subset it was not possible to determine the presence of the hummingbird for manual annotators).

From each subset of videos we extracted a set of frames using a sample rate that allowed us to gather at least 1000 positive and 1000 negative examples (that later were manually labeled), from which a frame centered on the hummingbird's nest was extracted and these frames were resized to 299 × 299 pixels. Finally, in order to label the adjusted frames, we applied to each of them the following

(a)   (b)   (c)   (d)

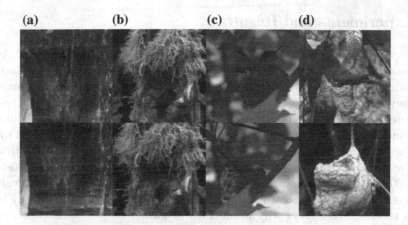

Fig. 3. The images in the upper row belong to the positive class and the ones in the lower row belong to the negative class. The columns, from left to right, correspond to the subsets **A**, **B**, **C** and **D**.

Fig. 4. Frames from the subset of videos that were omitted due to their poor resolution.

criterion: there were only two possible classes to be assigned, positive and negative classes. For a frame to be labeled as positive, a hummingbird should be in its nest. Otherwise, in order to label a frame as negative, no hummingbird nor any partial view of it should be captured within the image. As result, each set of frames was downsized due to those frames which did not satisfy any of the conditions previously described. To evaluate the classification performance of the models, the F1-Score was chosen.

Experimental Design: Being the main objective of this research to compare the performance of the features extraction method along with a classifier, and the fine-tuning method in the classification of images containing a hummingbird, we used *TensorFlow's* [32] implementation of the *Inception V3* CNN [33]. For the feature extraction approach, we opted for a SVM classifier and performed preliminary tests with several kernels, at the end we selected the linear kernel which was the one that reported the best results. On the other hand, with the fine-tuning approach, preliminary tests were carried out with different configurations in learning rate values and number of epochs to determine the appropriate parameters, the learning rate that reported better results was 0.01 and this was established as constant for the rest of the tests, while the optimal number of epochs ranged from 200 to 3000.

4   Experiments and Results

To compare both transfer learning methods, 14 tests have been defined, each one consisting of a combination of the four subsets of data, which we called **A**, **B**, **C** and **D**. In this way, the training and testing sets are not only disjoint, but also they come from different scenes making it more challenging. Each test is configured by the subsets used for training and those designated for evaluating the trained model, *i.e.* the test subsets. The number of training samples in every test was defined as 300, where of them 150 were positive and 150 of them were negative instances, randomly selected. Regarding the test samples, 1000 positive and 1000 negative samples were randomly selected for each test subset. Positive and negative examples of each of the subsets of images can be seen in Fig. 3. One of the main reasons of why we decided to gather only 1000 examples from each class is that in consecutive frames, even after sampling, the images have little noticeable differences, at least for the human eye.

The number of training samples for our models was determined experimentally after several preliminary tests, where the number of training samples was varied in each test. We observed that, with both approaches, for a number of examples greater than 400 the precision was high but with a low recall, and for less than 200 they had high recall but a very poor precision.

Table 1 shows the F1-Score obtained by the two evaluated methods. To compare the performance of the classifiers, the statistical Wilcoxon signed-rank test has been selected [34]. In order to apply this statistical test, we first defined the null hypothesis, $h_0 = $ *In the task of classifying hummingbird images, the performance of the features extraction method with SVM and the Fine-tuning method are not significantly distinct.* Then, the absolute values of the F1-Score difference in each test were assigned a range, starting with the lowest value with range 1, up to the largest of the differences with range 14. These values are used by the Wilcoxon test to calculate a sum for each classifier. In this case, the sums of the ranks of each classifier were $R_{SVM} = 88$ y $R_{FineTuning} = 16$. Checking Wilcoxon's table of critical values for a confidence of $\alpha = 0.05$ and $N = 14$ tests, the difference between the classifiers is significant if the lesser of the sums is less than or equal to 21. This last condition is met by $R_{FineTuning} \leqslant 21$, therefore, we reject the null hypothesis h_0 and we can affirm that the features extraction approach with SVM is significantly better than fine-tuning to classify hummingbird images when there are few sets of images. In addition, the average of the F1-Score of SVM (≈ 0.6837) is superior that fine-tuning (≈ 0.6384) with a difference of ≈ 0.0453.

The best result obtained by the fine-tuning method is experiment 11, which was trained with sets **B**, **C**, **D** and tested in set **A**. However, the best result was obtained by the SVM approach in the experiment 14, where the training was carried out with the sets **A**, **B**, **C** and tested in **D**, in Fig. 5 examples of frames for this configuration are shown.

Table 1. Performance of both classifiers

ID	Training subsets	Testing subsets	# of test examples	F1-Score Feat. ext. + SVM	Fine tuning	F1-Score abs. diff.
1	A	B, C, D	6,000	**0.6549**	0.6358	0.0191
2	B	A, C, D	6,000	**0.6913**	0.6744	0.0169
3	C	A, B, D	6,000	**0.7339**	0.6494	0.0845
4	D	A, B, C	6,000	0.6667	0.6667	0.0
5	A, B	C, D	4,000	**0.6667**	0.6665	0.0002
6	A, C	B, D	4,000	**0.6453**	0.5687	0.0766
7	A, D	B, C	4,000	**0.6026**	0.5235	0.0791
8	B, C	A, D	4,000	0.6715	**0.6921**	0.0206
9	B, D	A, C	4,000	0.6897	**0.7246**	0.0349
10	C, D	A, B	4,000	**0.6841**	0.6690	0.0151
11	B, C, D	A	2,000	**0.7502**	0.7281	0.0221
12	A, C, D	B	2,000	**0.6560**	0.3653	0.2907
13	A, B, D	C	2,000	**0.6682**	0.6675	0.0007
14	A, B, C	D	2,000	**0.7903**	0.7062	0.0841
Avg.				**0.6837**	0.6384	0.0453

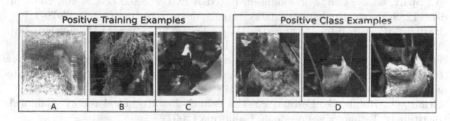

Fig. 5. Sample positive instances from the experiment 14.

5 Conclusions and Future Work

We presented a methodology for detecting hummingbirds in images. The goal of the study is to provide biologists with support tools that can help them to analyze animal behavior and make new discoveries. The problem was approached as one of classification and a real data set was considered for experimentation. Since the number of distinctive available images is scare for the considered domain, we relied on transfer learning techniques. We presented a comparative analysis on two image classification methods based on transfer learning in CNNs: features extraction along with a SVM and *fine tuning*. Given the nature of our data, which was a scenario with few and high-dimensional data, we observed a better performance from the SVM approach and noticed that the *fine tuning* approach requires a more variated set of training examples in order to increase its precision when classifying new unseen instances. We think F1-score values obtained from the SVM approach are acceptable considering the low variance within the training example sets. Moreover, we performed other tests where the training and test example were extracted from the same sub-set, the f1-score values obtained from the *fine tuning* approach vary over the range of 0.8654 to 1, while the SVM approach obtained values ranging from 0.7263 up to 0.9823, which indicate the great precision CNNs can achieve when they are trained under scenarios that are not as restricted as the ones designed in our analysis. It is worth mentioning that we started training a standard CNN (*Alexnet* [35]) from scratch to have a reference performance. However, we confirmed this procedure was too computationally expensive when compared to transfer learning (1 epoch for *Alexnet* took 25 min, while 1000 epochs for the transfer learning configuration lasted 86 s). This is in addition to the expected low performance of the network. As future work, we plan to train CNNs from scratch with data augmentation mechanisms, also, we will explore the use of methods that provide localization, in addition to recognition, of objects in images.

References

1. Duygulu, P., Barnard, K., de Freitas, J.F.G., Forsyth, D.A.: Object recognition as machine translation: learning a lexicon for a fixed image vocabulary. In: Heyden, A., Sparr, G., Nielsen, M., Johansen, P. (eds.) ECCV 2002. LNCS, vol. 2353, pp. 97–112. Springer, Heidelberg (2002). https://doi.org/10.1007/3-540-47979-1_7
2. Barnard, K., Duygulu, P., Forsyth, D., de Freitas, N., Blei, D.M., Jordan, M.I.: Matching words and pictures. J. Mach. Learn. Res. **3**(Feb), 1107–1135 (2003)
3. Fei-Fei, L., Fergus, R., Perona, P.: Learning generative visual models from few training examples: an incremental Bayesian approach tested on 101 object categories. In: Proceedings of CVPRW, p. 178 (2004)
4. Griffin, G., Holub, G., Perona, P.: The caltech-256. Technical report. California Institute of Technology, Pasadena, California (2007)
5. Everingham, M., Zisserman, A., Williams, C.K.I., Van Gool, L.: The PASCAL Visual Object Classes Challenge 2006 (VOC2006) Results. http://www.pascal-network.org/challenges/VOC/voc2006/results.pdf
6. Russakovsky, O., Deng, J., Hao, S., Krause, J., Satheesh, S., Ma, S., Huang, Z., Karpathy, A., Khosla, A., Bernstein, M., Berg, A.C., Fei-Fei, L.: ImageNet large scale visual recognition challenge. Int. J. Comput. Vis. **115**(3), 211–252 (2015)
7. Deng, J., Dong, W., Socher, R., Li, L.-J., Li, K., Fei-Fei, L.: ImageNet: a large-scale hierarchical image database. In: CVPR 2009 (2009)
8. Fink, M., Ullman, S.: From aardvark to zorro: a benchmark for mammal image classification. Int. J. Comput. Vis. **77**(1), 143–156 (2008)
9. Escalante, H.J., Hernández, C.A., Gonzalez, J.A., López-López, A., Montes, M., Morales, E.F., Sucar, L.E., Villaseñor, L., Grubinger, M.: The segmented and annotated IAPR TC-12 benchmark. Comput. Vis. Image Underst. **114**(4), 419–428 (2010)
10. Schroff, F., Kalenichenko, D., Philbin, J.: FaceNet: a unified embedding for face recognition and clustering. In: CVPR (2015)

11. LeCun, Y., Bengio, Y., Hinton, G.: Deep learning. Nature **521**, 436–444 (2015)
12. del Coro Arizmendi, M., Rodríguez-Flores, C.I.: How many plant species do hummingbirds visit? Ornitol. Neotrop. **23**, 71–75 (2012)
13. Elliott, A., del Hoyo, J., Sargatal, J.: Handbook of the Birds of the World, Volume 5, Barn-Owls to Hummingbirds, pp. 388–435. Lynx Edicions, Barcelona (1999)
14. Colwell, R.K.: Rensch's rule crosses the line: convergent allometry of sexual size dimorphism in hummingbirds and flower mites. Am. Nat. **156**(5), 495–510 (2000)
15. Bleiweiss, R.: Phylogeny, body mass, and genetic cponsequences of lek-mating behavior in hummingbirds (1998)
16. Johnsgard, P.A.: The Hummingbirds of North America. Smithsonian Institution, Washington (2016)
17. Vleck, C.M.: Hummingbird incubation: female attentiveness and egg temperature. Oecologia **51**(2), 199–205 (1981)
18. Baltosser, W.H.: Nesting success and productivity of hummingbirds in Southwestern New Mexico and Southeastern Arizona. Wilson Bull. **98**(3), 353–367 (1986)
19. Brown, B.T.: Nesting chronology, density and habitat use of black-chinned hummingbirds along the Colorado River Arizona. J. Field Ornithol. **63**(4), 393–400 (1992)
20. Greeney, H.F., Hough, E.R., Hamilton, C.E., Wethington, S.M.: Nestling growth and plumage development of the black-chinned hummingbird (Archilochus alexandri) in Southeastern Arizona. Huitzil. Revista Mexicana de Ornitología **9**(2), 35 42 (2008)
21. Greeney, H.F., Wethington, S.M.: Proximity to active accipiter nests reduces nest predation of black-chinned hummingbirds. Wilson J. Ornithol. **121**(4), 809–812 (2009)
22. Smith, D.M., Finch, D.M., Hawksworth, D.L.: Black-chinned hummingbird nest-site selection and nest survival in response to fuel reduction in a Southwestern Riparian forest. Condor **111**(4), 641–652 (2009)
23. Nair, V., Hinton, G.E.: Rectified linear units improve restricted Boltzmann machines. In: Proceedings of the 27th International Conference on Machine Learning, ICML 2010, pp. 807–814 (2010)
24. Memisevic, R., Zach, C., Pollefeys, M., Hinton, G.E.: Gated softmax classification. In: Advances in Neural Information Processing Systems, pp. 1603–1611 (2010)
25. Dai, W., Yang, Q., Xue, G.-R., Yu, Y.: Boosting for transfer learning. In: Proceedings of the 24th International Conference on Machine Learning, pp. 193–200. ACM (2007)
26. Raina, R., Battle, A., Lee, H., Packer, B., Ng, A.Y.: Self-taught learning: transfer learning from unlabeled data. In: Proceedings of the 24th International Conference on Machine Learning, pp. 759–766. ACM (2007)
27. Pan, S.J., Yang, Q.: A survey on transfer learning. IEEE Trans. Knowl. Data Eng. **22**(10), 1345–1359 (2010)
28. Taylor, M.E., Stone, P.: Transfer learning for reinforcement learning domains: a survey. J. Mach. Learn. Res. **10**(Jul), 1633–1685 (2009)
29. Oquab, M., Bottou, L., Laptev, I., Sivic, J.: Learning and transferring mid-level image representations using convolutional neural networks. In: Proceedings of the IEEE Conference on Computer Vision and Pattern Recognition, pp. 1717–1724 (2014)
30. Donahue, J., Jia, Y., Vinyals, O., Hoffman, J., Zhang, N., Tzeng, E., Darrell, T.: DeCAF: a deep convolutional activation feature for generic visual recognition. In: International Conference on Machine Learning, pp. 647–655 (2014)

31. Pasquale, G., Ciliberto, C., Rosasco, L., Natale, L.: Object identification from few examples by improving the invariance of a deep convolutional neural network. In: 2016 IEEE/RSJ International Conference on Intelligent Robots and Systems, IROS, pp. 4904–4911. IEEE (2016)
32. Abadi, M., Agarwal, A., Barham, P., Brevdo, E., Chen, Z., Citro, C., Corrado, G.S., Davis, A., Dean, J., Devin, M., et al.: TensorFlow: large-scale machine learning on heterogeneous distributed systems. arXiv preprint arXiv:1603.04467 (2016)
33. Szegedy, C., Vanhoucke, V., Ioffe, S., Shlens, J., Wojna, Z.: Rethinking the inception architecture for computer vision. In: Proceedings of CVPR, pp. 2818–2826 (2016)
34. Demšar, J.: Statistical comparisons of classifiers over multiple data sets. JMLR 7(Jan), 1–30 (2006)
35. Krizhevsky, A., Sutskever, I., Hinton, G.E.: ImageNet classification with deep convolutional neural networks. In: Advances in Neural Information Processing Systems, pp. 1097–1105 (2012)

Data Mining

Patterns in Poor Learning Engagement in Students While They Are Solving Mathematics Exercises in an Affective Tutoring System Related to Frustration

Gustavo Padron-Rivera[✉], Cristina Joaquin-Salas,
Jose-Luis Patoni-Nieves, and Juan-Carlos Bravo-Perez

Instituto Tecnologico Superior de Teziutlan, Puebla, Mexico
{gustavo.padron, cristina.joaquin, joseluis.patoni,
juancarlos.bravo}@itsteziutlan.edu.mx

Abstract. Nowadays, detection of learner's affective state is required for adaptive learning technologies that aim to support and regulate them, due emotions are important during learning process. An affective tutoring system (ATS) was developed, with capability to detect frustration and confusion mainly, because they are associated with low and high learning outcomes. In previous experiments with students while they were solving mathematics exercises using ATS, almost all of them got a low score. Therefore, it seems to be necessary to set up user profiles in order to improve learning, in those that usually show poor motivation and engagement, to design better learning environments and virtual helper assistant to attract and identify them for extra activities. A cluster analysis was applied, and it found a correlation between frustration, low scores and clicks on help. Then, a multilayer perceptron classified different examples getting a considerable percentage of accuracy.

Keywords: Affective tutoring system · Frustration · Patterns recognition

1 Introduction

Affective states are important during the learning process in students, some of them, such as boredom, have been shown to be associated with poor learning outcomes, mainly in science and mathematics. On the other side, concentration and even confusion have a beneficial role. Studies have explored affective states that occur during the complex learning, e.g. mathematics and science, identifying five: boredom, concentration/flow, confusion, frustration, and a neutral state [1]. The ability to detect a learner's affective states, while they are interacting with learning environment, it is required for adaptive learning technologies aim to support and regulate learners' affect in order to improve their learning engagement [2].

In general, students remain in a state of concentration/flow, while they are pursuing a goal, and enter a state of boredom if they leave it. There is an intermediate emotion from one affective state to another, and that is frustration, which plays an important role, and its level of presence can lead to the success or failure in students learning

© Springer International Publishing AG, part of Springer Nature 2018
J. F. Martínez-Trinidad et al. (Eds.): MCPR 2018, LNCS 10880, pp. 169–177, 2018.
https://doi.org/10.1007/978-3-319-92198-3_17

engagement. Frustration, is accompanied by a persistent state of confusion, considered as a negative affective state. However, also it has been shown that some episodes of confusion, lead to students to experience a cognitive imbalance, which forces them to reflect and solve the problem in course. Frustration, and even confusion, appears in shorter periods than concentration or flow, and these tend to persist over time, and arise when difficulties are encountered, which can lead to quit the goal. Therefore, to identify frustration or confusion, it is necessary to offer help and guide them, e.g. to argue with students, and take them from state of frustration or confusion, to concentration [3].

This research aims not just detect those negative affective states, but measuring patterns in student's activities to personalize the help in order to improve their engagement. Therefore, an affective tutoring system (ATS) was developed. An ATS is a kind of intelligent tutoring system (ITS), that enhance students into learning experiences in mathematics and science, creating successful affective responses depending of student's emotion, in activities that require a big effort, to detect student affect and to design appropriate responses to affect and motivate them [4]. An ITS is a friendly environment for learning, but it is necessary to adapt to the affective states of the learners too. Therefore, ATSs are ITSs with capability to adapt to the affective states of the learner [5]. The ATS was named Tamaxtil, which means «teacher», in Nahualt language, and it has the capability to detect frustration and confusion, mainly, because they have negative and positive impact in students. It teaches Eulers and Runge-Kutta Methods in an Spanish interface. A pilot experiment was made to test the ATS detecting affective states in students while they are solving mathematic exercises in order to regulate negative emotions. It was found that frustration was present in almost all students, perhaps by the complexity of the exercises, and it is necessary to improve the help assistant to avoid poor outcomes [6]. This document shows different cases of students with low scores, in order to develop a tool that responds appropriately to the negative affective states that a student goes through while they are stuck on a mathematical problem.

2 Methodology

The elements employed for this research consist of the ATS, for the exercises of Eulers and Runge-Kutta methods, with the capability to detect of automatic recognition of facial expressions in relation to affective states. It uses the open source software development kit, Affectiva/Affdex SDK [7], for recognition of Action Units (AU), which they are parts of the system for classifying human facial movements (FACS). An AU is defined as a contraction or relaxation of one or more muscles of face, and their combination can use to define human emotions [3].

The Fig. 1 shows the software detector for combinations of AUs, such as frustration defined by AU1+12 and AU2+12; and confusion by AU4+25 and AU4+26 [8].

The experiment was held in three days: day one, a human teacher mentions the Eulers and Runge-Kutta methods to students and they solve a pre-test of these topics; day two: students use Tamaxtil for practicing the methods, and at each five second student's faces were analyzed and saved into a database as AUs as it shows in Table 1, for a time lapse of 40 min. Due student position, in front of the display/screen, while

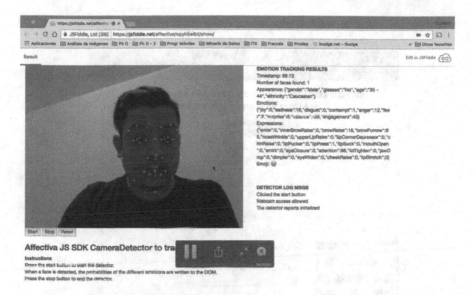

Fig. 1. Facial analysis of action units using Affectiva/Affdex SDK, for tracking muscle of faces for affective states recognition.

they are solving the exercises in a web browser, it was possible to analyze their faces (see Fig. 1). Finally, day three: students solve a post-test, similar to the pre-test, but with different exercises. The participants were 18 students of both genders, 19 years average, undergraduate from the Institute of Technology of Teziutlan, Puebla, Mexico. Tamaxtil has several exercises per each method, as well as a help assistant, that can be use by the student at any time.

Then, both exams were evaluated in order to verify the learning engagement progress. In this case, eleven examples got a low score, and seven examples, got high score. Therefore, it is important to detect and help them. Previous analysis, the affective state, frustration, got a correlation with those students that got a low score [6] and it also could affect learner motivations [9]. On the other hand, confusion, and engaged concentration persisted in both conditions «virtuous cycles» and «vicious cycles».

Tamaxtil, is an ATS that identifies negative affective states in students while they are solving mathematical exercises, to approach improving learning engagement, showing help in case of frustration or confusion, and congratulation messages per each correct answer. It was designed to improve the learning efficiency, trying to regulate negative emotions that present through the exercises, providing an accompaniment during learning process [6]. Frustration lead to students to boredom, and therefore to abandon the goal. To avoid this, it sends multiples messages to help them to move to the frustration state and, even if confusion, to keep to the students in a state of concentration/flow. Despite this, it offers help. As it notices, this did not work in all students, then it will be necessary to guide them with personalized help and motivation messages, that can lead them to abandon the frustration or confusion quickly and take them to a state of concentration. Figure 2 shows the interface of ATS and affective state

Fig. 2. ATS Tamaxtil user interface.

detector. As it notices, webcam is not mirroring user face, like in Fig. 1; students just can see an advertisement: *"Do not close this window, Tamaxtil is making an analysis. Thank you!"*.

3   Results

ATS save into dataset the AUs combinations related to frustration and confusion and clicks on help window. Table 1 shows the dataset for the experiment described above, with pre and post-test score, and labeled as high and low, for poor and high learning engagement. It is important to mention that during the tests there were problems with the internet bandwidth during the interaction with the ATS, only the data shown in Table 1 were collected, but it was enough for this early analysis.

The dataset was analyzed in order to patterns recognition on the statistical software R version 3.3.2, with the cluster dendrogram technique. The Fig. 3 shows, five clusters that allow identifying different user profiles, defined in relation to the number of clicks by the students during the interaction with Tamaxtil, as well as AUs related to frustration and confusion.

In Fig. 3, a tree diagram is shown to illustrate the arrangement groups, from left to right, produced by hierarchical clustering by the different students profiles and how

Table 1. Dataset for experiment of students using an ATS.

Student	Pre-test	Frustration_AU1 +12	Frustration_AU2 +12	Confusion_AU4 +25	Confusion_AU4 +26	Clicks_help	Post-test
1	Low	0	0	0	0	0	Low
2	Low	0	0	0	0	0	Low
3	Low	0	0	0	0	17	Low
4	Low	2	24	1	0	0	Low
5	Low	0	0	0	0	4	High
6	High	0	25	0	0	4	Low
7	Low	0	0	0	0	0	High
8	Low	0	2	0	0	0	High
9	Low	0	0	0	0	0	High
10	Low	0	41	0	0	9	Low
11	Low	0	19	0	0	10	Low
12	Low	0	3	0	0	13	Low
13	Low	1	16	0	0	2	Low
14	Low	0	21	0	0	3	High
15	Low	0	6	0	0	6	High
16	Low	0	18	0	0	0	Low
17	Low	0	16	0	0	0	High
18	Low	0	10	0	0	0	Low

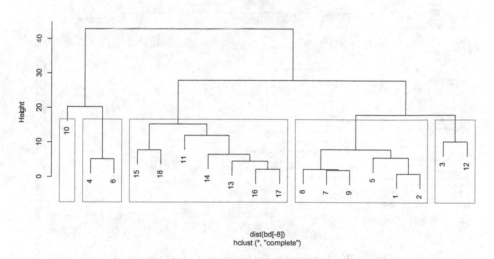

dist(bd[-8])
hclust (*, "complete")

Fig. 3. Cluster dendrogram for five group of students that have similar features.

affect the student engagements from pre-test to post-test, . Cluster #1 has just one student (student #10), it has the longest period of frustration, few times looking for help and low score in pre-test and post-test, therefore it is necessary to detect early this kind of users and help them to improve their learning engagement. On the other hand, the examples in cluster #2, apparently shows the same problem described previously, but student #6 has a high score in pre-test but low in post-test; both students had few times clicks on help; it is necessary to avoid these cases when they get high score, they seem to feel frustrated almost all the time while they were solving the exercises. The affective states detected were both combinations of frustration, AU1+12 and AU2+12, it seems to be another clue to detect this kind of users. For cluster #3, 50% of examples have a high score in post-test, in spite of their low score at pre-test. But, they have a lot of periods of frustration, specifically combination of AU2+12. In cluster #4, almost all students have a high score in post-test and no clicks in help, nor frustration time intervals, in spite of their low score in pre-test, they have been labeled as good students or high learning engagement. Finally, in cluster #5, both examples have low score in post-test, besides a lot of clicks on help, in spite of the lack of any combination of frustration.

Later, the dataset was analyzed on Weka, version 3.3.0, which is a collection of machine learning algorithms for data mining tasks. A multilayer perceptron was employed, as it shows in Fig. 4. This algorithm got 72.22%, and the confusion matrix (see Table 2), shows that the algorithm classified nine examples correctly, and missed twice, in «low score» examples; on the other side, it classified four examples correctly, and missed in three of «high score». Therefore, it was better classifying «low score» examples. The setup in this learning rate was equal to 0.3; momentum rate for backpropagation algorithm of 2.0; 500 epochs for training, and 5 hidden layers; the class label was «post-test»: High or Low score.

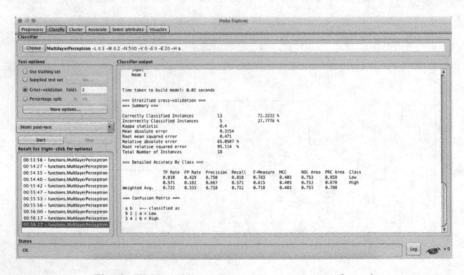

Fig. 4. Weka multilayer Perceptron outcomes performed.

As it shows, 13 examples of 18 were correctly classified. Therefore, there is a possibility to add a neural network to ATS, in order to detect students who likely will get a low score in post-test.

With a seven cross-validation, the accuracy arises to 77.77% (see Fig. 5), still modest, but it shows that it is possible to increase the accuracy, with more records. As shown in Table 2, it is possible to add this kind of algorithms into the ATS in order to detect students with patterns of frustration, sending different kind of messages offering help, and consequently, avoid low scores in post-test.

Table 2. Confusion matrix of multilayer perceptron outcomes.

a	b	Classified as
9	2	a = Low
3	4	b = High

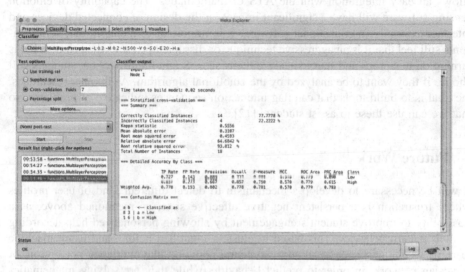

Fig. 5. Different accuracy of perceptron multilayer in Weka.

4 Conclusions

Results show that it is possible to define user profiles, from this five clusters, there is a chance to define user's behaviors while they are solving exercises, to offer personalized help. Previously, a lot of message were sent to the student with no positive impact on them. Therefore, it is necessary to develop an ATS that identifies specific features of learning engagement, that can lead from frustration to engagement, and to establish personalized help in relation to behavior patterns, thus it hope to reduce the learning curve that may block their school performance.

As it mentioned before, frustration has a negative correlation with student's learning engagement if is persists, however a few lapses of frustration can be addressed through an accompaniment that allow to the student to leave the transitory state and return to the confusion, an adequate stimuli of motivation can direct them to a state of concentration. When a multilayer perceptron was used, it shows a high accuracy detecting low score cases, so it is possible to detect this kind of students and to predict when they feel frustrated and provide important information to an ATS when inter-action was initiated. For example, an ATS uses this information to provide support who is likely to quit, and do not disturb to engaged learners for discover new things without interruption [10]. It is necessary to focus on to apply a machine learning techniques to classify different learning models or students' profiles, with out human teacher's help, frustration affect both genders equally [11].

This research is exploring a way to help students through the emotion detection and how to provide help to improve their capabilities in mathematics. The identification of affective states is often difficult and subjective because each human observer tends to have his own judgment, that is why this research uses Affectiva/Affdex SDK, that even has classifiers for determining gender and whether the person is wearing glasses, it allows an easy integration with the ATS of mathematics. The capability of emotion sensing software will have a significant impact on the design of connected devices and interfaces, meanly in educational software. It is important to mention that, some students still feel that it is an aggressive technique or disrupted privacy when camera led is turning on in laptops and start to analyze their faces. So, in future version, students will choose if they want to be analyzed by the emotional algorithm. As in other researches, the goal is to build tools that can flag interaction sequences indicative of problems, so that we can use these to assist students [12].

5   Future Work

It will be necessary to develop a mechanism to detect different kind of user profiles where frustration is a persistent negative affective state, as mentioned above, as a possibility to improve student's engagement by showing personalized help according to their pattern behavior. This based in clusters identified before, and using machine learning techniques, such as an artificial neural network, like multilayer perceptron, or Bayesian network, in order to predict behaviors while they are solving mathematics methods.

Tamaxtil has an assistant helper, but it is necessary to improve it, to offer a better learning environment interactions. This means a better user interface, to be more attractive, maybe using multimedia content. In another experimental results with learning tools, video-based multimedia material generated better learning performance and more positive emotion by students [13]. This approach will be considered, plus the model to identify low score students, in ATS next version. On the other side, it is necessary to remark that not all students used to learn in the same way, and there are different learning styles. Finally, it should be mentioned that ATS will be proposed as a complement learning tool in universities of Mexico, due these methods are important topics in engineering careers.

References

1. Craig, S., Graesser, A., Sullins, J., Gholson, B.: Affect and learning: an exploratory look into the role of affect in learning with AutoTutor. J. Educ. Media 29(3), 241–250 (2004)
2. D'Mello, S.K., Lehman, B., Person, N.: Monitoring affect states during effortful problem solving activities. Int. J. Artif. Intell. Educ. 20(4), 361–389 (2010)
3. Mello, S.D., Graesser, A.: The half-life of cognitive-affective states during complex learning. Cogn. Emot. 25(7), 1299–1309 (2011)
4. Defalco, J., Rowe, J.P., Mott, B.W.: Detecting and addressing frustration in a serious game for military training. Int. J. Artif. Intell. Educ. 28(2), 152–193 (2017)

5. Ben Ammar, M., Neji, M., Alimi, A.M., Gouardères, G.: The affective tutoring system. Expert Syst. Appl. **37**(4), 3013–3023 (2010)
6. Padron-Rivera, G., Joaquin-Salas, C.: Evaluation of affective states regulation in an intelligent tutoring system for mathematics. Res. Comput. Sci. **143**, 236–245 (2017)
7. McDuff, D., Mahmoud, A., Mavadati, M., Amr, M., Turcot, J., el Kaliouby R.: AFFDEX SDK: a cross-platform real-time multi-face expression recognition toolkit. In: Proceedings of 2016 CHI Conference Extended Abstracts on Human Factors in Computing Systems - CHI EA 2016, pp. 3723–3726 (2016)
8. Padrón-Rivera, G., Rebolledo-Mendez, G., Parra, P.P., Huerta-Pacheco, N.S.: Identification of action units related to affective states in a tutoring system for mathematics. Educ. Technol. Soc. **19**(2), 77–86 (2016)
9. Malekzadeh, M., Mustafa, M.B., Lahsasna, A.: A review of emotion regulation in intelligent tutoring systems. J. Educ. Technol. Soc. **18**(4), 435 (2015)
10. Kapoor, A., Burleson, W., Picard, R.W.: Automatic prediction of frustration. Int. J. Hum. Comput. Stud. **65**(8), 724–736 (2007)
11. Calkins, S.D., Dedmon, S.E., Gill, K.L., Lomax, L.E., Johnson, L.M.: Frustration in infancy: implications for emotion regulation, physiological processes, and temperament. Infancy **3**(2), 175–197 (2002)
12. Kay, J., Maisonneuve, N., Yacef, K.: Mining patterns of events in students' teamwork data. In: Educational Data Mining Workshop on Intelligent Tutoring Systems, pp. 1–8 (2006)
13. Chen, A.: Assessing the effects of different multimedia materials on emotions and learning performance for visual and verbal style learners, 38–40 (2017)

Pattern Discovery in Mixed Data Bases

Angel Kuri-Morales[(✉)]

Instituto Tecnológico Autónomo de México,
Río Hondo No. 1, 01000 Mexico, DF, Mexico
akuri@itam.mx

Abstract. Structured data bases may include both numerical and non-numerical attributes (categorical or CA). Databases which include CAs are called "mixed" databases (MD). Metric clustering algorithms are ineffectual when presented with MDs because, in such algorithms, the similarity between the objects is determined by measuring the differences between them, in accordance with some predefined metric. Nevertheless, the information contained in the CAs of MDs is fundamental to understand and identify the patterns therein. A practical alternative is to encode the instances of the CAs numerically. To do this we must consider the fact that there is a limited subset of codes which will preserve the patterns in the MD. To identify such pattern-preserving codes (PPC) we appeal to a statistical methodology. It is possible to statistically identify a set of PPCs by selectively sampling a bounded number of codes (corresponding to the different instances of the CAs) and demanding the method to set the size of the sample dynamically. Two issues have to be considered for this method to be defined in practice: (a) How to set the size of the sample and (b) How to define the adequateness of the codes. In this paper we discuss the method and present a case of study wherein the appropriateness of the method is illustrated.

Keywords: Mixed databases · Experimental probability distributions
Non-linear regression

1 Introduction

Cluster Analysis is the name given to a diverse collection of techniques that can be used to classify objects in a structured database. The classification will depend upon the particular method used because it is possible to measure similarity and dissimilarity (distance between the objects in the DB) in many ways. Once having selected the distance measure we must choose the clustering algorithm. There are many methods available. Five classical ones are (a) Average Linkage Clustering, (b) Complete Linkage Clustering, (c) Single Linkage Clustering, (d) Within Groups Clustering, (e) Ward's Method [1]. Alternative methods, based on computational intelligence, are (f) K-Means, (g) Fuzzy C-Means, (h) Self-Organizing Maps, (i) Fuzzy Learning Vector Quantization [2]. All of these methods have been designed to tackle the analysis of strictly numerical databases, i.e. those in which all the attributes are directly expressible as numbers.

If any of the attributes is non-numerical (i.e. categorical) none of the methods in the list is applicable. Clustering of categorical attributes (i.e., attributes whose domain is

© Springer International Publishing AG, part of Springer Nature 2018
J. F. Martínez-Trinidad et al. (Eds.): MCPR 2018, LNCS 10880, pp. 178–188, 2018.
https://doi.org/10.1007/978-3-319-92198-3_18

not numeric) is a difficult, yet important task: many fields, from statistics to psychology deal with categorical data. In spite of its importance, the task of categorical clustering has received relatively scant attention. Much of the published algorithms to cluster categorical data rely on the usage of a distance metric that captures the separation between two vectors of categorical attributes, such as the Jaccard coefficient [3]. An interesting alternative is explored in [4] where COOLCAT, a method which uses the notion of entropy to group records, is presented. It is based on information loss minimization. Another reason for the limited exploration of categorical clustering techniques is its inherent difficulty.

In [5] a different approach is taken by (a) Preserving the patterns embedded in the database and (b) Pinpointing the codes which preserve such patterns. These two steps result in the correct identification of a set of PPCs. The resulting algorithm is called CENG (Categorical Encoding with Neural Networks and Genetic Algorithms) and its parallelized version ParCENG [6].

However, this approach is computationally very demanding and, to boost its efficiency, it ought to be tackled in ensembles of multiple CPUs. Even so, when the number of CAs and/or the number of category's instances is large, execution time may grow exponentially. A practical alternative to ParCENG is the main subject of this paper.

Two notes are in order:

(a) As already pointed out, the execution time of CENG (and even ParCENG's) may grow exponentially.
(b) The PPCs are NOT to be assumed as an instance applicable to DBs other than the original one. That is to say: a set of PPCs (say PPC1) obtained from a DB (say DB1) is not applicable to a different DB (say DB2) even if DB1 and DB2 are structurally identical. In other words, PPC1 $\neq$ PPC2 for the same DB when the tuples of such DB are different,

The rest of the paper is organized as follows. In Sect. 2 we briefly describe (a) Pseudo-binary encoding alternative to our approach and (b) The optimization problem CENG solves. In Sect. 3 we present the statistical encoding methodology. In Sect. 4 we present some experimental results and, finally, in Sect. 5 we present our conclusions.

2   Encoding Mixed Databases

As stated in the introduction, the basic idea is to apply clustering algorithms designed for strictly numerical databases (ND) to MDs by encoding the instances of categorical variables with a number. This is by no means a new concept. MDs, however, offer a particular challenge when clustering is attempted because it is, in principle, impossible to impose a metric on CAs. There is no way in which numerical codes may be assigned to the CAs in general.

2.1   Pseudo-Binary Encoding

In what follows we denote the i instances of categorical variable c as ci; the number of categorical variables with c; the number of all attributes by n.

A common choice is to replace every CA variable by a set of binary variables, each corresponding to the cis. The CAs in the MD are replaced by numerical ones where every categorical variable is replaced by a set of ci binary numerical codes. An MD will be replaced by an ND with $n-c + c \cdot ci$ variables. This approach suffers from the following limitations:

(a) The number of attributes of ND will be larger than that of MD. In many cases this leads to unwieldy databases which are more difficult to store and handle.

(b) The type of coding system selected implies an *a priori* choice since all pseudo-binary variables may be assigned any two values (typically "0" denotes "absence"; "1" denotes "presence"). This choice is subjective. Any two different values are possible. Nevertheless, the mathematical properties of ND will vary with the different choices, thus leading to clusters which depend on the way in which "presence" or "absence" is encoded.

(c) Finally, with this sort of scheme the pseudo-binary variables do no longer reflect the essence of the idea conveyed by a category. A variable corresponding to the *i-th* instance of the category reflects the way a tuple is "affected" by belonging to the *i-th* categorical value, which is correct. But now the original issue "How does the behavior of the individuals change according to the category?" is replaced by "How does the behavior of the individuals change when the category's value is the *i-th*?" The two questions are not interchangeable.

2.2   Pattern Preserving Codes

An alternative goal is to assign codes (which we call Pattern Preserving Codes or PPCs) to each and all the instances of every class (category) which will preserve the patterns present for a given MD.

Consider a set of n-dimensional tuples (say U) whose cardinality is m. Assume there are n unknown functions of $n-1$ variables each, which we denote with

$$f_k(v_1, \ldots, v_{k-1}, v_{k+1}, \ldots, v_n); k = 1, \ldots, n$$

Let us also assume that there is a method which allows us to approximate f_k (from the tuples) with F_k. Denote the resulting n functions of $n-1$ independent variables with F_i, thus

$$F_k \approx f(v_1, \ldots, v_{k-1}, v_{k+1}, \ldots, v_n); k = 1, \ldots, n \tag{1}$$

The difference between f_k and F_k will be denoted with ε_k such that, for attribute k and the m tuples in the database

$$\varepsilon_k = \max[abs(f_{ki} - F_{ki})]; i = 1, \ldots, m \tag{2}$$

Our contention is that the PPCs are the ones which minimize ε_k for all k. This is so because only those codes which retain the relationships between variable k and the remaining $n-1$ variables AND do this for ALL variables in the ensemble will preserve the whole set of relations (i.e. patterns) present in the data base, as in (3).

$$\Xi = min[max\,(\varepsilon_k; k = 1, \ldots, n)] \tag{3}$$

Notice that this is a multi-objective optimization problem because complying with condition k in (2) for any given value of k may induce the non-compliance for a different possible k. Using the min-max expression of (3) equates to selecting a particular point in the Pareto's front [7].

To achieve the purported goal we must have a tool which is capable of identifying the F_k's in (1) and the codes which attain the minimization of (3). This is possible using NNs and GAs. Theoretical considerations (see, for instance, [8–11]) ensure the effectiveness of the method.

3   General Methodology

To avoid the high computational costs associated to CENG we designed a new algorithm (called "CESAMO": Categorical Encoding by Statistical Applied Modeling) which relies on statistical and numerical considerations making the application of NNs and GAs unnecessary, while achieving analogous results.

Here we denote the number of tuples in the DB by t and the number of categorical attributes by c; the number of numerical attributes by n; the i-th categorical variable by vi; the value obtained for variable i as a function of variable j by $yi(j)$.

We will sample the codes yielding yi as a function of a sought for relationship. This relationship and the model of the population it implies, will be selected so as to preserve the behavioral patterns embedded in the DB.

Two issues are of primordial importance in the proposed methodology:

(a) How to define the function which will preserve the patterns.
(b) How to determine the number of codes to sample.

Regarding (a), we use a mathematical model considering high order relations, as will be discussed below. Regarding (b), we know that, independently of the distribution of the yi's, the distribution of the means of the samples of yi (yi_{AVG}) will become Gaussian. Once the distribution of the yi_{AVG} becomes Gaussian, we will have achieved statistical stability, in the sense that further sampling of the yi's will not significantly modify the characterization of the population.

In essence, therefore, what we propose is to sample enough codes to guarantee the statistical stability of the values calculated from $yi \leftarrow f(vj)$. If $f(vj)$ is adequately chosen the codes corresponding to the best approximation will be those inserted in MD. Furthermore, CESAMO relies on a double level sampling: only pairs of variables are considered and every pair is, in itself, sampling the multivariate space. This avoids the need to explicitly solve the multi-objective optimization underlying problem. The clustering problem may be, then, numerically tackled.

3.1 The CESAMO Algorithm

The general algorithm for CESAMO is as follows:

- Specify the mixed database MD.
- Specify the sample size (ss)
- MD is analyzed to determine n, t and $ci(i)$ for $i = 1,...,c$.
- The numerical data are assumed to have been mapped into [0,1). Therefore, every ci will be, likewise, in [0,1).

$$
\begin{aligned}
&\text{for } i \leftarrow 1 \text{ to } c \\
&\qquad \text{Do until the distribution of } yi_{AVG} \text{ is Gaussian} \\
&\qquad\qquad \text{Randomly select variable } j \ (j \neq i) \\
&\qquad\qquad \text{Assign random values to all instances of } vi. \\
&\qquad\qquad yi_{AVG} \leftarrow 0 \\
&\qquad\qquad \text{For } k \leftarrow 1 \text{ to ss} \\
&\qquad\qquad\qquad yi \leftarrow f(vj) \\
&\qquad\qquad\qquad yi_{AVG} \leftarrow yi_{AVG} + yi \\
&\qquad\qquad \text{endfor} \\
&\qquad\qquad yi_{AVG} = yi_{AVG}/ss \\
&\qquad \text{enddo} \\
&\qquad \text{Select the codes corresponding to the best value of } yi \\
&\text{endfor}
\end{aligned}
$$

Notice that vj may be, itself, categorical. In that cases every categorical instance of vj is replaced by random codes so that we may calculate $f(vj)$.

4 Experimental Results

We illustrate the method with a simple DB (MD1) (Fig. 1).

V001	V002	V003	V004	V005	V006	V007	V008	V009
0.260522524543	0.509414653392	0.700915045452	0.707703920124	PUEBLA	0.943069979969	0.238061468236	0.139019787187	E
0.407041640749	0.637259876341	0.789221078153	0.556251922946	ZACATECAS	0.708160858038	0.421635467433	0.007609086010	E
0.535205277140	0.731029964609	0.648474125909	0.429007103388	JALISCO	0.961372002944	0.044127392956	0.101728142478	F
0.126772292602	0.354737576201	0.577610777361	0.852891723761	ZACATECAS	0.827321987848	0.334048866287	0.057648763948	E
0.469300405953	0.684411776614	0.819523265893	0.493880044410	MORELOS	0.896873485346	0.279710631585	0.103735589373	F
0.877291352488	0.936508870108	0.966276475038	0.108861371866	QUERETARO	0.323149913797	0.719992235632	0.223451376457	D
0.592027568409	0.768962277686	0.871359035707	0.373968286977	MORELOS	0.942230907053	0.026164386062	0.083310044031	A
0.933211797131	0.965959479230	0.982056648825	0.058890803985	JALISCO	0.993506894522	0.166548211151	0.169576293996	D

Fig. 1. Mixed data base 1 (MD1)

It consists of 9 variables. Two of them V005 and V009 are categorical. The rest are numerical. V005 has 10 instances: AGUASCALIENTES, BAJA CALIFORNIA, HIDALGO, JALISCO, MEXICO MORELOS, PUEBLA, QUERETARO, SAN LUIS, ZACATECAS; V009 has 6 instances: A, B, C, D, E, F.

4.1 First Order Relations (Pearson's Correlation)

To illustrate, we select Pearson's correlation coefficient as the approximation function from which we select the best codes. 36 samples/mean are selected; the compliance to Gaussian distribution is determined using the chi^2 goodness-of-fit test where 10 classes are defined. For this initial example we demand that maximum correlation is used as the best coding criterion. This is illustrated in Fig. 2.

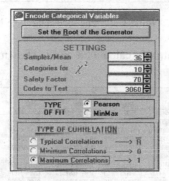

Fig. 2. Using Pearson's correlation

CESAMO is run. The codes of Fig. 3 are determined.

V005		V009	
Instance	Code	Instance	Code
AGUASCALIENTES	0.349731867	A	0.349731867
BAJA CALIFORNIA	0.954384493	B	0.954384493
HIDALGO	0.402948057	C	0.402948057
JALISCO	0.472595298	D	0.472595298
MEXICO	0.446255052	E	0.446255052
MORELOS	0.384697858	F	0.384697858
PUEBLA	0.216253521		
QUERETARO	0.140711205		
SAN LUIS	0.541695057		
ZACATECAS	0.276464318		

Fig. 3. Categorical codes for Pearson's correlation

The resulting encoded DB (ND1, with numerical values) is illustrated in Fig. 4. In this latter case, instead of calculating Pearson's correlation coefficient, we approximate variable yi as a function of variable of randomly selected independent variables using the so-called Ascent Algorithm [12, 13]. This algorithm has several useful properties: it allows us to determine the form of the approximant dynamically (that is, there is no pre-determined model for the function which approximates the data) and it does not need to store the whole data set in the computer's memory. It works by minimizing the L∞ norm rather than the more common L2. It is an exchange algorithm and requires a minimum amount of storage. This characteristic is most important when the data sets are large, as is often the case when mining DBs.

V001	V002	V003	V004	V005	V006	V007	V008	V009
0.2605252454300000	0.5094146533920000	0.7009150454520000	0.7077039201240000	0.21625	0.9430699799690000	0.2380614682360000	0.1380197871870000	0.44626
0.4070416407490000	0.6372589763410000	0.7892210781530000	0.5562519229460000	0.27645	0.7081608580380000	0.4216354674330000	0.0076090860100000	0.44626
0.5352052771400000	0.7310289646090000	0.8484741259090000	0.4290071033880000	0.47260	0.9613720029440000	0.0441273929580000	0.1017281424780000	0.38470
0.1267722926020000	0.3547375762010000	0.5776107773610000	0.8528917237610000	0.27646	0.8273219878480000	0.3340488662870000	0.0576487639480000	0.44626
0.4693004058530000	0.6844117766140000	0.8195232658930000	0.4938800444100000	0.38470	0.8968734853460000	0.2797106315850000	0.1037355893730000	0.38470
0.8772913524880000	0.9365089701080000	0.9662764750380000	0.1088613718660000	0.14071	0.3231499137970000	0.7199922356320000	0.2234513764570000	0.47260
0.5920275684090000	0.7689622776960000	0.8713590357070000	0.3739682869770000	0.38470	0.9422309070530000	0.0261643860620000	0.0833100440310000	0.34973
0.9332117971310000	0.9659594792300000	0.9820566488250000	0.0588908039850000	0.47260	0.9935068945220000	0.1665482111510000	0.1695762939960000	0.47260

Fig. 4. Numerically encoded data base ND1.

Pearson's correlation matrix is calculated and is shown in Fig. 5.

Correlated Variables	V001	V002	V003	V004	V005	V006	V007	V008	V009
V001	1.0000000000	0.9667892446	0.8983654887	-.9992139571	-.0252328986	-.0272705682	0.0340336531	-.0355132100	0.0069956907
V002	0.9667892446	1.0000000000	0.9784369164	-.9753008217	-.0264562494	-.0207185062	0.0298000972	-.0416465760	-.0011871033
V003	0.8983654887	0.9784369164	1.0000000000	-.9120617615	-.0251193560	-.0137345053	0.0243521074	-.0439454471	-.0061451268
V004	-.9992139571	-.9753008217	-.9120617615	1.0000000000	0.0254926026	0.0261284578	-.0333133847	0.0367530663	-.0059776316
V005	-.0252328986	-.0264562494	-.0251193560	0.0254926026	1.0000000000	-.0056924319	0.0104995665	0.0314667573	0.0017212012
V006	-.0272705682	-.0207185062	-.0137345053	0.0261284578	-.0056924319	1.0000000000	-.9692992222	-.6085091576	-.0186728830
V007	0.0340336531	0.0298000972	0.0243521074	-.0333133847	0.0104995665	-.9692992222	1.0000000000	0.5691163152	0.0039904819
V008	-.0355132100	-.0416465760	-.0439454471	0.0367530663	0.0314667573	-.6085091576	0.5691163152	1.0000000000	0.0283394586
V009	0.0069956907	-.0011871033	-.0061451268	-.0059776316	0.0017212012	-.0186728830	0.0039904819	0.0283394586	1.0000000000

Fig. 5. Correlation matrix.

From the table above we next obtain the table of relations, as shown in Fig. 6. Those variables exhibiting a value above a predetermined threshold are marked.

Significance % 90								
Correlated Variables	V001	V002	V003	V004	V005	V006	V007	V008	V009
V001		×		×					
V002			×	×					
V003				×					
V004									
V005									
V006							×		
V007									
V008									
V009									

Fig. 6. First order dependencies

As we can see, in ND1 variables V001, V002, V003 are "equivalent" with 90% confidence if only first order relations are preserved. Likewise, V006 and V007 are linearly equivalent.

4.2 Higher Order Relations (Functional Approximation)

Now we select an approximation function of 11th degree. In [14] it was shown that continuous data may be thusly approximated and its main components retained.

The codes obtained from high degree approximation are shown in Fig. 7. Notice that the codes do not seem to display any relation to the ones obtained from Pearsons's Correlation.

V005		V009	
Instance	Code	Instance	Code
AGUASCALIENTES	0.43963343	A	0.00517244
BAJA CALIFORNIA	0.44122174	B	0.60492887
HIDALGO	0.26234098	C	0.40085276
JALISCO	0.51601808	D	0.6773322
MEXICO	0.42692392	E	0.92045191
MORELOS	0.63528312	F	0.51587932
PUEBLA	0.8265257		
QUERETARO	0.20145042		
SAN LUIS	0.64382076		
ZACATECAS	0.60366524		

Fig. 7. Categorical codes for unbounded approximation

We, once again, calculate the correlation matrix as shown in Fig. 8.

	V001	V002	V003	V004	V005	V006	V007	V008	V009
V001	1.0000000000	0.9667892446	0.8983654887	-.9992139571	0.0592971389	-.0272705682	0.0340336531	-.0355132100	-.0075227681
V002	0.9667892446	1.0000000000	0.9784369164	-.9763008217	0.0502771788	-.0207185062	0.0298000872	.0416465760	-.0116309630
V003	0.8983654887	0.9784369164	1.0000000000	-.9120617615	0.0589621759	-.0137345053	0.0243521074	-.0439454471	-.0093939537
V004	-.9992139571	-.9753008217	-.9120617615	1.0000000000	-.0586083162	0.0261284578	-.0333133847	0.0367530663	0.0089823674
V005	0.0592971389	0.0582771788	0.0589621759	.0586003162	1.0000000000	0.0398152441	-.0263511824	-.0098329750	0.0358562580
V006	-.0272705682	-.0207185062	-.0137345053	0.0261284578	0.0398152441	1.0000000000	-.9692992222	-.6085091576	0.0430063404
V007	0.0340336531	0.0298000872	0.0243521074	-.0333133847	-.0263511824	-.9692992222	1.0000000000	0.5691163152	-.0493044161
V008	-.0355132100	-.0416465760	-.0439454471	0.0367530663	-.0098329750	-.6085091576	0.5691163152	1.0000000000	-.0483248681
V009	-.0075227681	-.0116309639	-.0093939537	0.0089823674	0.0358562580	0.0430063404	-.0493044161	-.0483248681	1.0000000000

Fig. 8. Pearson's correlation matrix for high order relation codes.

And, as expected, the variables display the same level of first order relations.

Significance %								
90								
Correlated Variables								
	V001	V002	V003	V004	V005	V006	V007	V008	V009
V001		X		X					
V002			X	X					
V003				X					
V004									
V005									
V006							X		
V007									
V008									
V009									

Fig. 9. First order dependencies

However, for the relations of order 3 codes from a) Pearson's and b) Functional codes we find the next scenario (shown in Fig. 10). Pearson's correlations miss third degree functional relations for variables V003 and V004. Likewise, (as shown in Fig. 11), 7th degree relations are hidden from Pearson's encoding but not so for Functional encoding. Note that in all the cases illustrated in Figs. 9, 10 and 11 functional relations are restricted to those of degree 1, 3 and 7, respectively.

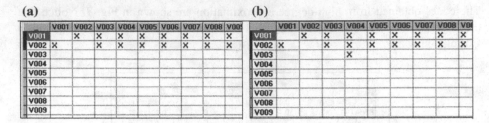

Fig. 10. Relations of degree 3 for (a) Pearson's codes and (b) Functional codes.

(a)

	V001	V002	V003	V004	V005	V006	V007	V008	V009
V001									
V002									
V003									
V004									
V005									
V006									
V007									
V008									
V009									

(b)

	V001	V002	V003	V004	V005	V006	V007	V008	V009
V001		×	×	×	×	×	×	×	×
V002	×		×	×	×	×	×	×	×
V003			×						
V004									
V005									
V006									
V007									
V008									
V009									

Fig. 11. Relations of degree 7 for (a) Pearson's codes and (b) Functional codes.

However, when functional codes consider all combinations of the powers of the function, we get the matrix illustrated in Fig. 12.

	V001	V002	V003	V004	V005	V006	V007	V008	V009
V001	1.0000000000	0.5351914557	0.5351914578	0.5351915232	0.5347595189	0.5351898425	0.5351871862	0.5351152174	0.2546840427
V002	0.5351805544	1.0000000000	0.5351862603	0.5351810995	0.5350538593	0.5351529387	0.5351530274	0.5317462920	0.5351522602
V003	0.5351037593	0.5351600780	1.0000000000	0.5351029048	0.5350206518	0.5350271954	0.5350221373	0.5098745497	0.4978701143
V004	0.5351915053	0.5351913809	0.5351910977	1.0000000000	0.5346712155	0.5351893965	0.5351573240	0.3457246016	0.0000000000
V005	0.5342934150	0.5342906928	0.5342924304	0.5342849135	1.0000000000	0.5342953904	0.5343094442	0.5342968509	0.5339350270
V006	0.5340588345	0.5340522215	0.5340606606	0.5340572362	0.5340503747	1.0000000000	0.5351446651	0.4881534669	0.5339557111
V007	0.5342328419	0.5342165796	0.5342032238	0.5342168610	0.5342194780	0.5348306875	1.0000000000	0.5151432500	0.5340178212
V008	0.5341517901	0.5342171171	0.5341199116	0.5340589879	0.5316718687	0.5351294259	0.5347265164	1.0000000000	0.5341438147
V009	0.5341523831	0.5341537751	0.5341471788	0.5341423750	0.5335682371	0.5341595085	0.5341553888	0.5341529202	1.0000000000

Fig. 12. Matrix of relations for full power combinations.

In this case the approximation is so accurate that all variables appear related EXCEPT for a few, as shown in Fig. 13.

	V001	V002	V003	V004	V005	V006	V007	V008	V009
V001		×	×	×	×	×	×	×	
V002	×		×	×	×	×	×	×	×
V003	×	×		×	×	×	×	×	
V004	×	×	×			×	×	×	
V005	×	×	×	×		×	×	×	×
V006	×	×		×	×		×	×	
V007	×	×	×	×	×		×	×	
V008	×	×	×	×	×	×		×	
V009	×	×	×	×	×	×	×		

Fig. 13. Independent variables.

It is the lack of simple relation of the variables remarked (with circles) which makes this case more interesting. For what we may see is that V001 and V009 have no detectable complex relations between them. That is the case for V003 and V009; V004 and V008 and so on. Notice also that this means that, for instance, V003 may not be expressed as a function of V009 but V009 may indeed be expressed as a function of V003. The preservation of these higher order relationships is what we mean by preserving the patterns in the data.

5 Conclusions

When mining arbitrary data it is very important to preserve the relation between their components. By approximating the elements in mixed DBs we have been able to do so. Given this we may now confidently look for the potential groupings that depend on functional dependencies.

The final goal of this methodology is to ensure that such hypothetical groups may be efficiently searched for.

We have focused on illustrating the behavior of a simple mixed database. But the algorithm behind this method is guaranteed to work smoothly even for very large data sets.

The mathematical description of the way the functional relationships are found is beyond the scope of this work. But we expect to report on this in a paper to appear soon.

References

1. Norusis, M.: SPSS 16.0 Statistical Procedures Companion. Prentice Hall Press, Upper Saddle River (2008)
2. Goebel, M., Gruenwald, L.: A survey of data mining and knowledge discovery software tools. ACM SIGKDD Explor. Newslett. 1(1), 20–33 (1999)
3. Sokal, R.R.: The principles of numerical taxonomy: twenty-five years later. Comput. Assist. Bact. Syst. 15, 1 (1985)
4. Barbará, D., Li, Y., Couto, J.: COOLCAT: an entropy-based algorithm for categorical clustering. In: Proceedings of the Eleventh International Conference on Information and Knowledge Management, pp. 582–589. ACM (2002)
5. Kuri-Morales, A.F.: Categorical encoding with neural networks and genetic algorithms. In: Zhuang, X., Guarnaccia, C. (eds.) WSEAS Proceedings of the 6th International Conference on Applied Informatics and Computing Theory, pp. 167–175 (2015). ISBN 9781618043139, ISBN 1790-5109
6. Kuri-Morales, A., Sagastuy-Breña, J.: A parallel genetic algorithm for pattern recognition in mixed databases. In: Carrasco-Ochoa, J.A., Martínez-Trinidad, J.F., Olvera-López, J.A. (eds.) MCPR 2017. LNCS, vol. 10267, pp. 13–21. Springer, Cham (2017). https://doi.org/10.1007/978-3-319-59226-8_2
7. Deb, K., Agrawal, S., Pratap, A., Meyarivan, T.: A fast elitist non-dominated sorting genetic algorithm for multi-objective optimization: NSGA-II. In: Schoenauer, M., Deb, K., Rudolph, G., Yao, X., Lutton, E., Merelo, J.J., Schwefel, H.-P. (eds.) PPSN 2000. LNCS, vol. 1917, pp. 849–858. Springer, Heidelberg (2000). https://doi.org/10.1007/3-540-45356-3_83

8. Cybenko, G.: Approximation by superpositions of a sigmoidal function. Math. Control Signals Syst. **2**(4), 303–314 (1989)
9. Rudolph, G.: Convergence analysis of canonical genetic algorithms. IEEE Trans. Neural Netw. **5**(1), 96–101 (1994)
10. Kuri-Morales, A., Aldana-Bobadilla, E.: The best genetic algorithm I. In: Castro, F., Gelbukh, A., González, M. (eds.) Advances in Soft Computing and Its Applications. LNCS (LNAI), vol. 8266, pp. 1–15. Springer, Heidelberg (2013). https://doi.org/10.1007/978-3-642-45111-9_1
11. Widrow, B., Lehr, M.A.: 30 years of adaptive neural networks: perceptron, madaline, and backpropagation. Proc. IEEE **78**(9), 1415–1442 (1990)
12. Cheney, E.W.: Multivariate Approximation Theory: Selected Topics. CBMS-NSF Regional Series in Applied Mathematics. S.I.A.M, Philadelphia (1986)
13. Cheney, E.W.: Introduction to Approximation Theory. McGraw-Hill Book Company, New York (1966)
14. Kuri-Morales, A., Cartas-Ayala, A.: Polynomial multivariate approximation with genetic algorithms. In: Sokolova, M., van Beek, P. (eds.) AI 2014. LNCS (LNAI), vol. 8436, pp. 307–312. Springer, Cham (2014). https://doi.org/10.1007/978-3-319-06483-3_30

Image Clustering Based on Frequent Approximate Subgraph Mining

Niusvel Acosta-Mendoza[1,2](✉), Jesús Ariel Carrasco-Ochoa[2],
José Fco. Martínez-Trinidad[2], Andrés Gago Alonso[1],
and José E. Medina-Pagola[1]

[1] Advanced Technologies Application Center (CENATAV),
7a # 21406 e/214 and 216, Siboney, Playa, CP: 12200 Havana, Cuba
{nacosta,agago,jmedina}@cenatav.co.cu
[2] Instituto Nacional de Astrofísica, Óptica y Electrónica (INAOE),
Luis Enrique Erro No. 1, Sta. María Tonantzintla, CP: 72840 Puebla, Mexico
{nacosta,ariel,fmartine}@ccc.inaoep.mx

Abstract. Frequent approximate subgraph (FAS) mining and graph clustering are important techniques in Data Mining with great practical relevance. In FAS mining, some approximations in data are allowed for identifying graph patterns, which could be used for solving other pattern recognition tasks like supervised classification and clustering. In this paper, we explore the use of the patterns identified by a FAS mining algorithm on a graph collection for image clustering. Some experiments are performed on image databases for showing that by using the FASs mined from a graph collection under the bag of features image approach, it is possible to improve the clustering results reported by other state-of-the-art methods.

Keywords: Approximate graph mining
Approximate graph matching · Graph clustering

1 Introduction

Frequent approximate subgraph (FAS) mining and graph clustering are important techniques in Data Mining with a wide spectrum of applications, such as: community detection, web image searching, and image categorization, among others [1–8]. In FAS mining, some approximation in data are allowed for identifying graph patterns which are missed when an exact graph matching is applied. Then, knowing that, in real-world applications, commonly there are data variations due to noise or natural variation on the study objects, several algorithms for mining FASs have been proposed [2,9–12]. These algorithms allow mining graph patterns, which, when used on supervised classification tasks, allow obtaining better results than using exact graph patterns [9,10,13,14]. However, the use of FASs has been little explored as a mean for extracting information useful for data

© Springer International Publishing AG, part of Springer Nature 2018
J. F. Martínez-Trinidad et al. (Eds.): MCPR 2018, LNCS 10880, pp. 189–198, 2018.
https://doi.org/10.1007/978-3-319-92198-3_19

clustering. To the best of our knowledge, only the work proposed in [1] introduces a method based on FAS mining for graph clustering. This method is based on FASs mined independently over each single-graph. However, we consider that FASs mined from a graph collection could provide more useful information for graph clustering tasks. For this reason, in this paper, unlike [1], we explore the use of the patterns identified by a FAS mining algorithm designed for mining FAS from a graph collection for image clustering.

The organization of this paper is the following. In Sect. 2, the related work is summarized. Our proposed method based on FAS mining for graph clustering is introduced in Sect. 3. Our experimentation is presented in Sect. 4. Finally, our conclusions and future work directions are discussed in Sect. 5.

2   Related Work

In the literature, some works have focused on graph clustering based on pattern mining [1,15,16]. In [15,16], emerging patterns are used as features for clustering, but only in [1], FAS mining has been used for graph clustering. In this later work, the authors take advantage of approximate graph mining to obtain useful patterns, which could be missed by using exact graph matching, and use this patterns for graph clustering.

In [1], after representing images as graphs, the authors used MaxAFG [17] for separately mining FASs from each single-graph of a collection. Later, joining all mined FASs, a vector representation is built for each image by comparing its representing graph to each FAS using a similarity function based on the graph edit distance [18–20]. Thus, a traditional clustering algorithm can be applied.

The graph clustering approach proposed in [1] is based on algorithms for mining FASs over a single-graph; allowing variations in vertex and edge labels, as well as approximations in the graph structure. However, allowing all these kinds of approximations highly increases the computational cost of the FASs mining process, because allowing label substitutions and approximations in the graph structure produces a combinatorial explosion of the number of candidate subgraphs. On the other hand, despite mining FASs separately into every single graphs has some advantages, it avoids detecting common parts among different graphs that are not frequent inside any of them. Thus, in this paper, we propose a FAS-based clustering method that uses FASs mined from graph collections, in order to allow detecting regularities among different graphs of the collection. Moreover, we propose using FAS mining algorithms where only approximations in vertex and edge labels are allowed but preserving the graph structure; in order to allow a faster mining process. However, only VEAM [13] allows mining this kind of FASs, in the next section, the VEAM algorithm will be briefly described.

2.1   The VEAM Algorithm

The VEAM (Vertex and Edge Approximate graph Miner) algorithm [13] mines all FASs in a graph collection allowing approximations in vertex and edge labels, keeping the graph structure. For allowing these approximations, VEAM uses substitution matrices (one for edge labels ME and another one for vertex labels MV), which contain the probability of a label to be replaced by another one. Based on these matrices, the similarity function between graphs used by VEAM is defined as follows.

Definition 1 (Similarity function $\Theta_{(f,g)}$ based on substitution matrices).
Let G_1 and G_2 be two graphs, and let MV and ME be two substitution matrices in L_V and L_E, respectively. The similarity function is defined as:

$$\Theta_{(f,g)}(G_1,G_2) = \prod_{v \in V_{G_1}} \frac{MV_{I_{G_1}(v),I_{G_2}(f(v))}}{MV_{I_{G_1}(v),I_{G_1}(v)}} * \prod_{e \in E_{G_1}} \frac{ME_{J_{G_1}(e),J_{G_2}(g(e))}}{ME_{J_{G_1}(e),J_{G_1}(e)}} \quad (1)$$

where (f,g) is an isomorphism between G_1 and G_2, $MV_{I_{G_1}(v),I_{G_2}(f(v))}$ and $MV_{I_{G_1}(v),I_{G_1}(v)}$ are the cells $MV_{i,j}$ and $MV_{i,i}$ respectively of the vertex substitution matrix with $i = I_{G_1}(v)$ and $j = I_{G_2}(f(v))$, and $ME_{J_{G_1}(e),J_{G_2}(g(e))}$ and $ME_{J_{G_1}(e),J_{G_1}(e)}$ are the cells $ME_{q,r}$ and $ME_{q,q}$ respectively of the edge substitution matrix with $q = J_{G_1}(e)$ and $r = J_{G_2}(g(e))$. Notice that, as the function $\Theta_{(f,g)}$ is based on substitution matrices and these matrices could be non-symmetric, then this similarity function also could be non symmetric.

Based on Definition 1, VEAM computes and stores all the occurrences of each subgraph candidate P_j in a graph collection D. Then, taking into account the occurrences of P_j, only the subset of graphs $D_j \subseteq D$, where P_j has at least one occurrence, is traversed for growing P_j. In this way, VEAM reduces the search space to D_j; speeding up the mining process.

VEAM uses adjacency matrices for representing each graph of a collection. Then, in order to simplify the graph representation based on adjacency matrices, VEAM uses the canonical adjacency matrix (CAM) code as a unique representation for isomorphic graphs [21,22].

The VEAM algorithm starts mining all frequent approximate single-vertex subgraphs. Then, following a *Depth-First Search* (DFS) approach, each frequent single-vertex G is extended by recursively adding a single-edge at a time; obtaining all children of G.

In the recursive pattern-growth step of VEAM, all children of each FAS G that satisfy the similarity constraint using Definition 1, are computed; each child of G is a candidate graph. As the same subgraph can be obtained from different candidate graphs, an isomorphism test over each computed candidate should be performed for eliminating duplicate candidates. For speeding up these isomorphism tests, each FAS is represented by its canonical form based on CAM. By comparing the CAM codes of the subgraphs, the isomorphic candidates (i.e., duplicate candidates) and only one of them is extended for exploring the search space. These comparisons between CAM codes allow us to eliminate duplicities in the candidate set. Once the candidate set is computed, only those frequent candidates that have not been not identified in previous steps, are stored as FASs in the collection and recursively extended. The stop condition in the recursion is supported by the downward closure property, which ensures that a non-frequent candidate cannot be extended to produce a FAS.

More details of VEAM can be found in [13].

3 Our Proposal

Our proposal for clustering images using FASs, mined from graph collections, as attributes is as follows. First, given a collection of images, each image is represented as a graph. Then, the VEAM algorithm [13] is applied over the graph collection obtained from the image collection, in order to identify the set of FASs. After, following the idea of the bag of features [23], the mined FASs are used as attributes for building a vectorial representation of each image. For an image, each element of its vectorial representation contains the similarity of a FAS with the graph representing the image. The similarity between a FASs and a graph is computed with the similarity function used in VEAM for the approximate graph mining process. In Fig. 1, we illustrate how the FASs are used for building the attribute vectors of the image collection.

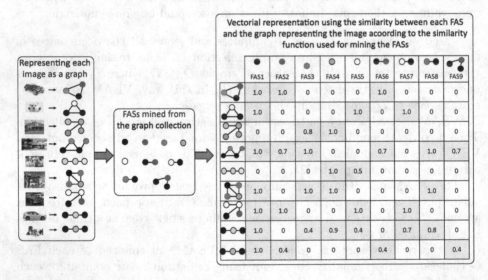

Fig. 1. Example of how the FASs are used for building the vectorial representation of the images.

Once the vectorial representation is built, a traditional clustering algorithm is applied on it for clustering the images according to their similarities computed on their FAS-based representation. A diagram of the workflow of our proposal is shown in Fig. 2.

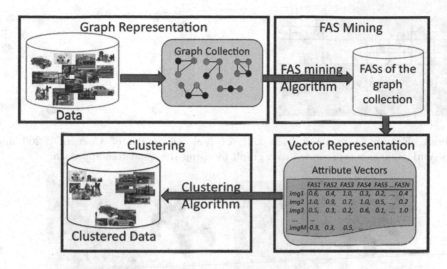

Fig. 2. Workflow of our proposal for image clustering based on FAS mining.

4 Experiments

Following the clustering method described in Sect. 3, we perform some experiments over three graph collections for showing the usefulness of using FASs computed from a graph collection in a clustering task. All our experiments were carried out on a personal computer with an Intel(R) Core(TM) i5-3317U CPU @1.70 GHz with 8 GB of RAM. All the algorithms were implemented in ANSI-C and executed on Microsoft Windows 10.

The three image collections used in our experiments are CoenenDB-200 and SkeletonDB used in [1], and CoenenDB-6000. Both CoenenDB-200 and CoenenDB-6000 image collections were generated with the Random image generator of Coenen[1]. CoenenDB-200 is composed by 200 images with two classes (100 images per class) and CoenenDB-6000 contains 6000 images also distributed in two classes. For our experiments, the class was not used as attribute. For both CoenenDB-200 and CoenenDB-6000, each image is represented as a graph following a quad-tree strategy of 4 and 3 levels respectively, using each quadrant as a vertex with the most frequent color as label with edges connecting neighboring vertices (vertices representing neighboring quadrants) using the angle respect to the horizontal axe as the label for the edges. In Fig. 3, we show an example of who an image of CoenenDB-200 is represented as a graph.

SkeletonDB is composed by 36 real-image silhouettes with nine classes (four images per class). In SkeletonDB, each image is represented as a graph extracted from its skeleton following [25], where the vertices are the junction and final points of the skeleton, labeled as body parts, and edges represent branches of

---

[1] www.csc.liv.ac.uk/~frans/KDD/Software/ImageGenerator/imageGenerator.html.

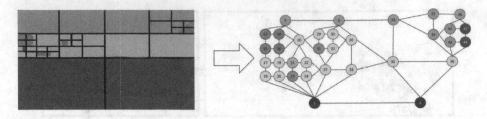

Fig. 3. Example, extracted from [24], of how an image of CoenenDB-200 and CoenenDB-6000 is represented as a graph by using the quad-tree approach.

Fig. 4. Example, extracted from [24], of how some images of SkeletonDB are represented as graphs.

the skeleton, labeled with the length of the branch in pixels. In Fig. 4, we show an example of who some images of SkeletonDB are represented as a graphs.

In Table 1, the description of the obtained graph collections is shown. The first column shows the collection identifier. The other columns show the number of graph in the collection, the average edges per graph, the average vertices per graph, and the number of classes of each collection, respectively.

Table 1. Description of the graph collections used in our experiments.

Collection	$|D|$	Average edges per graph	Average vertices per graph	Number of classes
CoenenDB-200	200	35	20	2
CoenenDB-6000	6000	12	8	2
SkeletonDB	36	6	7	9

In order to validate the clustering results, since we know the real classes of the graph collections, we apply the well known rand index measure [26] (see Definition 2), which is widely used in the literature as cluster quality index.

Definition 2 (Rand Index). Given a set of elements S, and two clusterings C and C', the rand index RI is defined as:

$$RI(C, C') = \frac{a + b}{a + b + c} \tag{2}$$

where:

- a is the number of pairs of elements in S that are in the same cluster in C and in the same cluster in C'
- b is the number of pairs of elements in S that are in different cluster in C and in different cluster in C'
- c is the number of pairs of elements in S that are not in a or b.

For mining FASs over graph collections, in our experiments we used VEAM [13] since this algorithm is the only one reported in the literature which allows label approximations preserving the graphs structures. For clustering, we used the well known k-means algorithm [27], specifically the WEKA implementation [28], where the value of k was fixed according to the number of classes in the used datasets.

With the aim of showing the usefulness of the FASs mined from a graph collection in an image clustering task, the results obtained by our method are compared against those reported in [1], where the usefulness of FASs separately mined from single-graphs was evaluated. We also compare our results against those obtained by applying the method reported in [29], which is based on spatial pyramid matching instead of FAS mining.

In Table 2, we show the clustering results obtained by our proposal, as well as using an approach based on separately mining FASs from single graphs [1], and the method proposed in [29]. In this table, the first column shows the graph collection identifier; the second one shows the clustering results, in terms of Rand Index, obtained by using the method proposed in [29]; the third column shows the clustering results, in terms of Rand Index, obtained by using the method proposed in [1]; and the last column shows the clustering results obtained by applying our proposal. The cells with "–" means that the method proposed in [1] cannot be applied since, due to the size of the collection, it was unable to mine the FASs after a weak; while our proposal only used less of two hours for processing this collection. In Table 2, the best results for each collection are highlighted in bold.

As we can see in Table 2, the clustering results obtained by the methods based on FASs are better than those obtained by the method proposed in [29] in all cases. In this way, the usefulness of the use of FAS mining for clustering tasks is shown. On the other hand, in CoenenDB-200 image collection, our proposal outperforms the results obtained by the using single graph FASs, as proposed in [1]. However, in the SkeletonDB image collection, the single graph FAS approach obtained slightly better results than our proposal. This fact takes place because the SkeletonDB image collection has very few graphs; thus, the graph collection FAS approach gets less information than the single graph approach. Nevertheless,

Table 2. Clustering results obtained by applying the k-means algorithm, evaluated with the rand index measure. The symbol "–" means that the corresponding method was unable to be applied.

Collection	The method proposed in [29]	The single graph [1]	Our proposed method
CoenenDB-200	0.657	0.768	**0.805**
SkeletonDB	0.652	**0.981**	0.978
CoenenDB-6000	0.705	–	**0.948**

as we can see in CoenenDB-6000 image collection, our proposal is able to process larger graph collections, which cannot be processed by the FAS-based method proposed in [1].

5   Conclusions

In this paper, we explore the usefulness of the FASs mined from a graph collection for clustering by introducing a FAS-based image clustering method that uses the mined FASs to represent images. Our proposal was tested over three image collections, comparing the obtained results against the results of two state-of-the-art clustering methods.

Based on our experiments, we conclude that FAS mining is useful for clustering tasks, outperforming the results obtained by a method based on spatial pyramid matching [29]. In our experiments, we have shown that using FASs mined from a graph collection as attributes, it is possible to obtain better results than those obtained by using FASs mined separately from single graphs.

As future work, we will corroborate our conclusions with a deeper and wider experimentation. Additionally, we plan to explore the usefulness of the FASs mined from multi-graph collections, for image clustering.

Acknowledgment. This work was partly supported by the National Council of Science and Technology of Mexico (CONACyT) through the scholarship grant 287045.

References

1. Flores-Garrido, M., Carrasco-Ochoa, J.A., Martínez-Trinidad, J.F.: Graph clustering via inexact patterns. In: Bayro-Corrochano, E., Hancock, E. (eds.) CIARP 2014. LNCS, vol. 8827, pp. 391–398. Springer, Cham (2014). https://doi.org/10.1007/978-3-319-12568-8_48
2. Morales-González, A., Acosta-Mendoza, N., Gago-Alonso, A., García-Reyes, E., Medina-Pagola, J.: A new proposal for graph-based image classification using frequent approximate subgraphs. Pattern Recogn. **47**(1), 169–177 (2014)
3. Herrera-Semenets, V., Acosta-Mendoza, N., Gago-Alonso, A.: A Framework for intrusion detection based on frequent subgraph mining. In: The 2nd SDM Workshop on Mining Networks and Graphs: A Big Data Analytic Challenge (SDM-Networks 2015), Vancouver, BC, Canada (2015)

4. Bai, L., Cheng, X., Liang, J., Guo, Y.: Fast graph clustering with a new description model for community detection. Inf. Sci. **388–389**, 37–47 (2017)
5. Yan, Y., Liu, G., Wang, S., Zhang, J., Zheng, K.: Graph-based clustering and ranking for diversified image search. Multimed. Syst. **23**, 41–52 (2017)
6. Viet-Vu, V., Hong-Quan, D.: Graph-based clustering with background knowledge. In: Proceedings of the Eighth International Symposium on Information and Communication Technology, SoICT 2017, pp. 167–172. ACM, New York (2017)
7. Ye, W., Zhou, L., Sun, X., Plant, C., Böhm, C.: Attributed graph clustering with unimodal normalized cut. In: Ceci, M., Hollmén, J., Todorovski, L., Vens, C., Džeroski, S. (eds.) ECML PKDD 2017. LNCS (LNAI), vol. 10534, pp. 601–616. Springer, Cham (2017). https://doi.org/10.1007/978-3-319-71249-9_36
8. Rao, B., Mishra, B.: An approach to clustering of text documents using graph mining techniques. Int. J. Rough Sets Data Anal. (IJRSDA) **4**(1), 18 (2017)
9. Jia, Y., Zhang, J., Huan, J.: An efficient graph-mining method for complicated and noisy data with real-world applications. Knowl. Inf. Syst. **28**(2), 423–447 (2011)
10. Flores-Garrido, M., Carrasco-Ochoa, J., Martínez-Trinidad, J.: AGraP: an algorithm for mining frequent patterns in a single graph using inexact matching. Knowl. Inf. Syst. **42**(2), 1–22 (2015)
11. Chen, C., Yan, X., Zhu, F., Han, J.: gApprox: mining frequent approximate patterns from a massive network. In: International Conference on Data Mining (ICDM 2007), pp. 445–450 (2007)
12. González, J., Holder, L., Cook, D.: Graph-based concept learning. In: Proceedings of the Fourteenth International Florida Artificial Intelligence Research Society Conference, pp. 377–381. AAAI Press, Key West (2001)
13. Acosta-Mendoza, N., Gago-Alonso, A., Medina-Pagola, J.: Frequent approximate subgraphs as features for graph-based image classification. Knowl. Based Syst. **27**, 381–392 (2012)
14. Emmert-Streib, F., Dehmer, M., Shi, Y.: Fifty years of graph matching, network alignment and network comparison. Inf. Sci. **346**, 1–22 (2016)
15. Gutierrez-Rodríguez, A., Martínez-Trinidad, J.F., García-Borroto, M., Carrasco-Ochoa, J.: Mining patterns for clustering on numerical datasets using unsupervised decision trees. Knowl. Based Syst. **82**, 70–79 (2015)
16. Gutierrez-Rodríguez, A., Martínez-Trinidad, J.F., García-Borroto, M., Carrasco-Ochoa, J.: Mining patterns for clustering using unsupervised decision trees. Intell. Data Anal. **19**(6), 1297–1310 (2015)
17. Flores-Garrido, M., Carrasco-Ochoa, J., Martínez-Trinidad, J.: Mining maximal frequent patterns in a single graph using inexact matching. Knowl. Based Syst. **66**, 166–177 (2014)
18. Ambauen, R., Fischer, S., Bunke, H.: Graph edit distance with node splitting and merging, and its application to diatom identification. In: Hancock, E., Vento, M. (eds.) GbRPR 2003. LNCS, vol. 2726, pp. 95–106. Springer, Heidelberg (2003). https://doi.org/10.1007/3-540-45028-9_9
19. Neuhaus, M., Bunke, H.: A probabilistic approach to learning costs for graph edit distance. In: Kittler, J., Petrou, M., Nixon, M. (eds.) Proceedings 17th International Conference on Pattern Recognition, Cambridge, United Kingdom, vol. 3, pp. 389–393 (2004)
20. Neuhaus, M., Bunke, H.: Automatic learning of cost functions for graph edit distance. Inf. Sci. **177**(1), 239–247 (2007)
21. Kuramochi, M., Karypis, G.: An efficient algorithm for discovering frequent subgraphs. Technical report, IEEE Transactions on Knowledge and Data Engineering (2002)

22. Gago-Alonso, A., Puentes-Luberta, A., Carrasco-Ochoa, J., Medina-Pagola, J., Martínez-Trinidad, J.: A new algorithm for mining frequent connected subgraphs based on adjacency matrices. Intell. Data Anal. **14**, 385–403 (2010)
23. O'Hara, S., Draper, B.: Introduction to the bag of features paradigm for image classification and retrieval. Computing Research Repository (CoRR) **abs/1101.3354** (2011)
24. Acosta-Mendoza, N.: Clasificación de imágenes basada en subconjunto de subgrafos frecuentes aproximados. Master's thesis, The National Institute of Astrophysics, Optics and Electronics of Mexico (INAOE), July 2013
25. Pinilla-Buitrago, L.A., Martínez-Trinidad, J.F., Carrasco-Ochoa, J.A.: New penalty scheme for optimal subsequence bijection. In: Ruiz-Shulcloper, J., Sanniti di Baja, G. (eds.) CIARP 2013. LNCS, vol. 8258, pp. 206–213. Springer, Heidelberg (2013). https://doi.org/10.1007/978-3-642-41822-8_26
26. Rand, M.: Objective criteria for the evaluation of clustering methods. J. Am. Stat. Assoc. **66**(336), 846–850 (1971)
27. McQueen, J.: Some methods for classification and analysis of multivariate observations. In: Proceedings of the Fifth Berkeley Symposium on Mathematical Statistics and Probability, Volume 1: Statistics, pp. 281–297. University of California Press (1967)
28. Arthur, D., Vassilvitskii, S.: K-means: the advantages of carefull seeding. In: Proceedings of the Eighteenth Annual ACM-SIAM Symposium on Discrete Algorithms, pp. 1027–1035. ACM (2007)
29. Lazebnik, S., Schmid, C., Ponce, J.: Beyond bags of features: spatial pyramid matching for recognizing natural scene categories. In: IEEE Computer Society Conference on Computer Vision and Pattern Recognition (CVPR), pp. 1–8. IEEE (2006)

Validation of Semantic Relation of Synonymy in Domain Ontologies Using Lexico-Syntactic Patterns and Acronyms

Mireya Tovar[1]([✉])(iD), Gerardo Flores[1](iD), José A. Reyes-Ortiz[2](iD),
and Meliza Contreras[1](iD)

[1] Faculty of Computer Science, Benemérita Universidad Autónoma de Puebla,
14 sur y Av. San Claudio, C.U., Puebla, Puebla, Mexico
{mtovar,mcontreras}@cs.buap.mx, gerardo.florespe@alumno.buap.mx
[2] Universidad Autónoma Metropolitana, Av. San Pablo Xalpa 180, Azcapotzalco,
02200 Mexico City, Mexico
jaro@correo.azc.uam.mx

Abstract. Synonymy is a relation of equivalence between the meanings of one or more words which allows the use of any word in an equivalent way depending on the context. Given the difficulty of defining the concordance between the meanings, the Natural Language Processing has focused on researching computational techniques that allow defining pairs of synonyms automatically. In this paper, a method based on lexico-syntactic patterns is proposed for the validation of semantic relations of synonymy between ontological concepts. An acronym will be considered a type of synonym within our paper. The results obtained by our proposed method were compared with the criterion of three experts, resulting above 80% of accuracy in the concordances of opinion between what is marked by the experts and the results of our proposed method.

Keywords: Patterns lexico-syntactic
Extraction of semantic relation · Synonymy

1 Introduction

The study of the meaning of words and how they are related is a task of the level-semantic of Natural Language Processing (NLP), the intention of such study is to discover the associations between words that allow defining whether a word can contain an implicit meaning of other words or two words can share a certain affinity that allows them to be used in the same context, these associations between meanings are known as a semantic relation.

Considering the best-known semantic relations, we find the synonymy, it is a relation of equivalence between the meaning of two or more words, Vidal [4]

This work is supported by the Sectoral Research Fund for Education with the CONA-CyT project 257357, and partially supported by the VIEP-BUAP 00478 project.

© Springer International Publishing AG, part of Springer Nature 2018
J. F. Martínez-Trinidad et al. (Eds.): MCPR 2018, LNCS 10880, pp. 199–208, 2018.
https://doi.org/10.1007/978-3-319-92198-3_20

mentions that the synonymy is a relation of identity between meanings and have two characteristics:

- The meaning is found in the same semantic field.
- The terms can be interchanged with each other, depending on the context.

To detect the synonymy between terms, the degree of agreement between the meanings of each term is measured to determine the degree of equivalence considering only the descriptive content of the meanings. An acronym will be considered a type of synonym within our paper. Authors such as García [3] remarks that given the nature of an acronym that is formed by the union of one or more elements can be established a relation of equivalence between terms that can be classified or signaling as synonymy.

Establishing the limits between the meaning of the concepts and considering special cases such as acronyms cause that the synonimy validation be a complex task for human experts because for define if exists a synonymy relation between two or more concepts they should evaluate each meaning for find equivalence between them for use a concept equally in a text without disrupting the main idea.

For the above, Natural Language Processing (NLP) proposes techniques that allow the automatic discovery and subsequent validation of the semantic relation of synonymy between terms applied to domain ontologies. NLP has intervened due to the difficulty that exists in the definition of limits that measure the descriptive content of meaning between terms to perform an automatic detection of synonymy between them and the treatment of particular cases of synonymy that exists such as acronyms.

In this paper, we propose a method that uses lexico-syntactic patterns to combine the extraction of acronyms with the validation of semantic relations of synonymy between terms that come from a domain ontology. The main objective is to create a method that is the independent semantic content of a concept and it is based only on the placement of the concepts within the corpus, which will allow migrating our system to other data sets.

The results of the proposed system were evaluated by comparison with respect to the criteria of three human experts who determined the validity of candidate semantic relations in terms of accuracy.

The content of the present paper is divided in the following way. In Sect. 2, the state of the art about the task of extracting semantic relations is briefly discussed. In Sect. 3 shows the approach addressed to the identification and validation of semantic relations of synonymy into domain ontologies. In Sect. 4, the data set considered, and the evaluation of the approach compared with the opinion of the experts is presented. Finally, we show the obtained conclusions and we expose the work in the future in Sect. 5.

2   Related Work

Natural Language Processing has been interested in searching for techniques for the automatic extraction and validation of semantic relations, the approaches considered starting from the use of lexico-syntactic patterns until techniques that involve supervised or unsupervised machine learning approaches.

Our analysis of the state of the art begins with Hearts [5], who makes an extraction of semantic relations of hyponymy/hyponymy from texts using lexico-syntactic patterns obtained by observation of the documents. Such research results in a list of extraction patterns for the English language, however, the technique used can be translated into other languages.

Ortega et al. [11] continues with the work of Hearts [5] by using patterns to find pairs of hyperonyms but translates the research into web texts in Spanish. Authors implement a method to assign a trust value to its patterns and thus discard those that do not have a minimum, this value changes as the list of patterns complements.

Simanovsky and Ulanov [12] keeps the pattern approach but translates it into semantic relations of synonymy. The searching for candidate patterns is done by extracting fragments of text about phrases that may contain references to synonymy from Wikipedia texts, each candidate is evaluated to know the value of trust and eliminate those that start with numbers or nouns.

On the other hand, Muller et al. [9] explores the identification of semantic relations using graphs and measuring the distance between the nodes to determine whether there is a semantic relation. Graphs are constructed based on the definitions of the words obtained from a dictionary.

Authors such as Lee et al. [8], use some machine learning approaches, specifically, Convolutional Neural Networks (CNN) for the extraction of semantic relations. CNNs are trained using characteristics such as position and a Part-of-Speech (PoS) tagging. After the classification by the Convolutional Neural Networks, the candidates are validated a second time using lexico-syntactic patterns.

In addition, Tovar et al. [7,13–19] carried out the evaluation and validation of semantic relations into ontologies, by pattern-based approaches or formal concept analysis.

This paper addresses the validation of semantic relations such as synonymy by a pattern-based approach. However, we consider acronyms as a special case of synonymy, all of them applied to domain ontologies. The main aim of this paper is to implement a system that is independent of the meaning words, which allows portability to different datasets.

3   Proposed Approach

The proposed method for the validation of semantic relations of synonymy type between ontological concepts is shown below:

1. **Preprocessing.**
   (a) *Ontology.* The concepts and semantic relations of synonymy type are extracted from a domain ontology using Jena[1].

---
[1] https://jena.apache.org.

Table 1. Extraction of lexico-syntactic patterns of semantic relations of synonymy between key phrases

<table>
<tr><td>1) Obtaining semantic relations of synonymy in the dataset</td><td colspan="3">...
T19 Material 1281 1308 N-dodecylpyridinium bromide
T20 Material 1310 1314 DDPB
* Synonym-of T20 T19

...</td></tr>
<tr><td></td><td>Keyphrase</td><td>Start</td><td>End</td></tr>
<tr><td></td><td>N-dodecylpyridinium bromidr</td><td>1281</td><td>1308</td></tr>
<tr><td></td><td>DDPB</td><td>1310</td><td>1314</td></tr>
<tr><td>2) Mapping of key phrases</td><td colspan="3">1. Positions: [1281, 1308, 1310 1314]
   Fragment of text to extract between the position 1281 - 1314
2. Text:
   ... [106]. A frequently employed surfactant was N-dodecylpyridinium bromide (DDPB) [9,60,61,108,109]. Anionic...
3. The part extracted
   N-dodecylpyridinium bromide (DDPB)</td></tr>
<tr><td>3) Obtaining the lexico-syntactic pattern</td><td colspan="3">1. Extract of text
   N-dodecylpyridinium bromide (DDPB)
2. Elimination of key phrases
   N-dodecylpyridinium bromide (DDPB)
3. Pattern:
   ( )

Final pattern: S_1 (S_2) Where S_1 and S_2 are key phrases identified</td></tr>
</table>

(b) *Corpus.* The domain corpus is split into sentences using the *sent_tokenize*[2] function of the Python NLTK package. Then, the sentences that have the two concepts that form the semantic relation of synonymy are used to form a subcorpus.

2. **Creation of a lexico-syntactic patterns list.** In this phase, we used the training dataset of Task 10, sub-task 3 of SemEval 2017 for the extraction of lexico-syntactic patterns of semantic relations of synonymy between pairs of key phrases. [2].

The pattern extraction process consists of the following phases:

(a) Obtaining semantic relations of synonymy in the dataset. From the training dataset, the start and end position of each pair of key phrases that make up the semantic relation of synonymy definite is extracted, see Table 1, row 1.

---

[2] http://www.nltk.org/api/nltk.tokenize.html.

Table 2. List of patterns gathered (where S_1 and S_2 are ontological concepts)

Pattern	Resource
S_1 (S_2)	
S_1 is often referred to as S_2	
S_1 is referred to as S_2	
S_1 alias S_2	
S_1 aka S_2	
S_1 as known as S_2	
S_1 frequently abbreviated as S_2	
S_1 usually called S_2	[6]
S_1 also called S_2	[6]
S_1 called as S_2	[6]
S_1 is called S_2	[6]
S_1 are called S_2	[6]
S_1 sometimes called S_2	[1]
S_1 known as S_2	[10]
S_1 also referred to as S_2	[6]
S_1 often described S_2	[20]
S_1 commonly known as S_2	[6]

(b) Mapping of key phrases. The positions are ordered from lowest to highest and the portion of text that is between the lowest value position and the highest value is extracted (see Table 1, row 2).

(c) Obtaining the lexico-syntactic pattern. From the text extract obtained in the previous step, the key phrases are removed to leave the text portion between them (see Table 1, row 3).

Through this method of extraction, a total of 7 extracted patterns was obtained, which were complemented with others from the literature, bringing together a total of 17 lexico-syntactic patterns [1,6,10,20]. The patterns obtained are shown in Table 2.

3. **Obtaining a list of acronyms from the domain corpus.** Since an acronym can represent an equivalence relation, which is cataloged as synonymy, we decided to implement the following algorithm to extract acronyms in the domain corpus; as a complement to the extraction of semantic relations of synonymy by lexico-syntactic patterns. The approach was applied directly in the domain corpus and produced as output a list of acronyms. The process is described below:

(a) The content of the document is split into sentences using regular expressions to take as a separator a sequence of alphanumeric symbols in parenthesis.

(b) For each sentence obtained, the sequence of alphanumeric symbols in parentheses is separated from the rest of the sentence. After the text obtained, the parentheses are removed to leave the internal content, which will be the acronym. The rest of the sentence is separated using the function *Word_tokenize* (see footnote 2). and the n terms are taken according to the length of the acronym extracted, starting from the end of the set of terms.

(c) The first letter of the terms extracted from the text is mapped to each element that makes up the acronym. If all the letters coincide, it is determined that these terms correspond to the acronym and the semantic relation of synonymy is established.

4. **Evaluation of semantic relations.** In this phase, for each semantic relation of synonymy existing in the domain ontology, the following two procedures are performed for its evaluation.

(a) **Evaluation using lexico-syntactic patterns.** In this phase, the concepts C_1 and C_2 of the ontology and the lexico-syntactic patterns of Table 2 are used to form regular expressions with the format C_1 *pattern* C_2. They are used to look for them at the domain corpus. If the regular expression matches with some sentence in the corpus; the semantic relation between the pair of concepts is considered synonymous and it is evaluated as true.

(b) **Evaluation using acronyms.** If the pair of concepts C_1 and C_2 are in the list of acronyms, it is determined that both form a semantic relation of synonymy and is evaluated as true.

With the purpose of verifying the results, we use the knowledge of experts for validating the semantic relations. In the next section, the results are presented.

4   Results and Discussion

The accuracy metric was used for the evaluation of the performance of the proposed system. The equation of accuracy is shown in the Eq. 1.

$$Accuracy = \frac{Quantity\ of\ correct\ cases}{Total\ of\ cases} \tag{1}$$

4.1   Dataset

The dataset consists of two ontologies, the first is in the domain of Artificial Intelligence (AI), and the second in the domain of e-Learning standard SCORM (SCORM) [21]. Each ontology contains a certain number of documents, tokens, and vocabulary (see Table 3). In addition, Table 4 shows the data of the subcorpora of assessment created for each domain.

Table 5 shows the total number of concepts, total of non-taxonomic relations and the total number of semantic relations of synonymy extracted from each domain ontology.

Table 3. Corpora of the domain

Domain	Documents	Tokens	Vocabulary
AI	8	11,370	1,510
SCORM	36	34,497	1,325

Table 4. Subcorpora of the domain

Domain	Sentences	Tokens	Vocabulary
AI	37	1,543	310
SCORM	39	1,680	325

Table 5. Elements extracted from the domain ontologies

Domain	Concepts	Non-taxonomic relations	Semantic relations of synonymy
AI	270	61	37
SCORM	1461	759	39

4.2 Experimental Results

Table 6 shows the results obtained from the approach using the accuracy measure. As can be seen, the system only considered as valid 22 of the 37 relations for the AI ontology obtaining an accuracy of 0.59. In the case of the SCORM ontology, only 13 of the 39 were obtained, achieving an accuracy of 0.33. Based on these results, it was decided to validate the semantic relations of synonymy by three experts.

Table 6. Experimental results obtained by the system

Ontology	Semantic relations of synonymy	Valid	Accuracy
AI	37	22	0.59
SCORM	39	13	0.33

Each human expert was provided with the subcorpora of evaluation with one or two samples of sentences, which contained the ontological concepts involved in the semantic relation.

In Table 7, the results of the evaluation for each ontology are shown. In each column, shows the number of relations that were classified as a synonym (column *Syn*) and which were not considered as a synonym (column *Not Syn*) in accordance with the experts (E_1, E_2, and E_3) under the subcorpora of evaluation.

According to the obtained results, for the case of the IA ontology, the system achieves an accuracy of 0.83 with the data recorded by the expert 1, 0.78 with

Table 7. Validation results of the semantic relations of synonymy by experts.

Ontology	System	E_1		E_2		E_3	
AI	Syn	Not Syn	Syn	Not Syn	Syn	Not Syn	Syn	Not Syn
	22	15	20	17	20	17	21	16
	Matches	31		29		36	
	Accuracy	0.83		0.78		0.97	
SCORM	Syn	Not Syn	Syn	Not Syn	Syn	Not Syn	Syn	Not Syn
	13	26	13	26	13	26	13	26
	Matches	33		33		31	
	Accuracy	0.85		0.85		0.80	

the data of the expert 2 and 0.97 with the data of the expert 3. The system has a greater coincidence with the expert 3 to achieve 36 results of 37, i.e., a 0.97 accuracy.

In the case of the SCORM ontology, it can be observed a behavior similar to that presented with the AI ontology, according to the results of Table 7. Under this ontology, the results of our system coincided with the first two experts (E_1, E_2) and obtaining an accuracy of 0.85, while the matches were lower with the third expert (E_3) which penalized the accuracy down to 0.80.

According to the results obtained with the SCORM ontology is observed abnormal behavior since the system and experts agree on 13 of the 26 relations evaluated and are considered synonyms. However, to make the comparison of results for the accuracy are observed different results.

According to the previous results, it can be concluded that the proposed system works properly for the extraction and validation of semantic relations of synonymy in the domain corpus. The system gives reliable results that coincide with the opinion of experts, which indicates that the intention to create a system that does a validation by patterns and consider the extraction of acronyms is reliable for the evaluation of semantic relations of synonymy in domain ontologies.

5   Conclusions

In this paper, a system is presented for the validation of semantic relations of synonymy between concepts from domain ontologies. For this work, two ontologies were considered with its corresponding domain corpus, the first is over the domain of Artificial Intelligence and the second in the domain of e-Learning standard SCORM, each with semantic relations of synonymy.

The proposed approach makes a validation of relations using lexico- syntactic patterns obtained from the dataset of the task 10 subtask 3 of SemEval 2017 and they are supplemented with other patterns obtained from the literature. In addition, a special case of synonymy was identified called acronym, which, according to some authors contains a degree of equivalence between terms that can be classified as synonyms. The goal was to create a system that does not take external resources for the evaluation, resulting in a system that is portable to other datasets.

The evaluation was carried out using the subcorpora created, however, the evaluation resulted in a low accuracy. So, we recourse to the criterion of human experts to validate manually relations and check whether the results obtained were reliable. The subcorpora was provided to three experts who issued its evaluation, which was compared with the results obtained by the system.

The results show that the system gives reliable results that match the criteria of experts, obtaining a 0.97 accuracy in the IA ontology and a 0.85 accuracy for the SCORM ontology. The evaluation shows that the system under the subcorpora give competitive assessment results in the validation of semantic relation of synonymy between concepts of domain ontologies and shows that the patterns-based approach and extraction of acronyms gives satisfactory results regarding the assessment issued by experts.

As a future scope of this work, it is planned to port the system to other datasets to measure performance. In addition, to make a comparison of the system against other approaches that use machine learning to make the detection of semantic relations of synonymy between concepts coming from a domain ontology.

References

1. Acosta, O.: Extracción automática de relaciones léxico-semánticas a partir de textos especializados. Ph.D. thesis, Universidad Nacional Autónoma de México, Posgrado en Ciencia e Ingeniería de la Computación (2013)
2. Augenstein, I., Das, M., Riedel, S., Vikraman, L., McCallum, A.: SemEval 2017 task 10: ScienceIE - extracting keyphrases and relations from scientific publications. In: Proceedings of the 11th International Workshop on Semantic Evaluation, SemEval-2017, pp. 546–555. Association for Computational Linguistics, Vancouver, August 2017. http://www.aclweb.org/anthology/S17-2091
3. Cardero, A.: Abreviaturas, acrónimos, iniciales, siglas y símbolos en los vocabularios especializados. Una propuesta. Debate Terminológico **2**, 1–10 (2006)
4. Escandell, M.: Apuntes de semántica léxica. Editorial UNED (2011)
5. Hearst, M.A.: Automatic acquisition of hyponyms from large text corpora. In: Proceedings of the 14th Conference on Computational Linguistics, COLING 1992, vol. 2, pp. 539–545. Association for Computational Linguistics, Stroudsburg (1992). https://doi.org/10.3115/992133.992154
6. Hu, F., Shao, Z., Ruan, T.: Self-supervised synonym extraction from the web. J. Inf. Sci. Eng. **31**(3), 1133–1148 (2015)
7. Chavez, H., Tovar, M.: Proposal for automatic extraction of taxonomic relations in domain corpus. Res. Comput. Sci. **133**, 29–39 (2017)
8. Lee, J.Y., Dernoncourt, F., Szolovits, P.: MIT at SemEval-2017 task 10: relation extraction with convolutional neural networks. In: Proceedings of the 11th International Workshop on Semantic Evaluation, SemEval-2017, pp. 978–984. Association for Computational Linguistics, Vancouver, August 2017. http://www.aclweb.org/anthology/S17-2171

9. Muller, P., Hathout, N., Gaume, B.: Synonym extraction using a semantic distance on a dictionary. In: Proceedings of the First Workshop on Graph Based Methods for Natural Language Processing, TextGraphs-1, pp. 65–72. Association for Computational Linguistics, Stroudsburg (2006). http://dl.acm.org/citation.cfm?id=1654758.1654773

10. Nazar, R., Renau, I.: A co-occurrence taxonomy from a general language corpus. In: Fjeld, R.V., Torjusen, J.M. (eds.) Proceedings of the 15th EURALEX International Congress, pp. 367–375. Department of Linguistics and Scandinavian Studies, University of Oslo, Oslo, August 2012

11. Ortega, R.M., Aguilar, C., Villaseñor, L., Montes, M., Sierra, G.: Hacia la identificación de relaciones de hiponimia/hiperonimia en internet. Revista signos **44**(75), 68–84 (2011). https://doi.org/10.4067/S0718-09342011000100006

12. Simanovsky, A., Ulanov, A.: Mining text patterns for synonyms extraction. In: Proceedings of the 2011 22nd International Workshop on Database and Expert Systems Applications, DEXA 2011, pp. 473–477. IEEE Computer Society, Washington (2011). https://doi.org/10.1109/DEXA.2011.53

13. Tovar, M.: Evaluación Automática de Ontologías de Dominio Restringido. Ph.D. thesis, Centro Nacional de Investigación y Desarrollo Tecnológico, Departamento de Ciencias Computacionales (2015)

14. Tovar, M., Pinto, D., Montes, A., González, G.: An approach based in LSA for evaluation of ontological relations on domain corpora. In: Carrasco-Ochoa, J.A., Martínez-Trinidad, J.F., Olvera-López, J.A. (eds.) MCPR 2017. LNCS, vol. 10267, pp. 225–233. Springer, Cham (2017). https://doi.org/10.1007/978-3-319-59226-8_22

15. Tovar, M., Pinto, D., Montes, A., González, G.: A metric for the evaluation of restricted domain ontologies. Computación y Sistemas **22**(1), 147–162 (2018). https://doi.org/10.13052/CyS-22-1-2792

16. Tovar, M., Pinto, D., Montes, A., González, G., Vilariño, D.: Evaluation of ontological relations in corpora of restricted domain. Computación y Sistemas **19**(1), 135–149 (2015). https://doi.org/10.13053/CyS-19-1-1954

17. Tovar, M., Pinto, D., Montes, A., González, G., Vilariño, D.: Identification of ontological relations in domain corpus using formal concept analysis. Eng. Lett. **23**(2), 72–76 (2015)

18. Tovar Vidal, M., Pinto, D., Montes, A., Serna, G., Vilariño, D.: Patterns used to identify relations in corpus using formal concept analysis. In: Carrasco-Ochoa, J.A., Martínez-Trinidad, J.F., Sossa-Azuela, J.H., Olvera López, J.A., Famili, F. (eds.) MCPR 2015. LNCS, vol. 9116, pp. 236–245. Springer, Cham (2015). https://doi.org/10.1007/978-3-319-19264-2_23

19. Tovar Vidal, M., Pinto, D., Montes, A., González, G., Vilariño, D., Beltrán, B.: Use of lexico-syntactic patterns for the evaluation of taxonomic relations. In: Martínez-Trinidad, J.F., Carrasco-Ochoa, J.A., Olvera-Lopez, J.A., Salas-Rodríguez, J., Suen, C.Y. (eds.) MCPR 2014. LNCS, vol. 8495, pp. 331–340. Springer, Cham (2014). https://doi.org/10.1007/978-3-319-07491-7_34

20. Yu, H., Agichtein, E.: Extracting synonymous gene and protein terms from biological literature. Bioinformatics **19**(1), 340–349 (2003). https://doi.org/10.7916/D8DN4DD5

21. Zouaq, A., Gasevic, D., Hatala, M.: Linguistic patterns for information extraction in OntoCmaps. In: Proceedings of the 3rd International Conference on Ontology Patterns, WOP 2012, vol. 929, pp. 61–72. CEUR-WS.org, Aachen (2012). http://dl.acm.org/citation.cfm?id=2887724.2887730

Computer Vision

Scene Text Segmentation Based on Local Image Phase Information and MSER Method

Julia Diaz-Escobar[⊠] and Vitaly Kober

Department of Computer Science, CICESE, 22860 Ensenada, BC, Mexico
jdiaz@cicese.edu.mx, vkober@cicese.mx

Abstract. The objective of text segmentation algorithms is a pixel-level separation of characters from the image background. This task is difficult due to several factors such as environmental aspects, image acquisition problems, and complex textual content. Up to now, the MSER technique has been widely used to solve the problem due to its invariance to geometric distortions, robustness to noise and illumination variations. However, when pixels intensities are too low, the MSER method often fails. In this paper, a new text segmentation method based on local phase information is proposed. Phase-based stable regions are obtained while the phase congruency values are used to select candidate regions. The computer simulation results show the robustness of the proposed method to different image degradations. Moreover, the method outperforms the MSER technique in most of the cases.

Keywords: Text segmentation · MSER · Phase congruency
Shadow degradation · Nonuniform illumination
Scale-space monogenic signal

1 Introduction

Despite the image text segmentation seems to be a trivial task for human beings, it is not such simple for computer vision systems. Besides, since the text segmentation is one of the first stages of "end-to-end" text detection and recognition applications, the segmentation accuracy plays an essential role in the overall performance of a system. Documents classification, industrial automation, language translator, traffic sign recognition, robotic navigation, multimedia retrieval, text to voice converter, and augmented reality are some of the applications related to text segmentation. Most of these applications utilize natural images without any restrictions, compromising the text segmentation task by environment aspects (nonuniform illumination, shadows, scene complexity), image acquisition problems (low resolution, blurring, perspective distortion), and text content (orientation, size, font style, texture, color) [1,2].

Until now, different techniques have been proposed for text segmentation such as image binarization, edge extraction, color clustering, and Maximally Stable

© Springer International Publishing AG, part of Springer Nature 2018
J. F. Martínez-Trinidad et al. (Eds.): MCPR 2018, LNCS 10880, pp. 211–220, 2018.
https://doi.org/10.1007/978-3-319-92198-3_21

Extremal Regions (MSER) extraction [1,2]. Nowadays, the MSER approach [3] has become the most utilized method for text segmentation in imagery due to its invariance to affine transformations and robustness to slight illumination variations. Basically, the MSER method extracts the image regions that remain stable under a certain number of thresholds. In particular, for text segmentation task the MSER method considers candidate regions and then classifies them into text or non-text components.

Recently, the use of all Extremal Regions (ER) was proposed [4,5]. Furthermore, since the MSER method works with any image that satisfies the totally ordered set condition [3], then it can be also applied to multiple channels images [6,7]. However, the use of all ER regions or multiple channels leads to appearance of numerous repeated regions. Furthermore, since the MSER technique is based on pixels intensities of the image, low contrast, shadows and high non-uniform illumination variations decrease the method performance. So, rather than being based on the local intensities variations, we propose a new text segmentation method utilizing the local image phase spectrum. It is well known that image phase contains most of the structural image information while it remains invariant to intensity variations [8]. Thus, it is robust to low contrast, high brightness, shadows, and illumination variations. The proposed phase-based segmentation is designed by applying the MSER technique to the local phase image instead of the intensity image. Additionally, the local phase congruency approach is used to control the candidate region selection. Computer simulation shows a superior performance (up to 20%) of the proposed method comparing to that of the MSER technique. Besides, the proposed method shows robustness to low contrast, illumination variations, and shadow degradations.

This paper is organized as follows. In Sect. 2, the theoretical background is presented. In Sect. 3, the proposed text segmentation method is described. In Sect. 4, computer simulation results are presented and discussed. Section 5, summarizes our conclusions.

2   Theoretical Background

For 1D signal, the local phase information is computed using the analytic signal model; however, for 2D signals, the analytic signal is not defined. In the latter case, 1D directional quadrature filters are usually used, but this approach is computationally expensive. Felsberg and Sommer [9] proposed the scale-space monogenic signal which can handle different structures of an image without changing the image size.

2.1   Scale-Space Monogenic Signal and Phase Congruency Approach

Let be $f(x,y)$ an image, and $F(u,v) = \mathcal{F}\{f(t)\}$ be its Fourier transform. The scale-space monogenic signal representation is defined as [9],

$$F_{Mbp}(u,v) = F_{bp}(u,v) + i\mathbf{H} \cdot F_{bp}(u,v). \tag{1}$$

where $\mathbf{H} = (H_1, H_2)$ is the transfer function of the first-order Riesz transform in the frequency domain:

$$H_1(u, v) = i\frac{u}{\sqrt{u^2 + v^2}}, H_2(u, v) = i\frac{v}{\sqrt{u^2 + v^2}}, \qquad (2)$$

and $F_{bp}(u, v) = B_{s_0, \lambda, k}(u, v) \cdot F(u, v)$ represents the image $F(u, v)$ filtered by the band-pass filter

$$B_{s_0, \lambda, k}(u, v) = \left(e^{-2\pi s_0 \lambda^k \sqrt{u^2 + v^2}} - e^{-2\pi s_0 \lambda^{k-1} \sqrt{u^2 + v^2}} \right), \qquad (3)$$

where $\lambda \in (0, 1)$ indicates the relative bandwidth, s_0 indicates the coarsest scale, and $k \in N$ indicates the bandpass number.

The local amplitude $A(x, y)$, local orientation $\theta(x, y)$, and local phase $\varphi(x, y)$[1] can be computed as follows:

$$A = \sqrt{(\mathcal{F}^{-1}\{F_{bp}\})^2 + (\mathcal{F}^{-1}\{H_1 \cdot F_{bp}\})^2 + (\mathcal{F}^{-1}\{H_2 \cdot F_{bp}\})^2}, \qquad (4)$$

$$\theta = \tan^{-1}\left(\frac{\mathcal{F}^{-1}\{H_2 \cdot F_{bp}\}}{\mathcal{F}^{-1}\{H_1 \cdot F_{bp}\}} \right), \qquad (5)$$

$$\varphi = atan2\left(\frac{\sqrt{(\mathcal{F}^{-1}\{H_1 \cdot F_{bp}\})^2 + (\mathcal{F}^{-1}\{H_2 \cdot F_{bp}\})^2}}{\mathcal{F}^{-1}\{F_{bp}\}} \right). \qquad (6)$$

Figure 1 shows a block-diagram of the scale-space monogenic signal framework.

A local energy model was proposed [10]. This model argues that the biological visual system locates features of interest by searching for maximum local energy, and identifies the feature type (shadow, edge or line) by evaluating the argument at that point. That is, edges, lines, and shadows can be detected at such points where the Fourier components of the signal are maximum in the phase distribution, called phase congruency. Continuing with this approach, a dimensionless measure of phase congruency was proposed [11] as follows:

$$PC(x) = max_{\overline{\varphi} \in [0, 2\pi]} \frac{\sum_n W(x) \lfloor A_n(x) [cos(\varphi_n(x) - \overline{\varphi}(x))] - T \rfloor}{\sum_n A_n(x) + \varepsilon}, \qquad (7)$$

where $W(x)$ is a weight for the frequency spread; ε is a small constant to avoid division by zero; T is a noise threshold parameter. The PC value indicates the significance of the current feature: unity means the most significant feature and zero indicates the lowest significance. We refer to the following papers [11,12] for more details.

---

[1] Note that the function $atan2(|y|/x) = sign(y) \cdot tan^{-1}(|y|/x)$, where the factor $sign(y)$ indicates the direction of rotation.

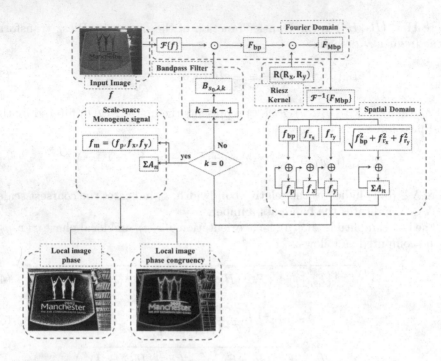

Fig. 1. Block-diagram of scale-space monogenic signal framework.

2.2   Maximally Stable External Regions

The MSER method was first introduced for grayscale images. Basically, the MSER method extracts the image regions that remain stable under a certain number of thresholds. Let $\mathcal{Q}_1, \mathcal{Q}_2, \ldots, \mathcal{Q}_{i-1}, \mathcal{Q}_i$, be a sequence of nested extremal regions, i.e. $\mathcal{Q}_i \subset \mathcal{Q}_{i+1}$. The extremal region $\mathcal{Q}_{i*}$ is *maximally stable* if only if $q(i) = \frac{|\mathcal{Q}_{i+\Delta} \setminus \mathcal{Q}_{i-\Delta}|}{|\mathcal{Q}_i|}$ has a local minimum at i^*, with $|\cdot|$ denotes cardinality, and $\Delta \in S$ is a parameter that considers the stability of the region under a certain number of thresholds. For a formal explanation, we refer to [3] for more details.

3   Text Segmentation Method

In this section, the proposed phase-based text segmentation method is described. Essentially, the phase-based regions are obtained by applying the MSER algorithm to the local image phase spectrum rather than to intensity image. The local phase congruency approach is used to control the candidate region selection.

As mentioned before, the local image phase $\varphi(x, y)$ contains most of the structural information of the image, while local amplitude gives an intensity measure of the structure. Moreover, the local phase information allows us to distinguish between edge, edge-line and line features [12].

A phase value of 0 indicates an upward going step, $\pi/2$ indicates a bright line feature, π corresponds to a downward going step, and $3\pi/2$ indicates a dark

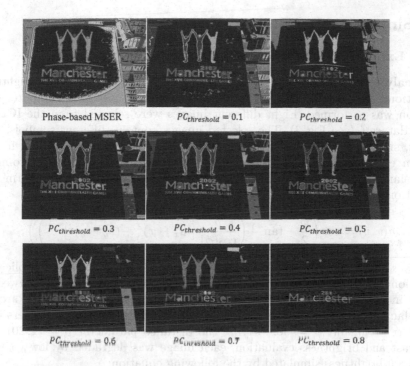

Fig. 2. Phase-based MSER regions filtered by different PC thresholds.

line feature. However, we are not interested to make a distinction between dark or bright lines features, but we are interested in finding upward and downward going step features for region detection. For this reason, we consider the range from 0 to π, mapping the angles grater then π back into the range. The proposed text segmentation method is explained below:

Step 1. Using the scale-space monogenic signal framework, the local phase (Eq. 6) and local phase congruency (Eq. 7) are computed (see Fig. 1).
Step 2. Once the local phase image is obtained, the phase-based MSER regions are formed by applying the MSER algorithm to the local image phase spectrum.
Step 3. The obtained phase regions are filtered by the mean phase congruency value (PC_{mean}) of the region contour (R_C). The PC_{mean} is computed as follows:

$$PC_{mean}(x,y) = \frac{1}{N} \sum_{i=1}^{N} PC(x,y) \cdot R_C, \qquad (8)$$

where $N = |R_C|$. If the $PC_{mean}(x,y)$ value is lower than a predefined threshold ($PC_{threshold}$), the region is discarded as a possible candidate region. Figure 2 shows an example of the phase-based MSER image under different $PC_{threshold}$ values.

4   Simulation Results

4.1   Experimental Setup

To analyze the tolerance of the proposed method to contrast and brightness variations, shadows, and non-uniform illumination degradations, computer simulation was performed. Eight different images were selected from the ICDAR 2013 dataset[2] (see Fig. 3). The selected images contain different symbols, font types, sizes, orientations, and backgrounds. For noise and non-uniform illumination evaluation, each grayscale image was degraded by additive zero-mean Gaussian noise with a Std. Dev. $\sigma = (0, 30)$; and distorted by nonuniform illumination using the Lambertian model defined as follows [13],

$$d(x,y) = \cos\left(\frac{\phi}{2} - \tan^{-1}\left(\frac{\rho}{\cos(\phi)}\left[(s_x - x)^2 + (s_y - y)^2\right]^{-\frac{1}{2}}\right)\right), \qquad (9)$$

where $s_x = \rho \cdot \tan(\phi)\cos(\psi)$ and $s_y = \rho \cdot \tan(\phi)\sin(\psi)$. The multiplicative function $d(x,y)$ depends on the parameter ρ that is the distance between a point in the surface and the light source, and the parameters ϕ and ψ are tilt and slang angles, respectively. In our experiments the following parameters were used: $\phi = 45$ and $\psi = 90$, varying the distance parameter $\rho \in (2, 20)$. For contrast and brightness evaluation, each image was degraded by low contrast and high brightness simulated by the following equation:

$$f'(x,y) = c \cdot f(x,y) + b, \qquad (10)$$

where $b \in (100, 200)$ and $c \in (0, 1)$ represent the brightness and contrast parameters, respectively. Figure 4 shows examples of the synthetic degradations. To evaluate the performance of the proposed method under shadow degradations,

Image 1   Image 2   Image 3   Image 4

Image 5   Image 6   Image 7   Image 8

Fig. 3. Images used for evaluation from ICDAR2013 dataset.

[2] http://rrc.cvc.uab.es/.

Fig. 4. Synthetic degradations. From up to down: low contrast, high brightness, nonuniform illumination, and additive noise. From left to right: degraded image, proposed method result, and MSER method result.

eight different shadow templates were utilized. Degraded shadow images are obtained by multiplying all the test images with shadow templates. Figure 5 shows an example of shadow degradations result.

4.2   Evaluation Protocol

The performance of the proposed text segmentation method is evaluated with the character-level Recall rate [14] defined as the ratio between the total correctly detected candidate regions and the ground truth characters. The recall measure is computed using two different approaches for a fair comparison with other methods. A region is considered as a character candidate: (1) if the bounding box of the detected character matches at least 90% of the area of the ground truth bounding box (R_1), (2) if the similarity value is up to 50% (R_2). The *similarity* value is defined as follows [5]:

$$similarity(D, GT) = \frac{area(D) \cap area(GT)}{area(D) \cup area(GT)}, \tag{11}$$

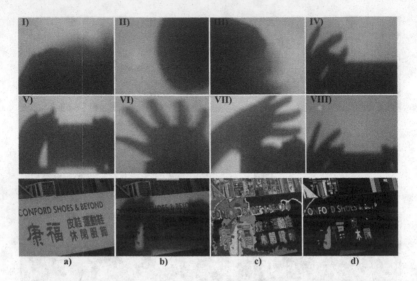

Fig. 5. Shadow degradations (I-VIII): (a) Original image, (b) image degraded by shadow (V), (c) the proposed method result, (d) the MSER method result.

where D and GT represent detected and ground truth bounding box, respectively. The similarity-Recall (R_2) reflects the detected character equality better than the R_1 approach.

For the MSER algorithm, two evaluations were carried out. Using the reported MSER parameter [15], that is, $\Delta = 4$, maximum variation $v = 0.5$, and minimum diversity $d = 0.1$ (denoted by param 1); and using the parameter setting $\Delta = 5$, maximum variation $v = 0.25$, and minimum diversity $d = 0.2$. The parameter values in [5,14] are not presented.

4.3   Results

The simulation results of the proposed text segmentation method under additive noise, low contrast, high brightness, non-uniform illumination variations, and shadow degradations are shown in Fig. 6. The proposed method shows a better performance up to 10% for low contrast and high brightness in most of the images, and up to 20% for non-uniform illumination. For additive noise degradations, the obtained results are similar, up to 90% in both cases. For shadow degradations, the proposed method outperforms up to 20% of the MSER method in most cases.

Finally, the proposed text segmentation method is compared with state-of-the-art methods on the ICDAR 2013 dataset. Neumann and Matas [14] and Sung et al. [5] methods are evaluated on ICDAR 2011 dataset (no longer available), but the differences between both datasets, ICDAR 2011 and ICDAR2013, are despicable. Comparison results are shown in Table 1 regarding character-level Recall.

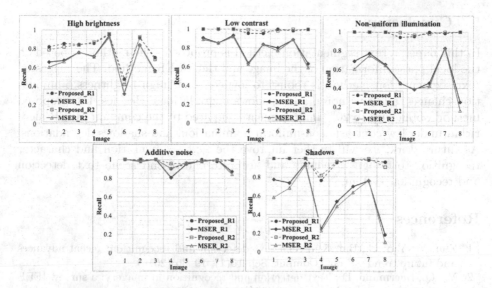

Fig. 6. Simulation performance of the proposed method and the MSER technique under high brightness, low contrast, non-uniform illumination, additive noise, and shadow degradations.

Table 1. Character-level recall

Method	R_1	R_2	# candidates
MSER (param 1)	0.82	0.78	12,359
Neumann [14]	0.85	-	-
Saric [15] (param 2)	0.89	-	17,940
Sung et al. [5]	0.99	0.86	75,124
Proposed method (param 1)	**0.89**	**0.88**	**16,956**
Proposed method (param 2)	**0.91**	**0.91**	**51,288**

The proposed text segmentation method obtains the best result regarding to the character-level similarity-Recall (R_2) evaluation. Despite Sung method achieves a better character-level Recall (R_1), the similarity-Recall (R_2) is lower than that of the proposed method. This means that the detected regions by the Sung method may not be completely correct and many detected regions are contained within a larger ground truth region. Furthermore, the proposed method obtains less candidate regions than that of the Sung method that means that the proposed method is more accurate. These results show that the proposed method yields more accurate segmentation performance than that of the tested methods.

5   Conclusion

In this paper, a text segmentation method is proposed. The method is based on the local phase information of the image and the MSER method. The suggested text segmentation method is robust to low contrast, high brightness, illumination changes, additive noise, and shadows degradations. Besides, the proposed method obtains up to 20% improvement compared to the common MSER algorithm under low contrast, non-uniform illumination, and shadows degradations. As future work, we will further improve the text segmentation and character recognition to design a reliable and accurate end-to-end scene text detection and recognition system.

References

1. Zhu, Y., Yao, C., Bai, X.: Scene text detection and recognition: recent advances and future trends. Front. Comput. Sci. **10**(1), 19–36 (2016)
2. Ye, Q., Doermann, D.: Text detection and recognition in imagery: a survey. IEEE Trans. Pattern Anal. Mach. Intell. **37**(7), 1480–1500 (2015)
3. Matas, J., Chum, O., Urban, M., Pajdla, T.: Robust wide-baseline stereo from maximally stable extremal regions. Image Vis. Comput. **22**(10), 761–767 (2004)
4. Neumann, L., Matas, J.: Real-time lexicon-free scene text localization and recognition. IEEE Trans. Pattern Anal. Mach. Intell. **38**(9), 1872–1885 (2016)
5. Sung, M.C., Jun, B., Cho, H., Kim, D.: Scene text detection with robust character candidate extraction method. In: 2015 13th International Conference on Document Analysis and Recognition, ICDAR, pp. 426–430. IEEE (2015)
6. Koo, H.I., Kim, D.H.: Scene text detection via connected component clustering and nontext filtering. IEEE Trans. Image Process. **22**(6), 2296–2305 (2013)
7. He, D., Yang, X., Huang, W., Zhou, Z., Kifer, D., Giles, C.L.: Aggregating local context for accurate scene text detection. In: Lai, S.-H., Lepetit, V., Nishino, K., Sato, Y. (eds.) ACCV 2016. LNCS, vol. 10115, pp. 280–296. Springer, Cham (2017). https://doi.org/10.1007/978-3-319-54193-8_18
8. Oppenheim, A.V., Lim, J.S.: The importance of phase in signals. Proc. IEEE **69**(5), 529–541 (1981)
9. Felsberg, M., Sommer, G.: The monogenic scale-space: a unifying approach to phase-based image processing in scale-space. J. Math. Imag. Vis. **21**(1), 5–26 (2004)
10. Morrone, M.C., Burr, D.: Feature detection in human vision: a phase-dependent energy model. Proc. Roy. Soc. Lond. B: Biol. Sci. **235**(1280), 221–245 (1988)
11. Kovesi, P.: Image features from phase congruency. Videre: J. Comput. Vis. Res. **1**(3), 1–26 (1999)
12. Kovesi, P., et al.: Edges are not just steps. In: Proceedings of the Fifth Asian Conference on Computer Vision, Melbourne, vol. 8, pp. 22–8 (2002)
13. Diaz-Ramirez, V.H., Picos, K., Kober, V.: Target tracking in nonuniform illumination conditions using locally adaptive correlation filters. Opt. Commun. **323**, 32–43 (2014)
14. Neumann, L., Matas, J.: Real-time scene text localization and recognition. In: 2012 IEEE Conference on Computer Vision and Pattern Recognition, CVPR, pp. 3538–3545. IEEE (2012)
15. Saric, M.: Scene text segmentation using low variation extremal regions and sorting based character grouping. Neurocomputing **266**, 56–65 (2017)

A Lightweight Library for Augmented Reality Applications

Luis Gerardo de la Fraga[1]([✉]) [iD], Nataly A. García-Morales[2],
Daybelis Jaramillo-Olivares[1], and Adrián J. Ramírez-Díaz[1]

[1] Computer Science Department, Cinvestav, Mexico City, Mexico
fraga@cs.cinvestav.mx
[2] Electrical Engineering Department, Cinvestav, Bioelectronics Unit,
Av. IPN 2508, 07360 Mexico City, Mexico

Abstract. To build an Augmented Reality (AR) application it is necessary to recognize a fiducial marker, then to calibrate the camera that is viewing the 3D scene on the marker, and finally to draw a virtual object over the image taken by the camera but in the virtual coordinate system supposed also on the fiducial marker. The camera calibration step give us the transformation matrix from 3D world to 2D on the screen, and the pose of the marker with respect to the virtual coordinate system. An AR application must run interactively with the user, and also in real time. Performing all these calculations in a embedded device such as a Single Board Computer (SBC), a tablet, or a smartphone, is a challenge because a normal numerical analysis library is huge, and it is not designed for such devices. In this article we present a lightweight numerical library, it has been developed thinking in such computing restricted devices. We show results on two AR applications developed for the Raspberry Pi 3 SBC.

Keywords: Augmented reality · Fiducial marker
Camera calibration · Homography estimation

1 Introduction

Augmented reality is a technology which superimposes computer generated images on top of a user's perception of the real world in real time [7]. AR has important applications in fields such as videogamming, interactive marketing and advertising, instructional aids and how-to for use, construction and maintenance, and navigation [7].

Perhaps one of most successful application of AR could be in education [3]. As a new technology, AR could help to students to learn more effectively and increase knowledge retention, relative to traditional 2D desktop interfaces. With the aid of AR could be build the virtual interaction with complex phenomena (showing the magnetic field, or the Earth layers, for example).

© Springer International Publishing AG, part of Springer Nature 2018
J. F. Martínez-Trinidad et al. (Eds.): MCPR 2018, LNCS 10880, pp. 221–228, 2018.
https://doi.org/10.1007/978-3-319-92198-3_22

In [4] authors analyze an AR application on sixty nine middle-school students. Their results show an increase in student's motivation, attention and motivation factors or the learning environment based on augmented reality technology compared with a more traditional learning environment. Authors also mention that AR is not mature enough to be used massively in education.

Users in AR application need to learn how to build 3D scenes, how to draw virtual objects, and how to manage, although amazing and exciting, a technology that is complex.

OpenCV [2] is the open tool to learn Image Processing, Computer Vision, and 3D user interfaces. This is the facto standard in this field. This library has more than 2500 optimized algorithms, which includes a comprehensive set of both classic and state-of-the-art computer vision and machine learning algorithms. But is the OpenCV library is far to be an easy tool, in its homepage there are listed 52 books about how to learn it.

The idea of this paper is to offer a simpler way to process fiducial markers. In Sect. 2 is presented the necessary components to build an AR application. Sect. 3 describes our proposed library that can be used in computationally restricted devices. Sect. 4 shows an AR application build with our library and running on the Raspberry Pi 3, a SBC that uses a 1.2 GHz 64-bits quad-core ARM Cortex-A53 CPU and 1 GB of RAM. Finally, in Sect. 5, some conclusions are drawn.

2 Augmented Reality Application

The following steps are performed in a typical AR application: (1) An image processing step to recognize a fiducial marker, (2) A computer vision step to calibrate the camera, this is, to obtain the projection matrix that transforms the 3D world viewing by the camera to a 2D plane that forms the viewed image; this step also obtains the pose, this is, the rotation and translation of the marker with to a virtual and global coordinate system. And finally, the step (3) that draws a virtual object over the coordinate system fixed in the marker. The augmented world is visualized only on the display, where it is possible to see the projection of the virtual objects on the image generated by the camera.

Two very simple fiducial markers are shown in Fig. 1: one is a simple black square, and the other is a pattern of two concentric circles [10]. The white area in the background of both markers help them to be recognized by a computer: it is a high contrast zone on the image. The black zone is supposed to be one of the biggest black objects on the scene. Marker detection is performed with image processing techniques: (1) a global threshold is applied to the input image which produce a binary (blank and white) image, (2) some morphological erosion and dilatation operations are applied to remove noise on the binarized image, and a labeling of the all black components in the image is performed. These image processing tasks were applied using library in [6].

Once we have the markers, the vertices positions must be calculated with the marker in Fig. 1(a), and the points of each ellipse must the extracted from marker in 1(b). With these data the homography can be estimated. Our library helps to perform easily these steps. Now, these Computer Vision steps will be described in detail.

(a) A black square marker

(b) Two concentric circles marker

Fig. 1. Images of two very simple fiducial markers in use.

3   Description of the Lightweight Library

Homography calculation. To obtain a homography by the *normalized DTL* algorithm [9] it is necessary to solve an overdetermined system of equations that forms a matrix of size $2n \times 8$, where n is the number of point correspondences between the marker model and an image of the same model. The easiest way to solve this problem is using the QR decomposition computed with the modified Gram?Schmidt algorithm [8]. In fact, this is the shortest code and easiest codification to solve the QR decomposition. If the overdetermined system of equations is expressed as $A\mathbf{h} = \mathbf{b}$, $\mathbf{h}$ is found using normal equations doing:

$$QR\mathbf{h} = \mathbf{b},$$
$$(QR)^{\mathrm{T}}QR\mathbf{h} = (QR)^{\mathrm{T}}\mathbf{b},$$
$$R^{\mathrm{T}}Q^{\mathrm{T}}QR\mathbf{h} = R^{\mathrm{T}}Q^{\mathrm{T}}\mathbf{b}, \qquad (1)$$
$$R\mathbf{h} = Q^{\mathrm{T}}\mathbf{b} = \mathbf{c}.$$

Here the system is already solved because matrix R is upper triangular and $\mathbf{h}$ values are found by back-substitution, staring with $h_{n-1} = c_a n / r_{nn}$.

We use here a further way to compact the calculations, such as it was suggested also by Golub and Van Loan [8]: the QR decomposition is calculated to the extended matrix $[A \mid b]$, of size $2n \times 9$, then one obtains $Q[R \mid Q^{\mathrm{T}}b]$, thus the product $Q^{\mathrm{T}}b$ is obtained in the last column. Notice here that matrix Q is not needed, thus the subroutine to solve the $A\mathbf{h} = \mathbf{b}$ is as (using the same notation that in [8]):

A notice here that is important. The calculation of the homography is a very well conditioned problem, then the use of the QR algorithm is justified. The only way to get a pour conditioned problem is to use repeated points correspondences to try to calculate the homography.

Eigendecomposition of a symmetric matrix of size 3×3. The eigendecomposition of a symmetric matrix A results in the matrices $V\ D\ V^{\mathrm{T}}$, where

---

Algorithm 1. Solving $Ah = b$ using QR decomposition

Require: Matrix A of size $2n \times 8$, vector b of size $2n$
Ensure: Vector h
 1: $B = [A \mid b]$ ▷ B has size $2n \times 9$
 2: **for** $k = 1 : 9$ **do**
 3:     $R(k, k) = \|B(1 : 2n, k)\|_2$ ▷ Norm of column vector k of B
 4:     $\mathbf{v} = B(1 : 2n, k)/R(k, k)$
 5:     **for** $j = k + 1 : 9$ **do**
 6:         $R(k, j) = \mathbf{v}^{\mathrm{T}} B(1 : 2n, j)$
 7:         $B(1 : 2n, j) = B(1 : 2n, j) - \mathbf{v}R(k, j)$
 8:     **end for**
 9: **end for**
10:   ▷ Back substitution stage:
11: $h(8) = B(8, 9)/B(8, 8)$
12: **for** $i = 7 : 1$ **do**
13:     $sum = 0$
14:     **for** $j = i + 1 : 8$ **do**
15:         $sum = sum + B(i, j)\mathbf{h}(j)$
16:     **end for**
17:     $h(i) = (B(i, 9) - sum)/B(i, i)$
18: **end for**

D is a diagonal matrix former with the eigenvalues of A, and V is a orthogonal matrix where its columns are the eigenvectors corresponding to each eigenvalue in D. This problem is simplified with matrices of size 3×3 because is equivalent to find the roots of a cubic equation [6,12].

SVD of a matrix of size 3×3. This problem is used to solve the orthogonalization of a matrix, specifically when this matrix is a matrix obtained with a linear method using a plane [13] or a circular marker [10]. The calibration of a camera with both linear methods produces a rotation matrix R far of being orthogonal, then to become orthogonal such matrix its Singular Value Decomposition is applied: $R = UD_1V^{\mathrm{T}}$, and $R' = UV^{\mathrm{T}}$ is obtained, where R' is already orthogonal. In [13] it is demonstrated that the obtained R' is the best orthogonal matrix which minimizes the Frobenius norm of $R' - R$.

Fitting an ellipse to a set of points. The fastest algorithm to fit a set of point to an ellipse is by solving a least square problem that minimizes the sum of squared algebraic distances [5]. Instead to solve this problem as an eigendecomposition of a 6×6 matrix, as it is in [5], this problem can be transformed easily to solve three times a eigendecomposition of 3×3 matrices, or to find three times the roots of three cubic equations [6].

Camera calibration using a marker of two concentric circles. This marker is presented in [10]. First, it is necessary to recognize two ellipses. For this task the previous method in the last paragraph can be used. With the two recognized ellipses, the homography can be obtained directly as it is explained in [10]. Here it is necessary to invert a 3×3 matrix, thus its eigendecomposition can be used because the used matrices in this method are the representation of a conic equation, which is symmetric and of 3×3 size.

4   Experiments and Results

To test our library against the results produced with a high level language, such as Octave, to demonstrate the correctness of its calculations. We generate two simulated images, each one from a square and two ellipses as the planar models of the markers. From these models we use the pinhole camera model in (2) with a known camera position to generate the two images shown in Fig. 2(b) and (c). The used pinhole camera model is

$$\lambda \mathbf{p} = KR[I| - \mathbf{c}]\mathbf{P}, \tag{2}$$

where $\mathbf{p} = [u, v, 1]^{\mathrm{T}}$ is a point over the image, $\mathbf{P} = [x, y, z, 1]\mathrm{T}$ is a point in the 3D scene, $\mathbf{c}$ is the position of the camera, and R is a rotation matrix. Markers are situated on the xy-plane, then $\mathbf{P} - [x, y, 0, 1]^{\mathrm{T}}$ and the camera model is reduced as:

$$\lambda \mathbf{p} = KR[\mathbf{e}_1, \ \mathbf{e}_2, \ -\mathbf{c}]\mathbf{P},$$
$$\lambda \mathbf{p} = K[\mathbf{r}_1, \ \mathbf{r}_2, \ -R\mathbf{c}]\mathbf{P},$$
$$\lambda \mathbf{p} = H\mathbf{P},$$

where I is the identity matrix $I = [\mathbf{e}_1, \ \mathbf{e}_2, \ \mathbf{e}_3]$, and $R = [\mathbf{r}_1, \ \mathbf{r}_2, \ \mathbf{r}_3]$, and we are abusing the notation on $\mathbf{P}$ to still denote a homogeneous 2D point on the model $\mathbf{P} = [x, y, 1]\mathrm{T}$. The used camera intrinsic parameters are in matrix K:

$$K = \begin{bmatrix} 1000 & 0 & -300 \\ 0 & 1000 & -200 \\ 0 & 0 & -1 \end{bmatrix},$$

to generate images of size 600×400 pixels, the principal point is situated in its center at $(300, 200)$.

Then we apply both codes, in C with out light library and with Octave, to estimate both homographies H, and recover the rotation matrix and camera position. Results are shown in Table 1.

Table 1. Results of camera calibration and pose estimation using the markers in Fig. 2

Language, marker	f	$R = R_z(\theta_3)R_y(\theta_2)R_z(\theta_1)$ $(\theta_3, \theta_2, \theta_1)$	Camera center
Ground truth	1000.0	(90.00, 57.69, -108.43)	$[20.00, -60.00, 40.00]^{\mathrm{T}}$
Octave (square)	1043.1	(89.44, 58.44, -107.70)	$[19.97, -62.71, 40.45]^{\mathrm{T}}$
C (square)	1043.1	(89.44, 58.44, -107.31)	$[19.74, -63.43, 40.44]^{\mathrm{T}}$
Octave (circles)	1012.0	(89.95, 57.70, -114.19)	$[26.20, -58.40, 40.50]^{\mathrm{T}}$
C (circles)	1005.5	(90.04, 57.67, -114.37)	$[26.27, -57.98, 40.30]^{\mathrm{T}}$

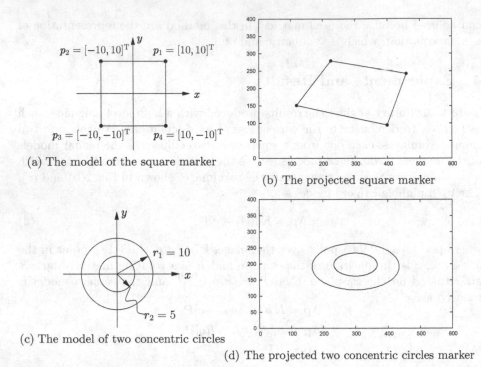

(a) The model of the square marker

(b) The projected square marker

(c) The model of two concentric circles

(d) The projected two concentric circles marker

Fig. 2. The square and two concentric circles markers and their projections used in the experiment. Images in (b) and (d) are generated with the parameters detailed in text.

Details for this first experiment are as follows: The square model has vertices $\{(10, 10), (-10, 10), (-10, -10), (10, -10)\}$. The two circles models have radius 10 and 5. Both markers are shown in Fig. 2(a) and (c), respectively. Both codes, in C and Octave, for this experiment are available in http://cs.cinvestav.mx/~fraga/LightLib.tar.gz.

The results shown in Table 1 are not the best with respect to the ground truth. This is because two reasons: (1) The marker images in Fig. 2(a) and (c) where generated rounding the pixels locations to the nearest integers, and (2) The pose calculated using the homography is based in a linear method which is not the best solution. The solutions obtained and shown in Table 1 must be refined with a non-linear method to improve their values. An alternative that will be explored as future work is to use a PnP algorithm such as the one in [11, 14] to calculate the pose. The inconvenience of using a PnP algorithm is that the camera must be calibrated in advance.

With the library were programmed two augmented reality applications shown in Fig. 3. A virtual object is shown above the corresponding marker. It is possible to move the marker in the real world, or to move, carefully, the camera. The virtual object follows the marker on the monitor screen. We used images with a resolution of 640×480 pixels, and then we obtained a processing frame rate of 30 frames per second. The Raspberry Pi 3 camera has a buildin autofocus feature [1], thus camera must be recalibrated at time to time. In our applications we recalibrate the camera at every frame because it is possible that focus change due this autofocus characteristic. In applications in Fig. 3 OpenGL 2.1 was used (this is the version that supports the Raspberry Pi 3) using glut for input/output. The glut function `glutTimerFunc` implements the timer that guide the main loop at 30 fps. Still could be possible to add a intelligent behavior to the application: perhaps it is not necessary to recalibrate if the reprojection error of the marker vertices is not to high. We are going to check this last possibility in the near future.

 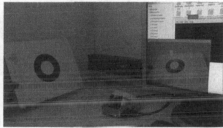

Fig. 3. Two pictures from two applications of augmented reality working on the Raspberry Pi 3

In OpenCV documentation in [2] it is available the SVD but not the QR decomposition. It seems now that OpenCV uses its own SVD implementation. In previous versions it used old Blas/Lapack numerical libraries (these libraries are used also by Octave). These old numerical libraries are written in Fortran language. We believe our small library uses memory more efficiently than Blas/Lapack and because of this reason, it can run very fast.

5   Conclusions

We have developed a light numerical library which can be applied in augmented reality application. We can calibrate a camera and calculate the pose for two different markers.

This library is programmed in C language and is intended for computing restricted devices such as smartphones, tablets and single board computers.

Results with our library are almost the same that the ones obtained with Octave that is a high level numerical language.

We tested our library in the Raspberry Pi 3 SBC. A frame rate of 30 frames per second with a camera resolution of 640 × 480 pixels was obtained.

As a future work we think it is necessary a function to calculate the marker pose solving the PnP problem [14]. PnP problem solves the pose if camera intrinsic parameters are known. The method to obtain the pose based in the homography, described in this article, is a linear method which has not the best results.

Otherwise, it is necessary to refine the solution using a non-linear method, which could be prohibitive in a real time application. It is necessary to investigate more about this problem of pose detection.

References

1. Camera model v2 documentation. https://www.raspberrypi.org/documentation/hardware/camera/. Accessed 9 Oct 2017
2. Open source computer vision library (OpenCV). http://opencv.org. Accessed 18 Sept 2017
3. Billinghurst, M., Dünser, A.: Augmented reality in the classroom. IEEE Mag. Comput. **45**, 56–63 (2012)
4. Di Serio, A., Blanca Ibáñez, M., Delgado Kloos, C.: Impact of an augmented reality system on students motivation for a visual art course. Comput. Educ. **68**, 586–596 (2013)
5. Fitzgibbon, A., Pilu, M., Fisher, R.: Direct least square fitting of ellipses. IEEE Trans. Pattern Anal. Mach. Intell. **21**(5), 476–480 (1999). https://doi.org/10.1109/34.765658
6. de la Fraga, L., Cruz Díaz, C.: Fitting an ellipse is equivalent to find the roots of a cubic equation. In: 2011 8th International Conference on Electrical Engineering, Computer Science and Automatic Control, pp. 1–4. IEEE (2011)
7. Gervautz, M., Schmalstieg, D.: Anywhere interfaces using handheld augmented reality. IEEE Mag. Comput. **45**, 26–31 (2012)
8. Golub, G., Van Loan, F.: Matrix Computations, 3rd edn. The Johns Hopkins University Press, Baltimore (1996)
9. Hartley, R., Zisserman, A.: Multiple View Geometry in Computer Vision, 2nd edn. Cambridge University Press, Cambridge (2003)
10. Kim, J.S., Gurdjos, P., Kweon, I.S.: Geometric and algebraic constraints of projected concentric circles and their applications to camera calibration. IEEE Trans. Pattern Anal. Mach. Intell. **27**(4), 637–642 (2005)
11. Kneip, L., Scaramuzza, D., Siegwart, R.: A novel parametrization of the perspective-three-point problem for a direct computation of absolute camera position and orientation. In: 2011 IEEE Conference on Computer Vision and Pattern Recognition (CVPR)(2011). https://doi.org/10.1109/CVPR.2011.5995464
12. Kopp, J.: Efficient numerical diagonalization of hermitian 3×3 matrices. Int. J. Mod. Phys. C **19**, 523–548 (2008)
13. Zhang, Z.: A flexible new technique for camera calibration. IEEE Trans. Pattern Anal. Mach. Intell. **22**(11), 1330–1334 (2000)
14. Zheng, Y., Kuang, Y., Sugimoto, S., Astrom, K., Okutomi, M.: Revisiting the PnP problem: a fast, general and optimal solution. In: The IEEE International Conference on Computer Vision (ICCV), December 2013

Point Set Matching with Order Type

Luis Gerardo de la Fraga$^{(\boxtimes)}$ and Heriberto Cruz Hernandez

Computer Science Department, CINVESTAV,
Av. IPN 2508, 07360 Mexico City, Mexico
fraga@cs.cinvestav.mx

Abstract. The problem to find the matching of two set of points in
the plane is solved in this paper, using a combinatorial invariant from
Computational Geometry called Order Type. The problem is solved even
if one of the set points has a general projective transformation. We show
an application of this problem to recognize fiducial markers that can be
used in augmented reality.

Keywords: Order Type · Augmented reality
Automatic identification · Rigid point registration

1 Introduction

The feature matching or feature correspondence is a very common subtask for
many tasks in Computer Vision. We find its application in camera calibration,
image aligning, image stitching, pattern recognition, 3D reconstruction, and augmented reality. The task consists in characterizing and identifying points through
different images of a same scene or object from distinct points of views (with
difference of angles, distances, changes of illumination and projective transformations). In the last decade the problem has been widely studied and many
approaches have been developed [13]. The selection of the method depends on
the final application since the methods exploit different image aspects to solve
the problem. Two of the most popular and used methods [1,11] are SIFT [12]
and SURF [4] along with epipolar geometry constraints [9]. These methods are
based in the analysis of local regions (the analysis of the neighborhood pixels of
a given feature). These methods generate a descriptor for each salient feature on
images. The matching with these methods consists in propose a putative correspondence between points of different images with the most similar descriptors.
Although SIFT and SURF are very popular and used, they are mainly suitable
to find matches between RGB images with high presence of textures.

In Computer Vision and Robotics, visual fiducials (artificial landmarks that
are easy to identify from images) are a very used tool to provide uncontrolled
scenarios of some reference to perform tasks as: automatic object identification,
SLAM [7,15], camera calibration [9], and camera pose estimation [9]. Visual
fiducials are commonly high reflectance (black and white) planar patterns that
encode a unique ID. Fiducials require of feature matching, specially to perform

© Springer International Publishing AG, part of Springer Nature 2018
J. F. Martínez-Trinidad et al. (Eds.): MCPR 2018, LNCS 10880, pp. 229–237, 2018.
https://doi.org/10.1007/978-3-319-92198-3_23

camera pose estimation but they lack of complex textures to use methods like SIFT of SURF. To perform the matching, some authors propose to exploit the known characteristics (constant features) of the tags, e.g., border corners, feature arrangements, distances, or colors.

When the two set of points are on planes, the translation, inplane rotation and scale to match both sets, can be recovered in a close form [14]. With our proposal it is possible to match the point sets even under a general rotation and perspective transformations. Given the matching, then it is possible to calculate the homography and from it to recover all the parameters for all the transformations [6,9].

This paper is structured as follows: in Sect. 2 we describe how Order Type can be used to perform the point matching. In Sect. 3 we present an application that validates our approach. Finally in Sect. 4 conclusions and future work are drawn.

2   Order Type for Point Matching

Goodman and Pollack [8] first introduced Order Type (OT) as a method to describe point sets in terms of the orientation of subsets of three points. OT can be understood as a conceptual way for describing point sets in the space and it is considered one of the most fundamental combinatorial descriptions of points on the plane. It encodes for each triplet of points its orientation and thus reflects most of the combinatorial properties of a given point set, avoiding the use of metric information.

The number of OTs is finite. In recent years OT has been widely studied and all existing OTs have been enumerated in the database provided in [2]. This database provides an instance of each existing OTs with point set cardinality up to eleven points (see Table 1). For simplicity, we denote as C^k the set with point subsets of the same cardinality k, and each instance in C^k as C_l^k, where l

Table 1. Number of OTs by the point set cardinality.

Set	$|C^k|$ = Number of OTs
C^3	1
C^4	2
C^5	3
C^6	16
C^7	135
C^8	3 315
C^9	158 817
C^{10}	14 309 547
C^{11}	2 334 512 907

is the number of instance. OTs in C^k with $k \leq 8$ are given in the database [2] with a precision of 8 bits per point.

OT can be described using an Order Type Representation (OTR). OTRs can be seen as data structures that quantify the triplets orientations. Many of them have been proposed [3] but one of the most compact is the λ-matrix.

λ-matrix is an OTR originally proposed by Goodman and Pollack [8]. It is a $n \times n$ matrix, for n points, in which each entry $\lambda(i, j)$ represents the number of points in the set that are on the left (positive) side of the oriented line through points p_i, p_j, for $i \neq j$. The orientation of a triplet of points (p_1, p_2, p_3) can be calculated by its *signed area* as the z value of the cross product of vectors $[p_2 - p_1, 0]$ and $[p_3 - p_1, 0]$. This cross product gives the double signed area of the triangle formed by the triplet.

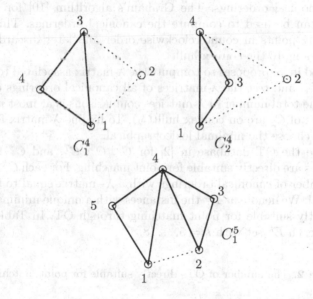

Fig. 1. The two OTs with the set of four points and the first OT that can be formed with five points.

In Fig. 1 it is shown the two OTs that can be obtained with four points, and one instance of the first OT with $n = 5$. These sets have not the same point positions that the sets in database in [2]. The lambda matrix for the labeling in C_4^1 shown in Fig. 1 is (do not care now about shown triangles, their utility will be explained later):

$$\begin{bmatrix} - & 2 & 1 & 0 \\ 0 & - & 2 & 1 \\ 1 & 0 & - & 2 \\ 2 & 1 & 0 & - \end{bmatrix} \tag{1}$$

An important aspect to mention is that λ-matrix depends on points labeling. Two different labelings of the same point set will correspond to two different λ-matrices. Although λ-matrix is sensible to point set labeling, the OT is not [8].

If two point sets C_1 and C_2 have the same λ-matrix and thus the same OT, C_1 and C_2 will be combinatorially equivalent. Since there are $n!$ possible labelings in a point set, for each point set there will be $n!$ associated λ-matrices. A naive method to determine if two unlabeled point sets are combinatorially equivalent is to fix a labeling in C_1, compute its associated λ-matrix and compute the $n!$ λ-matrices of C_2 until finding a coincidence of matrices.

A more efficient method is based in canonical order [8]. Canonical order is a way to label elements in a point set in a counterclockwise way starting by those points on the convex hull. All the three sets in Fig. 1 are labeled counterclockwise.

Since we can choose $m = |\text{convex\_hull}(C)|$ different initial points, there will also be m canonical orderings. The Graham's algorithm [10] for convex hull computation can be used to compute the canonical orderings. This algorithm start by sorting points in counterclockwise order and later discards all points that do not belong to the convex hull.

The method in [8] proposes to compute the λ-matrix associated to one canonical order of C_1, and test the λ-matrices of all canonical orderings of C_2. With this method the total number of λ-matrices comparisons is at most n in the case when all points of C_2 are on convex_hull(C_2). To fix one λ-matrix for both two sets, we could choose the minimal lexicographical.

We analyze the OT database in [2] for C^5, C^6, C^7, and C^8 for checking which instances are directly suitable for point matching. For each C_i^k instance we count the number of canonical orderings with a $\lambda-$matrix equal to the minimal lexicographical. We denote as E_i^k the instances with a unique minimal $\lambda-$matrix that are directly suitable for point matching through OT. In Table 2 we show the count for each E^k set with $k = 5, \ldots, 8$.

Table 2. The number of OTs directly suitable for point matching.

Set	$|E^K|$ =Number of OTs
E^5	2
E^6	11
E^7	13
E^8	3303

The two OTs in C^4 and the first in set C^5 (see Tables 1 and 2) are not suitable for direct point matching purposes. These three OTs are shown in Fig. 1. If the triangles shown in the same Fig. 1 are also stored, then it is possible to calculated similarly like λ-matrix but only checking of an edge exist between each pair of points p_i and p_j, for $i, j \in n$ and $i \neq j$. The three possible labelings and associated edge's matrix for the set C_2^4 are shown in Fig. 2. The second

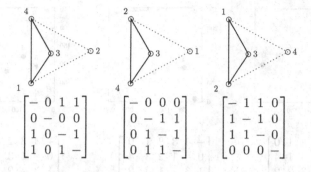

Fig. 2. The three possible canonical labelings for C^4 and their associated edges matrices. The second matrix is the minimal lexicographical, it corresponds to the invariant labeling, and can be used for matching purposes.

edges matrix is the minimal lexicographical and can be used to match two sets of points. The second labeling is invariant to geometrical transformations.

Pose Estimation. To perform the pose estimation between two set of points, three main steps must be performed: (1) *Point matching*: it consists in identifying each one of the points and their correspondences in image coordinates without ambiguity. (2) *Homography estimation*: it consists in estimating the projective transformation between the matched points on the model and the image. And (3) *Pose estimation*: it is to obtain the relative rotation and translation between two point sets through homography analysis. These three steps are described in detail in subsequent paragraphs.

Given two point sets C (points on the model) and C' (points on the image) we propose to perform the point to point matching using an invariant labeling. Each λ–matrix or edge's matrix has an associated point labeling. We propose to use the point labeling associated to the minimal lexicographical λ–matrix (or edge's matrix) as the invariant labeling. The idea is to compute the invariant labeling for the model point set $\mathcal{L}(C)$ and the invariant labeling for the point set on the image $\mathcal{L}(C')$. With this approach, the solution is given by the association (as matches) between the points in C with the same label in C', through $\mathcal{L}(C)$ and $\mathcal{L}(C)$.

The process to choose the invariant labeling is illustrated in Fig. 3. In the figure we show the 14-th point set in C^6. We show the tree possible λ–matrices, one for each canonical order (check out how the initial point is rotated in counterclockwise direction), since there are three points on convex hull, only three labelings are generated and three associated λ–matrices are obtained. In this instance, the labeling in the middle is the one with the minimal lexicographical λ–matrix, then the labeling in the middle is the invariant labeling that we use for point matching purposes.

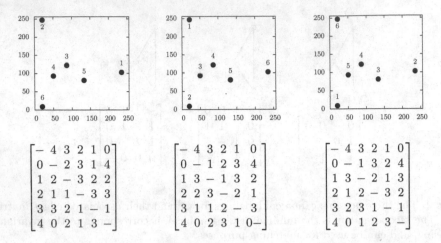

Fig. 3. The 14-th point set in C^6, its three canonical orderings, and their associated λ–matrix. The λ–matrix in the middle is the minimal lexicographical, thus the labeling in the middle is the invariant labeling.

Homography Estimation. To model the image generation process we use the camera pinhole model [9]. Given a point set C, it is transformed to the image coordinates by the expression: $\lambda C' = HC$, where C' is the transformed point set in image coordinates, $H \in \mathbb{R}^{3\times3}$ is an homography, i.e., a projective transformation that maps points on a plane (points in C) to another (pixels in the image), and λ is an unknown scale factor. $H = K[r_1 r_2, t]$ comprises the camera characteristics and also contains information about the relative pose between the camera and in our case the tag. $K = \begin{bmatrix} f_x & s & u_0 \\ 0 & f_y & v_0 \\ 0 & 0 & 1 \end{bmatrix}$, is known as the camera matrix and comprises the focal distances f_x, f_y, obliqueness s, and principal point $[u_0, v_0]^T$. $R = [r_1, r_3, r_3]$ is a rotation matrix with $r_i \in \mathbf{R}^{3\times1}$ columns, and $t \in \mathbf{R}^{3\times1}$ is a translation vector.

In this paper we estimate homography H through the normalized DTL algorithm [9] using all the matches between C and C'.

To obtain the pose between the camera and the tag, i.e., the rotation matrix R and the translation vector t from the decomposition of the homography H. We apply the Zhang's method in [16] using the model and only one image. With this method we obtain an approximation for the intrinsic parameters in matrix K and also the R and t for the pose.

3   Application

To test the feature matching we implemented an Augmented Reality demo. We take three feature suitable OT instances and we generate their respective fiducial marker using triangle vertexes to identify the point positions.

In our application we solve the feature matching using the procedure described previously, then we estimated homography by DTL and point normalization [9] using the seven vertexes inside data area, and finally we obtain the pose to place virtual objects. In Fig. 4 we show the result for this experiment, we observe the detected vertexes as green dots, tag axes: x (red), y (green), and three virtual objects (three cubes rotating in their own vertical axis), one placed at center of the tag and two other at two opposite corners.

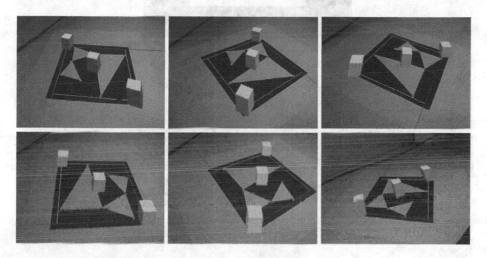

Fig. 4. Augmented reality application. Six images rotating the marker. The pose is fully obtained (check out how axes lines rotates with the marker).

Also, here we compare the pose estimated with two methods and four conditions: (a) the pose estimated using the homography with the four vertices of the square marker, (b) the pose estimated using the homography and the seven points of our fiducial marker, (c) and (d) the same conditions that in (a) and (b) but using the infinitesimal algorithm in [5]. Our fiducial marker at position $\theta_1 = 0$ is shown in Fig. 5. We used the camera model $\lambda_1 \mathbf{p} = \mathbf{K}[\mathbf{R}|\mathbf{t}]\mathbf{P}$, where λ_1 is an arbitrary scale factor, $\mathbf{p}$ a point on the image, K the matrix of camera intrinsic parameters, $R = R_z(\theta_3)R_y(\theta_2)R_z(\theta_1)$ a rotation matrix, and $\mathbf{P}$ a 3D point.

We add Gaussian noise with zero mean and a standard deviation of 1 pixel to each x and y point coordinate. The average of 30 estimations of the error in θ_1 angle, and the error in $\mathbf{t}$ position vector are shown in Fig. 6. The estimation of using Zhang's method described in Subsection 2 gives a lesser error using four points because the square (see Fig. 5) is bigger than the seven points pattern. The error is similar using the better, and refined, infinitesimal method (IPPE in Fig. 6) in [5]. In Fig. 6 to the left, it is also shown that the estimation of θ_1 only cover a range of 90° (the error is around 90° and it is not show on the graph) using four points; and this angle is fully recovered using the seven point of our marker.

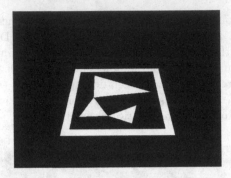

Fig. 5. Our fiducial marker in perspective at position $\theta_1 = 0$.

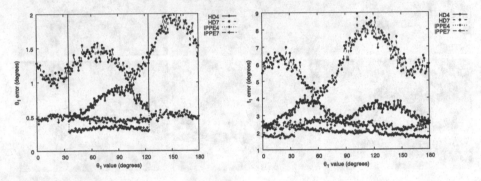

Fig. 6. The average of 30 estimations of θ_1 (to the left) and t (to the right).

4   Conclusion

In this work we study how Order Type can be used for point set matching. We have been used very low number of points (less than nine). We show an application in detection and pose estimation for a fiducial marker that can be used in augmented reality.

As future work we aim to develop an strategy to support occlusion in the markers, also to study OT behavior with more than eight points in real applications, and to investigate the use of OT to solve other Computer Vision tasks.

References

1. Vinay, A., Hebbar, D., Shekhar, V.S., Murthy, K.N.B., Natarajan, S.: Two novel detector-descriptor based approaches for face recognition using sift and surf. Proc. Comput. Sci. **70**, 185–197 (2015). Proceedings of the 4th International Conference on Eco-friendly Computing and Communication Systems. https://doi.org/10.1016/j.procs.2015.10.070
2. Aichholzer, O., Aurenhammer, F., Krasser, H.: Enumerating order types for small point sets with applications. Order **19**(3), 265–281. https://doi.org/10.1023/A:1021231927255. Accessed 15 Jan 2016

3. Aloupis, G., Iacono, J., Langerman, S., Özkan, O., Wuhrer, S.: The complexity of order type isomorphism. In: Proceedings of the Twenty-Fifth Annual ACM-SIAM Symposium on Discrete Algorithms, SODA 2014, pp. 405–415. SIAM (2014)
4. Bay, H., Ess, A., Tuytelaars, T., Van Gool, L.: Speeded-up robust features (SURF). Comput. Vis. Image Underst. 110(3), 346–359 (2008). https://doi.org/10.1016/j.cviu.2007.09.014
5. Collins, T., Bartoli, A.: Infinitesimal plane-based pose estimation. Int. J. Comput. Vis. 109(3), 252–286 (2014). https://doi.org/10.1007/s11263-014-0725-5
6. Fitzgibbon, A.: Robust registration of 2D and 3D point sets. Image Vis. Comput. 21, 1145–1153 (2003). https://doi.org/10.1016/j.imavis.2003.09.004
7. Gálvez-López, D., Salas, M., Tardós, J.D., Montiel, J.: Real-time monocular object slam. Robotics Auton. Syst. 75, 435–449 (2016). https://doi.org/10.1016/j.robot.2015.08.009
8. Goodman, J.E., Pollack, R.: Multidimensional sorting. SIAM J. Comput. 12(3), 484–507 (1983)
9. Hartley, R.I., Zisserman, A.: Multiple View Geometry in Computer Vision, 2nd edn. Cambridge University Press, Cambridge (2004). ISBN 0521540518
10. Johnsonbaugh, R.: Discrete Mathematics. Pearson/Prentice Hall, London/Upper Saddle River (2009). https://books.google.co.uk/books?id=KJwvt2Zz2R8C
11. Juan, L., Gwon, O.: A comparison of SIFT, PCA-SIFT and SURF. Int. J. Image Process. (IJIP) 3(4), 143–152 (2009). http://www.cscjournals.org/csc/manuscript/Journals/IJIP/volume3/Issue4/IJIP-51.pdf
12. Khan, N.Y., McCane, B., Wyvill, G.: Sift and surf performance evaluation against various image deformations on benchmark dataset. In: 2011 International Conference on Digital Image Computing: Techniques and Applications, pp. 501–506, December 2011. https://doi.org/10.1109/DICTA.2011.90
13. Krig, S.: Computer Vision Metrics: Survey, Taxonomy, and Analysis, 1st edn. Apress, Berkely (2014)
14. Shamsudin, S., Murray, A.: A closed-form solution for the similarity transformation parameters of two planar point sets. J. Mech. Eng. Technol. 5(1), 59–68 (2013)
15. Yang, S., Scherer, S.A., Yi, X., Zell, A.: Multi-camera visual slam for autonomous navigation of micro aerial vehicles. Robot. Auton. Syst. 93, 116–134 (2017). https://doi.org/10.1016/j.robot.2017.03.018
16. Zhang, Z.: A flexible new technique for camera calibration. IEEE Trans. Pattern Anal. Mach. Intell. 22(11), 1330–1334 (2000)

Including Foreground and Background Information in Maya Hieroglyph Representation

Laura Alejandra Pinilla-Buitrago$^{(\boxtimes)}$, Jesús A. Carrasco-Ochoa,
and José Fco. Martinez-Trinidad

Departamento de Ciencias Computacionales, Instituto Nacional de Astrofísica,
Óptica y Electrónica, Luis Enrique Erro # 1, Puebla, Mexico
{laurapin,ariel,fmartine}@inaoep.mx

Abstract. In the literature, all methods that represent Maya hieroglyphs compute local descriptors from the hieroglyph foreground. However, the background of a hieroglyph also contains information of its
shape. Therefore, in this paper, we propose a new Maya hieroglyph representation that includes information from both, the foreground and the
background. Our experimental results show that our proposal for representing Maya hieroglyphs allows obtaining better retrieval results than
those previously reported in the state of the art.

Keywords: Hieroglyphs · Maya hieroglyphs
Hieroglyph representation · Foreground · Background

1 Introduction

Hieroglyph representation has emerged from the need of carrying out tasks
that support or facilitate the study of inscriptions containing ancient writing.
In the literature, Maya hieroglyph representation has been faced following two
approaches: The first one consists in representing each hieroglyph by means
of multiple local descriptors [1,2]. The second one combines the local descriptors computed in the first approach with the *Bag of Visual Words* (BoVW)
model [3,4]. This last approach has reported the best results. In this approach,
the representation that reports the best results for image retrieval [3] starts
pre-processing the hieroglyph foreground by thinning it to one pixel with. The
foreground corresponds to all lines and strokes in the image. Then, a subset
of interest points is obtained from all points in the thinned foreground, and
for each interest point a HOOSC (*Histogram of Orientation Shape-Context*) [2]
local descriptor is computed. Finally, for each hieroglyph a vector-based representation is obtained through these local descriptors under the BoVW model [5].
In the literature, several works [3,4,6,7] compute local descriptors from thinned
Maya hieroglyph images. In all these works only the foreground is used. However,
the background of a hieroglyph also contains information of its shape. For this

J. F. Martínez-Trinidad et al. (Eds.): MCPR 2018, LNCS 10880, pp. 238–247, 2018.
https://doi.org/10.1007/978-3-319-92198-3_24

reason, in this work, we propose a new hieroglyph representation which includes foreground and background information. Our experiments show that our proposal obtains better hieroglyph retrieval results than other works reported in the state of the art.

This paper is organized as follows: In Sect. 2, we describe our proposal. Section 3 shows our experimental results. Finally, conclusions and future work are presented in Sect. 4.

2   Proposed Method

As we have already mentioned, the background of a hieroglyph also contains useful information, which could be used for Maya hieroglyph representation.

For this reason, in this work we propose including into the most successful Maya hieroglyph representation [3], information from the foreground and the background of a hieroglyph. Our proposal starts by pre-processing each hieroglyph by thinning separately its foreground and its background. The pre-processing of the image is described in Sect. 2.1. Then, a subset (a percentage) of interest points is randomly selected from the thinned foreground. After, from each interest point a local descriptor is computed, but considering both, the thinned foreground and the thinned background of the hieroglyph (Sect. 2.2). Once the local descriptors have been computed, each hieroglyph is represented following the BoVW model, in the same way as in [3] (Sect. 2.3).

2.1   Pre-processing a Maya Hieroglyph

Let H be the binary shape of a Maya hieroglyph, whose pixels can take 0 or 1 values. In this work, the *foreground* is the set of pixels with 1 value (white pixels), and the *background* is the set of pixels with 0 value (black pixels).

We obtain the thinned foreground and the thinned background by using the thinning process presented in [8]. To obtain the thinned foreground, we directly apply [8] in H (see Fig. 1a and b). For computing the thinned background, the complement of H is previously obtained (see Fig. 1c and d). The complement of

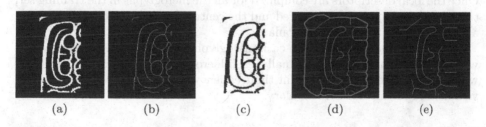

(a)   (b)   (c)   (d)   (e)

Fig. 1. Thinned foreground and background: (a) Original hieroglyph. (b) Thinned foreground. (c) Complement of (a). (d) Thinned background. Edges coming from the border are marked in red. (e) Final thinned background. (Color figure online)

a binary image is obtained by reversing all pixels values, which means that zeros become ones and viceversa. During the computation of the thinned background, there arise some branches coming from border (see Fig. 1d). Since these branches do not represent important details of the hieroglyphs, they are eliminated (see Fig. 1e).

2.2 Computing Local Descriptors

Once the thinned foreground and the thinned background have been computed, a set of local descriptors are computed as follows. Let P and Q be the sets of points in the thinned foreground and the thinned background, respectively. First, we compute a subset (i.e. a percentage) of interest points, denoted as P', from the thinned foreground, by uniform random sampling [3]. Then, for each point $p'_i \in P'$ a local descriptor is computed but unlike [3] by using all points in $P \cup Q$ (see Fig. 2).

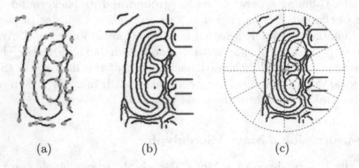

(a)   (b)   (c)

Fig. 2. Computing local descriptors: (a) Interest points (red) from thinned foreground. (b) Thinned foreground (black) and background (blue). (c) Local descriptor computed from a interest point using the thinned foreground and the thinned background (Color figure online)

2.3 Representing Maya Hieroglyphs

Once the local descriptors are computed for all the hieroglyphs in the training set, these local descriptors are clustered and the centroid of each cluster is considered a visual word in the visual vocabulary.

Then, each local descriptor in each hieroglyph is replaced by its closest visual word in the visual vocabulary. Finally, each hieroglyph is represented as a vector where the $i-$th entry will contain the frequency in the hieroglyph of the $i-$th visual word in the visual vocabulary.

3 Experiments

In this section, we compare our proposal, which represents Maya hieroglyphs by including foreground and background information, against the most successful method for representing Maya hieroglyphs reported in the literature [3], which only includes information from the foreground.

For our experiments, two Maya hieroglyph databases were used. The first database [4], denoted as *Maya-I*, contains 240 instances distributed over 24 categories (10 Maya hieroglyphs per category). An example from each category is shown in Fig. 3. The second database [3], denoted as *Maya-II*, contains 1043 instances distributed over 25 categories. A histogram with the number of hieroglyphs per category and an instance from each one, is shown in Fig. 4.

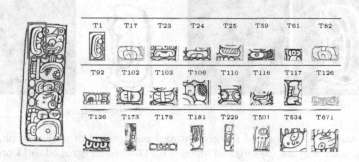

Fig. 3. Examples of hieroglyphs from the *Maya-I* database; an instance from each category is shown.

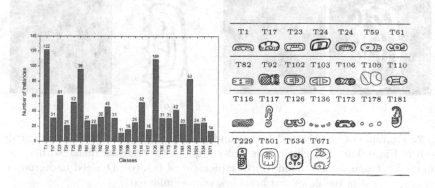

Fig. 4. Examples of hieroglyphs from the *Maya-II* database; an instance from each category is shown. The histogram shows the number of instances per category.

Since *Maya-I* and *Maya-II* databases contain hieroglyphs with different sizes, before pre-processing the hieroglyphs, all of them were resized to 256 × 256 pixels. n these databases, some hieroglyphs contain noisy regions (see Fig. 5), which often arise from the digitalization process. If these regions are not removed before the thinning process, many additional/unwanted branches that do not represent useful image information and that negatively affect the hieroglyph representation, can arise (see Fig. 6). In order to remove most of these noisy regions, we apply the noise filter proposed in [9] (see Fig. 7).

Fig. 5. Maya hieroglyphs with noisy regions, marked in red (Color figure online)

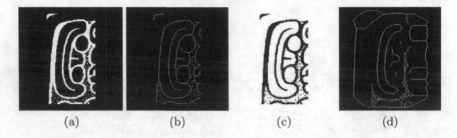

(a)   (b)   (c)   (d)

Fig. 6. Example of the thinned foreground and background of a hieroglyph, without eliminating noisy regions. (a) Original image. (b) Thinned foreground. (c) Complement of (a). (d) Thinned background. In both, (c) and (d), there are unwanted branches coming from noisy regions.

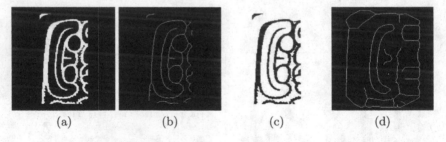

(a)   (b)   (c)   (d)

Fig. 7. Example of the thinned foreground and background of the same hieroglyph shown in Fig. 6, but after eliminating noisy regions. (a) Original image without noisy regions. (b) Thinned foreground. (c) Complement of (a). (d) Thinned background. In both cases, most of the unwanted branches were eliminated.

In our experiments, as well as in [3], we use 10% of the points in the thinned foreground as interest points, and we also use HOOSC4 [3] as local descriptor. We build a visual vocabulary with 1500 visual words by applying k-means, with $k = 1500$.

As we mentioned before, for showing the advantages of our proposed representation (denoted as "Foreground & Background"), we compare our proposal, in the context of image retrieval, against the method presented in [3], which will be denoted as "Foreground". All experiments were conducted using *five-fold cross-validation*. In each experiment, four folds (80% of Maya hieroglyphs from each class) were used as training set, and one fold (20% of Maya hieroglyphs from each class) was used as query images. From the training set, the visual vocabulary was computed. We run each experiment three times in each partition and the average of the mean average precision (average mAP) for all queries is reported. Table 1 shows the average mAP obtained for *Maya-I* and *Maya-II* databases, using the compared Maya hieroglyph representations for image retrieval.

Table 1. Average mAP of our proposal (Foreground & Background) and the method proposed in [3] (Foreground) for *Maya-I* and *Maya-II*

Method	Database	
	Maya-I	*Maya-II*
Foreground	0.2872	0.3131
Foreground & Background	0.3750	0.4564

As we can see in Table 1, in both databases, our proposal "Foreground & Background" outperformed the retrieval results (in terms of average mAP) obtained by "Foreground" [3].

In Fig. 8, we present graphs of the average of the average precision (average AP) *vs* standard recall, for the *Maya-I* and *Maya-II* databases. Each graph shows the results obtained by our proposal and the hieroglyph representation presented in [3], both using 10% of interest points (which are obtained from the thinned foreground) and HOOSC4 as local descriptor. These graphs correspond to the results presented in Table 1. As it can be seen in Fig. 8, our method in all intervals (standard recall), achieves the best average AP.

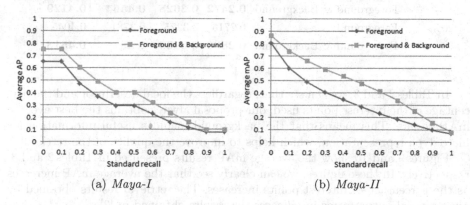

(a) *Maya-I*   (b) *Maya-II*

Fig. 8. Average AP *vs* standar recall of "Foreground & Background" (our proposal) and "Foreground" [3], using 10% of interest points and HOOSC4 local descriptors, for (a) *Maya-I* and (b) *Maya-II*.

We carry out an additional experiment, where our proposal is evaluated by using different local descriptors, including SC [10], HOOSC [2], HOOSC4 [3] and

HOOSC128 [11]. We also show the results using different percentages of interest points (5%, 10% and 20%). These results are shown in Tables 2 and 3 for *Maya-I* and *Maya-II*, respectively.

Table 2. Average mAP of our proposal (Foreground & Background) and the method proposed in [3] (Foreground) for Maya-I, using different local descriptors.

% Points	Method	Descriptor			
		SC	HOOSC	HOOSC4	HOOSC128
5%	Foreground	0.1448	0.1775	0.2339	0.1864
	Foreground & Background	**0.1847**	**0.2228**	**0.2972**	**0.2424**
10%	Foreground	0.1905	0.1977	0.2872	0.2262
	Foreground & Background	**0.2425**	**0.2583**	**0.3750**	**0.2969**
20%	Foreground	0.2515	0.2393	0.3341	0.2833
	Foreground & Background	**0.2543**	**0.2871**	0.4126	**0.3245**

Table 3. Average mAP of our proposal (Foreground & Background) and the method proposed in [3] (Foreground) for Maya-II, using different local descriptors.

% Points	Method	Descriptor			
		SC	HOOSC	HOOSC4	HOOSC128
5%	Foreground	0.1266	0.1759	0.2192	0.2460
	Foreground & Background	**0.1698**	**0.2975**	**0.3591**	**0.3319**
10%	Foreground	0.1797	0.2592	0.3131	0.3463
	Foreground & Background	**0.2472**	**0.3628**	**0.4564**	**0.4129**
20%	Foreground	0.2716	0.3275	0.3781	0.4045
	Foreground & Background	**0.2886**	**0.3969**	0.4979	**0.4513**

In Tables 2 and 3, we can see that, regardless the local descriptor and the percentage of the interest points used, our proposal always obtains the best average mAP results. This means that the background includes useful information for hieroglyph representation, which helps to improve the quality of the retrieval.

Figures 9 and 10 show the average mAP results presented in Tables 2 and 3, respectively. In these figures, we can clearly see that the average mAP increases as the percentage of interest points increases. The retrieval results obtained by our proposal outperforms in all cases the results obtained in [3].

In both databases, the best average mAP results were obtained with our proposal by using 20% of interest points with HOOSC4 local descriptors. In Fig. 11 we show these results for both databases, in terms of the average AP *vs* standard recall. In this figure we can see that the average AP obtained by our proposal outperforms, in all cases, the results obtained using only information from the foreground as in [3].

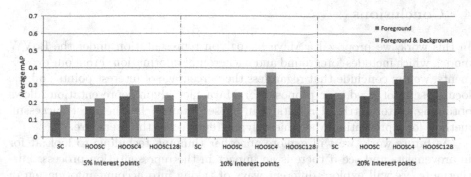

Fig. 9. Average mAP of our proposal (Foreground & Background) and the method proposed in [3] (Foreground) for *Maya-I*, using different percentages of interest points and different local descriptors.

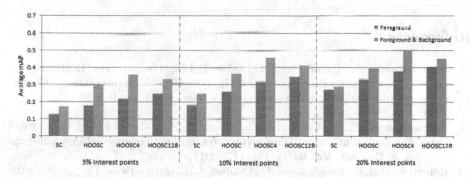

Fig. 10. Average mAP of our proposal (Foreground & Background) and the method proposed in [3] (Foreground) for *Maya-II*, using different percentages of interest points and different local descriptors.

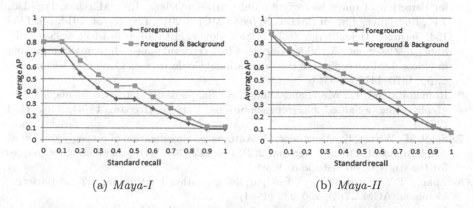

(a) *Maya-I*   (b) *Maya-II*

Fig. 11. Average mAP of our proposal (Foreground & Background) and the method proposed in [3] (Foreground) using 20% of interest points and HOOSC4 local descriptors, for (a) *Maya-I* and (b) *Maya-II*.

4   Conclusions

In this work, we proposed a Maya hieroglyph representation under the BoVW model, which includes foreground and background information. From our experiments, we can conclude that regardless the percentage of interest points and the local descriptor used, our proposal for Maya hieroglyph representation allows obtaining better retrieval results than those obtained by the most successful method for representing Maya hieroglyphs reported in the literature.

As future work, we will explore annother thinning technique to look at for improvements and see if there is an impact in the representation process. Furthermore, we will explore different ways of taking into account information of the background for building better hieroglyph representations.

Acknowledgment. This work was partly supported by the National Council of Science and Technology of México (CONACyT) under the scholarship grant 401885.

References

1. Roman-Rangel, E., Pallan Gayol, C., Odobez, J.M., Gatica-Perez, D.: Retrieving ancient Maya glyphs with shape context. In: 2009 IEEE 12th International Conference on Computer Vision Workshops, ICCV Workshops, pp. 988–995, September 2009
2. Roman-Rangel, E., Pallan Gayol, C., Odobez, J.M., Gatica-Perez, D., Gatica-Perez, D.: Analyzing ancient Maya glyph collections with contextual shape descriptors. Int. J. Comput. Vis. **94**(1), 101–117 (2011)
3. Roman-Rangel, E., Pallan Gayol, C., Odobez, J.M., Gatica-Perez, D.: Searching the past: an improved shape descriptor to retrieve Maya hieroglyphs. In: Proceedings of the 19th International Conference on Multimedia 2011, Scottsdale, AZ, USA, 28 November–1 December 2011, pp. 163–172 (2011)
4. Roman-Rangel, E., Odobez, J.-M., Gatica-Perez, D.: Evaluating shape descriptors for detection of maya hieroglyphs. In: Carrasco-Ochoa, J.A., Martínez-Trinidad, J.F., Rodríguez, J.S., di Baja, G.S. (eds.) MCPR 2013. LNCS, vol. 7914, pp. 145–154. Springer, Heidelberg (2013). https://doi.org/10.1007/978-3-642-38989-4_15
5. Sivic, J., Zisserman, A.: Video Google: a text retrieval approach to object matching in videos. In: Proceedings of the International Conference on Computer Vision, vol. 2, pp. 1470–1477 (2003)
6. Roman-Rangel, E., Marchand-Maillet, S.: Shape-based detection of maya hieroglyphs using weighted bag representations. Pattern Recogn. **48**(4), 1161–1173 (2015)
7. Seidl, M., Wieser, E., Alexander, C.: Automated classification of petroglyphs. Digit. Appl. Archaeol. Cultural Heritage **2**(2), 196–212 (2015). Digital imaging techniques for the study of prehistoric rock art.
8. Zhang, T.Y., Suen, C.Y.: A fast parallel algorithm for thinning digital patterns. Commun. ACM **27**(3), 236–239 (1984)
9. Vincent, L.: Morphological area openings and closings for grey-scale images. In: O, Y.-L., Toet, A., Foster, D., Heijmans, H.J.A.M., Meer, P. (eds.) Shape in Picture, pp. 197–208. Springer, Heidelberg (1994). https://doi.org/10.1007/978-3-662-03039-4_13

10. Belongie, S., Malik, J., Puzicha, J.: Shape context: a new descriptor for shape matching and object recognition. In: NIPS, pp. 831–837 (2000)
11. Roman-Rangel, E., Marchand-Maillet, S.: HOOSC128: a more robust local shape descriptor. In: Martínez-Trinidad, J.F., Carrasco-Ochoa, J.A., Olvera-Lopez, J.A., Salas-Rodríguez, J., Suen, C.Y. (eds.) MCPR 2014. LNCS, vol. 8495, pp. 172–181. Springer, Cham (2014). https://doi.org/10.1007/978-3-319-07491-7_18

A Fast Algorithm for Robot Localization Using Multiple Sensing Units

Reinier Oves García[✉], Luis Valentin, José Martínez-Carranza,
and L. Enrique Sucar

Computer Science Department,
Instituto Nacional de Astrofísica Óptica y Electrónica,
Sta. María Tonantzintla, 72840 Puebla, Mexico
{ovesreinier,luismvc,carranza,esucar}@inaoep.mx

Abstract. This paper presents a fast algorithm for camera selection in a robotic multi-camera localization system. The scenario we study is that where a robot is navigating in an indoor environment using a four-camera vision system to localize itself inside the world. In this context, when something occludes the current camera used for localization, the system has to switch to one of the other three available cameras to remain localized. In this context, the question that arises is that of "what camera should be selected?". We address this by proposing an approach that aims at selecting the next best view to carry on the localization. For that, the number of static features at each direction is estimated using the optical flow. In order to validate our approach, experiments in a real scenario with a mobile robot system are presented.

Keywords: Multi-camera navigation · Multi-camera localization
Guidance

1 Introduction

Nowadays, by using conventional cameras it is possible to obtain a set of images, which can be processed in order to obtain the estimated position of the robot in real time [7]. However, multi-camera approaches have also been proposed as having more than one camera observing different parts of the scene and constitute an attractive approach that can be helpful when autonomous navigation is performed. One application of these multi-camera approaches can be found in [15], where more than two cameras are used for eliminating motion ambiguity problems in a visual odometry system.

Motivated by the advantages of using multi-camera systems capable of capturing an approximate 360° field of view, in this work we explore the scenario of when the localization system is partially or totally occluded in the current active view, this is, in one of the cameras that is currently being used for feature tracking and localization. In this scenario, one of the available cameras has to be selected to avoid tracking loss. Motivated by this, we propose an efficient

© Springer International Publishing AG, part of Springer Nature 2018
J. F. Martínez-Trinidad et al. (Eds.): MCPR 2018, LNCS 10880, pp. 248–257, 2018.
https://doi.org/10.1007/978-3-319-92198-3_25

method for camera selection aiming at maintaining localization in the event of camera occlusion.

Our approach is based under the assumption that only one view is used for localization while the rest of the cameras are used for relocalization in case an obstruction in the main view is presented. Therefore, the contribution of this work is two fold: (i) a methodology based on the optical flow exhibited by the scene structure w.r.t. is presented in order to estimate the velocity of the visual texture observed by the camera and use it to distinguish motion from steadiness; and (ii) we present a histogram-based approach in order to quantify the evolution of the texture's motion frame by frame. This evolution is assessed in terms of how steady or unsteady scenes are along the time.

In order to present our contribution, this paper is organized as follows: Sect. 2 presents the related work; Sect. 3 provides a description of our system. In Sect. 4 the proposed algorithm is described while in Sect. 5 experiments are conducted in order to make clear the idea of this paper. Finally, in Sect. 6 conclusion and future work are included.

2   Related Work

Arguably, a multi-camera rig sensor may arises as a better choice than using an omni-directional camera [18] to address different problems, i.e. the localization [14]. The latter is due to the fact that several conventional cameras mounted in a rig can be set up to obtain a wider field of view. In contrast, an omni-directional system may have a superior field of view but at the expense of exhibiting a strong distortion, where calibration and measurement process are not straightforward.

In [15] the authors use a multi-camera stereo rig to solve motion ambiguity problems in their visual odometry process. In [12], a framework is described for 6D absolute scale motion and structure estimation for a stereo multi-camera system with non-overlapping fields of view in indoor environments. In [2] the authors introduces a testbed for sensor and robot network systems composed of 10 cameras and 5 mobile robots for self-localization and obstacle avoidance using machine vision and wireless communication. In [10] the authors present an extension of the monocular ORB-SLAM for multiple cameras alongside an inertial measurement unit *(IMU)* and a multi-camera SLAM is proposed in [11] based on a probabilistic approach for data association, that takes into account that features can also move between cameras under robot motion.

Several visual SLAM algorithms use keyframes to reduce the computational cost for developing online optimization. Entropy handling in the keyframes insertion improves significantly the system's ability to localize. This approach is recently presented by [5] and is implemented within the omni-directional multi-camera parallel tracking and mapping framework. Another interesting recent work is proposed by Harmat *et al.* [9]. They addressed the pose problem for UAV's using Multiple fish-eye cameras for tracking and mapping a small UAV in unstructured environment systems. Their approach improves the PTAM [13] pose estimation with the multi-camera rig.

Besides of localization, a multi-camera stereo rig may be used to address another kind of problems, like in the work proposed by Akash *et al.* [1], where a method for performing a fast 6-DOF head pose tracking using a cluster of rolling shutter cameras is proposed in order to deal with end-to-end latency challenge in Augmented Reality/Virtual Reality *(AR/VR)* applications.

3   System Overview

The architecture proposed in this paper counts of two parts (i) the *Guidance* sensor (see Fig. 1(a)) and (ii) a service robot (see Fig. 1(b)). Technically, the *Guidance* sensor is an upgraded version of Zhou et al.'s work [19] which is a visual mapping solution based on four cameras and a single processing chip-Altera's SoC FPGA. In our case, the *Guidance* is a multi-camera rig that captures up to 5 stereo pairs with a depth image associated to each stereo pair at a frequency of 18 fps.

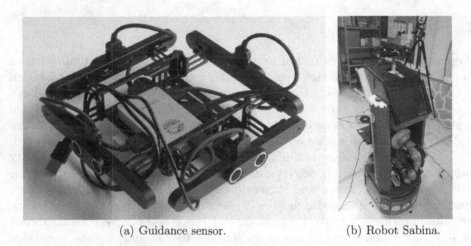

(a) Guidance sensor.   (b) Robot Sabina.

Fig. 1. (a) *Guidance* sensor: this image shows four of its five *stereo + ultrasound* cameras, which return gray and depth images, the sensor can be used to observe the scene in almost 360°. (b) Robot Sabina with the *Guidance* sensor on the top of it.

The way camera units are located in the rig enables the observation of the world in five directions *(front, back, left, right and top)*. The SDK, made available by the manufacturer [8], enables acquiering up to 10 gray images *(from the 5 stereo pairs)* simultaneously, with the caveat that only 2 depth images can be accessed simultaneously at a frequency of 18 Hz. Considering that we are interested in multi-camera localization within dynamic environments where laser-odometry may not be sufficient, we test our algorithm using a service robot based on a PatrolBot platform. The platform has a sonar ring, two wheels with independent motors with encoders, a Laser SICK LMS200, a video camera Canon

VCC5, speakers, and an integrated PC. The integration of this novel visual sensing platform with our multi-threading probabilistic visual odometry framework allows us to estimate the robot's localization in a more accurate way.

4   Velocity Map for Camera Selection

The algorithm proposed in this work is based on the extraction of the velocity map from each sensor unit through the optical flow computation [6]. For that, only left cameras of each stereo pair are enabled *(front, back, right, left)* in order to return grey images of the world in approximate 360°. However, even though we have four cameras observing the world at the same time, only one of these is used for localization *(main view)* in order to reduce computational times. The rest of the cameras are used as a backup in case the main view is obstructed. Obstructions are detected by the algorithm proposed in Sect. 4.1 and the way the next best view is selected is depicted in Sect. 4.2.

4.1   Camera-Blocking Detection

Let $C_i \in [front, back, right, left]$ with $i \in [1, 2, 3, 4]$ be the four different view directions taken from *Guidance*. For each C_i the optical flow O_{flow} is computed at every consecutive pair of frames f_i and f_{i+1}. After that, a set of ORB features [17] are computed and filtered by a threshold V_{min} (see Eq. 1). We choose ORB features because these are basically a fusion of FAST keypoints detector [16] and BRIEF descriptors [3] with several modifications to enhance the performance.

$$\mathbf{card}(\mathcal{F}^j)_i = \left| x \in F_i^j : \|O_{flow}(x)\| < V_{min} \right| \tag{1}$$

In Eq. 1, $\mathbf{card}(\cdot)$ represents the cardinality of the set $\mathcal{F}^j$, $\mathcal{F}^j$ is the set of all features such that their velocity are less than the threshold V_{min} *(static features)*, x is a feature computed by the ORB extractor, F_i^j represents the set of features computed in the jth frame of the ith camera, $\|O_{flow}(x)\|$ is the magnitude of the optical flow at x and V_{min} represents the maximum velocity for which a feature is considered static (see Fig. 2).

For every camera direction C_i a queue Q_i is created and filled with the number of static features of each frame $(\mathcal{F}_i^j)$. If the size of the Q_i queue is equal to a given number of frames *(NF)* the older value of Q_i is released for storing a new one. The number NF is directly related with the time window to be analyzed and the frequency of the video device. For instance, if the sensor have a frequency of 18 fps and you want to store the last 2 s, then you have to set $NF = 36$. In other words, $NF = \text{fps} \times (seconds\_to\_store)$.

$$Q_i = \left\{ \mathbf{card}(\mathcal{F}_i^0), \ \mathbf{card}(\mathcal{F}_i^1), \ ..., \ \mathbf{card}(\mathcal{F}_i^{NF}) \right\} \tag{2}$$

In order to perform the obstacle detection, a frequency analysis over each Q_i is done and a 1D histogram, H_i, is constructed with the values of each Q_i

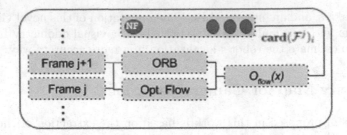

Fig. 2. In this picture $frame_j$ and $frame_{j+1}$ represent any consecutive pair of frames used for computing the optical flow O_{flow}. Over the $frame_j$ a set of ORB features are extracted and its velocities are computed using O_{flow} in order to extract the number of static features in $frame_j$. Finally, the number of static features per frame, **card**($frame_j$), is stored in the queue of its respective camera.

once the size of Q_i reaches NF. Once the queues are filled for first time, the histograms computation is performed at each frame. The idea of using histograms for counting the frequency of the values in the queue allows us to determine if an obstacle is blocking temporally the main view or not. For instance, if a person walks in front of the main camera and then stops so that the main view gets blocked, then the number of static features will start to decrease at every frame and hence the queue of the main camera's view will start to have many values near to 0. This situation produces a transformation in the histogram where the first bin will become in the biggest bin within the histogram. However, when the person starts to move far from the camera view, the number of static features per frame will increase and consequently the queue values. This another situation produces that the last histogram's bins being the largest. Finally, a camera change can be made at the moment in which all the values of the Q_i are in the first bin of the H_i.

4.2   Camera Selection

At this point of the algorithm, the main camera can be considered blocked and the system has to evaluate the other views in order to select the best one of the rest to continue localized inside the world. For this case, the best view is such in which its Q_i contains the largest amount of static features over a long period of time [4].

As mentioned before in Sect. 4.1, if all values of the main view's histogram are in its first bin, then it is not longer convenient to keep viewing in that direction. Following the proposed in [4] a new good view is such a view that conserves more static features over a time interval. Therefore, the new best camera's view to stay localized is such that its histogram contains the highest statistical mode (see Sect. 5.2).

5   Experiments

The experiments presented in this section describe the relation between cameras under specific situations as well as the frequency analysis of the static features within the scenes. For the sake of a better understanding of this model we divide the experimental section in static and dynamic testing.

5.1   Static Test

The goal in this experiment is to assess the performance of our camera selection approach. For that, the number of bins per histograms is set empirically to 5, $NF = 36$ and the upper left corner image in Fig. 3(a) is selected as main view. As mentioned before, the number of static features is computed *(points in blue)* over the four different directions in order to generate the queues and later the histograms. Once the system is running, we proceed to block the main view as is shown in Fig. 3(b) and the system is able to select the best of the remaining views. In this case, if we look at the Fig. 3(b), we might realize that the next best view will be the one at the bottom right because in that view the number of static features is highest during a period of time.

(a) Camera initialization.   (b) Camera blocking.

Fig. 3. (a) Initial state of the system and the main view is enclosed in a white rectangle. (b) Static and non-static features represented in blue and red color respectively. (Best seen in color)

As we have explained before in Sect. 4, our camera selection approach is based on the frequency analysis of the static features behavior. For that, a 1D histogram is built for each view and a continuously evaluation is performed in order to see if the number of static features in the main view is lower than a threshold; if this happens then the main view has been blocked. Figure 4 shows the histogram behavior over the time for the four views. At the beginning, the main view's histogram (see Fig. 4(a)) has all its values in the last bin as well as the other views, however, there is an instant marked with a red line where

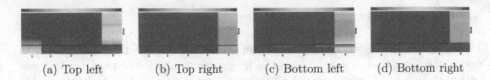

| (a) Top left | (b) Top right | (c) Bottom left | (d) Bottom right |

Fig. 4. Histogram behavior over time. The red horizontal line represents the moment in which a change of the main view has happened. The bar at the top of each histogram is used to represent the frequency in the histogram, higher values are in red while lower values appears in blue. The time sequence starts at the top. The bin number is shown at the horizontal axis. (Best seen in color)

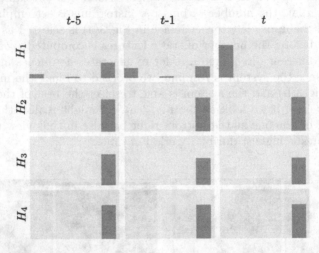

Fig. 5. Histograms evolution near the switching point. $H1$ represents the main view's histogram while $H2$, $H3$ and $H4$ the rest. Histograms are shown at frames t *(the switching point)*, $t - 1$ and $t - 5$. Note how the values in the histogram $H1$ move from the last bin to the first one from $t - 5$ to t. For this case the selected camera is C_4 because numerically this histogram keep the highest mode during the last 2 s.

the histogram distribution starts to change, this is because the camera is being blocked, and therefore, the first bin starts to grow. At this point the system realizes that the camera was blocked and selects from the remaining views, the best one to stay localized. Finally, the system selects the bottom right view (see Fig. 3(b)) because as can be observed in Fig. 4(d), is the view where the histogram have the larger statistical mode *(darkest red color)*. See Fig. 5 for a better understnding of the histogram behavior near the switching point.

In Fig. 4(d) after switching cameras *(red line)* appears a period of time with no static features. This situation is presented because the camera was blocked with a human hand which introduces a low motion over the sensor and hence a perturbation in the optical flow.

5.2   Dynamic Test

For this experiment, our robot system is navigating in an indoor scenario. The robot is moving with the *Guidance* attached at the top of it (see Fig. 1(b)) and the *front* camera is designated for staying localized by using ORB-SLAM. While robot is navigating all features velocities are affected by the displacement vector. There are always two views that are more affected than the others. The *front* and *back* views are less affected because the motion is normal to both planes while *left* and *right* views depend strictly on the displacement vector. For instance, if the robot is moving forward, the velocities of each feature from the *front* and *back* views will not be affected because the optical flow won't be perturbed. On the other hand, for lateral views, almost all the feature won't be statics, this effect is like if the robot was static and the world was in motion.

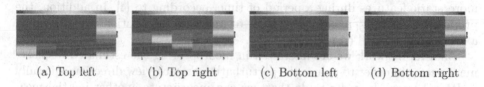

| (a) Top left | (b) Top right | (c) Bottom left | (d) Bottom right |

Fig. 6. Histogram behavior over the time when the sensor is mounted on the robot. The red horizontal line represents the moment in which a change of the main view has happened. (Best seen in color)

As in the first experiment, in Fig. 6 we depict the histograms behavior over the time. In this experiment the robot is initially static, hence, at the begging the amount of static features is high in each view. Once the robot starts moving the number of features starts to change. In this case it is more clear how the number of features on the main view (see Fig. 6(a)) starts to decrease while the robot is moving. Besides, in Fig. 6(c) it is possible to observe that the robot motion does not have effected the number of static features for this view, as we already mention above, this is because the motion is normal to this image plane. Finally, due to this effect, this view is the one that was selected as the new main view.

For lateral views (see Fig. 6(b) and (d)), we can distinguish a smooth transition in the last bin of the histograms which goes from orange to blue *(above to below)*. The above portion of the histograms, where the orange color remains constant is because we started to acquire data with the robot in an static state. In the histograms we can detect the starting robot motion when the orange color starts to turn in blue. Color changes in histograms implies that, at this time, the number of features with low velocities starts to decrease. This situation is presented because static features are apparently moving in the opposite direction that robot does.

The red line in Fig. 6 represents a stop in the robot motion produced by an obstruction in the current main view. At this point, the robot remains static during 2 s *(36 frames)* for acquiring the temporal distribution of the static ORB-features at each direction. With this tiny stop, the optical flow is finally stabilized and hence the features velocities.

6   Conclusions

In this paper we have presented a simple and effective camera selection algorithm for a multi-camera sensor systems when autonomous navigation is performed. Our approach aims at exploiting the visual capabilities offered by multi-camera sensors for visual-based localization, in scenarios where visual localization is obstructed. Experiments were conducted in static and dynamic scenarios. For the dynamic scenarios, we used a service robot platform *(Robot Sabina)*. In both cases, the results exhibit the same relation; the next best view is the one with more static features during a period of time, according to [4]. In addition, the proposed algorithm enables the system to maintain localization whilst keeping a low computational cost.

As a future work we are interested in incorporating the estimated displacement vector in order to reduce the perturbation at each view direction, specially in lateral views. In order to do that, we can incorporate another inertial measurement unit *(IMU)* and fuse its information with that of the robot odometry in order to enhance the selection of the best next main view.

Acknowledgments. This work was supported in part by FONCICYT (CONACYT and European Union) Project SmartSDK - No. 272727. Reinier Oves García is supported by a CONACYT Scholarship No.789638. Dr. J. Martinez-Carranza is thankful for the support received through the Newton Advanced Fellowship with reference NA140454.

References

1. Bapat, A., Dunn, E., Frahm, J.-M.: Towards kilo-hertz 6-DoF visual tracking using an egocentric cluster of rolling shutter cameras. IEEE Trans. Vis. Comput. Graph. **22**(11), 2358–2367 (2016)
2. Barbosa, M., Bernardino, A., Figueira, D., Gaspar, J., Gonçalves, N., Lima, P.U., Moreno, P., Pahliani, A., Santos-Victor, J., Spaan, M.T.J., Sequeira, J.: ISRobotNet: a testbed for sensor and robot network systems. In: IROS, pp. 2827–2833 (2009)
3. Calonder, M., Lepetit, V., Strecha, C., Fua, P.: BRIEF: binary robust independent elementary features. In: Daniilidis, K., Maragos, P., Paragios, N. (eds.) ECCV 2010. LNCS, vol. 6314, pp. 778–792. Springer, Heidelberg (2010). https://doi.org/10.1007/978-3-642-15561-1_56
4. Costante, G., Forster, C., Delmerico, J.A., Valigi, P., Scaramuzza, D.: Perception-aware path planning. IEEE Trans. Robot. (2016). arXiv preprint arXiv:1605.04151
5. Das, A., Waslander, S.L.: Entropy based keyframe selection for multi-camera visual slam. In: 2015 IEEE/RSJ International Conference on Intelligent Robots and Systems (IROS), pp. 3676–3681. IEEE (2015)

6. Farnebäck, G.: Two-frame motion estimation based on polynomial expansion. In: Bigun, J., Gustavsson, T. (eds.) SCIA 2003. LNCS, vol. 2749, pp. 363–370. Springer, Heidelberg (2003). https://doi.org/10.1007/3-540-45103-X_50
7. Forster, C., Pizzoli, M., Scaramuzza, D.: SVO: fast semi-direct monocular visual odometry. In: 2014 IEEE International Conference on Robotics and Automation (ICRA), pp. 15–22, May 2014
8. Guyue, Z., Lu, F., Ketan, T., Honghui, Z., Kai, W., Kang, Y.: Guidance: a visual sensing platform for robotic applications. In: 2015 IEEE Conference on Computer Vision and Pattern Recognition Workshops (CVPRW), pp. 9–14, June 2015
9. Harmat, A., Trentini, M., Sharf, I.: Multi-camera tracking and mapping for unmanned aerial vehicles in unstructured environments. J. Intell. Robot. Syst. **78**(2), 291–317 (2015)
10. Houben, S., Quenzel, J., Krombach, N., Behnke, S.: Efficient multi-camera visual-inertial slam for micro aerial vehicles. In: IROS 2016, pp. 1616–1622. IEEE (2016)
11. Kaess, M., Dellaert, F.: Probabilistic structure matching for visual SLAM with a multi-camera rig. Comput. Vis. Image Underst. **114**(2), 286–296 (2010). Special issue on Omnidirectional Vision, Camera Networks and Non-conventional Cameras
12. Kazik, T., Kneip, L., Nikolic, J., Pollefeys, M., Siegwart, R.: Real-time 6D stereo visual odometry with non-overlapping fields of view. In: 2012 IEEE Conference on Computer Vision and Pattern Recognition (CVPR), pp. 1529–1536. IEEE (2012)
13. Klein, G., Murray, D.: Parallel tracking and mapping for small AR workspaces. In: Mixed and Augmented Reality, ISMAR 2007, pp. 225–234. IEEE (2007)
14. Mur-Artal, R., Tardós, J.D.: ORB-SLAM2: an open-source slam system for monocular, stereo, and RGB-D cameras. IEEE Trans. Robot. **33**(5), 1255–1262 (2017)
15. Netramai, C., Roth, H., Sachenko, A.: High accuracy visual odometry using multi-camera systems. In: 2011 IEEE 6th International Conference on Intelligent Data Acquisition and Advanced Computing Systems (IDAACS), vol. 1, pp. 263–268. IEEE (2011)
16. Rosten, E., Drummond, T.: Machine learning for high-speed corner detection. In: Leonardis, A., Bischof, H., Pinz, A. (eds.) ECCV 2006. LNCS, vol. 3951, pp. 430–443. Springer, Heidelberg (2006). https://doi.org/10.1007/11744023_34
17. Rublee, E., Rabaud, V., Konolige, K., Bradski, G.: ORB: an efficient alternative to sift or surf. In: 2011 IEEE International Conference on Computer Vision (ICCV), pp. 2564–2571. IEEE (2011)
18. Tardif, J.-P., Pavlidis, Y., Daniilidis, K.: Monocular visual odometry in urban environments using an omnidirectional camera. In: IEEE/RSJ International Conference on Intelligent Robots and Systems, IROS 2008, pp. 2531–2538. IEEE (2008)
19. Zhou, G., Fang, L., Tang, K., Zhang, H., Wang, K., Yang, K.: Guidance: a visual sensing platform for robotic applications. In: CVPR, pp. 9–14 (2015)

Improving Breast Mass Classification Through Kernel Methods and the Fusion of Clinical Data and Image Descriptors

Saiveth Hernández-Hernández, Antonio Orantes-Molina,
and Raúl Cruz-Barbosa$^{(\boxtimes)}$

Computer Science Institute, Universidad Tecnológica de la Mixteca,
69000 Huajuapan de León, Oaxaca, Mexico
ps2016200001@ndikandi.utm.mx, {tonito,rcruz}@mixteco.utm.mx

Abstract. Breast cancer is a global health problem principally affecting the female population. Digital mammograms are an effective way to detect this disease. One of the main indicators of malignancy in a mammogram is the presence of masses. However, their detection and diagnosis remains a difficult task. In this study, the impact of the combination of image descriptors and clinical data on the performance of conventional and kernel methods is presented. These models are trained with a dataset extracted from the public database BCDR-D01. The experimental results have shown that the incorporation of clinical data to image descriptors improves the performance of classifiers better than using the descriptors alone. Likewise, this combination, but using a nonlinear kernel function, improves the performance similar to those reported in the literature for this dataset.

Keywords: Breast cancer · Clinical data · Mass classification
Kernel methods

1 Introduction

Breast cancer continues to be a growing health problem worldwide. It is considered to be the leading cause of death by malignancy in the female population with nearly 500,000 deaths each year [1,2]. To reduce the incidence of new cases due to this cancer, it must be detected and diagnosed at early stages. The use of mammograms is considered to be an effective method for the detection in an early stage [3,4]. The mammograms are analyzed by a radiologist who looks for anomalies related to this cancer. Such anomalies can be masses and microcalcifications, the former being the most difficult to detect. A mass is defined as a three-dimensional structure visible in two different projections [5], which can be characterized with respect to their size, shape, margins and density.

Both detection and diagnosis of masses are difficult tasks to perform due to the great variability of the characteristics they present. In addition, the success

© Springer International Publishing AG, part of Springer Nature 2018
J. F. Martínez Trinidad et al. (Eds.): MCPR 2018, LNCS 10880, pp. 258–266, 2018.
https://doi.org/10.1007/978-3-319-92198-3_26

of both tasks largely depends on the training and experience of the radiologists. Several studies report that radiologists are 75% successful at performing a mammographic analysis for cancer detection [4]. To aid in this process, detection and/or diagnosis systems have been developed (Computer Aided Detection, CADe and/or Computer Aided Diagnosis, CADx), which report a successful performance rate between 75% and 82% [3,6].

In the case of CADe or CAD systems, these are used to assist radiologists in the detection of anomalies in mammograms, that is, these systems aim to indicate the regions where a cancer-related lesion may possibly exist [7–9]. On the other hand, CADx systems are used to support the diagnosis of lesions. This task is more complex compared to the task carried out by a CAD system, as well as indicating the location of a possible lesion, the lesions must be characterized to determine the degree of malignancy or benignity [10–12].

Several works have addressed the problem of mass classification considering different approaches. One approach is only using image descriptors as input features for classifiers [3,11,13]. Other works combine each of the types of image descriptors with clinical data [14,15]. However, few studies have explored the combination between the best descriptors of intensity, shape and texture, reported in the literature, and merge this combination with clinical data. That is considering the three types of descriptors as a single set of characteristics and merge it with clinical data. The objective of this work, at first stage, is to compare the performance of the classifiers with the combination of image descriptors, considered as a single set, taking into account the cases with and without clinical data. As a second goal, we use a nonlinear kernel function implemented in a support vector machine (SVM) in order to improve the performance results compared to the obtained with a linear kernel.

This work is organized as follows. In Sect. 2, the image descriptors used to characterize the masses are explained. Likewise, Sect. 3 presents a brief description of the classifiers used for the mass classification. Section 4 describes the data set used, as well as the experimental results. Finally, Sect. 5 presents the conclusions and future work.

2   Image Descriptors

Two-dimensional images are used in this study and the image descriptors considered are those related to intensity, shape and texture [3,16,17]. These were used to characterize the masses and were chosen considering their high performance results in related work [11,14].

The intensity characteristics consider the level of gray of each pixel in the region and are the easiest to obtain. They are generally used to describe the mass density. Six intensity characteristics were calculated, namely, mean, standard deviation, asymmetry, kurtosis, and maximum and minimum gray level [3,11,14].

The shape, or morphological, characteristics are considered to be the most important descriptors of a mass. To describe a region inscribed in an image, two important properties must be considered, the first is through its external characteristics (its contour) and the second through its internal characteristics (the pixels that comprise the region). The calculated shape characteristics are divided into two subsets. The first set of characteristics obtained were: area, perimeter, center of mass, circularity, elongation, form, solidity and extent [3,14]. The second subset of characteristics obtained is related to the histograms of gradient divergence (HGD) [11]. When we talk about shape descriptors, we will be referring to the first subset as F, while the second subset will be named as an HGD descriptor.

Regarding texture characteristics, they describe the topology of an object at local level. The calculated characteristics were those related to the gray-level co-occurrence matrices (GLCM). The elements that make up the GLCM matrix are defined as the joint probability that gray levels i and j occur in the image, separated by a distance d and along a direction θ [3]. A total of thirteen characteristics were obtained from the GLCM matrix, namely, energy, contrast, correlation, homogeneity, entropy, sum of squares, sum average, sum entropy, sum variance, difference variance, difference entropy, information measure of correlation 1 and information measure of correlation 2.

3   Classifiers

In general, the objective of the classification stage is to detect or recognize objects in an image in terms of their characteristics or properties [18]. Within the framework of the classifiers, the most common in the literature are the statistical, neuronal and syntactic classifiers [3,19]. Regarding statistical classifiers, the objective is to design classifiers that are able to classify an unknown pattern in the most probable class [19].

The Bayesian (B) classifier is based on Bayes decision theory, and assumes that there is a sufficiently large number of training samples, so that a good estimate of the probability density function can be obtained. However, considering the dimension of the feature space, the data required for a good estimate grows exponentially. To overcome this drawback, the Naïve Bayes (NB) classifier considers that the individual characteristics are statistically independent, so the number of data required is less than that required for the Bayesian one.

Another classifier is called the K-Nearest Neighbor (KNN), which is that given to an unknown pattern, the k patterns (neighbors) closest to it are calculated, and the decision of the classification is made with respect to a majority vote of the classes that correspond to the k neighbors.

The SVMs are characterized by mapping the input data points to a high-dimensional feature space of by using functions such as kernels, so that a hyperplane is found that separates the classes [20]. Usually, there are four basic kernels in the literature, these are linear, polynomial, radial basis function (RBF) and sigmoid kernel. The RBF kernel maps non-linear examples in a high-dimensional space, so it can handle the case when class labels and attributes do not have a linear relationship [20,21].

4   Results and Discussion

The set of mammography images used for this study was taken from the public database BCDR-DO1 [14]. This database provides a total of 260 images of the right and left breast of each patient, with craniocaudal (CC) and mediolateral oblique (MLO) views, with the distribution presented in Table 1.

Table 1. Distribution of the images of the BCDR-D01 database.

View	Left	Right	Total
CC	64	65	129
MLO	63	68	131
Total	127	133	260

The database is composed of 79 lesions verified by biopsies in 64 women. These 79 lesions correspond to 79 masses, of which, 49 are benign and 30 are malignant. The masses can be seen in both CC and MLO views, so there is a total of 143 views of the 79 masses recorded by the radiologists. Table 2 shows this distribution.

Table 2. Distribution of the CC and MLO views, regarding the classification of the masses.

View	Malign	Benign	Total
CC	28	38	66
MLO	29	48	77
Total	57	86	143

For each of the registered masses there is information about the patient (clinical data), such as age at the time of the study, breast density presented, classification based on the Breast Imaging Reporting and Data Systems (BI-RADS) [22], as well as six binary variables that represent the presence or absence of a mass, calcifications, microcalcifications, axillary adenopathy, architectural distortion and stroma distortion.

In summary, the dataset considered has 143 instances related to the 79 masses, of which, 86 instances are related to the 49 benign masses, and 57 instances are related to the 30 malignant masses. Each mass is described by 44 image descriptors and 8 clinical data.

For computing the image descriptors, regions of interest (ROIs) were obtained by extracting the part of the mammogram within the bounding box containing a mass. The corresponding ROI coordinates are available and included in the BCDR-D01 database. Figure 1 shows three examples of the obtained regions.

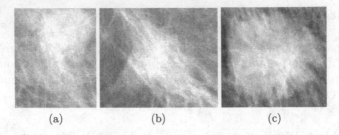

(a)   (b)   (c)

Fig. 1. ROIs extracted from mammograms: (a) img_3_4_1_LCC, (b) img_3_4_1_LO and (c) img_205_275_1_LO.

The methodology for mass classification used in this study is summarized in Fig. 2. The image descriptors are obtained from the ROIs and, optionally, in combination with the clinical data, they form the input of the classifier. Prior to the classification stage, a data preprocessing stage is carried out. After the classification, a evaluation stage is utilized to compute the performance of each classifier, using different validation measures.

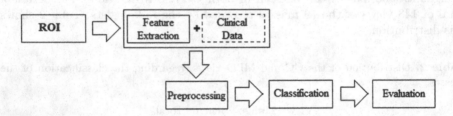

Fig. 2. Methodology for mass classification.

In the preprocessing stage, the first step was the elimination of instances with missing values, corresponding to the breast density information. A total of 11 instances were eliminated, of which, 5 of them corresponded with malignant masses while 6 with benign masses. After this step, the data set was reduced to 132 instances. As a second step in this preprocessing stage, we proceeded to normalize the data to transfer them to the interval $[0, 1]$ by using the maximum and minimum values of each of the descriptors.

In the case of the KNN classifier, the number of neighbors was taken in the interval $[5, 21]$, as suggested in [11], excluding cases for even numbers (since it is a binary classification task). In the case of the SVMs, the first kernel used was the linear kernel, and the value of the penalty parameter C, was searched in the interval $[10^{-2}, 10^3]$. The second kernel used was the RBF kernel. For this case, two grid searches were performed for the parameters C and γ, as suggested in [23]. The parameters were coarse searched in the intervals $[2^{-5}, 2^{15}]$ and $[2^{-15}, 2^3]$, for C and γ respectively. Once the best region of the grid was identified, a fine search of parameters was performed in the intervals $[10^{-2}, 10^3]$ and $[2^{-4}, 2^3]$.

For the validation of results stage, k-fold cross validation was used, with $k = 5$, so that each partition covered approximately 20% of the data set. Therefore, 80% of the data was used to train the classifier and the remaining 20% was used for validation in each fold, as suggested in [14]. The assessment measures that were used to calculate the performance of each of the classifiers presented in Sect. 3, were accuracy (Accu), precision (Prec), sensitivity (Sen), specificity (Spe), Matthews correlation coefficient (MCC), balanced error rate (BER), and Area Under the ROC curve (AUROC).

Classifiers B, NB, KNN and SVM (with linear kernel) were tested considering 6 cases, these are:

1. Test 1: Intensity, Form, Texture (IFT)
2. Test 2: Intensity, Form, Texture, HGD (IFT-HGD)
3. Test 3: Intensity (I)
4. Test 4: Form (F)
5. Test 5: HGD
6. Test 6: Texture (T).

Each of these cases was tested with and without clinical data, which makes a total of 12 tests.

Tables 3 and 4 show the best results obtained for each of the 12 tests above mentioned. Considering the maximum AUROC value, they correspond respectively to when clinical data is not used and when it is used. The last column shows the used classifier by which these measures were obtained.

In general, the incorporation of clinical data improves the performance of all classifiers, regardless of whether or not I, F, HGD or T image descriptors are combined (see Table 4). When clinical data are not incorporated, the KNN classifier, with $k = 11$, obtains the highest AUROC (0.89) using the combination of the four types of descriptors. Likewise, with this combination of characteristics, a sensitivity of 0.90 and a specificity of 0.89 is obtained. Although with the SVM, using the first subset of shape characteristics (F), a greater specificity is achieved compared with that obtained by KNN, the sensitivity recorded in this case is 0.75. When clinical data are incorporated, the highest AUROC result is 0.94 which is obtained using SVM with the combination of intensity, shape (F and HGD), and texture descriptors. Moreover, a very good sensitivity (0.93) and specificity (0.96) performance is obtained with this feature set.

From Table 4, it can be observed that the SVM-based classifier, with a linear kernel, shows the best performance in almost all tried Tests indicated by the corresponding assessment measures. In the case of the MCC, its value is in the interval [0.68, 0.89], which indicates good classification results. Regarding the BER reached by the SVM, this is in the interval [0.05, 0.21], which indicates that the error per class was small, which leads to a good classification by class. The highest sensitivity in this case was 0.93 showing that the SVM is acceptable for the detection of features obtained from malignant tumours. Regarding the registered specificity, this is in the interval [0.80, 0.99], that is, the SVM also has a good performance to detect healthy individuals. All these measures support the highest results obtained for the accuracy (0.95), precision (0.98) and AUROC (0.94).

Table 3. The best AUROC results obtained with classifiers only using image descriptors.

Feature	MCC	BER	Sen	Spe	Accu	Prec	AUROC	Classifier
IFT	0.7370	0.1337	0.8251	0.9075	0.8751	0.8523	0.8663	SVM
IFT-HGD	**0.7798**	**0.1058**	**0.9010**	0.8875	**0.8928**	0.8389	**0.8942**	KNN (11)
I	0.5070	0.2429	0.7547	0.7595	0.7576	0.6780	0.7571	KNN (11)
F	0.7150	0.1543	0.7547	**0.9367**	0.8636	**0.8889**	0.8457	SVM
HGD	0.3926	0.2999	0.7547	0.6456	0.6894	0.5882	0.7001	B
T	0.6091	0.1895	0.8868	0.7342	0.7955	0.6912	0.8105	NB

Table 4. The best AUROC results obtained with classifiers using image descriptors and clinical data.

Feature	MCC	BER	Sen	Spe	Accu	Prec	AUROC	Classifier
IFT	0.8213	0.1006	0.8288	0.9700	0.9144	0.9473	0.8994	SVM
IFT-HGD	**0.8865**	**0.0567**	**0.9303**	0.9563	**0.9462**	0.9303	**0.9433**	SVM
I	0.6764	0.2075	0.5849	0.7955	0.8333	0.6870	0.7925	SVM
F	0.8008	0.1195	0.7736	**0.9873**	0.9015	**0.9762**	0.8805	SVM
HGD	0.6919	0.2	0.6	0.7546	0.845	0.8285	0.8	KNN (11)
T	0.7802	0.1228	0.7925	0.9620	0.8939	0.9333	0.8772	NB

Based on the previously obtained results for each of the 6 Tests, an SVM with RBF kernel is used in particular with Tests 1 and 2, with and without clinical data. Tables 5 and 6 show the corresponding results. The last column of these tables shows the best values obtained for C and γ parameters.

From Tables 5 and 6 it can be observed that using a RBF kernel improves the AUROC measure results, regardless of whether image descriptors were merged or not with clinical data. Moreover, Test 2 (in both cases) obtained better AUROC results compared with those obtained by Test 1, which suggests that both the combination of intensity, shape, HGD and texture descriptors fused with clinical data and the SVM with kernel RBF make a good combination for mass diagnosis. This result is similar to that obtained in [14] but without using a majority vote technique among several classifiers as logistic model trees, random forest and linear SVM among others.

Table 5. The best AUROC results obtained for SVMs with RBF kernel using image descriptors without clinical data.

Feature	MCC	BER	Sen	Spe	Accu	Prec	AUROC	(C, γ)
IFT	0.7926	0.1019	0.8875	**0.9087**	0.9004	**0.8634**	0.8981	(10, 1)
IFT-HGD	**0.8131**	**0.0888**	**0.9217**	0.9006	**0.9089**	0.8571	**0.9112**	(1, 1)

Table 6. The best AUROC results obtained for SVMs with RBF kernel using image descriptors with clinical data.

Feature	MCC	BER	Sen	Spe	Accu	Prec	AUROC	(C, γ)
IFT	0.9066	0.0439	0.9615	**0.9506**	**0.9549**	**0.9268**	0.9561	(10, 1)
IFT-HGD	**0.9070**	**0.0413**	**0.9798**	0.9375	0.9542	0.9106	**0.9587**	(10, 1)

5   Conclusions

The impact of the combination of image descriptors (considering three types of descriptors as a single set of characteristics) fused with clinical data on the performance of mass classification was presented in this work. The experimental results have shown that linear SVM obtains the highest AUROC performance for the analyzed dataset when clinical data is fused with image descriptors information. Furthermore, the performance of the SVM is exceeded when the linear kernel is replaced by the RBF kernel which helps to model the nonlinearity relationship between class labels and input data.

As future work, motivated by the fact that the representation learning field using deep neural networks can automatically obtain good representations of image regions, a comparison of nonlinear kernel methods with deep learning methods for mass classification is considered.

References

1. GLOBOCAN: Breast cancer estimated incidence, mortality and prevalence worldwide in 2012. International Agency for Research on Cancer. http://globocan.iarc.fr/old/FactSheets/cancers/breast-new.asp. Accessed Feb 2018
2. Cárdenas-Sánchez, J., Bargalló-Rocha, J.E., Erazo-Valle, A., Chacón, A.P., Valero-Castillo, V., Pérez-Sánchez, V.: Consenso Mexicano sobre diagnóstico y tratamiento del cáncer mamario. Gaceta Mexicana de Oncología **14**(Suppl 2), 2–55 (2015)
3. Cheng, H., Shi, X., Min, R., Hu, L., Cai, X., Du, H.: Approaches for automated detection and classification of masses in mammograms. Pattern Recogn. **39**(4), 646–668 (2006)
4. Kom, G., Tiedeu, A., Kom, M.: Automated detection of masses in mammograms by local adaptive thresholding. Comput. Biol. Med. **37**(1), 37–48 (2007)
5. Liberman, L., Menell, J.H.: Breast imaging reporting and data system (BI-RADS). Radiol. Clin. **40**(3), 409–430 (2002)
6. Sampat, M.P., Markey, M.K., Bovik, A.C.: Computer-aided detection and diagnosis in mammography. In: Handbook of Image and Video Processing, vol. 2, no. 1, pp. 1195–1217 (2005)
7. Petrick, N., Chan, H.P., Wei, D., Sahiner, B., Helvie, M.A., Adler, D.D.: Automated detection of breast masses on mammograms using adaptive contrast enhancement and texture classification. Med. Phys. **23**(10), 1685–1696 (1996)
8. Wei, J., Sahiner, B., Hadjiiski, L.M., Chan, H.P., Petrick, N., Helvie, M.A., Roubidoux, M.A., Ge, J., Zhou, C.: Computer-aided detection of breast masses on full field digital mammograms. Med. Phys. **32**(9), 2827–2838 (2005)

9. Oliveira Martins, L., Braz Junior, G., Corrêa Silva, A., Cardoso de Paiva, A., Gattass, M.: Detection of masses in digital mammograms using k-means and support vector machine. ELCVIA: Electron. Lett. Comput. Vis. Image Anal. **8**(2), 39–50 (2009)

10. Varela, C., Tahoces, P.G., Méndez, A.J., Souto, M., Vidal, J.J.: Computerized detection of breast masses in digitized mammograms. Comput. Biol. Med. **37**(2), 214–226 (2007)

11. Moura, D.C., López, M.A.G.: An evaluation of image descriptors combined with clinical data for breast cancer diagnosis. Int. J. Comput. Assist. Radiol. Surg. **8**(4), 561–574 (2013)

12. Li, Y., Chen, H., Rohde, G.K., Yao, C., Cheng, L.: Texton analysis for mass classification in mammograms. Pattern Recogn. Lett. **52**, 87–93 (2015)

13. Rodríguez-López, V., Cruz-Barbosa, R.: On the breast mass diagnosis using Bayesian networks. In: Gelbukh, A., Espinoza, F.C., Galicia-Haro, S.N. (eds.) MICAI 2014. LNCS (LNAI), vol. 8857, pp. 474–485. Springer, Cham (2014). https://doi.org/10.1007/978-3-319-13650-9_41

14. Moura, D.C., et al.: Benchmarking datasets for breast cancer computer-aided diagnosis (CADx). In: Ruiz-Shulcloper, J., Sanniti di Baja, G. (eds.) CIARP 2013. LNCS, vol. 8258, pp. 326–333. Springer, Heidelberg (2013). https://doi.org/10.1007/978-3-642-41822-8_41

15. Rodríguez-López, V., Cruz-Barbosa, R.: Improving Bayesian networks breast mass diagnosis by using clinical data. In: Carrasco-Ochoa, J.A., Martínez-Trinidad, J.F., Sossa-Azuela, J.H., Olvera López, J.A., Famili, F. (eds.) MCPR 2015. LNCS, vol. 9116, pp. 292–301. Springer, Cham (2015). https://doi.org/10.1007/978-3-319-19264-2_28

16. Petrick, N., Chan, H.P., Sahiner, B., Helvie, M.A.: Combined adaptive enhancement and region-growing segmentation of breast masses on digitized mammograms. Med. Phys. **26**(8), 1642–1654 (1999)

17. Christoyianni, I., Dermatas, E., Kokkinakis, G.: Fast detection of masses in computer-aided mammography. IEEE Signal Process. Mag. **17**(1), 54–64 (2000)

18. Duda, R.O., Hart, P.E., Stork, D.G.: Pattern Classification. Wiley-Interscience, Hoboken (2001)

19. Bishop, C.M.: Pattern Recognition and Machine Learning, 1st edn. Springer, Heidelberg (2006)

20. Vapnik, V.N.: Statistical Learning Theory. Wiley, Hoboken (1998)

21. Burges, C.J.: A tutorial on support vector machines for pattern recognition. Data Min. Knowl. Disc. **2**(2), 121–167 (1998)

22. American College of Radiology (ACR): Breast Imaging Reporting and Data System. 4th edn. American College of Radiology, Reston (2003)

23. Hsu, C.W., Chang, C.C., Lin, C.J.: A practical guide to support vector classification. Technical report, Department of Computer Science, National Taiwan University, Taipei (2003)

An Improved Stroke Width Transform to Detect Race Bib Numbers

Wellington Moreira de Jesus[1] and Díbio Leandro Borges[2(✉)]

[1] Department of Mechanical Engineering, University of Brasília, Brasília, DF, Brazil
welmore@hotmail.com
[2] Department of Computer Science, University of Brasília, Brasília, DF, Brazil
dibio@unb.br

Abstract. We present modifications in a local operator known as stroke width transform (SWT) in order to improve its performance to detect Race Bib Numbers (RBNs) from natural images of running competitions. The original SWT algorithm is a simple and yet one of the top competitive algorithms for text detection. The proposal adds a Hue channel similarity test in the neighborhoods of edge borders candidates, and it limits the length of the stroke according to aimed characters at the images. We tested the proposed, and the original approach, using a publicly available database of 217 images in different conditions. The suggested approach outperformed the original one, both in sizes of width maps, and on RBNs detection. This research is not an end-to-end RBNs recognition system, so we focused on the improvements of the SWT algorithm in order to provide a more efficient method for future use in automated systems.

1 Introduction

In the sports world there is a variety of running competitions, across streets, mountains, trails, and marathons and shorter distances ones, where each competitor is identified by a numerical digit stripe, known as a Race Bib Number (RBN). These events are covered by professional photographers resulting in many pictures taken aiming to share and sell among individuals and broad media. It would be useful for these professionals to automatically identify the region of the numerical stripe in the images, and consequently be able to identify the runners.

The application of known techniques [1] for extracting text directly on these images is challenging because of the variability of views, number fonts and colors, occlusions, and lighting conditions besides the wiggling of the numbers in the racers shirts. Consequently, numbers are partially detected, completely missed, or very cluttered depending on the image. Figure 1 shows sample pictures of such races belonging to three sets of images exemplifying different image resolutions and RBNs formats with a ground truth target [2].

This paper investigates this issue and proposes to detect RBNs in running competitions by changing the finding letters and the grouping stages of the original Stroke Width Transform (SWT) [3] algorithm. This approach allows us to

© Springer International Publishing AG, part of Springer Nature 2018
J. F. Martínez-Trinidad et al. (Eds.): MCPR 2018, LNCS 10880, pp. 267–276, 2018.
https://doi.org/10.1007/978-3-319-92198-3_27

Fig. 1. Example images from different running competitions showing the RBNs to be detected (database from [2]).

discard a large amount of areas in the image and to find the most probable areas of numbers in it. This reduces the loss of numbers in the Connected Components (CC) stage and it increases the RBNs detection in the end. We ran tests on public images of running competitions in order to compare the results.

The rest of this article is organized as follows: in Sect. 2, we review works related to the detection of texts and numbers; in Sect. 3, we explain the methodology used to direct the SWT to the more related RBNs areas of the image, and then detect the RBNs; in Sect. 4, we present the results of the experiments; and finally, in Sect. 5, we show our conclusions and future directions.

2   Related Works

Detection of texts in images has been researched for a long time, resulting in several methods proposed. Many of these methods consist of four basic steps: (1) Detecting text candidates, which means locating regions with possible texts; (2) Reducing search area of regions, this means to extract the edges, for instance; (3) Unifying candidate pixels in components with similar characteristics, and (4) Eliminating non-text components.

In 2004, [4] Jung et al. carried out an extensive work on mapping techniques for detecting and extracting text in images and videos. In general, the Text Information Extraction (TIE) techniques are divided into three groups: texture-based methods, region-based methods, and hybrid methods. Texture-based methods scan texts in images for distinct properties, such as high border density, low gradient variation above and below the text, high contrast between letters and background, and so on.

Texture-based techniques scan the image several times by analyzing and classifying each pixel in function of its neighbors due to the characteristics listed generating a high computational cost. According to [4] Jung et al. region-based methods are a combination of edge extraction and Connected Components (CC) and their main assumption is that neighboring pixels show similarities in color, luminance, and texture. Then grouping between these neighboring pixels in components take place, followed by grouped components in regions, and later, regions are grouped into texts. However, these methods have great difficulty in separating text regions from non-text regions due to heuristics used to group pixels, and thus many image objects are similar to text. In terms of size and texture, they end up being identified as text, when they are not. This generates a high false positive rate.

2.1 Stroke Width Transform (SWT)

The Stroke Width Transformation technique was proposed by Epshtein et al. [3] as a method that transforms the pixel original values into the most likely stroke width they could belong to. In practice the SWT has two stages: (1) finding candidate letters by computing rays from the edges borders and selecting particular widths; (2) grouping letter candidates into text lines. In order to detect text, the SWT main premise is that text in the images appears as fixed stroke width. The SWT is a local operator that calculates from a pixel that is on the edge of the filtered image with the Canny edge operator, the stroke width in which the pixel is contained. For each pixel of the edge map, its direction is calculated. It assumes that at some point a pixel will be found on the opposite border edge with a similar gradient in the opposite direction.

Then the distance between them is attributed to these pixels, and, also to all the pixels that are between them. After the SWT detection stage, the pixels whose stroke width are similar, are then grouped into character candidates. First, candidate characters are grouped into pairs. Then grouped into text regions according to their color characteristics, stroke width, and distance from each other. An advantage of this technique is to perform only a single image scan, unlike texture-based techniques where it is necessary to convolve windows across the image several times. The transform is able to detect text regardless of size, direction, source or language. Their technique [3] is robust for detecting text in natural images and with low computational cost, but it may fail to detect texts that are not horizontal, such as texts written in arc form for example. Another difficulty is the need to make many adjustments based on the heuristics needed to cut non-text parts. The problem is that in many cases the filters also end up cutting regions of texts detected by the stroke stage.

Several other researches have been developed using variations of a SWT. In [5], Mosleh et al. changed the Canny edge detector by a bandlet-based detector and proposed that a more refined border map helps the SWT stage. In the case of RBNs it is crucial because the stripes with numbers change position at any moment. Yao et al. in [6] proposed a SWT-based algorithm that is capable of detecting texts in any language and in any direction using an extended set of characteristics of the CC filtering stage after the SWT stage, combined with a classifier based on a Random Forest algorithm. Paul et al. [7] developed an adaptive Stroke Filter with the proposition that there are many losses of candidate components when using a detector which stroke width is fixed, as it is the case of the Epshtein algorithm [3].

2.2   RBNs Detection

Regarding the detection of RBNs, Ben-Ami et al. [2] proposed an algorithm based on SWT that first seeks to reduce the area of search in the image by first locating the runner's face. Then from his/her face, a rectangular area is calculated that covers the runner's entire upper body where the stripe is possibly found. Thereafter, the reduced image is processed by a SWT. The SWT had been adjusted to set stroke width in proportion to the runners' face sizes. This facilitates the stroke detection of different sizes. After detection, the numbers are segmented, and each digit processed separately and passed to recognition through a Tesseract OCR algorithm. Two issues may arise from that technique: (1) the entire process is dependent on the face detection, since it is only after this that their system decides if it computes the SWT, and where based on the face detector output bounding box; (2) the computational overload of the face detection preprocessing, and the quality of its output since in many of those images there are plenty of false positives and false negatives to be dealt with. Our proposal here is to concentrate on improving the SWT only to provide it with means to more rapidly and efficiently detect characters (in this case RBNs) on natural images. Some preprocessing and postprocessing methods can be added in the future, and most of the systems in the literature do that, but in this presented research we aim to contribute to the SWT particularly.

3   Proposed SWT

Our working hypothesis here is that by having fewer rays in the image resulting from the SWT stage, it is possible to adjust the CC and filter parameters more accurately and improve the detection of numbers more evenly. In this sense, our approach works by reducing the amount of rays produced by the SWT stage on two fronts. First, a stroke when traversing a path from the pixel p, encounters an opposite pixel q that may be in the same character, or another object. In order to increase the chances that they may belong to the same character (i.e. RBN) it is conducted a color check in the neighborhoods of pixels p and q, and if the difference between their averages was greater than 50 degrees (using the Hue scale) this ray should be discarded. Second, also it is observed in the images used for tests that the number with the greater stroke width is around 37 pixels, then we can set to limit the maximum length of the rays. With those modifications we improve the SWT to provide less rays in the finding candidates stage, and a cleaner SWT preserving the RBNs detected, and to further be recognized. A comparison of the gains regarding this proposed SWT against the original SWT of [3] is made and shown in our experiments. Figure 2 shows a scheme of the p

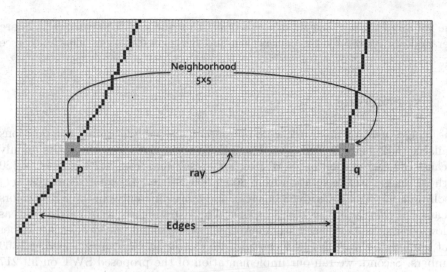

Fig. 2. Proposed new stroke scheme computation.

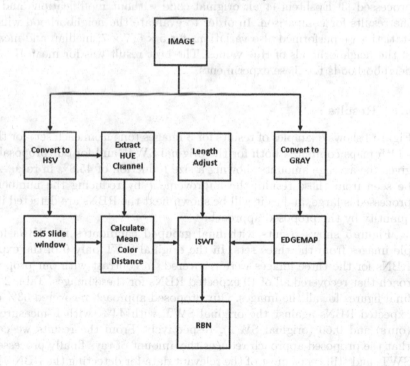

Fig. 3. Flowchart of the proposed SWT here.

and q pixels traversals and the computation of the rays for our proposal, and Fig. 3 gives a flowchart of the algorithm.

The HSV color space has less correlation between color and luminance channels [8], and because of this we transform the RGB image onto HSV and the

Hue values of the 5×5 neighborhoods of pixels p and q of the stroke (Fig. 2) are averaged and stored for the comparison and RBNs detection as mentioned (see Fig. 3).

4   Experiments

The images used in this work were obtained from public running competitions available in [2] being 217 images. The images are divided into three sets mainly because of image resolutions and sizes (set_1 resolution from 342×512–480×720 with 92 images, set_2 resolution from 800×530–850×1260 with 67 images, set_3 resolution of 768×1024 with 58 images), and more differences in the RBNs colors because of the variety of competitions. The experiments were carried out as follows. First, we performed a manual count (i.e. ground truth) of each number that composes the RBNs in focus and discernible in each image, having 1369 numbers. Second, we ran our implementation of the proposed SWT on all 217 images and annotated the hits, miss and the stroke width map sizes. Third, we processed [3] Epshtein et al. original code without modifications and counted the results for comparison. In order to evaluate the neighborhood window and statistics we performed also variations for $5 \times 5, 7 \times 7$, median and mean values of the neighborhoods of Hue values. The best result was for mean H, and 5×5 neighborhoods for these experiments.

4.1   Results

Figure 4 shows examples of results for 3 images (one from each set) for the stroke width maps computed both for the original SWT, and for our proposal. Table 1 gives the average amounts showing a size reduction of 45.8% in total. As it can be seen from these results the improvement by reducing the number of rays processed is large, and as it will be shown next the RBNs are detected in greater quantity by the proposed approach.

Figure 5 shows results with final grouped candidates for RBNs for example images from the three sets. In the original SWT only 9 of the expected 19 RBNs for the three images were recovered, in contrast with our proposed approach that recovered all of 19 expected RBNs for these images. Table 2 gives the final figures for all the images. Our proposed approach recovered 53% of all the expected RBNs against the original SWT with 44%, with F-measures of 0.69 (ours) and 0.60 (original SWT), respectively. From the results we can notice that the proposed approach reduces the amount of rays finally processed by the SWT, and still keeps most of the relevant data for detecting the RBNs. From the literature the original SWT [3] reported an F-measure of 0.66 considering text detection in ICDAR 2005 competition. The RBNs detection can be considered a particular case of text detection in natural images, but with context details far apart because the RBNs are attached in runners shirts, and color numbering, movements, occlusions, lighting conditions change from picture to picture frequently. Our results here are competitive since the original SWT is a well known

(a) Stroke width maps from original SWT

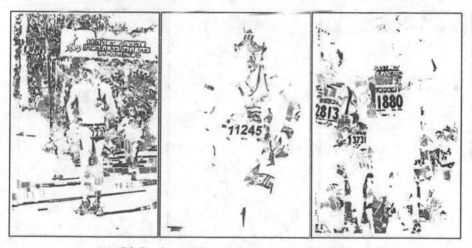

(b) Stroke width maps from proposed SWT

Fig. 4. Results for 3 images from the different sets showing the stroke width maps. Notice the reduction on rays for proposed SWT: (a) original SWT, (b) proposed SWT.

Table 1. Average sizes of stroke width maps produced by both approaches.

Images	Ours	SWT [3]	Reduction by ours
92 (set_1)	4.07 MB	6.76 MB	39.7%
67 (set_2)	3.83 MB	7.09 MB	45.9%
58 (set_3)	5.46 MB	10.8 MB	49.4%
Total			45.8%

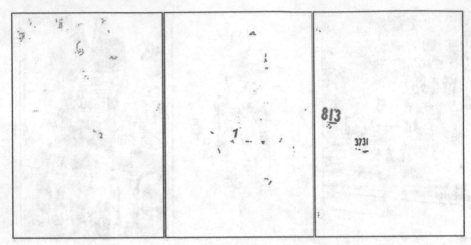

(a) Grouped characters candidates from original SWT

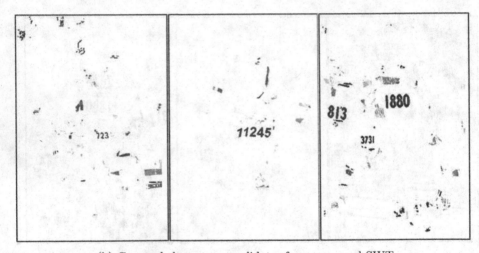

(b) Grouped characters candidates from proposed SWT

Fig. 5. Results for 3 images from the different sets showing the final grouped candidate characters for the RBNs: (a) original SWT, (b) proposed SWT.

and rated as a top efficient algorithm for text detection [3]. The improvements we have proposed here have to be incorporated into a complete end-to-end system for text and/or RBN recognition, with extra preprocessing for dealing with other scales, image acquisition stability compensation, and a specialized Optical Character Recognition (OCR) in the end. So far there are systems available with high performance for particular domains in text recognition, and [2] is one good example of it. However, our aim in this research is improving the SWT so it can provide a basis for RBNs detection in particular for future systems.

Table 2. Number of recovered RBNs for both approaches.

Images	Digits	Ours			SWT [3]		
		Hit	Missed	F-measure	Hit	Missed	F-measure
217	1369	732	637	0.69	600	769	0.60

5   Conclusions

In this paper, we proposed an improved stroke width transform (SWT) with the aim to detect RBNs in images from running competitions. The modifications were to reduce the number of rays computing to indicate the stroke width by checking Hue color similarity between stroke ends neighborhoods, and also by limiting the ray lengths. We have tested the approach with public available images (217) from running competitions, and compared those results with the original SWT. The proposed approach was superior by reducing the sizes of width maps by around 45.8%, and by detecting final RBNs with an F-measure of 0.69 against 0.60 from the original method. This research is not an end-to-end system for RBNs recognition, so the comparison with systems at this level was not made. Our research aimed to improve the SWT stage, and the results were positive in this direction. Particular types of scenes were noticed to be more difficult to deal with, especially those with many runners at large distances from each other, side pictures of corridors where RBNs are very distorted, and colors used in the RBNs that are more affected by sunlighting or even their sizes compared to other objects in the scene. We plan to work on those matters in the next steps and provide results with a database of a 1,000 images and to make it freely available. This scenario is challenging and this research aims to add a contribution in the use and performance of a modified SWT.

References

1. Ye, Q., Doermann, D.: Text detection and recognition in imagery: a survey. IEEE Trans. Pattern Anal. Mach. Intell. **37**, 1480–1500 (2015)
2. Ben-Ami, I., Basha, T., Avidan, S.: Racing bib numbers recognition. In: Proceedings of the British Machine Vision Conference, pp. 19.1–19.10. BMVA Press (2012)
3. Epshtein, B., Ofek, E., Wexler, Y.: Detecting text in natural scenes with stroke width transform. In: 2010 IEEE Conference on Computer Vision and Pattern Recognition (CVPR), pp. 2963–2970. IEEE (2010)
4. Jung, K., Kim, K.I., Jain, A.K.: Text information extraction in images and video: a survey. Pattern Recogn. **37**, 977–997 (2004)
5. Mosleh, A., Bouguila, N., Hamza, A.B.: Image text detection using a bandlet-based edge detector and stroke width transform. In: Proceedings of the British Machine Vision Conference, pp. 1–12. BMVA Press (2012)
6. Yao, C., Bai, X., Liu, W., Ma, Y., Tu, Z.: Detecting texts of arbitrary orientations in natural images. In: 2012 IEEE Conference on Computer Vision and Pattern Recognition (CVPR), pp. 1083–1090. IEEE (2012)

7. Paul, S., Saha, S., Basu, S., Nasipuri, M.: Text localization in camera captured images using adaptive stroke filter. In: Mandal, J.K., Satapathy, S.C., Sanyal, M.K., Sarkar, P.P., Mukhopadhyay, A. (eds.) Information Systems Design and Intelligent Applications. AISC, vol. 340, pp. 217–225. Springer, New Delhi (2015). https://doi.org/10.1007/978-81-322-2247-7_23
8. Koschan, A., Abidi, M.: Digital Color Image Processing. Wiley, Hoboken (2008)

Scaled CCR Histogram
for Scale-Invariant Texture Classification

Juan L. Alonso-Cuevas[1], Raul E. Sanchez-Yanez[1(✉)],
and Evguenii V. Kurmyshev[2]

[1] Universidad de Guanajuato DICIS, Comunidad de Palo Blanco,
36885 Salamanca, Guanajuato, Mexico
sanchezy@ugto.mx
[2] Universidad de Guadalajara, Centro Universitario de Lagos,
Av. Enrique Díaz de León 1144, Paseos de la Montaña,
47460 Lagos de Moreno, Jalisco, Mexico

Abstract. The Coordinated Clusters Representation (CCR) of images
is a statistical approach to texture description and analysis. In this work
a variation of the method, named the Scaled Coordinated Cluster Representation (SCCR), is proposed as a descriptor for scale-invariant texture
classification. The proposed method includes two phases. First, elements
in the CCR histogram are scaled giving more importance to the meaningful patterns of texture. Then, the histogram is filtered but preserving
the most representative patterns. The performance of the proposed algorithm is evaluated in three experiments. In the first one, a correlation
metric is used to assess the similarity among histograms of texture at different scales and evaluate the class discernibility of the CCR and SCCR
descriptors. The other experiments are classification tests, using a minimum distance classifier. One test compares the classification accuracy
of both descriptors at different scales; the other one compares the performance of the SCCR with the state-of-the-art methods, using images
of four well-known databases at different scale. The results show a high
performance of the SCCR in the scale-invariant texture classification.

Keywords: Texture classification · Scale invariance
Texture descriptor

1 Introduction

Texture analysis plays an important role in computer vision in areas such as pattern classification, image segmentation, image recognition, among others. Texture classification, as a branch of texture analysis, refers to assigning a texture
image to one of the classes we are interested in, and it consists of feature extraction and image recognition. The first is the acquisition of texture information
on a feature vector, which has to be discriminant for different textures. The
recognition is the tagging of an input texture image to a class it matches best.

© Springer International Publishing AG, part of Springer Nature 2018
J. F. Martínez-Trinidad et al. (Eds.): MCPR 2018, LNCS 10880, pp. 277–286, 2018.
https://doi.org/10.1007/978-3-319-92198-3_28

Texture classification has several applications where textural appearance is important such as industrial inspection to detect defects or aerial imagery to detect landscapes. Despite texture classification encompasses a large variety of algorithms, it remains one of the most challenging topics. The latter due to the problems of scale, illumination, viewing angle and resolution, between others. Variation of scale in images is a typical problem affecting classification because of changes in the visual appearance of texture.

A number of methods to obtain robust scale-invariant descriptors have been proposed. One of the commonly used methods is the wavelet transform and improved variants. Greatly related to this transform are the filter banks approaches, showing high performance but also high computational complexity. On the contrary, low computational cost is the attractive feature of statistical methods for obtaining efficient feature descriptors. A number of descriptors based on the concept of histograms of equivalent patterns (HEP) that represent the probability of occurrence of texture patterns, is given in [1]. Among them, the Local Binary Pattern (LBP) [2] and the Coordinated Clusters Representation (CCR) [3] are fundamental descriptors that have resulted in several variants.

A histogram-based approach frequently used to address the problem of scale in texture classification is the variant of LBP proposed by Ojala and Pietikäinen [4], which uses a combination of information obtained with circular LBP of different radii. Also, a scale-adaptive texton was proposed in [5,6], using the LBP as a descriptor. Qui et al. [7] suggested another variant of LBP, called MCLBP, which uses the correlation among different scales and rotation-invariant attributes. A different statistical approach was used in [8], adjusting the image to an optimal scale and calculating the CCR histogram from it.

Despite a notable success in solving the problem of scale-invariant texture classification, the approaches mentioned above cannot be considered as completely satisfactory or, as in the case of filtering methods, they are of significant computer complexity and time-consuming. To overcome such limitations, we propose a novel image representation for the scale-invariant texture classification. This representation is obtained from the CCR histogram, which registers the occurrence of binary patterns over an image. The feature vector is scaled giving preference to the most characteristic textural patterns; that results in a descriptor robust to scale changes.

The work is organized as follows. Section 2 describes the scaled CCR (SCCR) descriptor and the classifier used for the evaluation of the method. Experimental design is given in Sect. 3 followed by the results of experiments comparing the SCCR with the state-of-the-art approaches. Conclusions are given in Sect. 4.

2   Scale Invariant Descriptor

The Coordinated Clusters Representation of images [3], is a mathematical transform that extracts statistical information of binary images arranging it in a histogram of occurrences of local pattern units. To perform the scale-invariant texture classification, in this work the scaled CCR (SCCR) histogram is used as a feature vector. It is calculated according to the algorithm shown in Fig. 1. First, we transform the gray-level or color input image into a binary image. Then, the standard CCR histogram of the binary image is computed. Finally, the CCR histogram is adjusted using a two-step procedure. A detailed description of these steps is as follows.

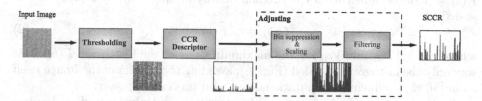

Fig. 1. Algorithm for calculating the SCCR histogram.

2.1 Coordinated Clusters Representation

The CCR of an image is calculated through the associated binary image obtained by the thresholding of the original image. The global thresholding of images proposed by Otsu [9] is used in our experiments. In the CCR representation, the histogram of occurrences of local patterns of a binary image is used as the feature vector of the image. Following [10] we present the CCR of binary images in an algorithmic way. Let $X = \{x(p,q)\}$ be a matrix of binary image intensities which elements $x(p,q)$ take values $(0, 1)$, where $p = 1, 2, \ldots, P$ and $q = 1, 2, \ldots, Q$. In order to calculate the CCR of a binary image X an inspection window W of size $I \times J$ $(I < P$ and $J < Q)$ pixels is used, moving it pixel by pixel all over the image X. As a custom the small 3×3 inspection window is used throughout this work. A row-ordered string of binary values is obtained at every locus of window W and that is transformed into a binary coded decimal (BCD). Then, this value is recorded in the histogram of occurrences $H(b)$ of 2^9 bins for the inspection window of 3×3. Here b is the decimal code that varies through $b = 0, 1, 2, \ldots, 511$. After the scanning, the histogram $H(b)$ is normalized accordingly to the total number of occurrences A, obtaining a probability density function:

$$F(b) = \frac{1}{A} H(b) \tag{1}$$

Analyzing the CCR histograms for an image in two different scales, we see that both histograms are quite similar, except the bins of totally black b_0 and white b_{511} local patterns. Totally black or white local patterns cover larger regions of a binary image when it is seen at higher scale. So, in calculating the CCR feature vector this information, having relatively high weight, will decrease the capacity to distinguish among different classes when the scale is varying. To compensate this effect, we propose the adjusting of histograms in two steps: (i) first we suppress bins of "black" and "white" patterns and scale the remaining bins, then, (ii) we filter the obtained vector.

2.2   Scaled CCR Histogram

As said before, adjusting of the CCR histogram is done in two steps. In the first one, the content of bins b_0 and b_{511} that represent the black and white patterns are set to be zero in the histogram $F(b)$, maintaining the bins between b_1 to b_{510} unchanged. Figure 2a and b depict the above procedure. The histogram $\widehat{F}(b) = F(b)$ obtained from the original one by setting $F(0) = F(511) = 0$ is scaled as,

$$G(b) = r \cdot \widehat{F}(b) \qquad (2)$$

where $r = 1/V_{max}$ and V_{max} is the maximum value of the histogram $\widehat{F}(b)$. This way only the histogram is scaled (Fig. 2c), avoiding the scaling of the image itself as in [8], thus reducing computational cost and processing power.

Scale changes on images may produce artifacts, mainly located on borders between regions. Such noisy patterns, like jagged edges, unseen lines, corners or blurred textures, usually show low occurrence and, hence, in the second step, they are removed from the feature vector $G(b)$. To filter them out, the bins with content lower than a threshold T_G (Fig. 2c) are set to be zero in the histogram $G(b)$. Different thresholds were tested, and the best result was obtained at $T_G = \mu_G + \sigma_G$, where μ_G and σ_G are the mean and the standard deviation of the histogram $G(b)$. Removing low values we obtain the SCCR histogram, where only the statistics of the most representative texture patterns are preserved (Fig. 2d).

$$S(b) = \begin{cases} G(b) & \text{if } G(b) \geq T_G \\ 0 & \text{otherwise} \end{cases} \qquad (3)$$

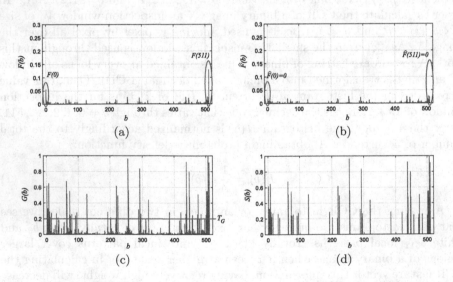

Fig. 2. Calculation of the SCCR for a texture image, D16 of the Brodatz album [11]. (a) The CCR histogram $F(b)$; (b) $\widehat{F}(b)$, after the suppression of bins b_0 and b_{511}; (c) the scaling of the remaining bins, in $G(b)$; and, (d) the SCCR $S(b)$ obtained by filtering $G(b)$.

2.3   Classifier

A minimum distance classifier is used in testing. In the learning stage, a set of N_c images of each texture class c ($c = 1, 2, \ldots, C$) is taken, and each image of the set is binarized to obtain its distribution function $F_{\alpha,c}(b)$ ($\alpha = 1, 2, \ldots, N_c$). Then, for each texture class the prototype histogram $F_c(b)$ is calculated as,

$$F_c(b) = \frac{1}{N_c} \sum_{\alpha=1}^{N_c} F_{\alpha,c}(b) \tag{4}$$

and the latter is scaled in accordance to Sect. 2.2 to obtain $S_c(b)$.

To calculate the distance between the two images X_α and X_β we use the Manhattan distance between the associated SCCR histograms in the SCCR space:

$$d(S_\alpha, S_\beta) = \sum_b |S_\alpha(b) - S_\beta(b)| \tag{5}$$

In classification test the Manhattan distance is calculated between the test image X_α with the scaled histogram $S_\alpha(b)$ and the prototype histogram of each class $S_c(b)$. The test image X_α will be assigned to class c^*, if and only if the distance is minimum,

$$d(S_\alpha, S_{c^*}) = \min_{c=1,2,\ldots,C} \{d(S_\alpha, S_c)\} \tag{6}$$

3   Experimental Design and Results

Three experiments are used to verify and validate the scale invariance of the SCCR descriptor in the classification of texture. In a first test, similarity matrices of the CCR and SCCR histograms describing textures at different scales are compared. The second test is a classification of scaled texture images using the CCR and SCCR as texture descriptors. In the final experiment, the scale invariance of the SCCR is compared with the state-of-the-art textural descriptors.

3.1   Experiment 1: Robustness of the SCCR to Scale Changes

A texture descriptor is said to be robust to scale changes if it remains almost unchanged describing texture images at different scale. The higher is the similarity between the feature vectors of a texture image at different scales, the better is the descriptor. To measure the similarity of feature vectors, representing texture images at different scales, we use the cosine amplitude method, yielding correlation values in the range $[0, 1]$.

To evaluate the robustness of descriptors to scale variations, a set of $C = 13$ texture images suggested by Riaz et al. [12] was selected from the Brodatz database [11], each image representing a particular class. These texture images were scaled by different factors ($\times 0.660$, $\times 0.800$, $\times 1.250$ and $\times 1.500$) using bilinear interpolation, resulting in images at five different scales for each class.

Table 1 shows the results for the intra- and inter-class similarities for the whole dataset. Each value in Table 1 is the average of the 25 values of intra- or inter-class similarity values. Elements in bold indicate possible confusion between different classes; say, if the difference is less than 0.01. Although inter-class similarity is lower in general, some samples of the category resulted in higher values than the intra-class average. From Table 1, we see that the CCR descriptor shows a high intra-class similarity and a high inter-class similarity. The latter can lead to confusion between classes. Meanwhile the SCCR descriptor shows slightly lower than the CCR intra-class similarity but substantially increased inter-class discernibility. This means that the SCCR feature vectors exhibit a high similarity rate among vectors of the same class at different scale, and an improvement for distinguishing textures from different classes. The SCCR descriptor maintains a high intra-class similarity, while maximizes the inter-class discernibility in the feature space.

Table 1. Similarity matrices for the CCR and the SCCR including average values for intra-class descriptors (along the diagonal) and inter-class descriptors (outside the diagonal).

					CCR														SCCR							
	D9	D12	D15	D16	D19	D24	D29	D38	D68	D84	D92	D94	D112		D9	D12	D15	D16	D19	D24	D29	D38	D68	D84	D92	D94	D112
D9	0.99	0.94	0.96	0.95	0.96	0.85	0.93	0.94	0.89	0.95	0.98	0.89	0.89	D9	0.98	0.96	0.76	0.92	0.89	0.86	0.89	0.69	0.52	0.73	0.86	0.79	0.89
D12	0.94	1.00	0.96	0.90	0.88	0.69	0.99	0.90	0.97	0.89	0.94	0.99	0.78	D12	0.96	0.97	0.77	0.92	0.87	0.84	0.90	0.71	0.55	0.77	0.87	0.81	0.89
D15	0.96	0.96	0.99	0.93	0.90	0.75	0.96	0.90	0.92	0.91	0.95	0.93	0.81	D15	0.76	0.77	0.94	0.70	0.60	0.52	0.77	0.43	0.27	0.61	0.64	0.56	0.73
D16	0.95	0.90	0.93	0.94	0.90	0.80	0.91	0.90	0.86	0.91	0.94	0.86	0.82	D16	0.92	0.92	0.70	0.96	0.84	0.77	0.89	0.64	0.49	0.84	0.88	0.74	0.90
D19	0.96	0.88	0.90	0.90	1.00	0.92	0.85	0.91	0.78	0.98	0.98	0.80	0.97	D19	0.89	0.87	0.60	0.84	0.97	0.83	0.82	0.54	0.37	0.73	0.90	0.69	0.89
D24	0.85	0.69	0.75	0.80	0.92	0.96	0.66	0.84	0.59	0.89	0.86	0.59	0.93	D24	0.86	0.84	0.52	0.77	0.83	0.98	0.66	0.82	0.65	0.55	0.71	0.74	0.74
D29	0.93	0.99	0.96	0.91	0.85	0.66	0.99	0.88	0.97	0.86	0.92	0.98	0.74	D29	0.89	0.90	0.77	0.89	0.82	0.66	0.95	0.50	0.36	0.78	0.88	0.75	0.87
D38	0.94	0.90	0.90	0.90	0.91	0.84	0.88	0.97	0.88	0.90	0.92	0.86	0.84	D38	0.69	0.71	0.43	0.64	0.54	0.82	0.50	0.99	0.93	0.41	0.46	0.79	0.52
D68	0.89	0.97	0.92	0.86	0.78	0.59	0.97	0.88	1.00	0.80	0.86	0.99	0.66	D68	0.52	0.55	0.27	0.49	0.37	0.65	0.36	0.93	0.97	0.30	0.31	0.72	0.35
D84	0.95	0.89	0.91	0.91	0.98	0.89	0.86	0.90	0.80	0.99	0.97	0.82	0.95	D84	0.73	0.77	0.61	0.84	0.73	0.55	0.78	0.41	0.30	0.99	0.86	0.51	0.88
D92	0.98	0.94	0.95	0.94	0.98	0.86	0.92	0.92	0.86	0.97	0.99	0.88	0.92	D92	0.86	0.87	0.64	0.88	0.90	0.71	0.88	0.46	0.31	0.86	0.97	0.65	0.93
D94	0.89	0.99	0.93	0.86	0.80	0.59	0.98	0.86	0.99	0.82	0.88	1.00	0.69	D94	0.79	0.81	0.56	0.74	0.69	0.74	0.75	0.79	0.72	0.51	0.65	0.95	0.62
D112	0.89	0.78	0.81	0.82	0.97	0.93	0.74	0.84	0.66	0.95	0.92	0.69	1.00	D112	0.89	0.89	0.73	0.90	0.89	0.74	0.87	0.52	0.35	0.88	0.93	0.62	0.98

3.2 Experiment 2: Classification Accuracy of CCR and SCCR

In the second test, the minimum distance classifier described in Sect. 2.3 is used in the CCR and SCCR feature spaces for the classification of scaled images. Images of the same set of classes ($C = 13$) are scaled by $\times 0.660$, $\times 0.800$, $\times 1.250$ and $\times 1.500$ factors for classification tests. In the learning phase, for each texture class only the original unscaled image of 337×337 pixels is used for generating randomly $N_c = 10$ sub-images of size 100×100 pixels, which are binarized and used to calculate the prototype vector. In the recognition phase, a set of $N_c = 10$ random sub-images of 100×100 pixels are taken from each scaled image ($\times 0.660$, $\times 0.800$, $\times 1.250$ and $\times 1.500$) corresponding to a class, getting $13 \times 4 \times 10 = 520$ test images in total for classification. For each test image, the feature vector is calculated and then the Manhattan distance to each texture prototype vector is computed, assigning the test image to the nearest class. If a test image from class c is assigned to class c it is considered a correct classification, otherwise, it is a classification error. Finally, the precision (positive predictive value) of each class is calculated, as well as the accuracy ($\frac{True Positive}{Total Population}$) for the testing set.

The results of classification of images at different scales using the CCR and SCCR are shown in Table 2, those are classification rates in the thirteen classes using a set of 520 test images. We see that the accuracy rate of the CCR based classifier is 0.736, while the accuracy rate using SCCR is over 0.862, improving the results in 12.6%. Using the SCCR the classification rate for each class is also improved, except for the classes D12, D38 where the classification rate decreases marginally. The D94 class represents a critical case because of the loss of local structure after image binarization, showing predominant white and black patches all over the texture. Despite this particular case, the improvement of the classification accuracy suggests that the scaling of the CCR histogram results in the SCCR descriptor robust to scale changes.

Table 2. Classification rates of the CCR and SCCR into the thirteen texture classes at four different scales.

Method	Image													
	D9	D12	D15	D16	D19	D24	D29	D38	D68	D84	D92	D94	D112	**Accuracy**
CCR	0.673	0.855	0.689	0.508	0.499	0.649	0.496	0.955	0.938	0.932	0.486	0.017	0.973	**0.736**
SCCR	0.827	0.832	0.968	0.838	0.863	0.984	0.689	0.926	0.993	0.999	0.845	0.449	0.990	**0.862**

Classification tests are performed at scales half to twice the original scale, to assess the robustness of the SCCR. Such tests compare the SCCR to standard CCR and results also enable us to estimate the range in which the SCCR properly handles the scale variation. Figure 3, shows classification rates for the SCCR and CCR at 9 scales (×0.660, ×0.800, ×1.250, ×1.500 plus ×0.500, ×0.750, ×1.750, ×2.000). We see that the SCCR responds better when the scale textures are highly unlike the original scale (at ×0.500 and in the range above ×1.250). In the range [×0.660, ×1.000], the CCR and SCCR show similar classification rates, having CCR slightly better results. We conclude that the SCCR maintains a better than CCR representation at large scale variations of texture images.

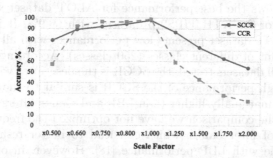

Fig. 3. Classification rates versus image scale using the CCR and SCCR descriptors. Results are obtained on 13 classes from the Brodatz database.

3.3 Experiment 3: Comparison with Other Approaches

In this experiment the SCCR method is compared with state-of-the-art textural descriptors. The local binary pattern (LBP) [2], a reference algorithm in texture analysis, and the MCLBP algorithm [7], as a powerful LBP variant that captures the correlation information between different scales. For this purpose, the MCLBP/C is used with two multi-scale co-occurrences pairs (LBP(8, 1) and LBP(8, 3); LBP(8, 1) and LBP(8, 4)). Also, as a part of our experiment, we include Gabor filter descriptors of textural information, as the homogeneous texture (HT) [13]. Furthermore, Gabor-Riaz 2D-DFT [12] and Gabor-Riaz 1D-DFT [14] are used in this comparison as efficient descriptors to deal with the invariance of scale and rotation. For this comparison, the three descriptors of Gabor filters were developed using the same filter design described in those references.

This experiment is performed on four well-known texture databases. **Brodatz** [11] - We select the same dataset used in [12], which includes 13 texture images, scaled using bilinear interpolation. **ALOT** [15] - For scale-invariant purposes, we only use the images in gray-scale that correspond to the camera 1 (c1) with 0 rotation degrees and the illumination condition I8; images are also scaled using bilinear interpolation. **Outex** [16] - In this experiment, the test suite TC_00011 (100 dpi and 120 dpi) was used, including resolutions of 300 dpi, 360 dpi, 500 dpi and 600 dpi for each texture. **KTH_TIPS2_b** [17] - We use the images that correspond to a frontal object position and ambient lighting condition, all of them at the 9 different scales from the sample a of the database. Finally, training and testing datasets consist of 130 and 520 images (Brodatz); 2,500 and 10,000 (ALOT); 240 and 1,200 (Outex); and 110 and 880 (KTH_TIPS2_b).

To have a fair comparison between descriptors, the classification test was performed using the minimum distance classifier, leaving out the use of classifiers that require the tuning of parameters specific to each descriptor. Each texture descriptor was tested over each dataset described previously. Furthermore, the reported results represent the mean accuracy over 30 test executions in order to give them a statistical significance. The results obtained from the classification test are presented in Table 3, where we observe that SCCR shows the best performance for Brodatz and Outex dataset with 85.6% and 62.8% respectively, while MCLBP shows the best performance for ALOT dataset with 25.7% and the LBP descriptor for KTH_TIPS2_b dataset with 68.9%. It is important to mention that ALOT dataset presents low performances with all algorithms due to the high amount of different classes (250 classes). According to the average performance on all datasets tested, the SCCR is the descriptor with the best performance. The high performance of the SCCR is similar to the state-of-the-art algorithms being marginally higher than LBP and Gabor filters.

Note that in the comparison we have not optimized the frequency and position parameters of filter banks, which can lead to better results with Gabor filters, comparable with LBP performance [18]. However, in order to make a fair comparison over all datasets, all descriptors were developed under the same parameters that are mentioned in the respective references.

Table 3. Classification accuracy for scale invariance on 4 different databases.

	CCR	SCCR	LBP	MCLBP	Gabor-Riaz 1D-DFT	Gabor-Riaz 2D-DFT	Gabor-HT
Brodatz	0.734	**0.856**	0.613	0.628	0.603	0.596	0.817
ALOT	0.151	0.179	0.246	**0.257**	0.139	0.158	0.230
Outex	0.414	**0.628**	0.581	0.437	0.282	0.385	0.345
KTH_TIPS2_b	0.552	0.575	**0.689**	0.612	0.554	0.534	0.644
Average	0.463	**0.559**	0.532	0.484	0.394	0.418	0.509

Run-Time Performance Analysis. To study the computational time of the methods used in Experiment 3.3, the average run-time for feature extraction is calculated using the full set of images in the corresponding database; the test was carried out on an Intel Corel i7-4720HQ processor at 2.60 GHz. Not all methods have been optimized, nonetheless, results lead to an idea of the computational complexity of them. Taking into account that feature extraction is faster on the KTH_TIPS2_b dataset and slower on Outex, the range of average consuming time on these datasets, given in seconds, are as follow: LBP, 0.006 to 0.054; SCCR, 0.012 to 0.103; CCR 0.013 to 0.104; MCLBP, 0.108 to 0.552; and, finally, the Gabor methods, 1.736 to 18.991. These results show that it is possible to get a high performance with lower computational cost.

4   Conclusions

In this work, the Scaled Coordinated Cluster Representation (SCCR) of images has been proposed as a descriptor for scale-invariant classification of visual texture. The method is a 2-step variation of the standard CCR. First, the CCR representation of the texture image is obtained. Afterward, the bins that represent the totally black or white regions in the texture are suppressed in the histogram and the remaining bins are scaled. Then, the low-occurrence patterns are filtered out. This adjustment leads to a descriptor robust to scale changes. Test series have been implemented to evaluate the performance of the proposed descriptor. Comparing the SCCR to the standard CCR, the results show that the SCCR provides a better representation, preserving a low intra-class variance and improving the inter-class discernibility. These properties of the SCCR are relevant when dealing with textures exhibiting large scale changes. The descriptor has been evaluated using a minimum distance classifier and texture images from four well-known databases. Compared with the standard CCR, the experiments show that the classification accuracy is improved substantially when the scale range is less than ×0.660 and higher than ×1.000. A comparison with the state-of-the-art algorithms was done, showing a high performance with a simpler representation than other scale invariant descriptors. This suggests that the SCCR may be used in applications when the scale variance has to be compensated and visual texture needs to be classified in a fast and accurate way, for example, in industrial inspection or mobile applications.

References

1. Fernández, A., Álvarez, M.X., Bianconi, F.: Texture description through histograms of equivalent patterns. J. Math. Imaging Vis. **45**(1), 76–102 (2013)
2. Ojala, T., Pietikäinen, M., Harwood, D.: A comparative study of texture measures with classification based on feature distributions. Pattern Recogn. **29**(1), 51–59 (1996)
3. Kurmyshev, E.V., Soto, R.: Digital pattern recognition in the coordinated cluster representation. In: 1996 Proceedings of the IEEE Nordic Signal Processing Symposium, Espoo, Finland, pp. 463–466 (1996)
4. Ojala, T., Pietikäinen, M., Mäenpää, T.: Multiresolution gray-scale and rotation invariant texture classification with local binary patterns. IEEE Trans. Pattern Anal. Mach. Intell. **24**(7), 971–987 (2002)
5. Li, Z., Liu, G., Yang, Y., You, J.: Scale- and rotation-invariant local binary pattern using scale-adaptive texton and subuniform-based circular shift. IEEE Trans. Image Process. **21**(4), 2130–2140 (2012)
6. Davarzani, R., Mozaffari, S., Yaghmaie, K.: Scale- and rotation-invariant texture description with improved local binary pattern features. Sig. Process. **111**, 274–293 (2014)
7. Qi, X., Shen, L., Zhao, G., Li, Q., Pietikäinen, M.: Globally rotation invariant multi-scale co-occurrence local binary pattern. Image Vis. Comput. **43**, 16–26 (2015)
8. Kurmyshev, E.V., Poterasu, M., Guillen-Bonilla, J.T.: Image scale determination for optimal texture classification using coordinated clusters representation. Appl. Opt. **46**(9), 1467–1476 (2007)
9. Otsu, N.: A threshold selection method from gray-level histograms. IEEE Trans. Syst. Man Cybern. **9**(1), 62–66 (1979)
10. Sanchez-Yanez, R.E., Kurmyshev, E.V., Cuevas, F.J.: A framework for texture classification using the coordinated clusters representation. Pattern Recogn. Lett. **24**(1–3), 21–31 (2003)
11. Brodatz, P.: Textures: A Photographic Album for Artists and Designers. Dover Publications, Mineola (1966)
12. Riaz, F., Hassan, A., Rehman, S., Qamar, U.: Texture classification using rotation- and scale-invariant gabor texture features. IEEE Signal Process. Lett. **20**(6), 607–610 (2013)
13. Manjunath, B.S., Ma, W.Y.: Texture features for browsing and retrieval of image data. IEEE Trans. Pattern Anal. Mach. Intell. **18**(8), 837–842 (1996)
14. Riaz, F., Hassan, A., Nisar, R., Dinis-Ribeiro, M., Coimbra, M.T.: Content-adaptive region-based color texture descriptors for medical images. IEEE J. Biomed. Health Inform. **21**(1), 162–171 (2017)
15. Burghouts, G.J., Geusebroek, J.M.: Material-specific adaptation of color invariant features. Pattern Recogn. Lett. **30**(3), 306–313 (2009)
16. Ojala, T., Mäenpää, T., Pietikäinen, M., Viertola, J., Kyllönen, J., Huovinen, S.: Outex - new framework for empirical evaluation of texture analysis algorithms. In: Proceedings of the 16th International Conference on Pattern Recognition, vol. 1, pp. 701–706 (2002)
17. Caputo, B., Hayman, E., Mallikarjuna, P.: Class-specific material categorisation. In: 10th IEEE International Conference on Computer Vision (ICCV 2005), vol. 1–2, pp. 1597–1604 (2005)
18. Ghita, O., Ilea, D., Fernandez, A., Whelan, P.: Local binary patterns versus signal processing texture analysis: a study from a performance evaluation perspective. Sens. Rev. **32**(2), 149–162 (2012)

Author Index

Printed in the United States
By Bookmasters

Printed in the United States
By Bookmasters